The Invisible War

The Invisible War

*Indigenous Devotions, Discipline, and Dissent
in Colonial Mexico*

David Tavárez

STANFORD UNIVERSITY PRESS

STANFORD, CALIFORNIA

Stanford University Press
Stanford, California

©2011 by the Board of Trustees of the Leland Stanford Junior University.
All rights reserved.

Published with the assistance of Vassar College and the Program for Cultural
Cooperation between Spain's Ministry of Culture and United States Universities.

Printed in the United States of America on acid-free, archival-quality paper.

Library of Congress Cataloging-in-Publication Data

Tavárez, David Eduardo.
The invisible war : indigenous devotions, discipline, and dissent in colonial
Mexico / David Tavárez.
p. cm.
Includes bibliographical references and index.
ISBN 978-0-8047-7328-7 (cloth : alk. paper)
1. Indians of Mexico--Religion. 2. Indians of Mexico--Rites and ceremonies.
3. Catholic Church--Mexico--History. 4. Idolatry--Mexico--History.
5. Inquisition--Mexico. 6. Christianity and other religions--Mexico.
7. Mexico--Religious life and customs. 8. Mexico--History--Spanish colony,
1540-1810. I. Title.
F1219.3.R38T38 2011
972'.02--dc22
2010039736

Typeset by Bruce Lundquist in 10/12 Sabon

A mi familia:
Elisabeth, Eva Isabel, David, Estela, Arturo, Irving,
y David A. Tavárez

Contents

Illustrations

Charts

Figures

Tables

Maps

Acknowledgments

This book owes its existence to the support of a diverse group of scholars, who share due credit for its usefulness, while I claim sole responsibility for its shortcomings. As an undergraduate, my early forays into Mesoamerican ethnohistory and Mexican history were kindly supervised by Alfredo López Austin, Rosemary Joyce, John Womack, Robert Preucel, and Ben Brown. At Chicago, I began my study of Nahuatl with a legendary figure in Mesoamerican linguistics, the sadly departed Norman McQuown. My always inspiring committee cochairs Paul Friedrich and Friedrich Katz, my unofficial cochair and tireless mentor and editor Susan Schroeder, and my steadfast adviser Tom Cummins each provided essential intellectual and personal support. I also had the privilege of counting on the insightful teaching and advice of Terry Turner, Bill Hanks, Ray Fogelson, Marshall Sahlins, and Manuela Carneiro da Cunha. As a Chicago-EHESS exchange fellow, I greatly benefited from the erudite suggestions of Serge Gruzinski and the prudent advice of Roger Chartier and Nathan Wachtel. In Spain, Italy, and Belgium, Jesús Bustamante, Mónica Quijada, Alessandro Lupo, and Eddy Stols opened doors and made important suggestions. As an ethnohistorian new to the field, my work was transformed by many illuminating exchanges with Kevin Terraciano, Michel Oudijk (who selflessly shared transcriptions and advice), John Chuchiak, William B. Taylor (who generously provided important archival leads), Louise Burkhart, María de los Ángeles Romero and Manuel Esparza, Juan Pedro Viqueira, Javier Urcid, Jorge Cañizares, Barry Sell, Matthew Restall, and Frank Salomon. My work on colonial Zapotec was improved by the gracious feedback of G. Aaron Broadwell, Pamela Munro, Juana Vásquez Vásquez, the Zapotexts group at UCLA, and by a commanding figure in Mesoamerican linguistics: the late Thomas Smith-Stark. A fruitful collaboration with John Justeson and some unpublished linguistic data graciously provided by Terry Kaufman helped me sharpen my analysis of the Villa Alta calendars. In Oaxaca, my research could not have taken place without the assistance of the unfailingly generous Lic. Luis Castañeda, Daniela Traffano, Michael Swanton, Bas van Doesburg, Ricardo Ambrosio, Pergentino Ruiz, Amador Teodocio, Israel Garrido, Isabel Grañén, Aurelia Cano, Fidel Cacho, and Vilma and Olga Diego. In Mexico City, I enjoyed the generous support of Solange Alberro, Miguel León-Portilla, Ramón Arzápalo, and Rafael Loyola Díaz. At presentations and conferences, I received important suggestions from Stafford Poole, R. Douglas Cope, John F. Schwaller, Kenneth Mills, Nancy Farriss, Alonso Barros, Yanna Yannakakis, Javier Villa-Flores, Lisa Sousa, Kris Lane, Alejandro Cañeque, Carmen Salazar-Soler, Sonia Rose, Aldo Lauria-Santiago, Kimbra Smith, and Paul Liffman. Besides providing an example of insightfulness, two reviewers helped me greatly improve this manuscript: John K. Chance made some crucial suggestions; and Judith Zeitlin provided many thoughtful comments. My colleagues at the Anthropology Department and the Latin American and Latino/a Studies Program at Vassar were a model of scholarly support and collegiality. My highly qualified assistants, Elise Stickles and Lynne Ciccaglione, carried out various research tasks, and Cristián Opazo generated an optimal set of charts. Many archivists provided inestimable help, particularly those at the Archivo General de la Nación, Archivo General de Indias, Archivo del Poder Judicial de Oaxaca, Archivo Histórico del Arzobispado de México, Archivo Histórico del Arzobispado de Oaxaca, the John Carter Brown Library, Archivio Segreto Vaticano, Archivio Generale dell'Ordine dei Predicatori, and the Fonds mexicain of the Bibliothèque nationale de France. My research and writing were rendered possible by funding from CONACYT, the John Carter Brown Library, the National Science Foundation, the Mellon and Hewlett Foundations, the Foundation for the Advancement of Mesoamerican Studies, the Research Institute for the Study of Man, the National Endowment for the Humanities, and Vassar College.

The love and support of my wife Elisabeth, my daughter Eva Isabel, my parents David and Estela Tavárez, my brother Arturo, my nephews Irving and David Aleksei, and my in-laws Harry and Maureen Weinberg sustained me throughout this decade-long enterprise. For this reason, I dedicate this work to all of them.

The Invisible War

CHAPTER I

Rethinking Indigenous Devotions in Central Mexico

INTRODUCTION

On April 18, 1665, several nocturnal comings and goings took place in Lachirioag, a Northern Zapotec community in Villa Alta, a district northeast of Oaxaca City in New Spain. These activities were uncanny from the vantage point of Antonio de Cabrera, an African slave whom Diego Villegas y Sandoval Castro, Villa Alta's *alcalde mayor,* or chief magistrate, had entrusted with the task of reporting any suspect activities. Cabrera's owner, the *encomendero* of Lachirioag, was also in town, discharging his duties as collector of indigenous tribute.[1] Cabrera's attention focused on several events that would have attracted little notice had they occurred at daytime or in an urban setting. He saw some natives enter the house of Lachirioag resident Gerónimo López late at night. They came in, passed two women at the door, placed a half *real*—a coin of moderate value—on the ground, and sat near two large pots in which deer meat simmered as a native stood nearby holding a reed shaft topped with a bloody rag, and another illuminated the scene with a torch.[2] As Cabrera drew closer, one of the women cried out a warning, and everyone left López's house in haste. A week later, Cabrera came across López and many adult residents of Lachirioag as they came down a hill and approached the town center early at night. Cabrera later noticed that some people were once again cooking deer meat in two large pots at López's house. Even later, just before dawn, Cabrera went past this dwelling and surprised several natives who were dividing the deer meat among themselves; as before, they exited the house in a rush.[3]

Even though these activities may seem innocuous when compared to the human sacrifices described in lavish detail in accounts of Central

Mexican idolatries since Cortés's time, this African slave's narrative provided the Spanish magistrate with the quintessential first step for a juridical inquiry into idolatry—a vivid denunciation of suspicious native activities. Cabrera would eventually turn out to be a less-than-reliable narrator, but the main question facing the alcalde mayor was deceitful in its plainness: Had Gerónimo López and his associates committed an idolatrous act? If so, what juridical proof could be offered of their guilt? Following the legal procedure observed in both ecclesiastical and civil idolatry trials, the magistrate arrested six defendants, collected testimony from witnesses, and sought to obtain idolatry confessions from the defendants in a spirited trial held between February and April 1666. To Villegas y Sandoval's surprise, unlike most Zapotec defendants in a similar predicament, López and his associates did not cooperate in the collective construction of an idolatry narrative in the courtroom. Instead, they insisted that none of the actions they had carried out were idolatrous, and they impeached Cabrera's testimony by noting he had been caught propositioning local women. The proceedings ended on an unusually ambivalent note, for Villegas y Sandoval absolved all the defendants, warning them they should avoid "any ceremony that may be suspected to be idolatrous."[4]

This case is, of course, highly unusual; not only did it involve civil rather than ecclesiastical justice, but it went against the dynamics of most other proceedings against native idolatry or superstition in Central Mexico, which often followed a predictable trajectory from discovery to conviction. This trial's unusual outcome and ambivalent depiction of the actions of the Lachirioag deer eaters—were the accused sharing hunting spoils or honoring a non-Christian entity?—force us to focus on seemingly pedestrian matters obscured from view by hurried avowals of guilt in other idolatry trials. Idolatry extirpators not merely sought to prove that a certain observable action had taken place; they also strove to adjudicate a mental state and convict on a crime of thought. Given such a burden of proof, idolatry as a legal and social category could only be willed into existence by the concerted action of accusers and suspects in a courtroom. Before indigenous defendants chose to confess that a particular action was indeed idolatrous, all their accusers possessed were suspicious ritual implements and troubling narratives proffered by witnesses. Colonial idolatry could be adjudicated into being only after accusers and defendants crossed this epistemic Rubicon.[5]

In New Spain, the venerable Christian preoccupation surrounding the assessment of intentionality in a sinner's mind during the act of confession faced large linguistic and cultural barriers.[6] The strange, fascinating—and, some interpreters feared, unknowable—motivations behind forms of worship in Mesoamerican communities posed a formidable challenge to Christian theological discourse and cultural categories, which turned to various reappraisals of pagan beliefs in classical antiquity during the ebullient intellectual climate of the early Renaissance.[7] In Central Mexico, a unique aspect of the response of Christian missionaries was the production of a vibrant doctrinal corpus in Nahuatl, Phurépecha, Zapotec, Mixtec, Otomi, and other indigenous languages with the assistance of scholars drawn from the ranks of the first native generations who lived under colonial rule. Furthermore, ecclesiastic and civil authorities developed institutional measures and discourses that sought to identify and publicly punish a broad range of indigenous activities that were labeled as idolatry, sorcery, or superstition.

Idolatry's opponents regarded their attacks on native beliefs as spiritual warfare—and this trope guided their efforts. In the phrasing of Bishop Diego de Hevia y Valdés of Oaxaca, idolatry extirpators would enter "this invisible war" by arming themselves "with God against the common enemy . . . fortified as he is in the hearts of natives."[8] To take Hevia y Valdés at his word, however, would be to adopt several troublesome assumptions: that the stakes in this war were evident and transparent to both sides, that native idolaters sought to present a united front against Christianity, and that this united front depended on an antipodal version of Christianity implanted by the devil in the natives' less discerning minds. Hence, the study of institutional attacks on indigenous beliefs and native responses in Central Mexico may appear to be an epistemic minefield: Did idolatry even exist? Should colonial idolatry be understood primarily as an expedient creation that merely advanced institutional interests and ecclesiastical career goals and fed on local enmities? Can we understand how native defendants thought about their ritual practices and about orthodox Christianity?

This work proposes an answer to these fundamental questions by means of three contentions. First, I argue that "idolatry" cannot be employed as a systematic analytic category, and that colonial idolatry had an uncertain ontological status that became attached to specific practices only through the conjunction of legal discourses, doctrinal rhetoric, and specific accusations and acts of avowal. In other words, public denunciation and confession, rather than the systematic application of a stable legal category, fixed what idolatry was as a thing in the world. Second, rather than employing a category like "indigenous religion," which implies an inherent agreement regarding a central core of beliefs, this work starts with the assumption that there existed local diversity in terms of indigenous beliefs and practices, and that any attempts to bracket this diversity should be based on detailed ethnohistorical evidence. Thus, I characterize the symbolic exchange between indigenous believers and their foci of worship as *devotions*, a flexible category encompassing rituals and observances. These devotions were shaped by a set of fundamental assumptions about the cosmos that sometimes, but not always, diverged in important ways from Christian cosmology. Third, native beliefs must be considered in their own terms through a close examination of available linguistic evidence. This work argues that the evidence about native ritual practices coming directly from documentary evidence produced by natives or recoverable from trustworthy nonindigenous sources through linguistic analysis has an epistemic status that differs from that of the descriptions of native ceremonies produced by less exacting chroniclers, doctrinal authors, parish priests, and civil or ecclesiastical judges. This is not to say that a pure, unmediated indigenous voice emerges from texts in indigenous languages. The evidence discussed in these pages allows only a partial and tentative reconstruction of the rich devotional worlds of indigenous communities in Central Mexico. However, an insightful reconstruction of them hinges on a serious consideration of the manner in which natives conceived, inhabited, and spoke about these domains in their own ways of speaking.[9]

This book builds on ground cleared by more than a hundred years of scholarship on anti-idolatry measures in Central Mexico, which has customarily examined the first decades after the Spanish conquest,[10] and treated developments in the seventeenth and the eighteenth centuries in a rather sporadic fashion,[11] due in part to the fragmentary nature of extant sources. Paradoxically, Hevia y Valdés's "invisible war" is a suitably sharp trope for our limited knowledge about the struggle against idolatry in Central Mexico after 1571. This is because my project seeks to heighten the visibility of extirpation campaigns and native responses in Central Mexico by focusing on the dioceses of Mexico and Oaxaca between the 1530s and the 1760s and by proposing a novel periodization of eradication efforts. Here, I analyze exceptionally rich ethnohistorical and linguistic evidence about the persistence of clandestine forms of worship in these two sees, with a focus on two major Mesoamerican linguistic groups—Nahuatl speakers in the Cohuixca-Tlalhuica region, the Basin of Mexico, and the Toluca Valley, and Zapotec speakers in the Valley of Oaxaca, the township of Sola, and the province of Villa Alta. My analysis is based on a decade of research in twenty-nine archival depositories in Mexico, Spain, the United States, France, Belgium, Italy, and the Vatican, and it addresses the activities of about 160 civil and ecclesiastical judges and approximately 896 native idolatry, sorcery, and superstition defendants for whom we have biographical information. Map 1.1 shows many of the towns in and near the diocese of Mexico discussed in this work, and Map 1.2 accomplishes the same task for the see of Oaxaca.

This chapter summarizes my approach to the vast panorama of colonial idolatry in Central Mexico. After presenting an interpretive model regarding indigenous devotions in preconquest Nahua and Zapotec communities, I analyze the conceptualization of idolatry and the procedural organization and punitive methods employed by its foes, propose a periodization of such efforts as a set of four distinct cycles, and provide a summary of quantitative and qualitative data regarding extirpation activities in the region between the 1520s and the 1760s. A final section contains a chapter overview.

THE SOCIAL ORGANIZATION OF DEVOTION IN POSTCLASSIC NAHUA AND ZAPOTEC COMMUNITIES

A variety of texts from the sixteenth and seventeenth centuries are the fundamental sources for any interpretation of Nahua and Zapotec devotional practices in the two centuries before the conquest. Although no Nahua or Zapotec pictographic codex or paper document of undisputed preconquest origin has survived,[12] a number of extant colonial pictorial and alphabetic documents record the Postclassic political history of several Northern, Valley, and Isthmus Zapotec communities.[13] A relatively large number of Nahua pictographic records based on preconquest texts and oral narratives were produced after the conquest, and several generations of indigenous and mestizo authors, which included anonymous chroniclers as well as Chimalpahin, Fernando de Alva Ixtlilxóchitl, Bartolomé de Alva, Fernando Alvarado Tezozómoc, Diego Muñoz Camargo, and Juan de Buenaventura Zapata y Mendoza, copied, modified, commented, and transcribed these records, as well as oral accounts, into alphabetic texts as early as the mid-sixteenth century. Moreover, Franciscans such as Andrés de Olmos, Toribio Benavente "Motolinia," Jerónimo de Mendieta, Bernardino de Sahagún, Martín de León, Juan de Torquemada, and Juan Bautista Viseo, Dominicans such as Diego Durán, Pedro de Feria, and Juan de Córdova, and Jesuits such as Juan de Tovar penned their own narratives based on native records.

Even though it is impossible to propose an overarching description of Mesoamerican devotional practices that does justice to local variations and historical transformations, any analysis of these practices must start with an axiomatic principle first embraced by Mesoamericanists

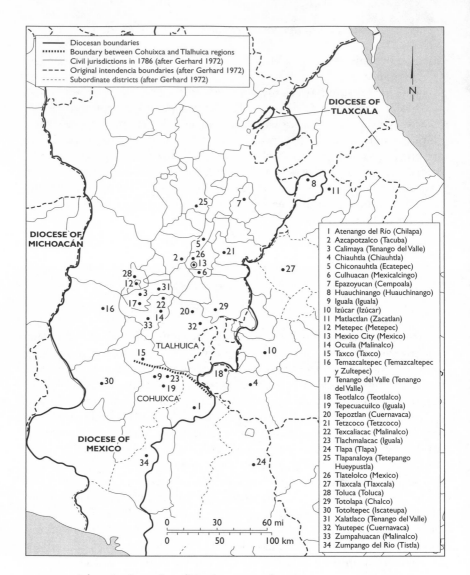

Diocesan boundaries
Boundary between Cohuixca and Tlalhuica regions
Civil jurisdictions in 1786 (after Gerhard 1972)
Original intendencia boundaries (after Gerhard 1972)
Subordinate districts (after Gerhard 1972)

N

DIOCESE OF
TLAXCALA

DIOCESE OF
MICHOACÁN

DIOCESE OF
MEXICO

TLALHUICA

COHUIXCA

1 Atenango del Río (Chilapa)
2 Azcapotzalco (Tacuba)
3 Calimaya (Tenango del Valle)
4 Chiauhtla (Chiauhtla)
5 Chiconauhtla (Ecatepec)
6 Culhuacan (Mexicalcingo)
7 Epazoyucan (Cempoala)
8 Huauchinango (Huauchinango)
9 Iguala (Iguala)
10 Izúcar (Izúcar)
11 Matlactlan (Zacatlan)
12 Metepec (Metepec)
13 Mexico City (Mexico)
14 Ocuila (Malinalco)
15 Taxco (Taxco)
16 Temazcaltepec (Temazcaltepec
   y Zultepec)
17 Tenango del Valle (Tenango
   del Valle)
18 Teotlalco (Teotlalco)
19 Tepecuacuilco (Iguala)
20 Tepoztlan (Cuernavaca)
21 Tetzcoco (Tetzcoco)
22 Texcaliacac (Malinalco)
23 Tlachmalacac (Iguala)
24 Tlapa (Tlapa)
25 Tlapanaloya (Tetepango
   Hueypustla)
26 Tlatelolco (Mexico)
27 Tlaxcala (Tlaxcala)
28 Toluca (Toluca)
29 Totolapa (Chalco)
30 Totoltepec (Iscateupa)
31 Xalatlaco (Tenango del Valle)
32 Yautepec (Cuernavaca)
33 Zumpahuacan (Malinalco)
34 Zumpango del Rio (Tistla)

0   30   60 mi
0   50   100 km

MAP 1.1 (above)   Some Localities in or near the
Diocese of Mexico Discussed in this Work
(Civil jurisdictions are listed in parentheses, and 1786 borders
are indicated. Chiauhtla, Izúcar, Matlactlan, Teotlalco, Tlapa,
and Tlaxcala were in the see of Tlaxcala after 1543.)
SOURCES: ACM; AGI; AGN; AHAM; BMNA; data from Gerhard 1972; NL

MAP 1.2 (right)   Some Localities in or near the
Diocese of Oaxaca Discussed in this Work
(Civil jurisdictions are listed in parentheses, and 1786 borders
are indicated. Santa Cruz Tlacotepec was in the see of Tlaxcala.)
SOURCES: AGI; AGN; AGOP; AHAO; ALC; AHJO;
Chance 1989; data from Gerhard 1972

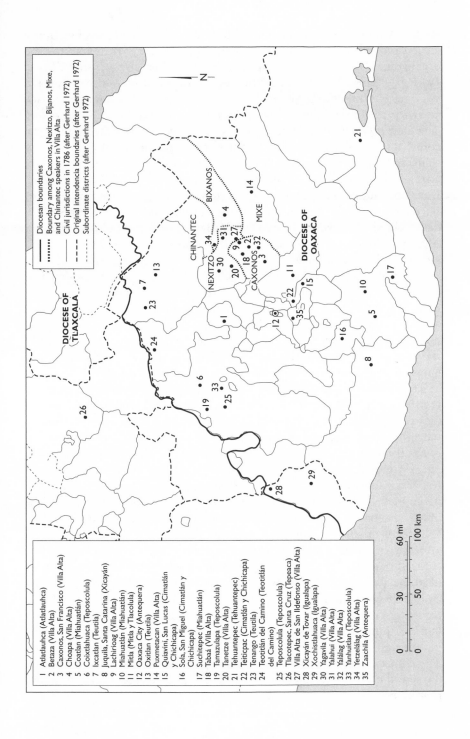

Diocesan boundaries
Boundary among Caxonos, Nexitzo, Bijanos, Mixe, and Chinantec speakers in Villa Alta
Civil jurisdictions in 1786 (after Gerhard 1972)
Original intendencia boundaries (after Gerhard 1972)
Subordinate districts (after Gerhard 1972)

—N—

DIOCESE OF TLAXCALA

CHINANTEC

BIXANOS

NEXITZO

CAXONOS

MIXE

DIOCESE OF OAXACA

1   Atlatlauhca (Atlatlauhca)
2   Betaza (Villa Alta)
3   Caxonos, San Francisco (Villa Alta)
4   Choapa (Villa Alta)
5   Coatlán (Miahuatlán)
6   Coixtlahuaca (Teposcolula)
7   Ixcatlán (Teutila)
8   Juquila, Santa Catarina (Xicayán)
9   Lachirioag (Villa Alta)
10 Miahuatlán (Miahuatlán)
11 Mitla (Mitla y Tlacolula)
12 Oaxaca City (Antequera)
13 Oxitlán (Teutila)
14 Puxmetacan (Villa Alta)
15 Quiavini, San Lucas (Cimatlán y Chichicapa)
16 Sola, San Miguel (Cimatlán y Chichicapa)
17 Suchitepec (Miahuatlán)
18 Tabaá (Villa Alta)
19 Tamazulapa (Teposcolula)
20 Tanetze (Villa Alta)
21 Tehuantepec (Tehuantepec)
22 Teiticpac (Cimatlán y Chichicapa)
23 Tenango (Teutila)
24 Teotitlán del Camino (Teotitlán del Camino)
25 Teposcolula (Teposcolula)
26 Tlacotepec, Santa Cruz (Tepeaca)
27 Villa Alta de San Ildefonso (Villa Alta)
28 Xicayán de Tovar (Igualapa)
29 Xochistlahuaca (Igualapa)
30 Yagavila (Villa Alta)
31 Yalahui (Villa Alta)
32 Yalálag (Villa Alta)
33 Yanhuitlán (Teposcolula)
34 Yetzelalág (Villa Alta)
35 Zaachila (Antequera)

0   30   60 mi
0   50   100 km

such as Alfonso Caso and Paul Kirchhoff: the widespread use of similarly structured calendrical systems. A central structuring principle for the organization of Nahua and Zapotec devotional practices in the Classic (200–800 CE) and Postclassic (800–1519 CE) periods was the use of two separate but interlocking calendrical systems known throughout Mesoamerica: a 260-day divinatory cycle, and a 365-day vague solar year.[14] The *tonalpohualli*, or Nahua 260-day count, designated each day in the count by combining the numbers one to thirteen with one of twenty day signs named after animals, natural forces, or objects (13 x 20 = 260), thus allowing for a division into twenty thirteen-day periods, or *trecenas*. Days and nights were thought to be under the respective influence of thirteen lords of the day and nine lords of the night.[15] The Zapotec 260-day cycle, designated as *piyè* in the Valley of Oaxaca and *biyè* in Villa Alta and glossed as "time" or "interval,"[16] mirrored the tonalpohualli's structure. Unlike other Mesoamerican systems, the piyè emphasized a division into four sixty-five-day periods, seen as powerful entities termed *cocijo* or *pitào*, which further subdivided into five trecenas.[17] The Zapotec count, perhaps the oldest known calendrical system in the Americas, is documented as early as 600 BCE,[18] and its antiquity is evident in the use of prefixes that combine with twenty day names to designate each of the 260 days in the count; unlike the Nahua count, which uses thirteen numerals, the Zapotec prefixes do not reflect extant numeral forms.[19]

The Nahua 365-day calendar, called *xihuitl*, was divided into eighteen groups of twenty days, or *veintenas*, commemorated with public ceremonies that propitiated divine entities. Since this count does not coincide with the exact duration of the solar year, 365.25 days, the rapport between this count and equinox and solstice events was probably a variable one, since there is little evidence regarding the existence of a preconquest leap-year adjustment.[20] The last five days in the count were regarded as *nemontemi*, or infelicitous days "lived in vain." In both systems, the use of the 365-day and the 260-day count as parallel cycles allowed calendrical specialists to name each 365-day year after a certain day in the 260-day calendar. The structural relationship between the two counts ensured that all of the names for the years would fall on a particular set of four day signs, or "year bearers." While both the Postclassic Nahua and Mixtec systems employed House, Rabbit, Reed, and Flint, the Zapotec system used Wind, Deer, Soaproot, and Earthquake.[21] The first day in the Zapotec system and the 360th day in the Nahua scheme provided a unique name for the 365-day year within a cycle of fifty-two such years. The concatenation of the two cycles resulted in fifty-two years of 365 days, and each of the days in this cycle could receive a unique designation by pairing the current year and date in the divinatory count, as in the formula 1-Earthquake, 1-Cayman, which refers, respectively, to the first in a cycle of fifty-two Zapotec years, and the first day of the 260-day count. The 52-year series, often ordered into four groups of thirteen years, was called *xiuhmolpilli*, "tied-up years," in Nahuatl, and piyè in Zapotec. The 260-day ritual day count was of utmost importance, and its management was a constant preoccupation for both commoners and elites. Both groups seemed to view the link between the two interlocking calendars and agriculture, the primary mode of subsistence, as a naturalized relationship between a body of traditional knowledge and the structure and history of the cosmos.

Late Postclassic Mesoamerican polities were defined as entities by one or more traditional lineages, land-holding rights, and the public worship of local deities and celebration of calendrical holidays. Each community had one or more hereditary rulers, and most were part of a highly structured and often modular political unit with a defined territory and a shared set of ancestors. The Nahua version of this unit, called *altepetl*, is comparable to its Zapotec counterpart, the *queche*,[22] even if the internal organization of the former is much better known than that of the latter.[23] Additionally, a set of relations linked a historically constituted community with its local deities and ancestors.[24] Thus, individuals were born into a set of naturalized relations with deities and local landscape features, were regarded as members of a particular altepetl or queche, and held various rights and responsibilities in their polity of residence. Major sustenance activities in the community, as well as each individual's life cycle, unfolded under the influence of the two-tiered calendrical system. In their role as mediators between deities and communities, or between deities and individuals, ritual specialists played a crucial role in the economy of ritual exchange. From a collective perspective, they were responsible for securing communal well-being through divination and public ceremonies tied to the 260-day and 365-day cycles. Ritual specialists were employed by individuals seeking to facilitate—or diminish, in the case of sorcerers—their own well-being.

How were these practices organized in social realms? A clear division of ritual labor seemingly existed in Postclassic times: rulers and priests provided for the well-being of the community through the performance of collective or state ritual practices, and individual ritual specialists with access to calendrical knowledge advised or performed ceremonies marking transitions in the socialization of individuals—birth, puberty, marriage, childbearing and child rearing, and death—addressing illnesses, personal misfortunes, and interpersonal conflict. Therefore, I propose here a rather broad model describing two distinct socially constituted realms in which ritual labor and ritual exchanges took place in Nahua and Zapotec communities: the *collective sphere* and the *elective sphere*. These terms are in part motivated by the dichotomy between what eighteenth-century Zapotecs called *sacrificios de particulares*, personal ritual practices performed with the assistance of ritual practitioners, and *sacrificios del común*, or communal sacrifices. Much like the religious field proposed by Pierre Bourdieu,[25] these two spheres were mapped out by the interaction of their participants and were therefore not rigidly isomorphic with public and private spaces (church versus household), legal criteria (licit or illicit), or theological distinctions (Christianity versus idolatry; religion versus magic). Ritual labor and ritual exchanges carried out in the collective sphere had a dual objective: the production of collective well-being, and the reproduction of a project of social order, which was presented as the guarantor of collective well-being. This proposal is in part informed by Nancy Farriss's well-known three-tiered model for colonial Yucatec devotions, which proposed a division between universal, corporate or parochial, and private ritual practices.[26] My model, however, assumes that the communal and private levels were vertically integrated with large-scale theories about the cosmological order, and that both intimate and public Nahua and Zapotec devotions were, in fact, oriented toward understanding, propitiating, or even manipulating important entities in the cosmos.[27] In other words, Nahua and Zapotec specialists believed that their ritual actions had a cosmological significance that could encompass familial, communal, and universal domains.

There are three rationales for positing a distinction between collective and elective rather than collective versus private. First, individuals and families participated in it on an elective basis, for there was no compulsion to participate, and the pragmatic objectives varied widely by individual and family situation. Second, such a label goes beyond a strict dichotomy between public and private domains. Ritual specialists in the elective sphere structured their practices according to a body of ritual knowledge perpetually in flux through exchange, circulation, imitation, and accretion, for the collective and elective spheres were neither rigid nor impermeable. Third, the opposition between elite specialists in the collective sphere and all other specialists elsewhere in Late Postclassic Mesoamerica could be strongly articulated in terms of political legitimacy and social stratification, but only weakly articulated in terms of an epistemological distinction between "true" and "false" devotions. Membership in a community of believers was not predicated on acceptance of dogma; instead, a core of corporate or state ritual practices articulated a claim to legitimate power made by elites. Heresy was an impossibility: if one follows Talal Asad's characterization of heresy as a willful rejection of the church's authority over the believer, and a rejection of an entire Christian community constituted by proper belief, such a dichotomy could not be articulated in Mesoamerica in terms of an epistemic divide between elite and nonelite ritual.[28]

In broad terms, the exchange of offerings depended on a recurring contract between human beings and Mesoamerican divine entities epitomized by Durkheim's influential formula *do ut des*, "I give so you may give."[29] Nevertheless, the Mesoamerican semantics of sacrifice were exceedingly complex, for the potency of offerings hinged not only on their substance but also on the multiple links between the sacrificer's aims, cosmological realms, the appropriateness of specific times in the calendrical cycles, an appraisal of the wishes of divine entities, the structuring of oral and bodily performances, and the presentation and arraying of human, animal, vegetal, and inert sacred gifts. The sacrificial acts described in further chapters offer a very limited glimpse at the colonial Mesoamerican universe of sacrificial offerings, but it may be helpful to emphasize some practices. In the collective realm, caves and mountains were sometimes associated with narratives of origin regarding founding ancestors, as shown in the *Historia Tolteca-Chichimeca*;[30] some important ceremonial structures were placed over caves that had been modified through human action, as it was the case for the largest temple in Teotihuacan, the most important ceremonial site in Central Mexico during the Classic period.[31] Important ceremonial complexes developed as layers of new architectural features built above older structures, sponsored by succeeding local rulers, and punctuated by elaborate arrays of inaugural human and animal sacrifices, as exemplified by the various building stages of the Mexica Templo Mayor.[32] The Mexica 365-day cycle had a fixed array of festivities overseen by rulers and high-ranking priests, which sometimes featured the scripted public performances of men and women who personified deities. In both the collective and elective spheres, specialists ingested mushrooms, peyote, ololiuhqui, and other hallucinogens in order to communicate with divine entities. Human blood was held in high esteem as an offering, although animal blood was also used as a viable proxy. The former was drawn from sacrificial victims, or in acts of self-sacrifice in which celebrants cut their earlobes, fingers, arms, legs, and genitalia with blades, spines, and thorns.[33] The latter was drawn from turkeys, dogs, eagles, small birds, and other creatures, and their bodies were also given as offerings. Besides blood, several items were appropriate gifts for the deities: copal, paper, cacao, maize, and other important cultigens. In the elective sphere, specialists instructed petitioners on the proper presentation of offerings, directed them to fast and abstain from sex before petitioning the deities, healed them and administered herbal remedies, and performed divination by a staggering array of techniques that included, just by way of an example, casting grains, measuring limbs with their hands, looking at water, reading ashes, and interpreting dreams.[34]

The received distinction in early modern Europe between magic and religion did not exist in Late Postclassic Mesoamerica. Categories such as sorcery, superstition, and idolatry were deployed in a heuristic manner by colonial observers after the conquest. Even analysts such as Nutini and Roberts, who use an aprioristic distinction between magic/religion and witchcraft/sorcery for colonial Nahua communities, acknowledge that no such distinction emerges from their sources.[35] This is not to say that there was no Late Postclassic category that corresponded, in some ways, with European notions of witchcraft or sorcery; there were, in fact, many terms and alleged procedures followed by malevolent ritual specialists.[36] This work, however, favors the term "sorcery" and avoids the use of "witchcraft" as an analytical category, due to three considerations. First, as argued below and in Chapters 2, 3, and 8, idolatry extirpators did not develop a sharp discursive or pragmatic distinction between sorcery and witchcraft. Second, the extirpators' skepticism toward the efficacy of native ritual led them to regard most malevolent ritual acts as sorcery. Finally, as discussed in Chapter 8, Nahua specialists and their clients believed that the boundary between healing and what they called "witchcraft and sorcery" was highly permeable. Another crucial distinction between European witchcraft and Mesoamerican malevolent specialists rests in the fact that the historicity of Mesoamerican ritual practices is beyond question. Even though there is a long-standing debate between those who emphasize the shamanistic roots of early modern European witchcraft and those who stress the legal construction of paganism by inquisitors,[37] Mesoamerican ritual practices cannot be bracketed by this dichotomy.

In this work, I use "ritual" as a term for the repetitive and highly creative performance of multilayered symbolic acts by individuals or groups in order to secure a number of pragmatic aims.[38] The primary effect of ritual practices may be the reproduction of a social or cultural order, but this does not mean that ritual re-creates an ahistorical ideological realm;[39] instead, endogenous ritual practices may respond to and assimilate exogenous events and thus result in the transformation of endogenous cultural categories.[40] While collective ritual may enhance, reenact, or reproduce representations of group identity and group cohesion, or situate communities and individuals within an unfolding life or yearly cycle,[41] private ritual may address a much narrower range of interests, dispositions, and representations. To avoid the appearance of an ontological demarcation between "pagan" ritual and Christian "religion," and the assumption that native practices could be easily sorted into separate religious and political domains, I employ "devotions" as shorthand for indigenous and European ritual practices, regardless of their relationship with Christian orthodoxy.

Finally, the collective-elective model moves beyond labels such as "syncretism" or "hybridity." In colonial Nahua and Zapotec communities, a subtle gradation of public and private spaces hosted ritual practices ranging from public Christian observances regarded as orthodox by civic and ecclesiastic authorities, to public and private acts of propitiation or divination perceived as suspect or as crimes against Christianity. A homogeneous analytical label like "syncretism" tends to efface, rather than elucidate, the specificity of such a range of native responses. Therefore, this work stresses the primacy of the collective and elective spheres as organizational principles for both native communities and the Spanish monarchy's diverse social body. The actual deployment of Mesoamerican practices in the collective and elective spheres is the crucial issue here, not their taxonomy. From this perspective, ecclesiastical and civil efforts to extirpate native idolatry and superstition was an attempt to absorb local indigenous collective spheres into the construction of a broader domain, that of Christianity, and to suppress myriad practices in local elective spheres through which exchanges of ritual labor and knowledge occurred among natives, Spaniards, and castas. Such collective spheres could certainly be called hybrid. Nonetheless, this label would collapse localities where ancestor worship was a dominant political project in the collective sphere (Lachirioag and Betaza, as shown in Chapter 7) with communities where traditional healing practices were conducted in the shadow of a more powerful Christian collective sphere (such as the Toluca towns discussed in Chapter 8). In the end, idolatry extirpation was the most visible aspect of a complex co-construction of local collective and elective spheres in Central Mexico.

CENTRAL MEXICAN IDOLATRIES: CONCEPTUALIZATION, PROCEDURE, AND COERCION

Since its origin in biblical texts, the notion of idolatry has followed the contours of a simple, ancient idea: only the one true God could be worshipped rightfully, as dictated by a special covenant joining God and his people. This belief, according to the Book of Exodus (32: 1–28), was linked to the notion of legitimate violence since its inception. After Moses descended from Mount Sinai to receive the Tables of the Law, he found many Israelites worshipping a golden calf that Aaron had made from their molten gold jewelry. Moses swiftly punished them by grinding the idol into powder and forcing the Israelites to drink it in water, and by having the "sons of Levi" slay three thousand idolaters. Indeed, the misguided or rebellious worship directed toward an entity other than God contradicted two key statements framing the uttering of the commandments: the giver of the commandments was the only true god, and no other deity could be worshipped. The Old Testament employed the trope of treason and infidelity to denounce those who broke this sacred compact. Like adulterous wives, idolaters betrayed the confidence placed on them to commit futile acts that were filthy and illegitimate.[42]

In the *Summa Theologiae*, Aquinas makes several influential contributions to the definition of idolatry, which is the opposite of rightful worship, or *latria*. First, Aquinas stresses a distinction between *idololatria*, concisely defined as "the cult of false gods," and superstition, which he sees as an excessive mode of worship often focusing on the forecasting of future events.[43] Second, Aquinas attributes idolatry to two primary causes: the *causa dispositiva*, which comes from humans, and the *causa consummativa*, introduced by the devil. Sixteenth- and seventeenth-century anti-idolatry rhetoric in Central Mexico would later echo the three Thomistic dispositive causes: the improper worship of dear, departed ancestors; the human enjoyment of images and representations; and the ignorance of the true God. Aquinas also emphasized the contributions of Satan, who deceived humans by answering their requests and performing miracles through false images. From his perspective, idolatry is "the cause, beginning, and end of all sins," since every known sin issued from its pursuit.[44]

An influential theological position articulated by the Dominican Bartolomé de las Casas in his *Apologética historia sumaria* also served as a recurring point of reference in anti-idolatry discourses in the Americas. Las Casas begins with the Thomistic argument that humans have a natural tendency to seek and worship God, but that the store of knowledge that natural law affords them is confusing and incomplete by definition. Since humankind cannot live without worshipping gods, the devil is able to exploit the essentially human drive to believe and worship by attracting them to false cults and propositions. Therefore, each form of worship developed by human beings can be assigned to the categories of latria or idolatria through a close examination of its origins. Bernand and Gruzinski observed the affinities between this position and the widespread Counter-Reformation definition of idolatry as the inversion of Christianity promoted through the devil's cunning. They also argued that the classification of indigenous devotional acts into latria and idolatria could be characterized as the casting of a "Lascasian" net. The casting of such a net, which portrayed idolatry as an inverted reflection of Christian beliefs, into an ocean of native practices resulted in a highly idiosyncratic yield. Bernand and Gruzinski noted, "This is an impossible operation, given that one may discover some idolatrous features on the ground, in all indigenous activities, however trivial. Under the weight of facts, idolatry then becomes a way of life radically different to that of Europeans."[45]

The very translation of the term "idolatry" into Nahuatl and Zapotec reflected its origins in Exodus, with some Thomistic echoes. Many doctrinal authors settled on the Nahua neologism *tlateotoquiliztli*, literally, "erroneously considering something to be a deity,"[46] as a translation of "idolatry." This choice is quite literal and may be contrasted with the translation for "devotion," *tlateomatiliztli*, "thinking or being concerned with a deity." In contrast, the most common Zapotec translation for idolatry was *quela huezete pitoo quiela (pitoo) yagala*, "the worship of stone deities and wooden deities,"[47] although some Nahua authors used a designation virtually parallel to this Zapotec rendering. While the first Nahua choice refers to Aquinas's concise definition of idolatry as "the worship of false gods," the Zapotec designation, which first appeared in print in Feria's 1567 *Doctrina*, establishes a direct link with a venerable rhetorical attack on idolatry on the part of the Old Testament prophets Isaiah, Jeremiah, and Habakkuk: the proposition that, in their foolishness, idolaters take mere representations made of wood and stone to be real gods.[48] The Nahua *tlateotoquiliztli* is both terse and concise; the Zapotec formula reflects the profound disdain with which biblical authors regarded their pagan neighbors.

How did ecclesiastic and civil judges define idolatry? Since the first half of the sixteenth century, native ritual practitioners were absorbed into a Christian classificatory scheme and received the terse designations of "idolaters," "sorcerers," or "superstitious healers," which covered both collective and elective ritual practices. In spite of an inquisitorial style that betrayed an unusual degree of intellectual curiosity, just as Italian inquisitors regarded peasant Friulian folk ideology as an organized witch cult,[49] the extirpators of New Spain often perceived native ritual practices as a unified antithesis of Christianity.[50] From the early seventeenth century onward, a divide appeared between two modes of eradication: an earlier one embraced by regulars, that is, Franciscans, Dominicans, and other mendicants, and a novel one advocated by seculars, or nonmendicant priests. In spite of a long-standing theological debate about New World idolatry, and a pragmatic focus on diverse ritual practices, most secular extirpators in Mexico and Oaxaca appeared to be unaware of the existence of earlier debates on idolatry and sorcery. For instance, two of the most procedurally oriented extirpators, Pedro Sánchez de Aguilar and Gonzalo de Balsalobre, cited specific Laws of the Indies, orders from the Mexican church councils, royal orders outlining idolatry extirpation policies, and a smattering of respected juridical

authorities, such as Barbosa, Vela, and Villadiego, to justify their procedural choices.[51] In an exceptional case, ecclesiastical judge Diego Jaimes
Ricardo Villavicencio contrasted a narrative about idolatry among the
Greeks and Romans with accounts about Mexica ritual practices drawn
from Torquemada and other printed sources available in the late seventeenth century.[52] For many of the secular extirpators, "idolatry" seemed
to be a self-evident juridical category requiring minimal explicit elucidation and maximal procedural clarity. To paraphrase a famous juridical
dictum regarding pornography,[53] many extirpators apparently believed
they knew idolatry when they saw it.

The local and regional attempts by mendicants, secular ministers, and
civil judges to eradicate what they regarded as idolatry in Central Mexico
should not be seen as unique projects, as they coincided with campaigns
against local Christian devotions and agrarian cults conducted in Spain,
France, and Italy in the late sixteenth and early seventeenth centuries.[54]
Unlike the idolatry campaigns in the archbishopric of Lima in the seventeenth century, which were conducted in a relatively compact region
inhabited by speakers of one major indigenous language,[55] the enemies
of idolatry in the New Spain orchestrated their campaigns in a rather
ad hoc manner in several regions inhabited by diverse linguistic communities. In New Spain, the exclusion of natives from the jurisdiction of
the Inquisition tribunal after its creation in Mexico in 1571 highlighted
two crucial juridical and procedural problems in ecclesiastical legisla-
tion. Which civil and ecclesiastic authorities possessed this mandate?
What was the juridical definition of an idolater? Throughout the seventeenth century, those who fought idolatry focused on the former question
and seldom addressed the latter in depth. After 1571, the prosecution of
natives for crimes against the Christian faith was, in principle, a task
reserved for bishops and their *provisores*, or chief prosecutors in the diocese. Toward the end of the seventeenth century, some bishops appointed
two provisores: a provisor *de indios*, and a provisor *de españoles*. These
magistrates were the most prominent executors of ecclesiastical justice
in the see, and their mandate for indigenous subjects included, in relative order of priority, tithes and contributions to the church, marriage
dispensations, bigamy accusations, pious works, and idolatry and sorcery accusations. I use *Provisorato* as shorthand for the ecclesiastical
juridical apparatus charged with investigating native heterodoxy from
1571 onward.[56] In some cases, the *ordinario*, or sitting (arch)bishop in
a diocese, misunderstood the extent of his faculties, leading to jurisdictional conflicts with the Mexican Holy Office and the civil justice.[57]
These confrontations are discussed in detail in Chapters 3, 4, and 8. The
Inquisition often received accusations against natives, and these were

turned over to the diocesan jurisdiction once it was determined that the suspects possessed the legal status of indigenous subjects.[58]

As a rule, ecclesiastical judges treated idolatry and superstition as *casos reservados*, or restricted cases that could not be instructed without the consent of a bishop or provisor. In fact, after 1571, the ordinarios of Mexico and Oaxaca began delegating the faculty of instructing idolatry and sorcery proceedings against natives to a select group of secular priests, many of whom had relevant experience or linguistic aptitudes, who received the titles of *jueces de comisión*, judges subject to a temporary appointment; these titles often included the phrase *contra las idolatrías*, thus specifying that the scope was limited to idolatry investigations.[59] Some clergy, mostly in Oaxaca, received a title naming them as *jueces de idolatrías*.[60] A small number of clergy were named *jueces de visita contra las idolatrías*, judges appointed in connection with a particular inspection.[61] If the priest in question already was *vicario y juez eclesiástico*, vicar and ecclesiastical judge, episcopal authorities sometimes provided him with additional faculties against idolatry.[62] Nevertheless, as discussed in Chapter 8, ecclesiastical judges in eighteenth-century Toluca did not cite specific faculties against idolatry and apparently proceeded *de oficio*, by the rights inherent to their position, but their counterparts in Oaxaca continued to receive specific commissions. Although idolatry was often regarded in principle as the exclusive province of ecclesiastical jurisdiction, a small but significant number of alcaldes mayores and *corregidores*, district governors appointed by the king, presided over idolatry trials in Mexico and Oaxaca as early as the 1530s. They continued to intervene in idolatry cases until the end of the eighteenth century.[63] Paradoxically, the largest extant set of idolatry trials in Oaxaca were heard not by ecclesiastical, but by civil justices in Villa Alta and Teposcolula.

Corporal punishment was a central component of idolatry eradication policies in Central Mexico. Nonetheless, the available data on juridical torture applied to native defendants accused of idolatry, sorcery, or superstition in New Spain between the 1520s and the early nineteenth century indicates that physical coercion and torture were highly unusual inquisitorial tools that were used in exceptional cases by a handful of ruthless or desperate inquisitors. In fact, in Central Mexico, juridical torture was applied to native idolatry or sorcery suspects during only seven trials: the trial against Phurépecha ruler Tzintzicha Tangaxoan by Nuño de Guzmán in 1530;[64] the trial of the former Nahua priest Alonso Tlilanci by fray Hernando de Oviedo in 1539;[65] the trial of Miguel the Pochtecatlailotlac by Bishop Juan de Zumárraga in 1540;[66] the trial of Nahua ritual specialist Tomás Tunalt by Gerónimo Flores in 1545;[67] the trial of four Zapotec residents of Teiticpac by fray Domingo Grijelmo in

1560;[68] the investigations on Zapotec idolatry in Villa Alta conducted by fray Pedro Guerrero in 1560;[69] and the civil trial of thirty-four residents of the Caxonos region in Villa Alta for rioting, murder, idolatry, and insubordination between 1700 and 1702.[70] Could physical coercion be regarded as an important factor in the extraction of confessions from native suspects? While torture was extremely infrequent, psychological coercion, public shame, fear of colonial authorities, and interpersonal conflict were much more likely to play a role in the extraction of confessions. In quantitative terms, the extant trial records reveal that only about 6 percent of all natives accused of idolatry and sorcery were subject to juridical torture in the dioceses of Mexico and Oaxaca between 1527 and 1759. In fact, juridical torture against idolaters was used primarily in the first half-century after the conquest, and its use decreased considerably after 1560.

PERIODIZATION AND QUANTITATIVE DATA
ABOUT IDOLATRY ERADICATION

From an institutional perspective, extirpation attempts in the ecclesiastical jurisdictions of Mexico and Oaxaca may be divided into four longitudinal "cycles," a term borrowed from Edward Spicer's analysis of "cycles of conquest" in the Greater Chichimeca.[71] The first cycle, denominated "the apostolic inquisition" by José Toribio Medina and Richard Greenleaf, begins with the public execution of several Tlaxcalteca lords circa 1527, comprises the idolatry trials of Zumárraga, Tello de Sandoval, and the Dominicans of Oaxaca between 1536 and the 1560s, and culminates with the transference of natives to episcopal jurisdiction after 1571, when separate inquisitorial tribunals were created in Mexico and Lima. The second cycle, from 1571 to about 1660, features a marked increase in the involvement of secular ministers in extirpation campaigns, epitomized by the activities of Hernando Ruiz de Alarcón and Jacinto de la Serna in Mexico, and Gonzalo de Balsalobre in Oaxaca, who along with Pedro Sánchez de Aguilar in Yucatán produced the first empirical extirpation manuals in New Spain. Paradoxically, this cycle's activities coincide with the lowest point in the demographic decline of indigenous populations in Central Mexico. The third cycle, between 1660 and the 1720s, begins with the suppression of a native rebellion in Tehuantepec, is characterized by the hardening of institutional punitive tactics exemplified by the establishment of a "perpetual prison" for idolaters in Oaxaca City, and leads to the multitudinous confessions secured by Bishop Maldonado in Villa Alta, the most ambitious and systematic extirpation campaign ever conducted in New Spain. The fourth and final cycle, which begins in the

1720s and extends until the end of colonial rule, introduces three novel strategies: the promotion of Spanish-language schools, the centralization of legal proceedings, and the requirement, from 1754 onward, to have a physician inspect any alleged victim of sorcery in Mexico. This period ends with a relative decrease in idolatry accusations.

This periodization rests on my interpretation of surviving data regarding allegations against indigenous specialists. The colonial record of native devotions in New Spain, as William B. Taylor noted in an erudite survey, "is most striking for its patchiness,"[72] a state of affairs stemming from the divergent preservation history of relevant archives. The set of indigenous trial records generated during the apostolic inquisition period (1520s–1550s) were generally archived with all other Mexican Holy Office records and have had a rather successful preservation history. Civil proceedings against indigenous specialists have been archived both in centralized locations (for instance, in various collections now residing at the Archivo General de la Nación [AGN] in Mexico City) and local judicial archives (such as proceedings heard by the alcaldes mayores of Villa Alta and Teposcolula in Oaxaca). In contrast, provisorato records in both Mexico and Oaxaca had a checkered preservation history, and of necessity this fact reduced their visibility in the historiography of idolatry extirpation in New Spain and encouraged the study of the apostolic inquisition. After more than a decade of research, I located a more substantial number of records relating to ecclesiastical and civil measures against native heterodoxy. I now turn to a brief quantitative characterization of these findings.

In a classical overview of microhistory, Carlo Ginzburg emphasizes the importance of biographical information about low-status, plebeian individuals by noting that "the lines that converge on the proper name, and that emanate from it in the manner of a tightly woven spider's web, give to the observer the graphic image of the network of social rapports in which the individual is placed."[73] The pages that follow will discuss the proper names and biographical information of an otherwise faceless host of natives, many of whom left little or no trace in records beyond their passage through colonial courtrooms. I turn to a quantitative accounting of these records, which provide a general perspective about the presence of these individuals as a group in the archives. I have kept Ginzburg's premise in mind during the tabulation process.

Charts 1.1 and 1.2 report the total number of individual natives accused of being ritual specialists for which name, gender, place of residence, and other biographical information exists. Each number on the right vertical axis represents a single accusation against a unique individual in a given decade. Hence, except for less than five renowned specialists whose careers resulted in two or three substantial separate investigations—such as Diego

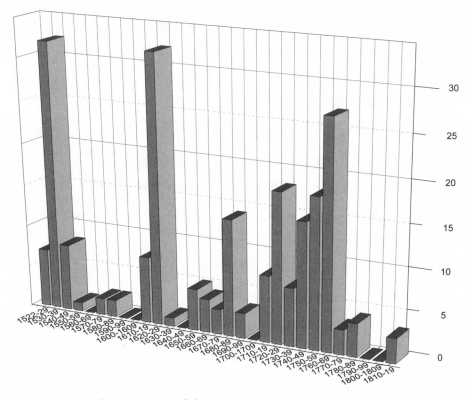

CHART 1.1   Extant Native Idolatry, Sorcery, or Superstition Accusations in Mexico, 1520s–1810s.

SOURCES: ACM; AGI; AGN; AGOP; AHAM; AHAO; ALC; AHJO; BMNA; NL

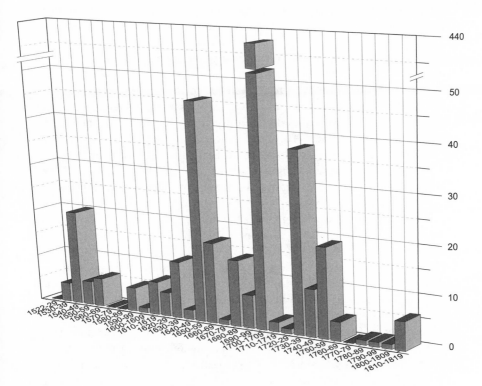

CHART 1.2 Extant Native Idolatry, Sorcery, or Superstition Accusations in Oaxaca, 1520s–1810s. 1700–1709 data not to scale (438 accusations).

SOURCES: ACM; AGI; AGN; AGOP; AHAM; AHAO; ALC; AHJO; BMNA; NL

Luis of San Miguel Sola—each specialist appears only once in this data set. In fact, this is an exacting and conservative reckoning, for I exclude about 103 idolatry convictions reported by ecclesiastical authorities in various documents, since no gender, linguistic, or biographical data about these specialists is extant and these figures cannot be confirmed through other sources.[74] I have focused on natives identified as specialists by those who denounced them, so these figures do not include clients. Furthermore, I have used accusations against specific individuals as an organizing principle, excluding any natives who did not figure directly in the proceedings.

These charts refer to juridical acts against natives within the diocesan boundaries of Mexico and Oaxaca and generally exclude accusations in neighboring sees, even when such cases are discussed in this work. Hence, at least three important cases heard outside the diocese of Mexico are not included in these graphs: the 1743 accusations against O'odham people from Ónavas and San Pedro de la Conquista;[75] the 1769 cult headed by Juan Diego in San Mateo Tututepec and investigated by civil and diocesan courts in Puebla;[76] and the 1796 hybrid observances at San Luis de la Paz in Michoacán led by Andrés Martínez.[77] I have also collected biographical information regarding approximately one hundred sixty ecclesiastical and civil justices who investigated and punished indigenous specialists, sixty-four active in Mexico and ninety-six in Oaxaca. Data about these eradicators have been incorporated throughout this work.

Charts 1.1 and 1.2 display all extant and corroborable native idolatry, sorcery, and superstition accusations made throughout colonial times by decade from the early 1520s until the early 1800s in the sees of Mexico and Oaxaca, respectively. There was some uncertainty as to the exact boundary between the dioceses of Mexico and Tlaxcala before the seat of the latter was moved from Tlaxcala to Puebla in 1543.[78] Hence, these charts include cases from four locations that fell under the jurisdiction of the bishop of Tlaxcala after 1543: Izúcar, Teotlalco, and Tlapa in Chart 1.1; and Tlacotepec in Chart 1.2.

For the diocese of Mexico, Chart 1.1 reflects allegations against 225 specialists contained in sixty-nine trials or proceeding summaries and in about thirty-seven accusations not resulting in full proceedings. A large majority of them, 172 specialists, or 76.45 percent, were Nahuatl speakers; the other linguistic groups represented are Otomi (25; 11.11 percent), Matlatzinca (5; 2.22 percent), Mazahua (2; 0.89 percent), Tlapanec (2; 0.89 percent), and Totonac (1; 0.44 percent). The rest of these cases in Mexico concern specialists whose linguistic affiliation is uncertain, given the predominant languages in their place of residence: Matlatzinca or Otomi (8; 3.56 percent); Otomi or Pame (5; 2.22 percent). Finally, the languages spoken by five, or 2.22 percent, of the accused are unknown.

For Oaxaca, Chart 1.2 portrays allegations against 673 ritual specialists compiled in three types of sources: fifty-seven trials or proceeding summaries, accusations against sixty native practitioners not resulting in full proceedings, and communal confessions signed by representatives of about one hundred native communities in Villa Alta in 1704–5. This set features an overwhelming majority of Zapotec speakers, 567 specialists, or 84.24 percent, with smaller concentrations of Mixe (37; 5.5 percent), Mixtec (30; 4.46 percent), Chinantec (20; 2.97 percent), Cuicatec (9; 1.34 percent), Chatino (8; 1.19 percent), and Tlapanec (1; 0.15 percent) speakers. The language spoken by only one specialist in this group (0.15 percent) is unknown. Given that the Villa Alta confessions and other sources for 1700–1709 in Oaxaca feature information about 438 specialists, this spike dwarfs information about all other periods, and hence this data point is shown not to scale, on a broken y-axis.

A quick comparison of Charts 1.1 and 1.2 demonstrates that, except for the 1750s, extirpation activities reached their peaks during separate periods in each diocese. In Mexico, the more active intervals are the 1530s, the 1620s, the 1750s, and the 1760s, and they depict the extirpatory zeal of Bishop Zumárraga (1536–40), Ruiz de Alarcón (1620s), and Toluca ecclesiastical judges Juan del Villar (1740s–50s) and George Martínez (1750s–60s). In Oaxaca, the most active periods besides 1700–1709 include the 1650s and 1660s, the 1730s, and the 1750s, reflecting proceedings heard by Balsalobre (1650s), several Villa Alta alcaldes mayores (1660s), and Bishop Maldonado (1700s), and important cases in Yalálag (1730s) and the Chinantla (1750s). Some of these fluctuations correlate with the transitional periods in the four extirpatory cycles that were proposed above: the shift from the apostolic inquisition to secular extirpations in the early seventeenth century, a transition in punitive tactics in the 1660s, and a set of institutional reforms in the 1720s and 1730s.

As will be argued in Chapters 2, 3, and 7, the increases in activity shown in Charts 1.1 and 1.2 were driven by political and ideological factors, for these rising trends cannot be easily linked to demographic patterns. In other words, the first half of the seventeenth century, when Central Mexican communities reached their demographic nadir, is characterized by a paradoxical increase in secular extirpation campaigns, which derived their urgency from the ideological climate established by Counter-Reformation policies in New Spain. Nonetheless, it is possible that the various periods of heightened activity between the 1700s and the 1750s correlate with a gradual recovery in Central Mexican population growth in the eighteenth century. Such a proposal would not be out of bounds; for instance, the quantitative analysis of a much larger set of witchcraft accusations in early modern Europe shows that changes in the pattern of witchcraft prosecutions before and after 1420 may have been shaped by demographic factors correlated with urban growth.[79]

CHAPTER OVERVIEW

This book's structure reflects my periodization and conceptual scheme for idolatry eradication in Central Mexico. Here, I have begun by presenting two complementary approaches. I started with a model that proposes two domains for the social reproduction of indigenous ritual practices: the collective and the elective spheres. I then sketched four periods in idolatry eradication efforts and provided a *longue-durée* perspective on quantitative data regarding accusations against native specialists. Chapter 2 opens with a brief look at the emergence of doctrinal discourses in Nahuatl and Zapotec before turning to the "apostolic inquisition" extirpatory cycle that unfolded between the late 1520s and 1571, the year when Holy Office tribunals in Mexico City and Lima were established, leading to the exclusion of indigenous subjects from inquisitorial jurisdiction. Chapter 2 also focuses on the disciplinary humanism of Bishop Zumárraga in Mexico, his use of public exemplary punishment, the execution of Nahua nobleman don Carlos Chichimecateuctli, and the transition to a less active extirpation under Tello de Sandoval and Archbishop Montúfar. These developments are contrasted with the Dominican order's disciplinary policies against idolaters in Oaxaca—particularly under Bishop Albuquerque—and with demographic data regarding population decline in the late sixteenth century.

Chapters 3 and 4 examine a second extirpatory cycle that began with the post-1571 transfer of jurisdiction over natives from the Inquisition to bishops and their diocesan tribunals, which was characterized by the participation of secular clergy as zealous investigators of indigenous heterodoxy. Chapter 3 investigates the careers of Ponce de León, Ruiz de Alarcón, and de la Serna in various Nahua-speaking regions in the see of Mexico and proposes a contextual analysis of the *nahualtocaitl*, a Nahua ritual genre through which specialists personified Postclassic deities. Chapter 4 analyzes the activities of various secular extirpators under Bishops Bohórquez and Hevia y Valdés in Oaxaca, with particular attention to the campaigns conducted by Balsalobre in south central Oaxaca, and the activities of the literate Zapotec specialist Diego Luis. This section examines Balsalobre's 1656 *Relación auténtica*, the first idolatry extirpation manual printed in New Spain, and then turns to an epochal jurisdictional dispute between the Holy Office and Hevia y Valdés.

Chapter 5 focuses on an unexpected development that began in the early seventeenth century: the appropriation of European literacy practices by indigenous specialists, which led to the clandestine circulation of ritual and devotional texts in Nahuatl and Zapotec. This topic is explored through four distinct case studies: the oral and written reproduction of Nahua ritual knowledge in the prayers collected by Ruiz de Alarcón, the emergence of a network of literate and partially literate users of calendrical texts around specialists like Diego Luis in south central Oaxaca, the appropriation of European almanacs and astrological texts by Nahua authors, and the circulation of the Northern Zapotec divinatory calendar in the seventeenth century.

Chapter 6 depicts two transitions at the beginning of a third cycle of idolatry eradication lasting from the 1660s into the second decade of the early eighteenth century. In the archbishopric of Mexico, there was a change in institutional practices that framed the consolidation of the diocesan tribunal into the Provisorato de Indios y Chinos. In Oaxaca, an escalation in punitive tactics in the 1670s and 1680s led to legal conflict between the Dominicans and alcaldes mayores on the one hand, and local specialists on the other, and to the establishment of a "perpetual prison for idolaters." Chapter 7 builds on the preceding chapter through an analysis of a bureaucratized extirpation campaign led by Bishop Maldonado in northern Oaxaca in 1702–6. I investigate native responses to this campaign, the most ambitious eradication effort ever conducted in New Spain, and I analyze Northern Zapotec clandestine devotions through two case studies: the clandestine worship of founding ancestors and Postclassic deities, and the appropriation of an indigenous ritual genre for catechistic purposes.

Chapter 8 discusses major trends characterizing a fourth and final extirpatory cycle, which extended from the 1720s into the early nineteenth century. In Mexico, this period entailed a modest increase in native sorcery accusations in the Toluca Valley, a more systematic approach to ecclesiastical juridical procedure during and after the tenure of Provisor Castorena y Urzúa, and the incipient medicalization of sorcery claims. In Oaxaca, the punitive experiment of the prison of idolaters came to an end, and an increase in local factionalism in various Zapotec and Chinantec communities impacted ecclesiastic and civil projects targeting native specialists and led to jurisdictional struggle. By way of a conclusion, Chapter 9 offers a reflection on the findings of this longitudinal, multidisciplinary inquiry into clandestine native observances in Central Mexico.

Before 1571

Disciplinary Humanism and Exemplary Punishment

On Sunday, November 30, 1539, a Nahua noble was led to a scaffold in Mexico City's main square. He had received the name don Carlos through Christian baptism; as a direct descendant of Tetzcoco's rulers, he bore the title of *Chichimecateuctli*, Chichimec Lord, inherited from his grandfather Nezahualcoyotl; following preconquest usage, his calendrical name was Ome Tochtli, 2-Rabbit.[1] He would be the last indigenous nobleman executed for crimes against the Christian faith in Central Mexico; in fact, no native convicted of crimes against Christianity would be punished in the public spaces of Mexico City again until 1714.[2] This execution epitomized an institutional attack on a style of native rulership that posed an obstacle to missionary evangelization enterprises. Fray Juan de Zumárraga, the first bishop of Mexico, intended don Carlos's execution to be an exemplary punishment to be witnessed by all native neophytes in the city. The bishop's disciplinary actions symbolically reclaimed public spaces: don Carlos was paraded from the inquisitorial jail to the scaffold on the city's main square bearing the markers of a Holy Office convict: the penitential robe and pointed cap respectively known as *sanbenito* and *coroza*, a tall candle in his hands, and a cross before him. A native interpreter proclaimed don Carlos's transgressions in Nahuatl, and the nobleman then reportedly repented from them in public.[3] Don Carlos's execution has been interpreted as a turning point in idolatry extirpation that led to the removal of natives from inquisitorial jurisdiction when Philip II established a Mexican Holy Office in 1571.[4] This chapter expands on this assessment by contextualizing Zumárraga's campaign within a first cycle of anti-idolatry efforts between the 1520s and 1571. It has also been argued that don Carlos's trial marks a transition from harsh public punishment to more subtle forms of discipline.[5] I will argue that this conclusion is not supported by existing evidence in the dioceses of Mexico and Oaxaca.

To paraphrase the Marxian bromide, the period between 1521 and 1571 in Central Mexico is one in which the historiographical tradition weighs like a nightmare in the brain of the living. This is a time of military conquests, early missionary projects, and emerging forms of colonial domination. Hence, this chapter has several mandates. It opens with an overview of early Christian literature in Nahuatl and Zapotec. Then, it examines Zumárraga's methods and plumbs other poorly known extirpation projects by building on insights drawn from five influential historiographical projects: Robert Ricard's exploration of missionary doctrinal enterprises; Richard Greenleaf's depiction of Zumárraga's age; Georges Baudot's portrayal of the intellectual background of early evangelization projects; Alberro's analysis of the institutional dynamics of the Mexican Holy Office; and Gruzinski's incisive interpretation of the impact of colonial rule in Central Mexico.[6] Then, the chapter focuses on the dynamics of extirpation projects led by Zumárraga, Tello de Sandoval, and Montúfar in Mexico, and Albuquerque in Oaxaca. The chapter closes with an assessment of the prosecution of native idolatry in the context of rapid population decline in Central Mexico.

NAHUA AND ZAPOTEC DOCTRINAL
DISCOURSES IN THE SIXTEENTH CENTURY

In the first two decades after the fall of Tenochtitlan, a small group of Franciscan, Dominican, and Augustinian missionaries faced a formidable task: not only did they pursue the indoctrination of millions of indigenous peoples, but they also attempted to break through multiple language barriers, apprehend indigenous cultural categories and social practices, and produce viable descriptions of indigenous languages through the transcription and grammatical practices afforded them by the intellectual repertoire of early Renaissance Europe. The reconstitution of European discourses on Christian practices into meaningful words in indigenous languages was the keystone of mendicant doctrinal strategies. From their perspective, their linguistic task addressed an ancient link between multilingualism and infidelity: Aquinas observed that idolatry began in the "second age" of the world—that is, after the Flood;[7] the Franciscan Sahagún concurred by noting in his 1583 *Psalmodia Christiana* that idolatry originated with the confusion of tongues after the fall of Babel.[8]

The trajectory of the Franciscan Pedro de Gante is a paradigmatic example of the multiple roles played by early missionary lexicographers.[9]

Gante arrived in Central Mexico in 1523 with two Flemish colleagues, ahead of the symbolic arrival of twelve Franciscans at the port of Veracruz in 1524.[10] By dividing the Basin of Mexico and Tlaxcala among them, these Franciscans secured their regions of influence before the 1526 arrival of the Dominicans and the 1533 entrance of the Augustinians in New Spain.[11] Gante became an influential educator in the Franciscan enterprise in Mexico: he founded an indigenous school known as San José de los Naturales, interceded on behalf of the Indians and the Franciscans before Charles V and Philip II, declined an opportunity to become archbishop of Mexico after Zumárraga's death in 1547,[12] and was widely mourned after his death in 1572. At the indigenous school of Santa Cruz in Tlatelolco, formally established in January 1536, Gante taught reading, writing, and singing during the day and doctrine and sermons in the evenings to noble Nahua children from the Basin of Mexico.[13] Perhaps beginning with his stay in Tetzcoco in 1523–26, but certainly when he moved to Tlatelolco after 1526, Gante pioneered the dual linguistic and visual approach that would characterize indigenous doctrinal instruction in the sixteenth century. His 1529 letter to members of his order in Flanders featured a Nahuatl sentence that is the oldest extant printed phrase in an indigenous language of the Americas.[14] Gante also composed an influential Nahuatl doctrine, which survives in a 1547 version and a revised 1553 edition. Moreover, Gante, like Jacobo de Tastera, used drawings to impress upon his native audience the basic tenets of the new faith in a genre that was later labeled "Testerian catechisms": brief texts with pictorial and ideographic representations that illustrated basic Christian tenets.[15]

The grouping of authors of Nahuatl and Zapotec printed doctrinal works during the sixteenth century sheds some light into the long-term transformation of doctrinal discourses. The most prominent authors of the first generation, who cover the decades between 1520 and 1550, are the Franciscans Francisco Ximénez, reputedly the first author of a Nahuatl grammar and vocabulary, Pedro de Gante, Andrés de Olmos, Toribio Benavente (known as Motolinia, "He Is Poor," in Nahuatl), Alonso de Escalona, Juan de Ribas, Juan de Romanones, Jean Focher, García de Cisneros, Arnold Basace, Alonso Rengel, and Alonso de Herrera.[16] There exist at least five texts that mark a transition in the emergence of textual genres in Nahuatl at midcentury: Gante's *Doctrina Christiana en lengua mexicana*;[17] a 1550 Nahuatl *Doctrina*, attributed to a group of Dominican writers rather than to a single author;[18] the 1552 *Libellus de medicinalibus indorum herbis*, a treatise on New Spain plants and their medicinal faculties by Nahua authors Martín de la Cruz and Juan Badiano;[19] a set of Nahuatl annals featuring personal observations about memorable public happenings,[20] and a monumental Nahuatl translation of the most popular devotional work in early modern Europe, Thomas à Kempis's *On the Imitation of Christ*, produced by and for a circle of Nahua authors probably associated with the Colegio de Santa Cruz in Tlatelolco and under the supervision of the Franciscan Luis Rodríguez.[21]

Even though there is no extant evidence of the output of missionary linguists who worked in colonial Zapotec variants before 1550, a Dominican cohort active between 1550 and 1590, which would correspond to the second generation of Nahua doctrinal authors, produced three foundational texts that shaped doctrinal discourses in Zapotec: Pedro de Feria's 1567 *Doctrina cristiana en lengua castellana y çapoteca*, and Juan de Córdova's *Arte del idioma zapoteco* and *Vocabvlario en lengua çapoteca*, both first printed in 1578. Some references to no longer extant works suggest that the range of Zapotec genres the Dominicans cultivated was rather broad: songs and sacramental plays,[22] a biblical drama, a work on the martyrdom of Saint Catherine of Alexandria,[23] and various other doctrinal works. An even greater diversity is in evidence in the works of the second generation of authors of Nahuatl doctrinal works (1550 to 1590). The production of missionary texts and the genres covered—catechisms, sermons, moral treatises, historical narratives, translations of devotional works, rewordings of pre-Hispanic songs—reached its apex through the works of missionaries from various orders: Domingo de la Anunciación, Juan de la Anunciación, Alonso de Escalona, Juan de Gaona, Jerónimo de Mendieta, Alonso de Molina, Bernardino de Sahagún, Alonso de Truxillo, and Miguel de Zárate.[24]

James Lockhart's three-stage interpretation of changes in Nahuatl textual genres provides a useful vantage point for long-term language change in Central Mexico: Stage 1 (1530s to 1540s) is characterized by the use of Nahuatl neologisms for notions unfamiliar to Nahuatl speakers; Stage 2 (1540s to 1640) is marked by the appropriation of Spanish loan words and expressions; Stage 3 (1640–present) is characterized by growing Spanish syntactic, semantic, and phonological influence on Nahuatl.[25] Colonial Mixtec may have gone through a similar set of changes, exhibiting a more gradual transformation between stages 2 and 3.[26] Colonial Zapotec has not yet been the subject of longitudinal philological analysis.

BEFORE ZUMÁRRAGA: MARTYRDOM NARRATIVES AND PUBLIC EXECUTIONS

During the 1520s and early 1530s, inquisitorial faculties were exercised by several clerics in New Spain or Hispaniola who held Holy Office commissions. These powers existed alongside various extraordinary faculties

that allowed ecclesiastics without such a commission to act as inquisitors. Since the regular orders were the only ecclesiastics capable of following the accelerated pace of military conquest, in 1522 Pope Adrian VI
issued *Exponi nobis*, also known as *Omnímoda*, a bull giving temporary episcopal powers, excepting ordination and other faculties reserved
for consecrated bishops, to all regulars living beyond a two-day journey
from a diocesan seat.[27] In 1535, Paul III extended these faculties to all
regulars located within this radius, if their bishop consented to such
an arrangement.[28] Indeed, Martín de Valencia, leader of the celebrated
group of twelve Franciscans who arrived in New Spain in 1524, exercised
faculties as inquisitorial commissioner between 1524 and 1526, but the
circumstances surrounding his appointment are unclear.[29] After Valencia, the Dominican Tomás Ortiz briefly assumed this office before ceding
inquisitorial obligations to another Dominican, Domingo de Betanzos,
who tried a total of nineteen cases, none dealing with idolatry or superstition. In July 1528, Vicente de Santa María, the vicar general of the
New Spain Dominicans, became the inquisitorial commissioner upon
Betanzos's departure to Guatemala.[30] Hence, it is not a surprise to find
only one extant idolatry trial before 1535: Santa María's proceedings
against a Spanish clerk.[31]

The multitudinous period between the arrival of the Franciscan order
in Central Mexico in 1523–24 and 1536, the year when fray Juan de
Zumárraga returned from Spain to assume his post as first bishop of the
diocese of Mexico, was dominated by a missionary obsession with gathering natives for mass baptisms and indoctrination. The Franciscan drive
to baptize multitudes of indigenous converts was influenced by millenarist tendencies informed by the works of the Italian twelfth-century author Joachim de Fiore. By the first decades of the sixteenth century, some
Franciscans believed that, after human history had completed the Age
of the Father, as narrated in the Old Testament, and the Age of the Son,
which began with Christ's sacrifice, the age they lived in belonged to the
Holy Spirit. A sign this age had arrived was the unparalleled opportunity
to convert the many natives living in recently uncovered lands. Some
missionaries even thought that Christ's second coming would occur soon
after these nonbelievers were baptized.[32]

The pulse of that age in Mexico is captured by three letters that were
translated into Latin and printed in Amandus van Zierikzee's *Chronica
compendiosissima*, a 1534 volume celebrating the spread of Christianity
to Africa and the Americas by the Franciscans. One of these letters was
the one composed by Gante in 1529 and cited above; it contained an account of his efforts to establish a Christian curriculum for young native
neophytes. Moreover, in a July 1531 letter to the Franciscan Cismountain

provincial, or chief administrator of a mendicant province, Zumárraga asserted that he and other coreligionists had baptized two hundred and fifty thousand natives, destroyed fifty temples, and smashed and burned twenty thousand "images of the devil." Finally, in a 1531 letter, Valencia, who still believed he was residing in *magna Asia*, boasted of the baptism of "more than one million" natives and stated that diligent missionaries such as Francisco de los Ángeles were responsible for at least one hundred thousand neophyte baptisms.[33] Nonetheless, no extant documentation corroborates these Franciscans' hyperbolic statements.[34]

Valencia was so impatient to push forward with evangelization that some of his dreams, as reported by Mendieta, feature premonitions of native peoples in Asia better prepared to receive the Christian word. In fact, these visions reveal disillusion with the natives of Central Mexico. In one of them, Valencia witnesses the efforts of two types of beasts of burden. The first ones barely finish their journey due to exhaustion, but the second ones "walked with a lightness in their step and seemingly without suffering." Valencia later understood that the former group stood for the natives of Central Mexico, while the latter "were other peoples that would soon be discovered . . . who would convert without compulsion or fear and would gracefully bear the yoke of the Lord and His holy faith." Furthermore, another evocative dream portrayed the natives of New Spain as an ugly woman and a crusty-eyed child who barely reach salvation after crossing a river.[35]

Although Valencia did not hold an inquisitorial commission between 1527 and 1531, he led several measures against relapsed Nahua neophytes in Tlaxcala.[36] These attacks began in 1525, when the Franciscans expelled the Nahua priests of Tetzcoco from their temples, which were then demolished.[37] Three well-known accounts by Mendieta portray early struggles against idolatry as a contest between eager neophytes and recalcitrant elders. Mendieta praised the Christian ardor of some children from the first Franciscan school in Tlaxcala, who stoned to death a priest who walked through a crowded market chewing on obsidian blades while dressed as Ome Tochtli, or 2-Rabbit, the Mexica deity associated with *pulque*, an alcoholic beverage. Mendieta also recounted a confrontation between Acxotecatl, a nobleman from the Tlaxcalteca town of Atlihuetzia, and his recently baptized son Cristóbal. When Cristóbal broke Acxotecatl's idols due to a relapse after being baptized, Acxotecatl threw him into a fire and had Cristóbal's mother killed. Motivated by a Spaniard's complaint about being mistreated by Acxotecatl, Cortés commissioned Martín de Calahorra to prosecute this lord. Calahorra eventually uncovered evidence of the murders and sentenced Acxotecatl to death by hanging, with Cortés's approval.[38] Other

Tlaxcalteca elites were also executed in the same year. According to the *Anales de Tlaxcala*, in the year 8-Rabbit, circa 1527, four other lords were hanged: they were Cuauhtlahtoa, lord of Atempan; Tenamaz, lord of Tepeyanco and Ocotelulco; Cuicuiltzin; and Atlontzin.[39] In fact, a late sixteenth-century Tlaxcalteca source depicted the burning of two other natives and the hanging of one woman and five idolatrous *caciques*, or native chiefs, by order of Cortés and with the approval of the four lords of Tlaxcala.[40]

Mendieta's third narrative focuses on the martyrdom of Nahua children. Valencia gave the Dominicans Bernardino de Minaya and Gonzalo Lucero three children to assist them in their journey to Oaxaca: Antonio, the grandson of Tlaxcalteca ruler Xicotencatl, his servant Juan, and Diego. After Antonio and Juan destroyed idols in Cuauhtinchan and Tecali, several noblemen beat them to death and threw their bodies in a ravine. These murders resulted in the hanging of the lord of Cuauhtinchan and his associates.[41] Some Nahua annals date these events to 13-Reed, circa 1531, and reveal that Tochayotl and the *tlacochcalcatl* Huilacapitzin were among those executed.[42] The alleged martyrdom of these children became a leitmotif in evangelization narratives; besides a work by Motolinia translated into Nahuatl by Juan Bautista Viseo,[43] several late colonial paintings at the church of Atlihuetzia rehearsed this account.

In a complicating turn for early idolatry eradication, civil judges in New Spain could claim jurisdiction over indigenous idolaters and sorcerers, following Castilian precedents. Spanish possessions in the New World were regarded as part of the kingdom of Castile,[44] and Castilian law was an important source for juridical principles in the Indies. Title 23, Law I of the *Siete Partidas*, a compilation of early Castilian law, distinguished between "astronomy," a legitimate pursuit, and "auguries" and "sorcery," which were forbidden; Title 23, Law II denounced necromancy and love magic; Title 23, Law III, charged the civil justice with punishing these transgressions, but permitted exorcists and specialists who cast spells against impotence, hail, or locusts to practice their trades.[45] This precedent was expanded upon by a June 1523 *cédula*, or royal decree, from Charles V, which asked the viceroy and the American *Audiencias*, or high civil courts, to destroy idols and temples and punish natives engaging in idolatry, ritual sacrifice, and cannibalism. This decree gave rise to a similar statute in the Laws of Indies: under the provisions of Law 35, Book VI, Title V of the *Recopilación de Leyes de Indias*, the royal justice could intervene in sorcery cases if they involved *maleficio*, or damage or death caused by an implicit or explicit pact between a sorcerer and the devil.

Two civil cases from the 1530s demonstrate both the latitude civil justices enjoyed and the potential for abuses. The better-known case is that of Nuño de Guzmán, the infamously ruthless president of the first Audiencia of Mexico, the highest civil court in New Spain. In early February 1530, Guzmán tried, tortured, and executed Tzintzicha Tangaxoan, the *Caltzontzi*, or native ruler, of the most powerful Phurépecha state in Michoacán. The once mighty Caltzontzi, along with his associates don Pedro Panza, don Alonso Vise, and Gonzalo Xuárez, were submitted to water and binding tortures, and they confessed afterward to killing several Christians and drying their skins in order to wear them during ritual practices. Nuño de Guzmán, who profited personally from the confiscation of the Caltzontzi's riches, had him executed a few days later.[46]

A lesser known but equally controversial case involved a Zapotec ruler and high priest in Yagavila, in the Oaxacan province of Villa Alta. In February 1537, the Audiencia heard some disquieting testimony from several natives as part of the *residencia*, or final audit of an outgoing administrator, of Francisco López Tenorio, corregidor of Yagavila.[47] After being sworn to veracity not through Christian means, but "according to their own laws," these witnesses brought forth serious accusations. According to them, after imprisoning Yagaeche, ruler of Yagavila, Tenorio subjected him to the brutal punishment termed *aperreamiento*, the siccing of trained dogs on a defenseless victim,[48] and then hanged him while still alive. Tenorio used the same punishment against a Zapotec boy, had a woman called Bineche or Guezalao hanged, cut a porter's ears, and jailed a *principal*, or prominent person, named Nalao.[49] Asked to explain himself, Tenorio surrendered his trial records, arguing he carried out severe punishments because these defendants were idolaters, cannibals, sodomites, and sorcerers who plotted to kill him and his associates by becoming mountain lions. While cannibalism and sodomy could be prosecuted by civil judges, Yagaeche's idolatry technically fell under the jurisdiction of fray Juan López de Zárate, who became the first bishop of Oaxaca in 1535,[50] the same year when the Dominican province of Santiago was constituted and celebrated its first chapter, and Oaxaca City established as a Dominican vicariate.[51] Native cannibalism and sodomy had been entwined in Spanish minds ever since Columbus mobilized such accusations as a pretext for slaying natives,[52] and even Gante proposed a link between sodomy and indigenous priesthood.[53] Although Tenorio's trials bore detailed confessions of cannibalism and sodomy, the highly coercive nature of the proceedings casts a shadow over these avowals. According to trial records and Tenorio's residencia, Yagaeche was a high priest who occasionally performed human sacrifices and lived with four young male attendants, with whom he committed "nefarious acts"; allegedly, Yagaeche and Nalao killed and ate three of Tenorio's and the encomendero's servants. During a swift three-day trial in January 1537, Yagaeche confessed to being a cult effigy keeper and a sodomite after Tenorio threatened him with torture. In the end, Tenorio's actions were regarded as abuses: after weighing the testimony against Tenorio, the Audiencia forbade him from holding public office and exiled him from Oaxaca.

ZUMÁRRAGA'S EXTIRPATION EFFORTS, OR DISCIPLINARY HUMANISM

Richard Greenleaf aptly summarized Zumárraga's character by stating he was "a man of contradiction, a segmented thinker."[54] Indeed, the same man who admired Erasmus and advocated the diffusion of the Scriptures in his *Doctrina christiana*[55] had arrived in the Americas an accomplished inquisitor. In 1527, as a native Euskara (Basque) speaker, he was tapped by Charles V and Inquisition officials to conduct an investigation on the extent of witchcraft and sorcery in his homeland, which was completed in a discrete and mature manner, according to Mendieta. It was during this early assignment that Zumárraga began collaborating with Andrés de Olmos, a Franciscan who would become one of the most accomplished missionaries and doctrinal authors in New Spain. On the one hand, Zumárraga held a deep concern for the natives: as Protector of Indians, he engaged in a ferocious dispute with Nuño de Guzmán and the first Audiencia.[56] On the other hand, Zumárraga's resolve against idolatry found an outlet in a series of idolatry trials in the late 1530s discussed below.

Zumárraga arrived in Mexico in December 1528 after being appointed first bishop of New Mexico, returned to Spain for his consecration in 1533, and in June 1535 he received the title of "apostolic inquisitor," which he retained until 1543, from Alonso Manrique, archbishop of Seville and apostolic inquisitor general.[57] As New Spain's sole inquisitorial judge, he either presided over or granted faculties regarding all Holy Office proceedings in New Spain between 1536 and 1543. Zumárraga himself heard nearly every extant proceeding against native defendants, with three exceptions. In October 1538, the parish priest Bernardo de Isla initiated proceedings against the Nahua cacique don Diego of Tlapanaloya, a locality northeast of Mexico City.[58] Isla could try natives and Spaniards, given his appointment as juez de comisión by Zumárraga, and this is in fact the earliest known commission against native idolatries given to a parish priest in New Spain. Additionally, in 1539, Olmos, then chaplain of Hueytlalpan, tried and punished don Juan, cacique of the Totonac locality of Matlactlan near the north-central Gulf coast. Among the various ceremonies reported during this trial, two events stand out: a celebration on behalf of a deity called 8-Monkey on a day 1-Reed in 1538, and the feast of Panquetzaliztli, "the Raising of the Flags," held on November 16, 1539.[59] The third case concerns an incomplete November 1538 *información*, or formal accusation, compiled by the vicar of Totoltepec, a Chontal town southwest of Taxco, against the cacique don Juan for idolatry, incest, drunkenness, and mocking Christianity.[60] Around the time of Advent in 1539, the Augustinian Antonio de Aguilar staged an *auto de fe*, or public inquisitorial punishment, in Ocuila, a Nahua town west of Cuernavaca, which featured flogging and the burning of effigies.[61] News of this event soon reached the bishop, who warned the Augustinians to either produce a commission against idolaters, or "refrain from acting in cases over which they had no jurisdiction."[62] Eventually, Aguilar apologized to Zumárraga, and the bishop tried the Ocuila defendants in 1540.

Between 1536 and 1543, Zumárraga presided over or reviewed nineteen inquests involving natives, two of which concerned bigamy or cohabitation.[63] The remaining seventeen proceedings, involving idolatry, sorcery, heresy, or superstition, are the most closely scrutinized records regarding indigenous crimes of faith in New Spain. Ten of these proceedings were transcribed and published in 1910 and 1912, and several influential scholars have scrutinized them in detail.[64] My analysis highlights three components that are essential to our understanding of these trials as a display of Zumárraga's disciplinary humanism: an emphasis on the public humiliation of native nobles and officeholders, a near fetishistic form of iconoclasty, and a concern for procedural formality. Zumárraga's experiment came to a premature end with the trials of don Carlos in 1539 and don Pedro and Antón in 1540. While the former marks the climax of Zumárraga's disciplinary regime, the latter showcases procedural innovations unthinkable before don Carlos's demise.

Zumárraga's focus on native lords was echoed in a translation of a sorcery manual by his associate Andrés de Olmos.[65] In the early 1530s, Olmos began translating Franciscan author Martín de Castañega's influential 1529 *Tratado de las supersticiones y hechizerías* into Nahuatl, concluding this monumental task around 1553. In this work, Olmos argued that the rapport between "pagan" deities and ritual specialists issued from a deliberate pact with the devil, rather than from mere ignorance, an argument resembling the assessment of dangerous forms of sorcery espoused both by Castañega and by renowned theologian Pedro Ciruelo in his *Reprobación de las supersticiones y hechizerías*.[66] In an

important passage from his Nahuatl *Tratado*, Olmos reports an uncanny meeting with the devil in the guise of a Nahua ruler, or *tlahtoani*.
According to Olmos, a Nahua man described his deeply unsettling encounter in a forest near Cuernavaca with a powerful supernatural who
demanded offerings, decried the arrival of the friars, and chided a local
lord for not heeding his call. The unnamed informant claims that, when
"the devil" came before him, "he was arrayed like a tlahtoani, arrayed
like the tlahtoqueh long ago when they danced."[67] Following Fernando
Cervantes's interpretation, this narrative may be interpreted as a nomi-
nalist appraisal of the devil's power. Cervantes argues that the rapport
between pagan deities and ritual specialists depicted by Castañega and
Olmos issued from an explicit pact with the devil, and not from ignorance.[68] In Cervantes's view, this interpretation derived from an emerging theological consensus that gradually replaced the Thomistic view of
vice as the simple absence of divine grace with a dichotomous notion
of good and evil. This turn to Franciscan nominalism, which regarded
evil as an principle independent from Christian grace, would account for
Olmos's depiction of indigenous practices as the opposite of Christianity:
if Christians had sacraments, the Nahua necessarily had "exsacraments."

Perhaps Olmos's characterization of a tlahtoani derived from collective
memories of rulers as depositories of wondrous powers. A vivid example
of a lord who also was a *nahualli*,[69] a powerful shape-changing sorcerer,
appears in a 1539 trial. During this proceeding, don Andrés of Culhuacan
volunteered an account about a divination performed by Tetepanquetzal,
lord of Tlacopan, in August 1521.[70] As the battle for Tenochtitlan raged
on, Tetepanquetzal visited Huitzilopochtli's temple along with the lords
of Tetzcoco and Atzcapotzalco, but Cuauhtemoc stayed behind in fright.
After saying some words before a *nahualtezcatl*, or divining mirror, the
mirror darkened and in a small section, "a few commoners appeared,
crying,"[71] signaling the Mexica would lose the struggle. Along with a
premonition allegedly made to the Mexica ruler Moteuczoma Xocoyotzin
(henceforth Moteuczoma) by the specialist Martín Ocelotl, which the latter reported at his 1537 trial, these are the two earliest extant narratives
regarding omens about the fall of Tenochtitlan.[72]

A slight majority of Zumárraga's cases centered on allegations
against officeholders and culminated in their public exemplary punishment. Out of thirty-five defendants in seventeen trials, eight of them
were caciques or principales, and ten more held either a preconquest
title or public office. Between 1536 and 1539, eight indigenous men and
one woman of high social status were disciplined in public,[73] a warning
was issued to one cacique, and only the tribute collector Alonso Tlilanci
received an absolution. No details are known about the sentencing of

the remaining five officeholders. The degree of punishment varied considerably: Olmos sentenced a lord to receive four lashes and sit among children at a doctrinal school, but other officeholders were condemned to one hundred lashes and ten years' exile.

One may understand Zumárraga's public disciplining of indigenous elites, following Foucault's influential inquiry into public punishment, as the open display of the might of the colonial state on the bodies of its subjects, for the whip "trace[d] around or, rather, on the very body of the condemned man signs that must not be effaced."[74] This administration of discipline had to be an overwhelming spectacle, since "from the point of view of the law that imposes it, public torture and execution must be spectacular, it must be seen by all almost as its triumph."[75] Since natives were accustomed to elaborate displays of deference to preconquest elites, even a single lash on a lord's back was a redoubtable display of colonial might. Hence, it would appear that Zumárraga's disciplinary acts had a metonymical quality not present in the punishments analyzed by Foucault, which were inflicted on bodies belonging to a lower social echelon: by subjecting Nahua elites to humiliation and physical penance, Zumárraga also targeted their subjects' collective remembrance of the power their bodies once held. Indeed, Zumárraga's disciplining of Nahua noblemen was duly memorialized in indigenous narratives. For instance, the prolific Nahua historian Chimalpahin reported that don Carlos of Tetzcoco was executed in 1539 and pithily noted, "And through this, idolatry was burned along with him."[76] In addition, the author of a set of Nahua annals drafted in Mexico City circa 1596 wrote that in 1539 the Tenochca migrated to Yancuictlalpan, "when they burned the lord of Tetzcoco, don Carlos."[77]

INQUISITORIAL MISRECOGNITIONS

Paradoxically, Zumárraga and his associates frequently misread preconquest office titles as personal names during their trials.[78] As a result of this misrecognition, the bishop failed to inquire into evidence that may have afforded him a better understanding of the Nahua collective ritual sphere. Two appellations that recur in several trials, *Tacatetle* and *Tacustetle*, were garbled versions of the titles *tlacateccatl* and tlacochcalcatl, two meritocratic titles designating warriors who took captives in battle and exercised local political duties.[79] Mexica emperor Itzcoatl was himself a tlacateccatl,[80] a broadly used title referring to military or judicial duties.[81] Ironically, the bishop and his translators, which included a young Sahagún, did not have a clear idea of the status these titles indexed. In Zumárraga's first idolatry trial, the Otomi specialists Antonio Tacatecle and Alonso Tanixtecle were accused of organizing worship practices involving self-sacrifice and the use of copal every twenty days.[82] In the 1538 preliminary investigation against don Diego of Tlapanaloya, he is called both "Tacateca" and "Lord of Tlapanaloya," and one of the witnesses against him is called "Martín Cortés . . . *tacustecle* and principal." In a 1548 proceeding, the defendant is referred to as "don Pablo Tacatecle," a principal of the mines of Zumpango. In 1537, the specialist Andrés Mixcoatl received deferential treatment from a "tlacuxcalcatl" and a "tlacatecutli" in Metepec, and from two men in Cuauhchinanco: a Pedro Mixcoatl Tlailotlac Teuctli, and a Juan Tlailotlac, also called by a variant of the military title *achcautli*.[83]

A more substantial misrecognition, discussed at length by Gruzinski, was the ecclesiastical conviction that native beliefs hinged on the physical shape of cult effigies; once the most venerated and visible idols were destroyed, the argument went, idolatry itself would die. Such a conviction originated a dynamic of inquisitorial questioning that made various assumptions about the structure and motivations of native ritual observances. Trial after trial, idols were regarded as transparent visual representations of nonhuman entities in the shape of figurines, statues, or carved shapes on rocks. Following deeply seated notions about idols in Genesis, Exodus, and other biblical books, each image was believed to stand for one discrete entity with a single name.[84] From this perspective, to understand what the idol referenced was to understand "native religion." An exchange between Zumárraga and don Pedro, ruler of Totolapa, epitomizes this belief in the transparency of idols. During Zumárraga's last extant idolatry trial, which has been rarely examined by scholars, native witnesses swore that don Pedro, who had been baptized fifteen years earlier, buried various cult effigies circa 1530 under some maize fields near his house. During his interrogation in January 1540, the following exchange between the bishop and don Juan took place through a Nahuatl interpreter:

His Lordship asked whether a black figurine of a man seated on a high-backed seat, which he showed to him, is recognized by him as an idol, and whether he has had it in his house, and what is its name. [Don Juan] said that he recognizes said figurine not as an idol, but as a candle holder, which he has kept in his house, and that his name is Black Hunchback. When asked to confess how long he has had said figurine in his house, he said that he has kept it for more than sixty days, as far as he remembers, and that he kept it by a window. [85]

Apparently satisfied with these answers, the bishop then steers his questions toward two other figures: a black figure with a robe, and another figure that was destroyed by the vicar. This passage suggests that the visibility of the figure indexes, in Zumárraga's view, its status as an idol. Since the Black Hunchback was not hidden, it must not have embodied a deity. Was don Juan concealing a cult effigy in plain sight? We will never know. The description of the figure, black and hunched over, brings to mind a representation of Huehueteotl, the elder fire deity, but its placement on a ruler's high-backed seat and its alleged use as a candle holder complicate any potential identification.

Zumárraga's unsuccessful attempts to track down several cult effigies from Tenochtitlan's Templo Mayor illuminates his concern with seizing and destroying concealed images. These efforts, which began with a proceeding against Miguel the Pochtecatlailotlac of Mexico City in July 1539 and continued with an *información* against don Baltasar of Culhuacan five months later, exposed confidential exchanges among officeholders in the Basin of Mexico.[86] The bishop started his inquiry when he learned from Mateo, a Nahua painter residing in Mexico City, that several cult effigies had been taken from the Templo Mayor after the fall of Tenochtitlan in August 1521. According to Mateo, his father Atolatl, also called Tlatolatl, was a confidant to Moteuczoma and the keeper of a Mexica-Tenochca tutelary deity bundle named as Huitzilopochtli in a single-leaf pictorial testimony drawn for the proceeding.[87] Atolatl hid this sacred bundle in Atzcapotzalco. Don Carlos Oquiztzin, then ruler of Atzcapotzalco,[88] gave Atolatl four other effigies for safekeeping: Cihuacoatl; Telpochtli (a Tezcatlipoca epithet); Tlatlauhqui Tezcatlipoca; and Tepehuan. Oquiztzin and Atolatl died as they traveled with Cortés in his expedition against Cristóbal de Olid in 1524–26. During this time of upheaval, Nanahuatzin the Tlacochcalcatl, whom several witnesses identified as the "lord of Mexico" at that time,[89] and Uxcuecuetzin, lord of Tula, had these five effigies transferred to the house of Miguel the Pochtecatlailotlac in Mexico City. Eventually, the Pochtecatlailotlac admitted that Nanahuatzin brought these images to his home, but he claimed to be unaware of their significance, since they were wrapped in mats; he also claimed that Nanahuatzin carried them away to another, unknown place ten days later.[90] Since Tlailotlac was a title held by some rulers and by the heads of the kin or corporate groups known as *calpolli*, Miguel's designation as Pochtecatlailotlac suggests that his role in these events was connected to his office.[91]

Ironically, Zumárraga's concern with images resulted in a jumble of idol sightings that he did not pursue further, for he was removed from his post as inquisitor in 1543. First, Francisco of Chiconauhtla, who had testified against don Carlos of Tetzcoco four months earlier, volunteered the names of seven Nahua men regarded as "prophets" who "knew about all the idols of the land."[92] Two of these men were summoned before the bishop. The first one, an unbaptized man designated only with the title Colhua Tlapixqui, "Colhua Keeper," admitted to being a calendar specialist and deflected the bishop's questions by suggesting that four associates of the sitting indigenous governor of Mexico City, don Diego de Alvarado Huanitzin, probably held these idols, as their fathers were their appointed keepers. He further stated that, a decade earlier, another "prophet" called Achacatl refused to surrender an image of Huitzilopochtli. Zumárraga dropped this line of inquiry after Achacatl denied Tlapixqui's accusation and instead sentenced the Pochtecatlailotlac to juridical torture. Eventually, in May 1540, he was tied to a rack, and his limbs were distended by one turn of the wheel. Still, the Pochtecatlailotlac continued to plead his innocence, and the provisor released him into the care of some Franciscans on account of his age and health.

A December 1539 proceeding against don Baltasar, cacique of Culhuacan, offered more details about the spiriting of idols. Don Baltasar declared that, circa 1522, the effigies of Huitzilopochtli, Cihuacoatl, and "other idols" were transported as bundles from Mexico to Culhuacan, and then on to Xilotepec and Xaltocan before their placement in a cave near Lake Tepetzinco. This witness also provided a veritable catalogue of idols hidden in various localities: Huitzilopochtli and Quetzalcoatl in Talchico; "Macuyl Masiciual" in Puxtlan; "the figure of the wind" in Ecanaco; Macuiltonale (*Macuyl Tunal*) in Xochicalco; "Yzmain" and the "Heart of the Community" in Uluicatitlan; four "demons" in Tetenmapan; and Chalmecatl and Ecinacatl in Tecanalcanco.[93] Nevertheless, this inquest by Zumárraga did not result in the recovery of any of the cult effigies mentioned above.

ZUMÁRRAGA AGAINST THE NAHUA MAN-GODS

During the 1536–37 hearings against Martín Ocelotl, a specialist who accumulated great personal wealth by offering advice to several lords, the bishop heard a long list of transgressions: he foretold lean years and life spans, propitiated divinities for rain, kept cult objects devoted to the deity Camaxtli, spoke against the teachings of the friars, and claimed to have gone through the shamanistic feat of dismemberment and reconstitution after Moteuczoma had him executed for foretelling the coming of the Spaniards.[94] Ocelotl was regarded as so pernicious an element that Zumárraga eventually decided to hand him over to the Holy Office tribunal in Seville, but his ship was lost at sea "near the port" as it sailed to Spain.[95] Nonetheless, Ocelotl returned to Mexico under a different guise.

In a related proceeding that began five months after Ocelotl's departure, several witnesses reported that a certain Andrés Mixcoatl claimed he was the true Martín Ocelotl. Mixcoatl also spoke of Ocelotl as a personal "messenger" he had sent to Castile. He also mocked the words of the Credo and asked his clients for sixteen hundred metal tacks to be used in arrows for a rebellion against the Spanish headed by Ocelotl.[96] Like Ocelotl, Mixcoatl had unusual personal wealth, earned from his activities as a specialist.

In a lucid analysis of the Ocelotl and Mixcoatl cases, Gruzinski proposed that they should be characterized as "man-gods" freed from the ceremonial constraints that bracketed the actions of preconquest ritual representatives of Mexica deities, designated as *teixiptla* (singular) or *teixiptlameh* (plural).[97] Gruzinski bases this characterization on the strength of several observations made during their trials. Witnesses claimed that Ocelotl called himself Telpochtli, "Young Man," a Tezcatlipoca epithet, and said he was one hundred years old, or even immortal.[98] Andrés bore the name of the deity Mixcoatl and was reported to say "we who are gods never die."[99]

Andrés's claim raises the issue of preconquest links between a *teotl*, a deified ancestor or deity, and his or her teixiptlameh, or representations. Who was a teotl, and what was the boundary between teotl and human being? According to some of Sahagún's informants, a human could in fact become a teotl, and some ancestors had achieved such a transition during the Mexica migrations: "Thus the old men said: those who died, *teot*-ed; it was said: 'Truly they teot-ed'; it means, truly they died. And thus they confused themselves, perhaps so that the lords were obeyed: all thought themselves teotl when they died. Some represented the Sun; others, the Moon."[100] Indeed, as López Austin argued, some ancestors who died during Postclassic migration events apparently achieved the position of tutelary deity,[101] as it was the case for Huitzilopochtli, Ehecatl, and Itzpapalotl.[102] However, teixiptla is related to corporeal representation, etymologically: its root is probably derived from *ix-*, "face, surface" and *xip-*, "peel, skin." Molina's Nahuatl dictionary provides two translations that suggest a distinction between standing in for someone—teixiptla, "someone's image, substitute, or delegate"—and portraying someone by acting—*teixiptlatini*, "a person's representative in a play."[103] These two terms mark an important ontological distinction between representing, being the delegate of, or standing in for someone on the one hand, and impersonating or playing a role on the other. For instance, Sahagún observed that during the celebration of the feast of Tititl, Ilamateuctli's teixiptla danced atop the temple; through this performance, "truly she was made a teotl on earth."[104] I will henceforth refer to teixiptlameh not as impersonators, but as representatives or delegates of absent entities.

In Mexica state ritual practices, a teixiptla designated both human beings and objects that stood in for a divine entity, particularly in the case of deities in rituals performed at the end of twenty-day periods in the 365-day year, such as Centeotl, Tezcatlipoca, Ilamateuctli, Xipe Totec, and Xiuhteuctli-Milintoc.[105] Objects also represented deities; for example, people who died by drowning had edible teixiptlameh of them eaten during the feast of Tepeilhuitl.[106] The most celebrated deity substitute was Tezcatlipoca's *iixiptla*, who represented this deity for an entire 365-day year, wore his dress and was attended to by four female servants; at the end of the cycle, he was sacrificed in public during the feast of Toxcatl.[107] Hvidtfeldt emphasized the legitimization of the teixiptla's role by rulers.[108] For instance, during Toxcatl, after Tezcatlipoca's iixiptla came out dancing, Moteuczoma approached him and gave him presents, "because truly already he considered him his dear teotl."[109]

Given this legitimation procedure, it is crucial to ask what strategies conferred Ocelotl and Mixcoatl their status as deity delegates. Mixcoatl's career provides insights into how he positioned himself as a mediator between deities and humans. In 1533, as he was passing by Tepehualco, he learned that, in spite of the propitiatory practices of a local specialist, rain had not come. That night, Mixcoatl burned copal and paper and performed his incantations; the following day, it rained abundantly at noon, "and for this they thought him a god, and then they killed the said specialist they had there, because they said that it would not rain because of him."[110] This communal understanding of Mixcoatl's power brings to mind Max Weber's influential characterization of a charismatic leader, one who "must work miracles, if he wants to be a prophet. He must perform heroic deeds, if he wants to be a warlord. Most of all, his divine mission must prove itself by bringing well-being to his faithful followers."[111] Teixiptla roles were rooted in the practices of specific altepetl; nevertheless, Ocelotl and Mixcoatl, as itinerant specialists, were bound to no particular community. Therefore, their purchase on authority relied entirely on charismatic authority's fragile foundation: the measure of well-being their clients attributed to their actions. From this vantage point, they both appear to be not only "man-gods" liberated from the yoke of preconquest pageantry but also to have an unstable form of charismatic authority, instigated through their insinuation of their status as teixiptlameh and sustained only through pragmatic results.

Moreover, Mixcoatl and Ocelotl innovated on ritual practice by assuming roles that belonged to native priests, even though their status as commoners and itinerant specialists would have in fact barred them from holding such roles before the conquest. Mixcoatl often spoke to his clients on behalf of Tezcatlipoca, announcing rain, and he reminded his followers of an ancient contract that bound them with their deities. During a particularly eloquent speech, after giving his followers *nanacatl*, or hallucinogenic mushrooms, Mixcoatl asserted that friars did not provide sustenance to the natives because "they do not know us and we do not know them. Did our grandfathers and our fathers perhaps know these Fathers? Did they perhaps see what they preach, and what is that God they mention? This is not so, for they lie. We eat what the gods give us; they sustain you, and bring you up."[112] Mixcoatl's epistemological premise was strikingly similar to one adduced by the Mexica priests confronted by Franciscan missionaries circa 1524, as reported by Sahagún forty years later in *Colloquios y doctrina christiana*: "Truly it is through the deities that one lives . . . truly they themselves give us our supper, our breakfast, and everything that is drunk, that is eaten, our sustenance; maize, beans, amaranth, chia. It is they that we ask for water, for rain, with which [everything] is made on earth."[113]

THE EXECUTION OF
DON CARLOS OF TETZCOCO

Zumárraga's most contentious trial, which passed judgment on don Carlos Chichimecateuctli, was fueled by allegations from nobles and commoners from Tetzcoco and Chiconauhtla.[114] For this trial, the bishop employed various translators, three of which would later become leading doctrinal authors: Antonio de Ciudad Rodrigo, Alonso de Molina, and Bernardino de Sahagún. The trial opened with reports of a heated exchange between don Carlos and several noblemen. In early June 1539, a few days before Corpus Christi, the Franciscan provincial Antonio de Ciudad Rodrigo organized a procession in Chiconauhtla to ask for rain and deliverance from a pandemic, which coincided with a visit don Carlos paid to his sister doña María, wife of don Alonso, ruler of Chiconauhtla. Late at night, don Carlos came to drink with don Alonso and asked all the commoners in the room to leave. This left in the room the Chiconauhtla don Alonso, Melchor Aculnahuacatl, Francisco Maldonado, and Cristóbal, and the Tetzcoca Coaunochitli, Zacanpatl, and Poyoma. Since Francisco was an assistant to the friars, don Carlos lectured him by asking, "What are the things of God? They are nothing. . . . I will let you know that my father and grandfather were great prophets, and they foretold many things in the past and the future, and they said nothing, nothing about this." The Tetzcoca's words upset Zacanpatl,

who stormed out of the room. Francisco claimed don Carlos then suggested killing Zacanpatl and others because of their Christian beliefs;
when don Alonso noted a friar had praised his son's progress in the new
faith, an angry don Carlos suggested murdering the boy.[115] Finally, don
Carlos admonished his own sister to allow don Alonso to take women as
concubines if he wished to do so.

By claiming the authority of two legendary Tetzcoco rulers, his father
Nezahualpilli and his grandfather Nezahualcoyotl, don Carlos questioned the epistemological basis of Christianity, according to Cristóbal's
testimony:

What truth is this divinity we desire? Perhaps it is nothing. Here we have three
ways, which are *cartillas* [reading primers], *romance* [Spanish], and grammar, and
in the cartilla there is the a b c, and *pater noster* and *ave María*, *credo*, and *salve
regina*, articles and commandments. Perhaps everything perishes here? Nothing
is to be done; the fathers of Saint Francis have one type of habit, those of Saint
Dominic another one, those of Saint Augustine another one, the clergy another
one, and each of them teaches in his own way.[116]

Don Carlos's maieutic tone calls for an explanation. Using the subtle
tones of preconquest *huehuehtlahtolli*, "ancient words," don Carlos
chided his audience for embracing Spanish writing and abandoning ancestral practices. This was an elegant, if not unique, attack on Spanish writing; a year earlier, don Juan of Totoltepec had been accused by his wife
of dressing up as a Spaniard, pretending to read books in Spanish before
the principales, and then smashing the books on the floor in derision.[117]

In an ironic turn, the very technology don Carlos denounced was
turned against him by Francisco, the prosecution's main witness. In July
1539, Zumárraga asked Francisco to read a copy of his Nahuatl testimony so it could be translated and entered into the record. According
to this text, probably the earliest instance of alphabetic testimony by
a native in Central Mexico, after noting the different manners of worship of the mendicants, don Carlos proposed that, if this heterodoxy
was acceptable, then people from different regions should be allowed to
worship in their own ways.[118] According to Francisco and Alonso, don
Carlos stated that, in the time of the ancestors, commoners did not dare
sit on *petlatl icpalli*, "the mat, the high-backed seat," the metonymical
representation of rulership in Nahua rhetoric.[119] Still, Francisco was not
the only zealous neophyte to disagree with the Chichimecateuctli. Don
Lorenzo Luna, who was both Tetzcoco's native governor and don Carlos's nephew, was so accepting of Christianity that don Carlos chided
him, calling him by his preconquest Nahua name and complaining that
he no longer understood what Luna did or said.[120] In fact, Luna's fer-

vor helped him secure a commission from Viceroy Mendoza circa 1538 to compel all Tetzcoco residents to attend mass every Sunday and thus avoid idolatry and bigamy.[121] After some effigies of Tlaloc, Quetzalcoatl, Xipe Totec, and other deities were discovered embedded in the walls of one of don Carlos's houses, the zealous Luna conducted a search for Tlaloc cult objects in a nearby mountain range. The prosecutor used these implements and the discovery of a *tonalamatl*, a 260-day calendar, to accuse don Carlos of idolatry, but his possession of these objects was not proven in court.

A traditional assessment of don Carlos's status holds that he was the ruler of Tetzcoco for several years before his trial. This view is based in part on Chimalpahin's statement that in 1539, "he was just burned, the person of don Carlos Ahuachpitzactzin, tlahtoani of Tetzcoco; he had ruled for nine years. . . . He was a *fiscal* when don Fr[ay] Juan de Zumárraga [was] the first bishop of Mexico."[122] Nevertheless, Chimalpahin's claim that don Carlos was a tlahtoani and a fiscal are in direct conflict with virtually every single statement made about don Carlos's status in the only extant document concerning him that was drafted in his lifetime: his 1539 trial. What follows is a summary of evidence demonstrating that, between the death of Tetzcoco ruler don Pedro around late April of 1539 and the beginning of don Carlos's trial in late June, the latter failed to be appointed as ruler. This interpretation is congruent with Gibson's claim that don Carlos did not accede to the throne, even if he did "proclaim himself successor" to don Pedro, his half-brother.[123]

First, don Carlos describes himself as the legitimate but still unconfirmed heir to Tetzcoco's throne. At the end of his trial, he adduced that the testimonies against him were proffered "so that I may not become lord of [Tetzcoco] and *gobernador* [local native ruler], which comes to me through a legitimate succession, since my brother, the former lord of said town, named me as such legitimate heir in his testament; and also because, once I am gobernador, I have to punish and rectify the abuses and bad habits of those who testified against me."[124] Second, nowhere in don Carlos's trial do we find an unambiguous reference to him as ruler or cacique. On the one hand, this document often referred to don Pedro as the late señor, or recently deceased ruler, of Tetzcoco and identified don Lorenzo de Luna as gobernador, or native ruler. On the other, the trial records systematically designated don Carlos as either a native, a principal, or a *vecino*, a local resident.[125] Whenever a defendant in Zumárraga's trials was a cacique, this fact was duly noted, as occurred during the trials of the caciques of Culhuacan, Iguala, Matlactlan, Tlapanaloya, Totolapa, and Totoltepec. Hence, not designating don Carlos as a ruler if he was one would have strongly contradicted Zumárraga's usual procedure. Third, an account written by several Tetzcoca nobles later in the sixteenth century asserted that don Pedro, which they called by his proper Nahua name, Tetlahuehuetzquititzin, "designated no one to be ruler" of Tetzcoco. Moreover, this document provided an ordered succession of early postconquest rulers—Coanacochtzin, don Hernando Tecocoltzin, don Fernando Ixtlilxochitzin, don Jorge Yoyontzin, don Pedro Tetlahuehuetzquititzin, and after don Pedro's death, don Antonio Pimentel—that pointedly excluded don Carlos.[126]

A further contradiction of Chimalpahin's statement comes from the fact that there is no evidence that don Carlos ever was a *fiscal*, a native official who monitored local compliance with Christian precepts. Indeed, his reported preaching against Christian beliefs contrasted with the fiscal-like fervor of his nephew don Lorenzo Luna. Finally, Chimalpahin may have in fact conflated accounts about two separate Tetzcoca nobles called don Carlos Ahuachpitzactzin—our defendant, and another one who briefly ruled Tetzcoco in 1521—in his statement. The aforementioned Tetzcoca account states that, after the fall of Tenochtitlan in 1521, Cortés installed a don Carlos Ahuachpitzactzin as ruler of Tetzcoco, only to remove him later because "he did not heed [the Spaniards]." This earlier Ahuachpitzactzin was, in all likelihood, not the don Carlos tried by Zumárraga, since the latter was a young, inexperienced man in 1521.[127]

Accounts given by two Nahua noblewomen during the trial portray don Carlos as engaging in an active campaign to succeed his brother don Pedro. The most damning testimony came from don Pedro's widow, doña María. This widow stated that her husband had died "about two months" before her testimony of July 8, 1539. This testimony places don Pedro's demise in late April or early May, or less than eight weeks before the beginning of don Carlos's trial on June 22. She accused don Carlos of sending her flowers as presents as she grieved don Pedro's passing and gave a detailed account of don Carlos's four attempts to force himself on her, as "our fathers used to do with their sisters-in-law."[128] A second doña María, wife of Antonio de Pomar and one of don Carlos's sisters, testified that the Chichimecateuctli had taken his own niece doña Inés as a concubine. More importantly, she also stated that "when don Pedro, her brother, was still alive and was lord of Tetzcoco, the said don Carlos would ask [don Pedro] repeatedly to appoint him as lord at the end of his days . . . and that said don Carlos has always attempted to rule and forcibly command everyone, and to become lord of Tetzcoco."[129]

To be sure, while he was alive, don Pedro apparently favored don Carlos. At the time of the trial, don Carlos testified he was residing in a grand house at Oztoticpac that had belonged to his father Nezahualpilli, "with the permission of don Pedro." Moreover, a 1564 letter by the Tetzcoca writer Juan de San Antonio portrayed with indignation don Pedro's decision to grant don Carlos a cultivated field at Yahualiuhcan that had earlier been assigned to another nobleman by one of don Pedro's predecessors.[130] Although such favors suggest that don Pedro may have intended don Carlos to succeed him, nothing in the extant evidence allows us to corroborate this decision. In any case, San Antonio's letter vividly displayed local resentment regarding don Carlos's privileges. Furthermore, the testimony of two women closely associated with don Pedro depicted don Carlos's frantic attempts to obtain recognition as heir both during don Pedro's last days and in the brief period between the latter's passing and the former's trial.[131]

Don Carlos's attempts to take his brother's widow may have seemed an outrage from a Christian viewpoint, but it was a legitimate Postclassic strategy for the polygamous, alliance-oriented lords of Central Mexico.[132] In the 1538 información against don Diego Tlacatec[c]atl, cacique of Tlapanaloya, his wife Ana revealed that one of his three wives was her own sister, and a principal confirmed that don Diego sired a child with his own sister, provoked an abortion, and tried to take another man's wife.[133] In November 1538, don Juan, ruler of Tototepec, was accused of having taken his own sister and his wife's sister as concubines.[134] Don Juan, ruler of Iguala, was accused in 1540 by his wife doña Ana and two noblemen of forcing himself on doña Ana's sister, his own half-sister, his aunt, and a very young girl.[135] Furthermore, in the proceedings against don Pedro, ruler of Totolapa, and his brother Antón, a commoner called Cecilia recounted her sexual servitude to the Totolapa lineage. She denounced don Melchor—who was don Pedro and Antón's father—for deflowering her by force. After his father's death, don Pedro forced Cecilia to be his concubine until he married a noblewoman, while Cecilia terminated two pregnancies when don Pedro denied his paternity. Afterward, Antón also used her as a concubine until his marriage, and he left her pregnant.[136]

Hence, Don Carlos's speeches may be interpreted as an attempt to present himself as a traditional Tetzcoca nobleman as he asserted his claim to the rulership. Nonetheless, his elegant words fell on deaf ears, for no one supported his cause before Zumárraga. While the testimony against don Carlos was not necessarily a complot, this trial depicts a common store of ill will against him as potential ruler. On the one hand, as seen above, the testimonies portrayed him as an imperious nobleman who attacked Christianity and the emerging political order. On the other, his defense was marred by the absence of any favorable witnesses. Following procedure, Zumárraga stipulated a one-month

recepción de prueba in September 1529, which allowed for the recording of testimony on the defendant's behalf. Since no favorable witness
came forward, don Carlos's attorney asked for two consecutive extensions, but he was denied a second one in November. In spite of don
Carlos's protests, Zumárraga closed the proceedings a week after this
denial occurred.[137]

Given the case's high profile, the viceroy, the Audiencia, the Dominican provincial, and the Franciscan guardian reviewed the trial records.
These deliberations do not appear on the record, but the bishop used
them for his ruling: given don Carlos's refusal to confess and his status as
a heretic, he would be turned over to the secular justice to be executed.
Fortuitously, Don Carlos's auto took place only a few months after two
lavish public reenactments of Christian victories performed by indigenous actors: the Conquest of Jerusalem in Tlaxcala, and the Capture of
Rhodes in Mexico.[138]

The Chichimecateuctli's execution generated a public outcry that
reached the Audiencia and the Council of Indies. Furthermore, there
was a growing consensus that natives should be removed from the Holy
Office's jurisdiction.[139] An unusual motion at the end of Zumárraga's
last two idolatry trials reflects a procedural innovation possibly motivated by this backlash. Between January and November 1540, as news
of don Carlos's demise circulated in Mexico and Spain, don Pedro, ruler
of Totolapa, and his brother don Antón were investigated for idolatry,
fornication, and incest. Two leading Augustinians provided favorable
testimony to no avail,[140] for the bishop ruled both of them guilty in May
1540. Zumárraga's sentencing revealed an interesting punitive calculus: don Pedro was condemned to fifty lashes and a five-year exile from
Totolapa, but don Antón, who had committed incest, was sentenced to
one hundred lashes and a ten-year exile. At this point their defense attorney Vicencio de Riverol, who had also represented don Carlos and
other idolatry defendants, introduced a peculiar writ: separate motions
in which each defendant, claiming to have been "aggrieved" by the sentence, appealed to the inquisitor general and cardinal of Toledo, the head
of the Holy Office in Spain.[141] This move was a truly innovative defense
strategy, as no other indigenous defendant had ever attempted to appeal
the bishop's rulings. Zumárraga approved this petition, but his hand may
have been forced by the tone of the new guidelines he received from the
crown in 1540, which forbade him to confiscate the natives' property
and instructed him to ensure they were treated with gentleness.[142] In any
event, this motion reached an anticlimactic end: in October 1540, both
don Pedro and don Antón abandoned their appeals in exchange for their
release from prison to a guarantor.[143]

TELLO DE SANDOVAL
AND THE FIGHT AGAINST IDOLATRY

In light of the Council of Indies' review of Zumárraga's sentencing of don Carlos, the crown removed him from his post as apostolic inquisitor in 1543. He occasionally participated in trials against idolaters and was created archbishop of Mexico by Paul III in July 1547,[144] a post he held until his death in June 1548.[145] The end of Zumárraga's tenure as inquisitor coincided with a *visita*, or official inspection, by Francisco Tello de Sandoval, a member of the Council of the Indies and former Toledo inquisitor also appointed as New Spain's apostolic inquisitor in 1544.[146] Tello de Sandoval's multiple obligations and short tenure as *visitador*, or royal inspector, in 1544–47 allowed him to supervise only five idolatry proceedings: the case against don Domingo, don Francisco, and don Juan, lords of Yanhuitlan, for idolatry and human sacrifices (1544–47); a denunciation by the corregidor of Izúcar against Tomás Tunalt for making ritual offerings (1545); a case against the caciques of Coatlan in Oaxaca for engaging in idolatry and human sacrifices (1544); the trial of don Juan, gobernador of Iguala (1546–47); and a case against don Pablo Tacatecle, principal of Zumpango del Río, and two of his associates, for engaging in propitiatory rituals (1547).[147]

Three Mixtec caciques were tried as two political conflicts unfolded in their *ñuu*, or community, of Yanhuitlan (Yodzocahi in Mixtec). Their cases have been analyzed by Kevin Terraciano and summarized by María Sepúlveda y Herrera.[148] On the one hand, there existed a deep enmity between Francisco de las Casas, corregidor of Yanhuitlan, and the local Dominicans; on the other, various rivalries existed among the lords of Yanhuitlan, the residents of Etlatongo, and the three neighboring communities of Xaltepec, Nochistlan, and Suchitepec. According to the testimony of fray Domingo de Santa María, vicar of Yanhuitlan, which was corroborated by several ecclesiastics and Spaniards, de las Casas obstructed Dominican attempts to erect and provide ornaments for local churches.[149] De las Casas was also accused of allowing don Francisco, don Domingo, and don Juan, rulers of Yanhuitlan, to engage in traditional ritual practices in exchange for tribute and native laborers for the corregidor. An official inquiry into such practices began after Gonzalo, son of don Francisco, and Juan de las Casas, son of the local encomendero, confronted the *alguaciles*, or constables, of Etlatongo due to the disputed possession of several slaves. After this quarrel, the royal justice issued an arrest order against Gonzalo, which a royal *escribano*, or notary, and the *bachiller* (university degree holder) Pedro Gómez de Maraver attempted to carry out. During a search of don Francisco's dwelling, the two officials uncovered bloodied feathers, idols, and one hundred portions of food offerings. After Maraver began an inquiry with the support of local Dominicans, don Francisco and don Domingo were arrested in January 1545 and brought as prisoners to Mexico City in March. Don Juan was arrested a year later, in April 1546.

These detentions uncovered a network of ritual specialists in the employment of the rulers of Yanhuitlan. Four priests called Siquii, Caco, Quio, and Cahvio were in residence at don Juan's home; don Domingo kept a priest called Joseph Xaco and at least twenty deity bundles in his house. Four priests also lived in don Francisco's house: Cocoa, Numav, Cocoane, and a female diviner called Xihua; don Francisco's unbaptized son was also a ritual specialist. As Terraciano indicates in his lucid description of the ritual practices uncovered during this trial, four main entities were the most visible foci within a much larger devotional complex at Yanhuitlan: Dzahui or Dzavi, a rain deity comparable to the Nahua Tlaloc and the Zapotec Cocijo; Tidzono, an entity comparable to the deities called "Heart of the Town" in both Nahuatl and Zapotec; Toyna, an entity linked by its name to two merchant deities from the Mixteca Baja; and Xitondodzo, a deity associated with trade.[150] Furthermore, don Francisco was the keeper of four *cuacu*, or images, representing the tutelary deities of Yanhuitlan that were the focus of four public yearly celebrations. These effigies were preserved clandestinely after the Dominican Domingo de Santa María ordered the demolition of Yanhuitlan's temples. Every three years, a new group of specialists was put in charge of these tutelary deities; in 1544, the specialists were Diego Cumizo, Cocoa, Domingo Xixa, Catucha, and Caco.[151]

According to the depositions in this case, human sacrifice was a relatively common technique for propitiating the "deity of bread" and Dzahui. Human sacrifices were also performed after the death of the wives, mothers-in-law, and other family members of the three caciques, and to commemorate the death circa 1539 of 8-House, or Caltzin, who had been the local ruler and don Domingo's uncle. Some of the witnesses gave detailed accounts of these sacrifices, but the details remained contradictory. For example, in an earlier confession from April 1546, Juan Caco the Elder declared that, upon the orders of don Juan and don Francisco, he sacrificed five boys to stave off famine.[152] Two months later, Caco the Elder admitted performing a total of thirteen human sacrifices in behalf of Xicoa, the deceased cacique of Cuxcatepec, but denied having performed sacrifices for the rulers of Yanhuitlan.[153] Other witnesses admitted to the frequent performance of sacrifices for the caciques. Joseph Xaco acknowledged that he and other specialists immolated four boys to the deities of rain and "bread" twice by order of don Francisco and don Domingo. Xaco also sacrificed a child on behalf of Yanhuitlan, and another boy on behalf of his patron don Domingo.

These proceedings lasted from October 1544 until January 1547, but the final sentences are not included in surviving records. Apparently, a sentence against don Francisco, singled out as the most influential organizer of sacrifices, was handed down in November 1545 by a group that included, as in don Carlos's trial, Tello de Sandoval, Zumárraga, Audiencia members, and Franciscan and Dominican representatives; don Juan's trial was concluded in early 1547. Don Domingo's fate is better known: after he fell ill while imprisoned in Mexico City, Tello de Sandoval released him into the care of three Mexico City residents, who would pay 2,000 *pesos de oro* if don Domingo escaped.[154]

Two other fragmentary proceedings record idolatry and cannibalism accusations against Mixtec lords in this period; unfortunately, both cases have no extant outcome. The first one was instigated by the priest Pedro de Olmos against don Fernando, don Alonso, don Juan, and don Andrés, caciques of Coatlan. Olmos collected accounts about the ritual sacrifice of slaves by these caciques. More importantly, on the road between Coatlan and Tototepec, Olmos found a stone idol covered in blood that still held a child's heart in its mouth, surrounded by sixteen human heads. The rulers of Coatlan eventually confessed that, circa 1538, they had surrendered some of their lesser images to a visiting priest to save their main cult effigies, which they placated with human sacrifices.[155] The second case involved an investigation circa 1546 of human sacrifices by the principales of Tamazulapa, near Teposcolula. According to testimony compiled by the vicar Julián Carrasco, the cacique don Hernando and the former gobernador don Domingo of Tamazulapa, ordered the brother of Tequecistepec's cacique and a *tequitlahto*, or labor draft official, to punish a Coixtlahuaca native because "he became a god and asked for doves, turtledoves, quails, puppies, and copal in order to perform sacrifices." The two delegates beat the specialist to death; his body was eaten and his bones buried. The noblemen of Tamazulapa claimed that several Coixtlahuaca natives, including don Diego, had recently sacrificed and eaten one of their own; therefore, they argued, they were now entitled to a Coixtlahuaca, and don Hernando in fact used the Nahuatl verb *quipatla*, "to exchange a human being."[156]

Between 1545 and 1547, three idolatry inquiries took place in three Nahua regions southwest of the Basin of Mexico: Cohuixcatlalpan (Zumpango del Río), Tlalhuicatlalpan (Teotlalco), and Coatlalpan (Izúcar). These regions would again draw the attention of idolatry eradicators in 1584 and in the 1620s. In October 1545, the corregidor Gerónimo Flores notified Tello de Sandoval about the activities of the commoner specialist

Tomás Tunalt and his associates in Izúcar, a polity with a ruling lineage related to those of Tenochtitlan and Quauhquechollan.[157] After Flores imprisoned and tortured Tunalt, he confessed to making ritual offerings to an aspect of Tezcatlipoca designated by the epithet Titlacahuan, "We Are People Who Belong to Him." Titlacahuan's image was kept in a cave in the sierra of Teponahuaztli; he could assume the figure of a youth or an old man at will, and was also known as "the lord of all things, . . . Molcuyuyaçin or Moyuicuyaçin." Providentially, some Izúcar residents freed Tunalt from jail, and he fled the area along with his family.[158]

Tello de Sandoval's final idolatry trial involved a Nahua ruler. Don Juan, gobernador of Teotlalco, a town to the south of the Tlalhuica region,[159] was accused in late 1546 of organizing ceremonies on a hill in the town's outskirts to propitiate the rain god during a dry spell in the area. Don Juan alleged that his enemies were behind these charges. He repeatedly denied having worshipped an effigy of Ome Tochtli during the previous ten years, stating instead that he had not engaged in such devotions after his baptism. Even though a witness who assisted him in these rituals was called to corroborate these accusations, he stated instead that don Juan was guilty of the lesser charge of consuming meat during Lent. To prove himself a true Christian, don Juan crossed himself and then recited the Ave María, the Pater Noster, and the Credo in Latin. There is no determination of guilt in the extant proceedings, which ended in March 1547.[160]

Another proceeding from this period shows that parish priests, the driving force behind extirpation efforts in the seventeenth century, began investigating idolatry as early as 1547. Between May and November 1547—that is, after Tello de Sandoval's departure from New Spain—the vicar and ecclesiastic judge Rodrigo de Gallegos carried out a trial under the guise of an *información* against a nobleman from the Cohuixca Nahua mining town of Zumpango del Río.[161] In violation of juridical procedure reserving such faculties for inquisitors, Gallegos compiled testimony and dictated a sentence. Like many of Zumárraga's defendants, the accused held a preconquest title; he was called don Pablo the Tlacateuctli, and Gallegos accused him of performing a propitiation ritual along with two other *principales*. The observance took place on the Central Mexican icon of rulership, a woven mat, and during its course the defendants employed a pictographic text painted on a deer hide to perform acts of divination and chewed on *tenexietl*, a type of tobacco with a wide ritual usage. This ceremony's objective was to ensure that don Pablo would become the new cacique of Zumpango. Gallegos handed down a sentence that did not involve corporal punishment: after being given a hefty fine, don Pablo was admonished not to engage in such practices again.[162]

EXTIRPATORS AT REST UNDER MONTÚFAR

The gap in extant native idolatry proceedings in Mexico between 1548 and 1571 is roughly coterminous with the tenure of the Dominican fray Alonso de Montúfar, a former Inquisition official in Granada, who was named archbishop in 1551 and began exercising inquisitorial faculties in 1556.[163] Unlike Zumárraga and Tello de Sandoval, he was not ever named apostolic inquisitor and may have been allowed by the crown to act as inquisitor in his capacity as ordinario.[164] In fact, the creation of a separate Mexican inquisitorial tribunal meant he would be the last judge in Central Mexico who could legitimately claim to be an ordinario inquisitor.

The establishment in the see of Mexico of two important ecclesiastic offices, that of provisor de españoles and provisor de indios, seems to date to Montúfar's administration. Provisor de Españoles and Vicario General Doctor Anguis and Provisor de Indios Marañón, respectively aided by an indigenous and a nonindigenous constable, conducted two cases regarding the cohabitation of Spanish men with indigenous women in 1559 and 1564, but only the former dictated a final sentence.[165] Significantly, this early date for the appointment of a provisor de indios antedates the reorganization of juridical procedure after the establishment of a Mexican Holy Office in 1571.[166] The early years of the Provisorato de Indios were apparently marked by jurisdictional struggle; thus, in 1574, Provisor de Indios Pedro Gutiérrez de Pisa complained that, in spite of three cédulas issued in 1552, 1562, and 1563 instructing the Franciscans to turn over any cases against indigenous believers to the ordinario's jurisdiction, these mendicants persisted in conducting proceedings against natives and even forbade them to appear before the provisor or the archbishop.[167]

Complicating the jurisdictional picture, the civil justice investigated alleged indigenous sorcerers during Montúfar's administration; for instance, a June 1550 order from Viceroy Mendoza sought the apprehension of several Nahua itinerant specialists who wandered through Tepecuacuilco and Taxco as they became "sorcerers, tigers, and lions."[168] During his tenure as de facto inquisitor, which lasted until his death in 1569, Montúfar dedicated most of his efforts to the prosecution of Protestants and crypto-Jews throughout Central Mexico, Guatemala, Nicaragua, and Yucatán. This emphasis was a clear departure from the idolatry eradication policies of Zumárraga and Tello de Sandoval.

Hence, there is only one extant significant idolatry that dates to Montúfar's tenure. According to a two-folio section in a mid-sixteenth-century set of Nahua annals, in 1558 Juan Teton of Michmaloyan was apprehended after having "washed away [the] baptism" of several cabildo officials from Atlapolco and Coatepec, located southeast of the Toluca

Valley. Strikingly, the Nahua Christian writer who recounted Teton's activities characterized his ritual act as the antithesis of Christian baptism,
thus aligning himself with Olmo's claim that Nahua idolaters possessed
"exsacraments." In any case, Teton voiced his concerns regarding the end
of the Nahua 52-year count around 1558 by predicting that the feared *tzitzimimeh*, the skeletal supernaturals who appeared during important cosmological transitions, would descend and devour people. Afterward, all
natives who had been baptized and believed in the Christian God would
be transformed into the European food staple they habitually ate: those
who ate beef would become cows, pork eaters would turn into pigs, and
mutton eaters would be sheep. Teton contended that such had been the
fate of some of the first converts in Xalatlaco in the Toluca Valley and also
warned of a future famine and provided his followers with a list of native
plants that would ward off a powerful Nahua supernatural associated
with the tzitzimimeh, the *tlantepozilama*, or "Old Woman with Metal
Teeth." These annals conclude their account of Teton's case by reporting
that he was imprisoned in Xalatlaco by the priest Pedro Hernández, and
brought before Provisor Francisco Manjarrés and Archbishop Montúfar.[169]

Some mendicants stepped into the vacuum created by Montúfar's lack
of juridical interest on indigenous practices and acted with great severity and little accountability in Oaxaca and Yucatán in the 1560s. The
most egregious abuses were committed by Dominican friars in Oaxaca
under Bishop Albuquerque and by fray Diego de Landa, the Franciscan
provincial who would become the second bishop of Yucatán. As is well
known, in 1562 Landa and his associates used harsh methods to prosecute a large group of Yucatec Maya idolatry suspects. Landa's opponents argued that, as a result of his indiscriminate use of torture, some
157 natives perished.[170]

During Montúfar's tenure, projects other than outright extirpation
had a greater impact on the social reproduction of native ritual practices. Montúfar presided over the First Mexican Church Council of 1555,
the first comprehensive discussion of doctrinal policies by ecclesiastical
authorities in New Spain. Moreover, shortly before and during the mid-
sixteenth century, the crown successfully pursued a policy of displac-
ing lineage rulers in order to clear the ground for the introduction of a
cabildo, or town council. After the political reorganization of Central
Mexico in the 1520s, the crown had to contend with local lineages and
traditional notions of rulership. At first, it allowed for the appointment
of "natural lords" as both native and colonial rulers, reflected in the
designation of a ruler as "cacique and gobernador." The crown rarely
interfered with the election of native rulers for the first two postconquest
generations, but it prepared the ground for their demise with a number

of ordinances, such as a 1549 royal order calling for the formation of cabildos headed by indigenous alcaldes.[171] The crown seized the initiative at times of native inheritance crises and imposed commoners and outsiders as gobernadores, thus separating political authority from the office of the native ruler.[172] The actual date of rupture varies by region; it occurred in 1564 in Tetzcoco, around 1560 in Pátzcuaro, and in the 1560s in Toluca and Cuernavaca.[173]

DOMINICAN PUNITIVE EXPERIMENTS IN OAXACA UNDER ALBUQUERQUE

Archbishop Montúfar's evangelization policies shared some ground with those of the second bishop of Oaxaca, the Dominican Bernardo de Albuquerque (1555–79). Both prelates attempted to systematize the teaching of the Christian doctrine in native communities through the First Mexican Council of 1555; both were determined to police the political and moral behavior of the dominant mendicant orders in their jurisdiction. Otherwise, Albuquerque and Montúfar had dissimilar backgrounds and goals. Montúfar was the scion of a prominent family that included a president of the Council of Indies, a viceroy, and an ambassador to Rome; Albuquerque rose through the Dominican ranks through missionary labor: he learned Zapotec, lived as a missionary in Villa Alta, and served as his order's provincial and prior in Oaxaca. His zeal was rewarded when he was nominated as incoming bishop of Oaxaca by the crown in 1559, receiving his consecration in 1562.[174]

The fragmentary quality of records regarding sixteenth-century idolatry extirpation attempts in Oaxaca stands in contrast with the vivid portrayals of early evangelization efforts penned in the seventeenth-century by Dominican author Francisco de Burgoa. In his majestic *Palestra historial* (1670) and *Geográfica descripción* (1674), Burgoa crafts an evangelization narrative in Oaxaca in which God's will is the ultimate and omnipresent protagonist. Burgoa's hagiographic rhetoric about idolatry extirpation campaigns follows, as a matter of procedure, three stages in an entirely predictable dramatic structure. First, there is Discovery: a bold missionary enters a new region and surprises an idolater *in medias res*, or uncovers a cache of idols. Then, there is Punishment: the idols are burned or pulverized, and the idolater, almost always a male, is paraded in an auto, and corporal punishment is administered. Finally, there is Contrition: if the idolater survives his ordeal, he repents, and the public spectacle of his punishment and reconciliation compels a faceless group of natives to embrace Catholicism with sincerity. Although the Teiticpac episode introduces a slight departure in this model—here, contrition is experienced both by the natives and by their vicar—all of Burgoa's extirpation accounts fit this narrative model and provide us with little else beyond a providential narrative, the names of sixteenth-century idolatry eradicators, and the regions where they operated: fray Alonso de Espinosa in Yabela; Gonzalo de Grijalva in Yagavila and Teotlaxco; fray Vicente Rodríguez in Quegochono; fray Luis de San Miguel in Nejapa, Quije Colani, and Mixtepec; and fray Jordán de Santa Catarina in Chuapa and Comaltepec.[175]

Burgoa also memorialized the two most important proceedings against idolaters under Albuquerque: the discovery and punishment of the clandestine ritual practices of don Juan Cortés Cosijopij and a mock auto de fe held at Teiticpac in 1560. According to Burgoa's received account,[176] Cosijoeza, ruler of Zaachila, conquered the Tehuantepec region not long before the Spanish conquest, and he installed his son Cosijopij as its ruler. Upon the arrival of the Spaniards, Cosijoeza abdicated his kingdom in favor of the crown, thus avoiding a military conquest; he then returned to Zaachila and died in the region in 1529, while his son Cosijopij was baptized as don Juan Cortés.[177] In a detailed analysis of don Juan Cortés's attempts to maintain a measure of his preconquest political and economic privileges under Spanish rule, Judith Zeitlin noted that the crown allowed the Zapotec ruler to continue receiving tribute from subjects who lived near the salt fields on the Isthmus coast and granted him the right to ride a horse and bear arms.[178] In 1553, don Juan was imprisoned and faced a secret residencia due to complaints from some of his subjects regarding tribute misappropriation and allegations of mistreatment made by Nahua residents in Tehuantepec. In spite of such a serious legal challenge to his authority, don Juan appears to have exercised political or diplomatic pressures over the complainants, given that they dropped their charges only two weeks after the original accusation.[179] In the end, don Juan retained his title and office as gobernador.

According to Burgoa, don Juan Cortés Cosijopij brought to his residence in Tehuantepec a high priest who bore the title of *Huija too*, "Great Seer," and several *Copa bitao*, or "deity keepers," from the temple complex at Mitla.[180] Burgoa narrated the unveiling of don Juan as idolater using a highly dramatic tone. After a Spaniard in disguise stole into don Juan's house dressed as an Indian and witnessed clandestine celebrations, the vicar of Tehuantepec, fray Bernardo de Santa María, decided to confront don Juan at his house. One evening, he and some associates went stealthily into don Juan's dwelling and surprised him as he sacrificed some fowl at an altar before six of the priests from Mitla; don Juan was wearing a white robe and a feathered headdress. After his imprisonment, don Juan explained that he expected the Spaniards to let him engage in traditional ritual practices, so long as he paid his tribute in gold and silver.

Both Santa María and Albuquerque recognized that this was a delicate case, since it involved a ruler who had cooperated with ecclesiastical and civil authorities, and they had two renowned Dominicans appointed as judges: the lexicographer Juan de Córdova, and Juan de Mata. Nonetheless, in a prudent move perhaps inspired by the outcry following don Carlos's execution a decade earlier, the Audiencia soon intervened and had don Juan brought to Mexico City, where he was judged and sentenced to lose both his office as ruler and the income from his tributary towns. According to Burgoa, this sentence broke don Juan's spirit, and he died in Nejapa as he was making his way back to Tehuantepec. Santa María also destroyed a renowned cult effigy in Tehuantepec, a tutelary deity known as "Heart of the community,"[181] located on an islet in the neighboring lagoon of San Dionisio.[182]

Burgoa's account of the auto de fe at Teiticpac fulfills a role as an exemplary narrative, even as it reflects the embellishment of contradicting extant sources.[183] According to Burgoa, fray Domingo Grijelmo, vicar of Teiticpac, reprimanded nine specialists for engaging in ritual practices. When they mocked his words and refused to listen, Grijelmo consulted Bishop Albuquerque, who allowed him to stage a simulated auto de fe with the support of the secular justice. After Grijelmo passed a sentence and released the defendants to the secular justice, the defendants were placed at the stake in order to simulate a public burning. As the judges pronounced the final sentence, the fire started of its own accord, burning the chief idolater and leaving the other defendants unharmed.[184]

In a marked contrast with this providential narrative, on August 1560 don Juan Ruiz Martínez, provisor and vicario general of Oaxaca, heard a different account from six Teiticpac native officials. In June 1560, Juan Pérez, alcalde of Teiticpac, denounced the ritual practices of four residents of the neighboring settlement of San Dionisio before Grijelmo and three other Dominicans. The allegation was that the tequitlahto Andrés, Juan Yoquipitela, Juan Ticopia, and Juan Tepeo employed three *pigana*, or young male assistants, to perform sacrifices before cult effigies. Like the Augustinians who pursued idolaters in Mexico two decades earlier, Grijelmo mistakenly believed that Dominicans could punish idolaters without the authorization of their bishop; thus, he asked town officials not to intervene and consulted his provincial after imprisoning these four defendants. The proposed solution was to perform a simulated auto during which proximity to the flames would convey to the audience the dangers of idolatry for the soul. Thus, on Sunday, August 4,

1560, the defendants were brought out, tied to stakes at the local market, and a large bonfire was started in between them; a breeze fanned the flames, and the fire surrounded the four defendants. One of them, Juan Tiquipela, died from the burns the following day; the three others barely survived. Neither the provisor of Oaxaca nor the Dominican provincial embraced the heavenly fire theory, as the former sent a report to the Audiencia and the latter rescinded Grijelmo's appointment as vicar.[185]

During this time Villa Alta, an alcaldía mayor northeast of Oaxaca City, became a frequent staging ground for Dominican actions against native practitioners. Ever since the first stages of colonization, Villa Alta was regarded as a region in which doctrinal projects were confronted with native hostility; in Burgoa's words, in this territory, "due to its roughness and inhospitableness, the errors were harsher, and the barbarity was less civilized; the land was more receptive to idolatry, and the people were more prone to superstition."[186] Fray Gonzalo Lucero was the first resident missionary in Villa Alta, but the missionary enterprise achieved a critical mass only with the arrival of fray Jordán de Santa Catarina and three other Dominicans in 1558.[187] Burgoa depicted the earliest extirpation attempts in Villa Alta as gentle but firm confrontations between Santa Catarina and local rulers: thus, he allegedly persuaded don Alonso, cacique of Comaltepec, to yield his cult effigies peacefully. Indeed, one of Santa Catarina's students recalled the following admonition he gave to novices in 1589: "The apostles faced steel blades, every sort of torment and imprisonment, while you, if you go to native communities, you shall fight [fragrant flowers], roads covered with flower arches, the multitude of repasts and gifts."[188]

Other Dominicans under Santa Catarina's supervision took a more violent approach. According to an información collected in July 1560 by Diego Trujillo, vicar of Villa Alta and visitador, several Dominicans whipped and tortured natives in an attempt to confiscate cult effigies. Foremost among them was fray Pedro Guerrero, who stood accused of whipping a pregnant woman who lost her fetus. Guerrero had also driven don Pedro of Yojovi to suicide after several whippings and had the body incinerated at night to avoid further scandal. Both Santa Catarina and Guerrero experimented with potentially troublesome innovations: for instance, they delegated some preaching and visiting responsibilities to the first generation of fiscales to be appointed in the region.[189] Trujillo's claim about the naming of these officials is corroborated by fiscal appointments made by Guerrero at Lachixila, Petlapa, and Tizatepec between April 1559 and May 1560, which granted them the authority to punish fellow villagers engaging in "cohabitation, drunkenness or sacrifices," among other transgressions.[190]

The decade of the 1560s was characterized by disagreements between civil authorities on the one hand, and the Dominicans of Oaxaca and Bishop Albuquerque on the other. The accusations against the mendicants suggest that in the previous three decades they had enjoyed greater latitude in anti-idolatry measures than their counterparts in Mexico. By late 1560, several grave accusations against the Dominicans of Oaxaca, which included the cruel Teiticpac auto, Guerrero's lavish use of the whip, and miscellaneous abuses by the friars of Guaxolotitlan,[191] had reached the king. Furthermore, in April 1562, the provisor and vicar general of Oaxaca reported that some Dominicans were refusing to bury natives in a Christian manner in Teotila and other communities.[192]

In fact, the Dominicans were not the only order accused of abuses against natives in that period. In June 1561, the archbishop of Mexico received a cédula that forbid regulars from having prisons, whipping or shearing Indians, and admonished them to respect the ecclesiastical jurisdiction. This order was apparently addressed to Franciscans, Dominicans, and Augustinians, and their response was one of outrage. In an April 1562 letter to the crown, Montúfar reported that this cédula was regarded as an affront by the mendicants, who called secret meetings with the viceroy in order to confront both the ordinario and the Audiencia. In subsequent letters drafted in March and May 1563, Montúfar complained the regulars were attempting to discredit his authority.[193]

In Oaxaca, mendicant resistance to the Audiencia was compounded by the fact that the Dominicans were then engaged in a protracted battle against what they regarded as unnecessary political scrutiny and by an attempt by the crown to reassess native tributary obligations in an effort spearheaded by Visitador Valderrama. In fact, Valderrama and Albuquerque clashed on three major points: the reassessment of tributary obligations, the reduction of native patrimonial service to lineage rulers, and the preservation of local community funds for collective needs.[194] Although the political context contemporaneous to the transfer of native peoples to episcopal jurisdiction after 1571 was more contentious in Oaxaca than in Mexico, this transfer did not seem to cause further conflicts in late sixteenth-century Oaxaca.

IDOLATRY ERADICATION IN CENTRAL MEXICO BEFORE 1571

Are there any correlations between idolatry, superstition, and sorcery prosecution patterns, and dramatic population losses in sixteenth-century Central Mexico? Even though we may never know the exact scale of indigenous demographic decline between 1519 and the early seventeenth century in Central Mexico due to epidemics, warfare, and exploitative labor conditions, several estimates provide a general basis for assessing demographic change for this period. Cook and Borah's classic study provides the most devastating estimate, with an indigenous population estimate of 16.8 million for Central Mexico in 1532 that declined to 1.075 million by 1605.[195] Some critical assessments of this work argue for less drastic reductions, based on lower initial population estimates obtained through archaeological and simulation methods. For the late sixteenth-century Basin of Mexico, Sanders calculated a descent to 18 percent of the preconquest total based on archaeological survey data.[196] Whitmore calculated a descent to 11.5 percent of the preconquest population through a computer simulation.[197] The broader picture was rather dismal; according to Cook and Borah, the lowest point in Central Mexican indigenous population was reached circa 1650, with less than 900,000 individuals, and demographic recovery was not detectable until 1671. The major single factor behind this decrease was a series of pandemics and epidemics affecting almost exclusively indigenous peoples.

As argued in Chapter 1, the fluctuations in accusations against native ritual specialists in Central Mexico follow sociopolitical developments rather than population decline. Nonetheless, such decreases, compounded by *congregaciones*, or the consolidation of native population centers in the late sixteenth century, resulted in the creation of more compact native social spaces in which ritual practices might have been more readily visible to clergy by the early seventeenth century.[198] The tallying of native ritual practitioners investigated in Mexico and Oaxaca until 1571 shows that a majority were interrogated during the administrations of Zumárraga and Tello de Sandoval in 1536–early 1547, a period accounting for 78 percent of all such defendants between 1521 and 1571. By contrast, the period between 1548 and 1571 encompasses only about 16 percent of this total. The least represented period is, not surprisingly, the earliest mendicant inquisition (1521–36), with only about 7 percent of the total. The marked decrease in prosecutions in Mexico between the 1550s and the 1571 may be due to two factors: first, the lack of inquisitorial interest in native practices displayed by Montúfar; second, the growing impact of epidemics and pandemics on native population levels after 1545.[199] Paradoxically, in Oaxaca, extirpation campaigns prospered under Albuquerque.

Zumárraga's idolatry and superstition proceedings stand out as the most systematic idolatry eradication experiment in sixteenth-century Central Mexico. In one of the most concise analysis to date of extirpation campaigns between 1536 and 1540, Klor de Alva noted that this period, characterized by the meting out of bodily punishment against idolaters, was followed by the rise of "penitential discipline": that is, the attempt to eliminate idolatrous behavior through the establishment of confessional dynamics in Nahuatl leading to the emergence of a Nahua Christian self who would voluntarily identify and suppress instances of idolatry.[200] According to Klor de Alva, the rise of sacramental confession was seen as an alternative to bodily punishment, which would have fallen out of favor in ecclesiastical circles after the 1539 execution of don Carlos. A crucial element in this argument is an elaborate reading of the instructions sent by the king to Zumárraga in 1540, which Klor de Alva interprets as a mandate to focus on the self rather than the body, to conceal the source of discipline, and to apply discipline evenly throughout the social body. This interpretation is a pitch-perfect echo of Foucault's celebrated hypothesis about a transition in the punishment methods employed by the state after the Enlightenment.[201]

Nevertheless, no decisive transition to more introspective methods followed don Carlos's burning. To be sure, this case's repercussions motivated a faltering in punitive efforts, exemplified by Zumárraga's granting of an appeal injunction by the Totolapa principales in 1540, and by Tello de Sandoval's preference for fines over corporal punishments. However, in Oaxaca, the three decades after don Carlos's passing were characterized by a recrudescence of corporal punishment against idolatry defendants. The Dominicans resorted to the whip, the shears, and the bonfire in order to reform indigenous social behavior. By contrast, the Audiencia's criticism of Dominican punishments was motivated by the intention to rein in the powers of this order in Oaxaca and to avoid scandal; their objective was not to phase out corporal punishment, but rather to punish with lesser violence. Klor de Alva's hypothesis rests on the remarkable but temporary lull in extirpation campaigns against native specialists in the archbishopric of Mexico between 1547 and 1571. Nonetheless, the rise in secular extirpation campaigns in the late sixteenth and early seventeenth centuries was characterized by a constant reliance on the punitive strategies Zumárraga pioneered: public shaming and corporal punishment, exile from one's community, forced labor, financial penalties, and exclusion from elective public office. Indeed, a new round of confrontations between Nahua and Zapotec specialists and their parish priests was just about to begin.

CHAPTER 3

Local Cosmologies and Secular Extirpators in Nahua Communities, 1571–1662

AFTER 1571: FROM INQUISITORIAL TO DIOCESAN TRIBUNALS

Between 1571 and the middle years of the seventeenth century, ecclesiastical policies toward traditional native devotions underwent an epochal transition in the see of Mexico. While indigenous nobles would no longer be the centerpiece of exemplary punishment, a new generation of secular foes of idolatry submitted native commoners's bodies to similar forms of discipline, and their devotional practices to novel forms of scrutiny. Although these changes were certainly informed by Counter-Reformation policies, a deep understanding of them calls for a nuanced analysis of the social and intellectual exchanges between a relatively small number of native specialists and ecclesiastic actors. Hence, this chapter investigates the modifications in idolatry eradicators' policies, methodology, and objectives by focusing on the careers of Pedro Ponce de León, Hernando Ruiz de Alarcón, and Jacinto de la Serna, three important secular extirpators in the Cohuixca-Tlalhuica region and the Toluca Valley. These transformations were echoed by no less dramatic changes in the Nahua collective and elective ritual spheres. In an attempt to plumb this transition, I discuss below a ritual genre that allowed specialists to personify Nahua deities, and provide a demographic and sociocultural interpretation of its highly gendered patterns of usage. The chapter closes with an overview of ecclesiastical and medical discourses regarding the indigenous use of several plants with hallucinogenic effects, and with a discussion of Nahua hybrid healing practices and the clandestine market that emerged around them.

Many ecclesiastical actors in New Spain supported the establishment of a separate Inquisition tribunal in Spanish America, but this transition was not accomplished systematically. Greenleaf cites a 1545 letter stressing the need for a Mexican Holy Office from Tello de Sandoval to Prince Philip, later Philip II;[1] Medina mentions various petitions submitted by colonial authorities and the Franciscan order;[2] Lea points out that not all regional bishops were willing to cede inquisitorial faculties and areas of jurisdiction to the Mexican Inquisition and notes that a preemptive 1570 order to cease delegating such powers to their subalterns had to be issued again in 1585.[3]

Once the crown and the Council of Indies decided there were strong political and demographic reasons for establishing separate Holy Office tribunals in Mexico and in Peru,[4] the formal exclusion of native peoples from inquisitorial jurisdiction on December 1571 was an expedient but logical corollary to legal arguments that accorded a position of moral fragility and inferiority to indigenous subjects.[5] The establishment of a colonial legal system that distinguished between two legal and political spheres, the *república de españoles* and the *república de indios*, bracketed indigenous people into a separate and relatively constrained juridical and moral space. As human beings, the rational and moral capacities of natives were doubted by the theologian Ginés de Sepúlveda, defended by Las Casas, and eventually acknowledged by the Vatican; as colonial subjects, they were regarded as vulnerable and accorded the status of minors under the crown's protection; as new Christians, they were expected to falter in the faith; as devotional weaklings, they were expected to observe only ten of the canonical forty-one yearly Christian holidays and keep a partial fast during Lent.[6] The exclusion of natives from inquisitorial jurisdiction was another step toward the consolidation of an exclusive legal sphere for colonial native subjects, which was reinforced through the creation in 1592 of an indigenous tribunal, the General Indian Court, which provided natives with legal assistance and was funded with their contributions.[7]

The transfer of jurisdiction over native crimes against the faith from inquisitorial to episcopal authorities led to the emergence of dissimilar legal interpretations within the episcopal, inquisitorial, and civil jurisdictions, a status of affairs Richard Greenleaf famously characterized as "jurisdictional confusion." In theory, the post–1571 jurisdictional situation was simple: only the Holy Office of Mexico City held or delegated jurisdiction over crimes of faith committed by nonindigenous subjects, and only the bishop or archbishop and his provisores, who presided over ecclesiastical courts, had faculties to act against native crimes of faith, which included bigamy, sexual transgressions, failure to tithe, idolatry, sorcery, and superstition. In practice, the boundaries between ecclesiastic and early Mexican inquisitorial justice were rather amorphous: some bishops misunderstood the extent of their faculties; some regular and secular local ministers acted against natives without the proper granting of faculties; a few ecclesiastic officials assumed inquisitorial and episcopal faculties; and a few impostors even impersonated inquisitorial commissioners and ecclesiastics for personal gain.[8]

An emblematic instance of the confused reception of the post-1571 jurisdictional transfer is the conflict surrounding Bishop Albuquerque's idolatry eradication policies in Oaxaca. A February 1576 letter from the Audiencia of Mexico to the crown illustrates Albuquerque's incomplete and immoderate interpretation of his new juridical mandate. According to this document, in the mid-1570s Albuquerque had given commissions against idolaters to all Dominican vicars in Oaxaca, who now conducted autos de fe patterned after inquisitorial usage. They also carried out a corporal punishment program traditionally reserved for civil justice: the Dominicans now placed Indians in stocks, whipped them, and imprisoned them. The earlier controversies noted above regarding Dominican punishments in the 1560s demonstrate that, rather than being an innovation, these punitive practices were an extension of long-standing Dominican disciplinary strategies. Albuquerque's Dominicans also confiscated objects made of gold and precious stones, adducing they were idols. When confronted by the Audiencia's prosecutor, Albuquerque argued that he now had an inquisitorial mandate to prosecute native heresies that functioned as an *inquisición ordinaria*. This was a legal fiction, since after 1571 there was only one inquisitorial tribunal in New Spain, now located in Mexico City, but there was no "ordinary" one in existence elsewhere. In fact, the Oaxacan bishop did possess jurisdiction against indigenous crimes of faith, not as inquisitor, but as part of his newfangled faculties as bishop. Consequently, the Audiencia asked the crown to order Albuquerque to suspend his commissions, to take into account the "scarce capacities and discretion" of neophytes, to refrain from confiscating gold and jewels, and to submit both trial records and confiscated items for review.[9]

This disagreement triggered a haughty response from Albuquerque in 1577, who justified his policies by summoning tropes that subsequent generations of Oaxacan extirpators would later invoke. First, he argued, there were substantial obstacles to evangelization efforts: his bishopric extended for two hundred leagues of rugged territory, large distances separated indigenous communities, and, according to Albuquerque, there existed at least twenty-two different native languages. Second, he accused some corregidores of preventing the Dominicans from enforcing "order, proper instruction, and good customs" among the natives. Due to this, indigenous people "have returned to their vices, drunkenness, and superstitions as dogs go back to their own vomit."

The lapidary image of a dog lapping its own vomit was meant to capture the profound disdain with which Albuquerque regarded the natives' perfidious character. Moreover, such transgressions carried a divine penalty, according to the bishop, since indigenous drunkenness was to blame for the epidemics of the 1560s and 1570s. Third, civil authorities were not supportive of the bishop's evangelization efforts. Even though ministers were scarce, the Audiencia refused to grant stipends for new ministers, opposed the policy of appointing native fiscales to police local customs, and required Albuquerque, who was sixty years old, to conduct laborious visitas. Moreover, the Audiencia's prosecutor had pledged to appeal any punishments handed down by the bishop. Finally, Albuquerque justified a policy of exemplary punishment—imposing stocks on and taking political posts away from natives—to avoid pecuniary penalties.[10] The crown reacted favorably to Albuquerque's exposition and pledged to increase the number of ministers. Presciently, Albuquerque also argued in favor of congregaciones. Throughout the end of the sixteenth century and the first decade of the seventeenth century, this resettlement policy would indeed transform the social and political landscape of many native communities in Central Mexico.

FROM CONGREGACIONES TO THE
THIRD MEXICAN CHURCH COUNCIL

The last decade of the sixteenth century and the first of the seventeenth were one of the most difficult periods for the social and demographic reproduction of native communities in Central Mexico. It is not surprising, therefore, that there are virtually no extant inquiries about idolatry and native sorcery in Nahua communities during this period.[11] Quite possibly, this void reflects the impact of two major demographic changes in ecclesiastical and juridical projects: a recurrent series of epidemics and pandemics,[12] and congregaciones, which displaced many previously existing native communities. Various letters to the crown from Archbishop Pedro Moya de Contreras (1573–91) suggest that, even from the comfort of the episcopal residence, native epidemics proved a frightful spectacle.[13] In an April 1576 letter, Moya de Contreras noted that the disease not only afflicted Indians but also mestizos, Africans, and Spaniards, and stated that he would not perform a visita under such conditions. An October 1576 letter from the Audiencia echoed the archbishop's concerns and reported charitable acts toward Indians performed by the viceroy.[14] In another letter dated March 1577, the archbishop stated that indigenous mortality diminished in the Basin of Mexico, just as the epidemic expanded to Michoacán and Nueva Galicia; after completing a visita of Taxco, he postponed any further journeys in the diocese.[15] By March 1578, Moya de Contreras observed that the epidemic has ceased, and in an October 1583 missive, he contended that demographic decline and congregaciones would result in more compact and manageable *doctrinas*, or parishes:

> Even if more than half of all the Indians have died, one cannot decrease the number of doctrinas, since the Indians have not been aggregated, and they are still quite scattered about. Before the plague, there were so many of them, that one would have had to duplicate the doctrinas; now, if the Indians were congregated as Your Majesty has ordered, they would be well instructed, and would live in civility and not as barbarians, and this with a much smaller number of ministers.[16]

As this passage suggests, Moya de Contreras was interested in assuming greater institutional control over indigenous everyday activities, and this preoccupation also found its outlet in a serious critique of indigenous education under the mendicants. The archbishop's interest in closer regulation of indigenous indoctrination coincides with three processes that facilitated new measures of control: the consolidation of the Holy Office in New Spain; the proliferation of seculars in parishes formerly served by regulars; and the early application of directives issued by the councils at Trent and Mexico.[17] Moya de Contreras's conservative attitude toward indigenous education was displayed in a January 1585 letter to the crown, where, in a dismissal of the Franciscan educational experiment at the Colegio de Santa Cruz, he opined it was not wise to teach Latin, rhetoric, philosophy, or other liberal arts to the natives until the Christian faith had deeper roots in them.[18]

Furthermore, the archbishop attempted to review and restrict the circulation of mendicant accounts about indigenous ritual practices. This point is best illustrated by Moya de Contreras's interest in the work of Bernardino de Sahagún, who, after several decades of patient collaborative authorship with Nahua metropolitan elites associated with the Colegio de Santa Cruz in Tlatelolco, was completing a draft of an encyclopedic work on the history, cosmology, devotions, customs, and literature of Nahua communities in the Basin of Mexico.[19] Between 1576 and 1578, the archbishop ordered the Franciscan commissary Rodrigo de Sequera to secure a Spanish translation of Sahagún's *Historia General*, and ordered that all the original Sahagún manuscripts and translations be sent to Spain, "without leaving a transcription or a printed copy here, due to fair considerations."[20] According to Moya de Contreras, Sahagún's monumental task could serve two institutional purposes. First, since the Franciscan knew "the most elegant and proper usage in the land" of Nahuatl, his project would preserve rapidly fading ancient Nahua rhetoric. Second, "the curiosity of this friar may be of great benefit at some point in time, particularly because the Inquisition will thus have an account of rituals by the time that it arrives here to investigate cases involving Indians."[21] The archbishop's statement, which viewed Spanish knowledge of native ritual practices as a central motivation for eradication efforts, also erred in its interpretation of inquisitorial jurisdiction over natives after 1571. Four decades later, the Franciscan Torquemada would agree with the archbishop's first point by insisting that Sahagún sought to preserve ancient Nahuatl speech "because it was becoming corrupted by mixture with our own, and because the Indians were losing their natural and curious way of speaking," but offered a sarcastic rejoinder to Moya de Contrera's request to send Sahagún's papers overseas. Since no one understood Nahuatl in Spain, he reasoned, "they will serve as papers for [wrapping] spices."[22]

The development of institutional and judicial means of control over the production and circulation of doctrinal works in printed and manuscript form during the second half of the sixteenth century strengthened and formalized review mechanisms for doctrinal texts written in native languages. This turn toward greater scrutiny was certainly fostered by Counter-Reformation policies seeking a dramatic reorientation of how the faithful interacted with ecclesiastical institutions through modifications in doctrinal education and the administration of sacraments.

The printing and selling of books in New Spain was closely regulated by inquisitorial and secular authorities, who sought out copies of books forbidden by the inquisitorial indices, as well as any books not bearing an authorization granted by a bishop, or the *licencia del ordinario*. After the First Mexican Council of 1555, manuscript copies of translations of doctrinal works in indigenous languages were the focus of intense regulation: the Mexican conclave stipulated that all doctrinal works in native languages in circulation be removed from native hands, that any new translations bear the approval of an ecclesiastical language expert, and that any such works be signed with the author's name.

An example of this shift is found in the censorship of fray Maturino Gilberti's doctrinal writings. In 1559, Gilberti's work was seized by orders of the bishop of Michoacán, and several censors argued there existed substantial differences between the Phurépecha and the Spanish, as well as "things impertinent and ill-sounding to our ears."[23] Such measures placed overt attempts at translating doctrinal works into native languages at the mercy of multiple linguistic and ecclesiastical reviews. This tendency was also exemplified by a 1577 consultation the Mexican Inquisition made to a group of mendicants that included Nahuatl doctrinal authors Molina, Sahagún, and Domingo de la Anunciación regarding the wisdom of rendering Ecclesiastes and other biblical books into indigenous languages.[24] A more rigorous form of ecclesiastical control over doctrinal texts and educational enterprises was embraced by the 1585 Third Mexican Church Council, which enforced previous directives by threatening to excommunicate anybody involved in the circulation of doctrinal works in native languages not authorized by the ordinario.

Nonetheless, the capacity of inquisitorial indices and ecclesiastical ordinances to effectively control the circulation of texts, particularly in the form of manuscript copies, should not be overstated.[25] The use of lists of forbidden works, such as the Holy Office Index of 1583–84, which expanded on the 1559 index, constituted a means of ideological control seeking to regulate anything a Spanish subject should read and emphasize an orthodox intellectual orientation.[26] Henry Kamen's revisionist view of the Inquisition holds that the Holy Office's attempt at restricting intellectual production "looked imposing in theory but was unimpressive in practice."[27] Kamen also contends that gauging the impact of inquisitorial censorship is a difficult task, that the indices often featured works that were nearly impossible to find in Spain, and that few of the most popular devotional texts appeared on these lists. Additionally, Fernando Bouza's work on private libraries and the activities of copyists, particularly in Madrid and in university circles, demonstrates that the production and compilation of manuscript versions of a variety of works was an extremely dynamic endeavor in sixteenth-century Spain.[28]

SECULAR CLERGY AS IDOLATRY INVESTIGATORS AFTER 1571

Even though Hernando Ruiz de Alarcón's investigation of Nahua ritual practices between 1614 and the 1630s constitute the center of gravity of known extirpation efforts in the diocese of Mexico in the early seventeenth century, three separate cases, along with Pedro Ponce de León's inquiries in the Toluca Valley, depict growing interest on the part of extirpators regarding the empirical basis of native ritual knowledge. These three proceedings, in fact, portray a significant change in the attitudes of civil and secular authorities. While Zumárraga, Tello de Sandoval, Albuquerque, and other sixteenth-century extirpators focused on ritual practices that offered broad parallels with classical antiquity, such as concealment of idols in caves and houses, offerings to idols, human sacrifice, or cannibalism, secular and civil authorities who began conducting inquiries into Nahua and Zapotec ritual practices after 1571 focused on more discrete units of behavior—specific utterances, ritual practices tied to specific social contexts, or ritual implements. What remained to be done, as this new generation of secular extirpators soon realized, was to make detailed inquiries into the dynamics and meaning of these uncanny observances. Even if this change did exemplify the renewed inspection of parishioners' devotional practices by resident priests that Counter-Reformation policies inspired, these extirpators' engagement with their subjects' beliefs and actions went well beyond that of their contemporary fellow priests.

For instance, a case from Epazoyucan featured a detailed inter-rogation focusing on the meaning of a single ritual object.[29] Around 2:00 a.m. on a January night in 1572, Andrés del Rincón and Alonso Reyes, native alguaciles of the Nahua town of Epazoyucan on the north-east of the Basin of Mexico, came across a house in Tezcacoac in which lights and voices betrayed an unusual degree of activity for that hour. Fearing a clandestine drinking session, they rushed in as the house's in-habitants extinguished their fire, finding a series of objects that suggested an offering: pulque, tamales, cooked meat, and some strange pieces of straw. The officials arrested the men found in the house and turned them over to the acting corregidor of Cempoala, Pedro Martínez de Perea, who began a civil inquest.[30] Through interpreters and acting as a civil judge, Martínez de Perea interrogated two natives: Francisco Tezca, the owner of the house that had been raided, and Pedro Xochitonal, a native of Tecuauhtla whose son and daughter had recently passed away. The narrative that emerged out of the inquest was simple: Xochitonal and others were preparing burial offerings for his dead son and daughter under the supervision of Tezca. Martínez de Perea was not satisfied with eliciting a canonical narrative about acts of superstition. Under interro-gation, Xochitonal instructed the judge on the hidden meanings of the implements he had seized: a length of straw with paper knots was "a lad-der for descending into hell" for his deceased offspring; a piece of bark paper tied to the straw was the ladder's runner; finally, two small straw brooms he had made were for sweeping the place where they would place an offering of tamales and a skewered rabbit for the nourishment of his dead son and daughter.[31] The judge was unaware of recent jurisdictional changes and therefore sent the two defendants to the Holy Office.

Two cases that took place a decade later suggest that secular parish priests had already begun to assume a mandate against native idolaters. In 1584, two separate cases against native ritual specialists were heard in Teotlalco,[32] a parish located just across diocesan borders in the bishopric of Tlaxcala, near the Nahuatl-speaking region of Tlalhuicatlalpan.[33] In

October 1584, Mateo de Zepeda questioned a ritual specialist called Joseph Chicon. Zepeda was a *beneficiado*, or clergy appointed to a curate
endowed with an income. During a stay in a nearby town called Tlachco,
Zepeda found evidence that Chicon prepared a brew with *temecatl*, a
dried seed, which he drank in order to address an entity who instructed
him on healing treatments. Thus, temecatl usage resembled that of a
widely used hallucinogen called *ololiuhqui*. The temecatl entity often
instructed Chicon to bleed the patient, a practice suggesting some familiarity with European medical practices, and to apply ground temecatl
on wounds. Chicon learned about the virtues of temecatl eighteen years
earlier from Lorenzo Tlilancatl, his brother-in-law; unlike other specialists, he had no set fee for his cures and accepted gifts of food from his
clients instead. More importantly, Chicon recited an incantation before
taking temecatl in which he addressed the seed as *Coaxoxohuic*, "Green
Snake," an epithet also used for ololiuhqui.[34]

Only a month later, an idolatry trial in the same parish investigated
a much more experienced ritual specialist, a sixty-year-old woman
called Magdalena Papalo Coaxochitl of Cuitlatenamic. In scrupulous
observance of episcopal jurisdiction, Francisco León Carvajal had been
granted faculties as *juez de comisión contra los idólatras*, or commissioned judge against idolatry, by Diego Romano, bishop of Tlaxcala, and
as such he began investigating Papalo's activities by interrogating María
Teycuh at the mines of Tlautzinco. Teycuh was married to Papalo's son,
a church alguacil in Cuitlatenamic called Jerónimo Antón, and she volunteered ample details about Papalo's activities. Teycuh identified her
mother-in-law as a *ticitl*, or healer, and as a midwife who performed
bathing and naming ceremonies in behalf of infants, used forearm measuring to diagnose illnesses, and performed ritual cleanings with cotton
balls to protect clients from sorcery. After being admonished to give a
full account of her activities in exchange for merciful treatment, Papalo
complied, providing León Carvajal not only with descriptions of her ritual practices but also with the words of five separate incantations in Nahuatl, which represent an oral genre known as *nahualtocaitl*, or Nahual
Names. Due to this judge's providential curiosity, five Nahuatl incantations were entered into trial records: one for easing childbirth through
which Papalo embodied the creator couple Ohxomoco-Cipactonal, two
more for an infant's first bath and naming ceremony, another for providing a prognosis of a child's illness through forearm measuring, and
another for staving off acts of sorcery by rubbing the client's body with
cotton balls. Papalo also explained she had placed pulque and food offerings by her granary in order to honor Tlalteuctli, Lord of the Earth,
who was customarily given the first pulque and fruits of every season.

In the end, Papalo attempted to turn suspicion away from her by stating that her main accuser, her daughter-in-law, made food offerings to an image of Saint John.

A more systematic regional campaign against idolatry was conducted in 1610 by Pedro Ponce de León, a beneficiado of Zumpahuacan of Nahua origin who used his fluency in the language and familiarity with local customs to his advantage. Ponce de León also wrote a succinct treatise about native ritual practices entitled *Relación de los dioses y ritos de la gentilidad mexicana*.[35] The most detailed surviving account of Ponce de León's activities appears in an unpublished extirpation manual written by another leading eradicator, Jacinto de la Serna, before 1656, and called *Manual para los ministros de indios para el conocimiento de sus idolatrías y extirpación dellas* (henceforth *Manual*). In this work, de la Serna noted that neither epidemic disease, nor famine, nor congregaciones had eliminated native ritual practices, and characterized eradication efforts in the early seventeenth century as a logical response to the fact that "idolatry was so deeply rooted in the heart of the Indians, that it began to sprout once again . . . throughout the Marquesado [of Toluca]."[36] According to de la Serna, Ponce de León "punished some, and taught others" with the assistance of the Jesuit Juan de Tovar, a distinguished preacher, chronicler, and author of Nahuatl doctrinal texts; another Jesuit, Antonio del Rincón, assisted Tovar. In 1610, de la Serna recounted, a "great complicity of idolaters" was uncovered in various Toluca Valley towns where Otomi, Nahuatl, and Matlatzinca were spoken: Teotenango, San Mateo Texcaliacac, Xalatlaco, and Calimaya.[37]

These inquests arose as a result of a visita in Toluca by the Mexican archbishop fray García Guerra. During his brief tenure as archbishop (1607–12) and viceroy (1611–12), the Dominican Guerra made idolatry prosecution a priority by personally overseeing these campaigns, instead of delegating that function to his provisor.[38] García Guerra designated Ponce de León and Diego Gutiérrez Bocanegra, the Matlatzinca-speaking beneficiado of Xalatlaco,[39] as commissioned judges; the beneficiado Gaspar de Prabes acted as an assistant. The archbishop described this campaign in a May 1610 letter to Philip III, where he mentioned Ponce de León and Bocanegra's appointments and noted he had charged "a qualified person" to tour the diocese in order to punish idolaters. Viceroy Luis de Velasco the Younger praised García Guerra's inquiry in an October 1610 letter to the crown in which he reported that idolatries had been uncovered in "two or three doctrinas" in Mexico and in one parish in Tlaxcala.[40]

Ponce de León's campaign report was forwarded to the crown along with a letter from the archbishop. In a rhetorical move later echoed by idolatry eradicators, at an auto de fe held in Tenango del Valle on May 16, 1610, Ponce de León compared idolatry eradication in the Toluca Valley with the Israelites's struggle against their polytheistic enemies:

[The defendants] were punished according to Your Excellency's instructions; there were seven corozas, besides the ones that were taken out for public penance, and whipped. A solemn absolution and due punishment was administered in a manner that caused great fright. A Franciscan father preached in the Matlatzinca language, and I in the Mexican language, the gospel corresponding to that Sunday, together with the sixth and seventh chapter of Joshua, in which it is recounted the prohibition of idolatry, and the punishment that God brought on the people of Israel for having embraced idolatrous customs.[41]

Although no copy of Ponce de León's oration survives, perhaps his choice of Joshua was motivated by a rather intricate parallel between the penitents' seven corozas and the "seven trumpets of rams' horns" with which the priests of Israel brought down the walls of Jericho. Moreover, in keeping with the link between infidelity and heavenly punishment proposed earlier by Moya de Contreras and later embraced by de la Serna and Ruiz de Alarcón, Ponce de León proposed that the epidemics affecting natives in the 1610s were divine retribution for their idolatries.

De la Serna's narrative complements our knowledge of Ponce de León's extirpations, which preceded Ruiz de Alarcón's activities by four years.[42] Some ritual specialists in the Toluca Valley molded amaranth seeds, or *huauhtli*, into figurines, which were then propitiated and ingested.[43] Other specialists performed ritual songs to the beat of the wooden drum known as *teponaztli* and uttered "unintelligible words." Even some variations of Christian practices that may seem hybrid from our vantage point belonged to a separate elective realm, according to both practitioners and extirpators. Some specialists used Latin prayer formulae, propitiated the Virgin Mary and Santiago de Compostela, and recited prayers composed "with the very words of the Roman Manual." In fact, a miscellany of texts by native authors that was eventually acquired by the scholar and collector Lorenzo Boturini in the eighteenth century (BNF-Mex 381), may contain some clandestine writings similar to those confiscated in the Toluca Valley in 1610.

Another particularly vivid example comes from a document seized by Ponce de León in 1610. As an iconographic reference to indigenous interest in Spanish heraldic insignia,[44] this text featured a seal consisting of a creature half eagle and half ocelot with the Eucharist, a chalice, and a suspended fleece at its center. According to de la Serna, the figure of an ax represented the obligations of married men. A Nahuatl inscription read, "Here one tells the prayer of Our Lord Jesus Christ and the prayer of His dear mother Saint Mary, which the true Christian shall recite and listen. They [true Christians] are called the eagle, the ocelot, the commoners' wings, the vassals, the little cripples, the poor ones, the commoners who live amidst the grass."[45] This excerpt provides a glimmer of Nahua authors' attempts to embrace Christianity through a novel iconography and a peculiar description of their status. Through the deployment of metaphorical terms used for commoners in Nahua rhetoric, such as "the eagle, the ocelot, the commoners' wings,"[46] these anonymous writers indicated this work was addressed to a group of literate, indigenous Christian commoners—perhaps an unofficial *cofradía*, or confraternity. In spite of the manifold distinctions between these writings and devotional songs celebrating Nahua deities, such a literate appropriation of Christian beliefs seemed intolerable to a secular eradicator of native heterodoxy.

HERNANDO RUIZ DE ALARCÓN, AMATEUR INQUISITOR

The scarce biographical data on Hernando Ruiz de Alarcón contrasts with his status as one of the most resourceful idolatry extirpators in Central Mexico. His parents, the miner Pedro Ruiz de Alarcón and his wife Leonor de Mendoza, took residence in the mining town of Taxco toward the middle of the sixteenth century, and Hernando was born in 1574. His maternal grandparents, Hernando Hernández de Casalla and María de Mendoza, were among the first settlers of Taxco, arriving by the early 1540s.[47] All of Pedro Ruiz de Alarcón's sons—Pedro, Hernando, Gaspar, García, and Juan—were raised in Taxco, and at least three of them took university degrees. This family embraced the usual diversification strategy favored by Spanish families of certain means: Pedro and Hernando embraced a career in the priesthood, and Juan took a degree in law. Pedro received a *bachillerato*, or first degree, in philosophy on February 25, 1594;[48] Hernando followed his lead by matriculating at the Royal University in May 1597 and obtaining a first degree in theology.[49]

Two of Hernando's brothers pursued extremely successful careers in the ecclesiastical and civil spheres. One of them was the exceptionally talented Juan Ruiz de Alarcón, the well-known Golden Age playwright, author, and wit, who overcame two major obstacles to success in Philip III's court—his status as a *criollo* (one born in the Indies to Spanish parents) and an unseemly hunch on his back—and became a member of the Council of Indies and Lope de Vega's most prominent literary rival. The other illustrious brother was Pedro Ruiz de Alarcón, who served for two years as priest and vicar of Xalticpac, obtained the relatively profitable *beneficio*, or curate endowed with an income, of Tenango near Taxco by 1604,[50] and ended his distinguished ecclesiastical career as chaplain of the Royal College for Children in Mexico City.[51] If Hernando was indeed challenged to greatness by Juan's and Pedro's merits, he chose a relatively lackluster endeavor to make his mark: the extirpation of native ritual practices and their recording for the benefit of future crusaders. In contrast with documentary evidence about Juan's and Pedro's achievements, there is no extant documentation regarding Hernando's two turning points in his career: his acquisition of an outstanding command of Nahuatl, and his appointment, which occurred in the first decade of the seventeenth century, as one of the first beneficiados at San Juan Atenango del Río, fifteen leagues southeast of Taxco in the jurisdiction of Chilapa.[52]

By 1613, Hernando (henceforth Ruiz de Alarcón) was already conducting autos against ritual specialists. On February 1614, the itinerant Spanish weaver Juan Ponce Zambrano approached the apostolic inquisitor Juan Gutiérrez Flores in Mexico City and recounted several transgressions against the faith. One of his accusations was referred to him by a "scandalized" Spaniard from Comala, who said that, on Palm Sunday of 1613, the beneficiado of Atenango del Río had made "an inquisitorial auto" by parading an unspecified number of native convicts.[53] Gutiérrez waited four months before ordering Bernardino de Rojas, the inquisitorial commissary at the Dominican convent in Tepoztlan, to investigate this newfangled inquisitor. In July 1614, don Toribio de la Cruz, gobernador of Atenango, was interrogated by Rojas. His deposition provides a detailed account of Ruiz de Alarcón's activities as amateur inquisitor. On Palm Sunday 1613, as he waited for mass to begin, a native *alguacil mayor*, or constable,

brought from the town's prison to its church two Indian women, each with a rope around her neck, her hands tied up, a coroza on her head, and a candle in her hands. In this manner and with these symbols, they were put before the altar, where they heard Mass. Then . . . the alguacil mayor had the Indian women brought out; they were led around the church, along the way that processions customarily follow, with an Indian crier who said in their language and in a loud voice that the beneficiado had ordered their punishment for certain crimes. . . . When Mass ended, Hernando Ruiz de Alarcón turned to the people, and said in the Mexican language to those present that they should take stock of the punishment he had given those women. . . . Then, the said beneficiado stated that, if others committed such a crime, he would punish them in the same way. . . . This witness then said the corozas were painted with images of flames, and that . . . two Indians flogged one Indian women each, having disrobed them from the waist up.[54]

According to don Toribio, these women from the neighboring town of Comala had not been the beneficiado's only disciplinary targets, for he had also punished a man and a woman in a separate auto. These descriptions demonstrate that Ruiz de Alarcón's punishments were scaled-down, modest replicas of inquisitorial autos carried out in Mexico City. The procession began and ended at the jail's door, tracing a communal movement through the parish's most important public spaces, the same spaces that Christian observance reclaimed during the processions of Corpus Christi. Just as inquisitors were assisted by the secular arm, Ruiz de Alarcón relied on native officials to mete out punishment. As a visual complement to the sermon, the penitents heard mass wearing corozas decorated with the flames of hell and holding an expensive wax candle that was returned to the priest at the end of the auto. A crier announced in Nahuatl the crimes committed by the penitents, just as their disciplined bodies were led back to jail. Paradoxically, such pageant was not an effective didactic vehicle, for don Toribio could not—or would not—recall the defendants' transgressions a year later.

Rojas forwarded to his superiors a positive report about the beneficiado in July 1614, "because [his parishioners] say that he is very good minister and a saint"; he eventually concluded that Ruiz de Alarcón acted "out of ignorance and not out of malice."[55] Archbishop Juan Pérez de la Serna (1613–27) did not punish Ruiz de Alarcón's judicial entrepreneurship; instead, he granted him a commission to instruct legal proceedings against idolatry and superstition in his parish before 1624, a milestone the beneficiado later mentioned in his writings.[56] At the time when Ruiz de Alarcón obtained this commission, the archbishop was embroiled in a conflict against regulars regarding indigenous tongues. Pérez de la Serna directed all regular preachers and priests to appear before him in 1618 and 1619 to present proof of their fluency in the indigenous language of their parishes, a move that led to a suit before the Audiencia and to a cédula instructing the archbishop to continue with these examinations "following the dictates of . . . his own conscience."[57] Hence, it is plausible that Pérez de la Serna regarded Ruiz de Alarcón's mastery of Nahuatl as an important and relatively scarce qualification.

It is telling that Ruiz de Alarcón repeatedly referred to a "commission" granted him by the archbishop of Mexico, which would have made him a commissioned judge against idolatries. Although he held an appointment as vicar and ecclesiastical judge, in the early seventeenth century and in the see of Mexico, this post did not include faculties to proceed against native idolaters. As an illustrative example, one could compare the 1613 appointment of Hernando's brother as beneficiado and ecclesiastical judge of Tenango with the faculties granted to Ponce de León in 1610. Pedro Ruiz de Alarcón's appointment bears a stern clause forbidding him to act on "reserved cases" and does not mention any faculties against idolaters;[58] by contrast, Archbishop García Guerra explicitly reported to the crown he had commissioned Ponce de León to act as "ecclesiastical judge against idolatry" in the Toluca Valley.[59]

In any case, Ruiz de Alarcón kept the archbishop informed about his activities. In a 1624 missive, he referred to his extirpation efforts as "what His Illustrious Lordship has charged me to do, which is what concerns the tribunal of the ordinary inquisition of the Indians."[60] This phrase reveals a common misunderstanding regarding late sixteenth-century changes in ecclesiastical jurisdiction. In referring to his jurisdictional realm as the "ordinary inquisition of the Indians," Ruiz de Alarcón proffered a garbled truth: his activities were the province of the ordinario, or diocesan, tribunal for natives, but he had no justification for using the term "inquisition," as the Holy Office and diocesan tribunals had separate mandates after 1571. Further proof of Ruiz de Alarcón's confusion is given by the fact that in this communication he also notified the archbishop about a mulatto who hired a native to drink ololiuhqui in order to diagnose sorcery acts and asked if he could prosecute Spaniards and mulattos. Even if Pérez de la Serna's response is not extant, it is likely that he would have instructed the beneficiado to forward his accusation to the Inquisition, for the archbishop did have a clear understanding of jurisdictional boundaries. In a 1628 letter to the crown, the archbishop praised the king for not allowing the Inquisition to punish "that which belonged to it by its very nature, the investigation of native heresy and superstition. Rather, this jurisdiction was given to the ordinary ecclesiastical judges, who prosecute these cases."[61]

Although no trial conducted by Ruiz de Alarcón is extant, he left behind a far more valuable record: a detailed depiction of the Nahua rhetorical and ritual practices he investigated between 1613 and 1629, the last date mentioned in his text. He titled his manuscript *Tratado de las supersticiones y costumbres gentílicas que oy biven entre los indios naturales desta Nueva España* (henceforth *Tratado*).[62] Ruiz de Alarcón transcribed about sixty-six Nahuatl incantations employed by an unspecified number of anonymous specialists and by nine male and seventeen female ritual practitioners designated by their names in the *Tratado*. These specialists resided in thirty communities located mostly within Cohuixcatlalpan and Tlalhuicatlalpan,[63] two Nahuatl-speaking regions within the colonial jurisdictions of Chilapa, Cuauhtla Amilpas, Cuernavaca, Iguala, Taxco, and Tistla, and now part of the states of Guerrero, Mexico, and Morelos. The sixty-six incantations in the *Tratado* covered a broad range of propitiatory and divinatory objectives, which Ruiz de Alarcón used as his main organizational criteria. Treatise I recorded general observations on communal religious practices, the consumption of hallucinogens like ololiuhqui and peyotl, and the use of the piciyetl, tenexietl, and *yauhtli* plants, omens, self-sacrificial practices, and a regional variant of a Nahua account about the most recent creation of the world. Treatise II recorded, unusually, an incantation used for malevolent purposes by *temacpalihtotiqueh*, or hypnotists,[64] as well as prayers used by hunters, fishermen, and gatherers. Treatise III was devoted to incantations for agriculturists; Treatise IV, to prayers used to inspire affections and to clear illnesses caused by sexual desire or sexual excesses. Treatise V was devoted to divining techniques through forearm-measuring and maize-throwing, and Treatise VI considered bleeding and herbal cures for fevers, fatigue, scorpion bites, and various bodily ailments. The social and performative context in which these practices occurred was described only so far as it would give its implied reader, a fellow priest, an understanding of each performance.[65]

RHETORICAL STRUCTURE AND AUTHORITY IN THE NAHUAL NAMES GENRE

The ritual oral genre Ruiz de Alarcón transcribed in his *Tratado* was characterized by a highly sophisticated manner of designating various entities with names: there existed an astounding number of epithets composed by two parallel elements for referring to oneself as a Nahua deity, calling forth propitiated entities, and designating a range of objects and entities during the course of the incantation. The native label for the genre was quite transparent: ritual specialists reported this manner of speaking was called nahualtocaitl, or Nahual Names. Our current understanding of the obscure metaphorical expressions in this genre rests on a brilliant early study by López Austin and on an exhaustive critical edition of the *Tratado* by Andrews and Hassig, as well as on an edition by Coe and Whittaker.[66] Since these scholars have already addressed the production, organization, and literal meaning of this incantation corpus, I now turn to an analysis of its social and cultural context.

An undated letter from Ruiz de Alarcón to Archbishop Pérez de la Serna highlights the mystifying nature of the nahualtocaitl and exposes some of his methodology as an interpreter of Nahua ritual speech.[67] In this document, Ruiz de Alarcón reports the existence of a perplexing, hermetic language in which "disguised names" refer to the patient and the propitiated entities. Although he eventually understood the ritual logic of *matlapouhqueh*, specialists who performed divination by measuring the patient's forearm with their fingers, and transcribed a more complete selection of matlapouhqueh incantations in Part V of his

Tratado, his discussion denotes some lack of knowledge about Nahua deities. For example, in the aforementioned letter, Ruiz de Alarcón translated the phrase *nomatca nehuatl, nixulutl,* "I myself, I am Xolotl," as "I as my own person; I, a deranged one," even if this sentence clearly refers to the deity Xolotl.[68] Moreover, he rendered the phrase *nicenTeotl,* "I am Centeotl," as "somebody who is like a deity," instead of identifying the Nahua maize deity Centeotl. Thus, although Ruiz de Alarcón's transcriptions highlight his linguistic acuity, his analysis was hampered by his imprecise knowledge of Nahua cosmology and his dismissive approach to Nahua ritual. For instance, even though he spent years studying these cryptic prayers, he believed that Nahua specialists made only a minimal investment on the nahualtocaitl, stating with derision that, "since the profession does not cost them any money, but only the memorization of a fortune-telling incantation . . . , they easily enter into the profession."[69]

Andrews and Hassig regard the nahualtocaitl as an almost theatrical oral performance, and point out that no evidence suggests that singing, keening, or music accompanied these recitations. They do draw the genre line at poetry by asserting that "if these incantations are poems, we have been unable to determine the parameters that define them as such."[70] Even though this genre does not bear a structural similarity with Nahua song genres, I argue here that the nahualtocaitl was a Nahua oral genre that employed highly characteristic rhetorical and stylistic devices. Some of these are found in other Nahua oral genres, while others are particular to this genre. In order to place the practice of the nahualtocaitl in a broad context, I begin with a consideration of Nahua oral genres and then discuss several parallel epithets used by Nahua specialists to embody deities in the nahualtocaitl. Finally, I contend that the peculiar gender dynamics of verbal personification in the *Tratado* relate to specific demographic and social changes in that period.

Preconquest Nahua oral genres, according to Garibay, León-Portilla, and Karttunen and Lockhart,[71] were related to various performative practices and social contexts—for instance, festivities in which deity representatives engaged in elaborate oral performances, as recorded by Sahagún and Durán, or a range of social occasions that called for elegant speech. León-Portilla proposed a major division into two metagenres: *cuicatl,* "songs"; and *tlahtolli,* "words."[72] Colonial cuicatl were transcriptions of songs performed to the beat of an upright drum called *huehuetl,* and the teponaztli, a cylindrical wooden drum with two tones. Both these compositions and a corpus of colonial Zapotec songs featured sung syllables, such as *ohuaya* or *ahuayo,* and the syllabic transcription of percussion patterns.[73] Tlahtolli encompassed a wider range of oral performances, including various accounts and prayers compiled by

Sahagún,[74] historical narratives, and *huehuehtlahtolli*, "Ancient Words," the elite orations compiled by Olmos and published by Bautista Viseo in 1601.[75] López Austin subsumes nahualtocaitl under the tlahtolli label.[76]

Ritual speech has been characterized as a creative combination of memorized, parallel formulae pragmatically attuned to the needs of a specialist's performance.[77] Morphological, syntactic, and semantic parallel constructions are a particularly well attested rhetorical device in Mesoamerican and other Amerindian oral genres.[78] Garibay coined the term *difrasismo* to denote the "pairing of two metaphors, which together yield a symbolic medium for the expression of a single thought."[79] In an influential work on parallelism, Bricker noted that, as in Nahuatl poetry, Tzotzil Maya notions are expressed in syntactically or semantically parallel expressions, a structuring device she called "couplet," which occurred at the beginning and end of important segments in certain Tzotzil speech genres.[80] In the nahualtocaitl, the content and tone of propitiatory speech acts varies considerably, but the use of parallel epithets remains a constant. An important language ideology underlies this genre: every entity in the world, including deities, animals, natural features and objects, bears a unique personal or calendrical name associated with specific mythohistorical narratives, and uttering the appropriate name conferred on practitioners a form of authority. Furthermore, the epithets employed to refer to various entities are almost always structured in a parallel manner. Nahualtocaitl is thus characterized by the specialist's (*nahualli*) utterance of names (*tocaitl*) composed of two or more verbal or nominal phrases that exhibit parallel features at the morphological, syntactic, semantic, or syllabic levels, and it distinguishes itself from other tlahtolli genres by its systematic recourse to such epithets.

Nahualtocaitl epithets may be illustrated by the appellation for flames and skin rashes in a written transcript for a deer-hunting incantation:[81]

Notah	Nahui Acatl	Milinticah
My father	*Four Reed*	*He Is Shining*

This parallel expression was not a formula that could be creatively altered: through its utterance, the specialist referred to one and only one entity that could be designated as *Nahui Acatl / Milinticah*, two syllabically parallel names with four syllables each.[82] Saul Kripke's analysis of the referential properties of proper names may be invoked to argue that, as in the case of "Cortés" or "Moteuczoma Xocoyotzin," this utterance acted as a rigid designation for a particular entity in the world, creating an unambiguous link between it and a Nahual Name.[83] The importance of parallel epithets as part of Nahua ritual knowledge is shown by their broad distribution in the Cohuixca and Tlalhuica regions. In 1584, the epithet *Nahui Acatl / Milinticah* was uttered by Magdalena Papalo before giving an infant its first bath, and it was also transcribed during her trial; thirty years later, it was still used by deer hunters and lime kiln makers.[84]

Specific deity personification epithets were used by several Nahua specialists to embody particular deities through verbal performance. For example, practitioners frequently used the following epithet, which appears in an incantation for sowing sweet potatoes:[85]

Nohmatca	nehhuatl	N[i]	Icnopiltzintli	Ni	Centeotl
My person,	*I myself*	*I am*	*Orphan Child*	*I am*	*Centeotl*

Centeotl, derived from *cen-tli*, "dried maize ear," named the male aspect of a Postclassic Mexica maize deity, and "Orphan Child" was an epithet often associated with this deity. As noted above, Ruiz de Alarcón did not recognize it as a name, confusing it with its near homophone *ce teotl*, "one deity," and glossed it as "I who am one god."

Deity personification epithets played a salient role in the performative framework of the nahualtocaitl due to their investment in a cardinal Nahua ritual practice: the propitiation of deities through their personification by ritual specialists in both the collective and elective spheres. The Nahua practice of personifying deities in a specific ritual context reenacted a primordial relation between deities and elements in nature, justified and historicized by creation narratives in Nahua cosmology. Deity personification seemed to be an exalted and particularly powerful manner of propitiating a deity. To invoke J.L. Austin's influential analysis of speech acts,[86] Nahua specialists believed that the effectiveness of their divination and propitiation activities derived from the illocutionary force of the speech act through which they designated themselves as deities: in saying "I am Centeotl, I am Icnopiltzintli," they became conduits for Centeotl and Icnopiltzintli within the discrete parameters of a ritual act. Certainly, the rhetorical act of designating oneself as a particular deity through epithets was a significant departure from the deity personification practices of *teixiptlameh* in preconquest Mexica public ritual practices. The differences between both sets of practices highlight the contrast between the collective and elective spheres: Mexica state ceremonies targeted the well-being of the entire altepetl; colonial verbal deity personification was oriented toward pragmatic outcomes for an individual or family.

Some deity personification epithets were part of an archaic oral repertoire that specialists no longer recognized. Ruiz de Alarcón protested that "artificial words are inserted in all these incantations . . . never heard in everyday language. The devil must have put them in."[87] As an example, he cited the word *nisocomoniz*, employed in a divination ritual:

Nohmatca	nehhuatl	Ni-xocomoniz	Ni-Cipactonal
My person,	*I myself*	*I am [Ohxomocotzin]*	*I am Cipactonal*

Here, "xocomoniz" is a nonstandard spelling of Ohxomoco(tzin);[88] in Nahua cosmology, Ohxomoco and Cipactonal were the names of a deity couple associated with the creation of the world and diviners by profession.[89] This epithet occurred only once elsewhere in the *Tratado*,[90] in an incantation where "Cipactonal" was reanalyzed into two names, "I am Cipac, I am Tonal."[91] Ruiz de Alarcón was not acquainted with the names of this creator couple either, since he translated "I am Tonal" as "I am the one of superior science."

GENDER, DEITY REPRESENTATIVES, AND DEMOGRAPHIC DECLINE

This section analyzes a most striking feature in the nahualtocaitl: a revealing set of patterns of gendered dynamics for verbal deity personification. Even though Ruiz de Alarcón volunteered little biographical information about the specialists he investigated, he identified twenty-six of them by name and at times noted their age and place of residence. Similar biographical data was preserved in the 1584 idolatry trials from Teotlalco, and in de la Serna's *Manual*. These data, which allow us to match individuals with specific incantations and thus with specific deity personification epithets, are summarized in Tables 3.1–3.2.

The verbal personification of Centeotl, a deity associated with maize crops and fertility in Nahua cosmology, illustrates the gendered dynamics of deity personification. The importance of Centeotl is emphasized in a well-known passage of André Thévet's 1575 *Cosmographie universelle*, which glosses in French a now-vanished but authoritative Spanish-language description of Central Mexican cosmology, Andrés de Olmos's enigmatic *Tratado de las Antigüedades Mexicanas*.[92] According to this account, which combined accounts from Nahua, Otomi, and other Central Mexican linguistic groups, Centeotl, born out of the union of Piltzinteuctli and Xochiquetzal, hid himself under the earth. Many plants issued from Centeotl's body; his hair became cotton, his nose gave rise to chia, his fingers became sweet potatoes, his nails turned into an elongated form of maize, each of his eyes produced various seeds, and

TABLE 3.1 Specialists in Ruiz de Alarcón's Tratado Who Personified Deities

Name or occupation	Gender	Town	Reference (Tratado)	Pragmatic objective	Deity-personification epithets	Other entities named with epithets
1. Agustín Jacobo	M	Oapan	II: 9	Deer hunting with bow and arrow	Ni Centeotl, N[i] Icnopiltzintli	Bow, flint, deer, Xochiquetzal
2. Juan Matheo	M	Comala	II: 16 II: 3	Fishing with fish hooks Wood cutting	None Ni Tlamacazqui Ni Nahualteuctli Ni Quetzalcoatl	Fish (6 epithets), piciyetl Piciyetl, wood, ax
3. Juan Bernal	M	Iguala	II: 1	For defending himself from highwaymen	Ni Quetzalcoatl Ni Matl Ni Yaotl Ni Moquehqueloatzin	Earth, knife, road, clubs
4. Deacon of Cuetlaxxochitla	M	Cuetlax-xochitla	II: 4	For carrying loads and traveling	Ni Nahualteuctli Ni Quetzalcoatl	Piciyetl, pain, road, load, earth
5. Baltasar de Aquino, cacique	M	Atenango	I: 4	Instructions to one who performs sacrifice, or tlamaceuhqui	Ni [O]hxomoco Ni Huehueh Ni Cipac Ni Tonal	None
6. Diego de San Matheo	M	Atenango?	I: 4			
7. Don Martín Sebastián y Cerón	M	Chilapa	VI: 32	Cure for scorpion sting, based on Yappan myth	Ni Xochiquetzal Ni Tlamacazqui Ni ChicomeXochitl (deer)	Yappan, scorpion, dust, earth
8. Magdalena Papalo, ticitl and midwife	F	Teotlalco	AGN, U. E., 1584	To facilitate childbirth	Ni [O]hxomoco Ni Cipactonal	Hands

9. Francisca Juana, *tetonaltiqui*, wife of Juan Bautista	F	Mescaltepec	IV: 3	Bathing of child after birth	Ni Nahualteuctli Ni Xolotl Ni Capanilli	Water, piciyetl, fire, copal, child
10. Magdalena Juana, *tlaolximiani*, wife of Melchor Gutiérrez	F	Oapan	Tratado, V: 3	Divination with maize grains	Ni Cipactonal Ni Huehueh	Maize grains, hands and fingers, maize grain patterns on mat
11. María Madalena, *tlapouhqui*, wife of don Diego de la Cruz	F	Ozomahtlan	V: 2	Divination by looking at fire	Ni [O]hoxomocotzin Ni Cipactonal Ni Mictlanmati Ni Topanmati	Fire, forearms, hands and fingers (6 epithets)
Seducers of women	Unknown; M	?	IV: 2	Attracting women	Ni Telpochtli Ni Yaotl	Woman
Deer hunters	Unknown; M?	?	II: 8	Deer hunting with snare	Ni Centeotl, N[i] Icnopiltzintli	Xochiquetzal, earth, rope, deer, piciyetl, hands
Fishermen (Juan Matheo?)	Unknown; M?	?	II: 15	Fishing with fish hooks	NiCenteotl, N[i] Icnopiltzintli	Piciyetl, tutelar deities, fishing rod, broom, worms, fish hook, Xochiquetzal
Hypnotists, or *temacpalihtotiqueh*	Unknown; M?	?	II: 2	Inducing sleep in robbery and rape victims	Ni Moyohualihtoatzin Ni Xolotl Ni Capanilli Ni Yohuallahuantzin Ni Yaotl Ni Moquehqueloatzin	*Temicxoch*, or dream flower

SOURCE: BMN-ColAnt 160

TABLE 3.2 Specialists in Ruiz de Alarcón's Tratado Who Did Not Personify Deities

Name or occupation	Gender	Town	Reference (Tratado)	Pragmatic objective	Self-referential epithets	Other entities named with epithets
1. Joseph Chicon, healer and diviner	M	Teotlalco	AGN, U. E., 1584	Healing and divination	None	Temecatl seeds
2. Martín de Luna, "almost 110 years old"	M	Temimiltzinco	II: 2	Protecting oneself during sleep	None	mat
3. Don Martín Sebastián y Cerón	M	Chilapa	III: 4	Maize sowing	Nomatca Nehhuatl Ni Tlamacazqui	Seed, earth
			VI: 30	Fever cure with atlinan herb	Nomatca Nehhuatl Ni Tlamacazqui	water, patient, atlinan herb, stomach, maize
4. Catharina Juana	F	Tecuacuilco	VI: 4	Cure for headaches	Ni Tlamacazqui; Ni Nahualteuctli	Water, hands, four Tlazohteteoh deities
5. María Salomé, wife of Gaspar Rodríguez	F	Tetelpan	VI: 5	Cure for eye illnesses	None	Eyes, water, veins
6. Marta Mónica	F	Teteltzinco (Oapan)	VI: 6	Curing eyes with mezquite sap	Ni Tlamacazqui; Ni Nahualteuctli	Eyes, hands and fingers, mezquite sap, piciyetl and copal
7. Marta Mónica, wife of Juan Matheo, alcalde	F	Teteltzinco	VI: 13	Curing chest pains with coanenepilli herb and atolli drink	None	Chest pains, medicines, stomach, breath
8. Catalina María, wife of Agustín Bartolomé	F	Teteltzinco				

	Sex	Location	Ref.	Description	Materials	Symptoms/Notes
9. Doña Catalina Paula	F	Huitzuco	VI: 15	Pachollztli, curing chest pains in children	None	Chest pains
10. Anonymous woman	F	Mayanala	VI: 12	Cupping cure	None	Cotton, fire, intestines, pain
11. Isabel María	F	Temimiltzinco	VI: 24	Curing with needle pricks	None	Body, needle, and piciyetl
12. Magdalena Juana, wife of Pedro Mayor	F	Tepecuacuilco	VI: 28	Cure for urinary disease	None	Herbs, patient
13. Isabel Luisa (Mazahua)	F	?	VI: 29	Curing fever with four-herb remedy, or tlanechchilcopahtli	None	Herbs, fever
14. Magdalena Petronila Xochiquetzal	F	Huitzoco	VI: 31	Enema for fatigue, or cuacuauhtiliztli	None	Muscles, rigidity
15. Justina	F	Huitzoco	VI: 31	Tzopillotl herb enema for fatigue	None	Rigidity, tzopillotl
16. María Madalena, tlapouhqui, wife of Baltasar Melchor	F	Comala	V: 2	Divining thefts	?	Incantation not transcribed
17. Ana María, tlaolxiniani, Gaspar de Morales's wife	F	Xoxouhtla	V: 4	Divination by throwing maize grains into water	?	Incantation not transcribed

SOURCE: BMN-ColAnt 160

other cultigens emerged from other body parts; "for this reason, this God was loved by others, and he was called [Tlazohpilli], that is, Beloved Lord."[93] Additionally, Centeotl was propitiated during the feast of Huey Tozoztli in the Mexica 365-day calendar. According to Sahagún's informants, commoners visited their land plots and selected maize ears that would be dried and used as seeds for sowing. Then, they took the maize ears (*cintli* or *centli* in Nahuatl) to their homes and propitiated them, addressing each of them as Centeotl's iixiptla, or representative; later, these ears were deposited in their granaries.[94] Centeotl or Cinteotl was the name of one aspect of this deity, probably male, and the feminine aspect bore the calendrical name Chicome Coatl, 7-Snake.[95]

In the *Tratado*, Chicome Coatl designates maize and appears with one of the epithets Thévet recorded for Centeotl, Tlazohpilli.[96] The Mexica also believed that four previous creations and apocalypses had preceded the current age of the world, which featured a sun with the calendrical name Nahui Ollin, 4-Movement.[97] In a Cohuixca version of this narrative in the *Tratado*,[98] Ruiz de Alarcón's informants employed an epithet that recurred in other incantations, Centeotl Icnopiltzintli, "Centeotl the Orphan Child." In the Cohuixca narrative, Centeotl plays an important role as the deity who motivates Nanahuatzin to plunge into a bonfire so that 4-Movement may be born. Centeotl and Nanahuatzin were the only deities mentioned by name in this narrative, and their names were employed in various incantations in the *Tratado*, thus showcasing their importance for local cosmologies.[99]

Ritual specialists followed a gendered logic in their personification practices. Most of the specialists whose biographical data is recorded in the *Tratado*, the Teotlalco trials, and de la Serna's work seem to adhere to similar gender distinctions in their acts of verbal personification. The anonymous and probably male author of a written incantation for capturing deer with a snare stood for Centeotl during an incantation, as did both an anonymous fisherman and Agustín Jacobo when hunting deer with bow and arrow. In a performance resembling the propitiation of Centeotl during Huey Tozoztli, an anonymous peasant claimed to be Centeotl as he shelled fresh maize after a harvest; additionally, another anonymous specialist designated himself as Centeotl-Icnopiltzintli when sowing sweet potatoes and thus reenacted the mythohistorical origin of this plant. Furthermore, while Centeotl, the male aspect of the maize and fertility deity, was embodied by several male ritual specialists listed in Table 3.1, Chicome Coatl, the deity's female aspect, was propitiated when addressing maize seeds, but never verbally personified by males.[100]

As shown in Tables 3.1–3.2, there was a major gender difference between male and female verbal personification patterns. Even though male specialists embodied a broad range of ten Nahua deities and entities—Centeotl-Icnopiltzintli, Quetzalcoatl, Ohxomoco-Cipactonal, Huehueh, Xochiquetzal, Tezcatlipoca (as Telpochtli and Yaotl), Moyohualihtoatzin, Xolotl-Capanilli, Yohuallahuantzin, and Moquehqueloatzin—female specialists stood for a much more restricted range of four deities: Ohxomoco-Cipactonal, Xolotl-Capanilli, Huehueh, and Mictlanmati-Topanmati. These acts of personification were tied to highly specific contexts. Juan Matheo and the deacon of Cuetlaxxochitla embodied Quetzalcoatl when cutting wood or traveling with loads. In order to perform individual acts of penitence, Baltasar Aquino and Diego de San Matheo became the representative of both Huehueh and the deity couple Ohxomoco-Cipactonal. In order to ward off highwaymen, Juan Bernal claimed to be Quetzalcoatl and Tezcatlipoca. Men stood for Tezcatlipoca during an incantation for seducing women, and the feared hypnotists known as temacpalihtotiqueh designated themselves as Xolotl-Capanilli and used epithets linked to Tezcatlipoca and Xipe. Male specialists tended to embody male deities, with one important cross-dressing exception: during a reenactment of a cosmological narrative performed to cure scorpion bites, don Martín Sebastián y Cerón embodied a male deer through its calendrical name 7-Flower and then tied a shawl around his body in lieu of a skirt in order to personify the female deity Xochiquetzal.[101]

Most of the women in this sample, fifteen out of nineteen, did not act as stand-ins for a deity. Many of them were designated as *titicih*, or healers, and employed the most frequently used personification epithet in the *Tratado*:

Nohmatca	nehhuatl	Ni-tlamacazqui	Ni-nahual-teuctli
My person,	*I myself*	*I am a priest*	*I am Nahual Lord*

This epithet did not refer to a specific deity, but the specialist who uttered it claimed to be both a priest and a powerful shape-changing specialist. In contrast with these female healers, the four female specialists who embodied deities had various ritual specializations. Magdalena Papalo was not only a ticitl: she also represented Ohxomoco-Cipactonal as a midwife, and performed acts of divination resembling the activities of a *matlapouhqui*, or forearm measurer. Francisca Juana was a *tetonaltiqui*, or a finder of errant day signs who stood for Xolotl, a deity associated with twins and monsters who guided the dead to Mictlan, the Land of the Dead.[102] María Magdalena and Magdalena Juana used fire and maize grains to make auguries, and both embodied the primordial diviners Ohxomoco-Cipactonal.[103]

This gendered divide may reflect Nahua collective responses to demographic decrease during the first third of the seventeenth century. Even a cursory look at available demographic data for the Cohuixca and Tlalhuica regions shows that the native population of many of these communities was at least halved during the last quarter of the sixteenth century. The major cause is well known: in south Central Mexico, epidemics affected indigenous communities in 1544–45, 1576–77, the 1590s, and in 1630–33.[104] The population of Tepecuacuilco, the main military and tributary center in the Cohuixca region during the Late Postclassic went from 6,468 to 2,650 residents,[105] probably due to the epidemics of 1544–45 and 1576–77, which particularly affected their neighbor, Tlachco.[106] Not only epidemics contributed to population descent, for forced labor obligations in the mines of Zacualpa, Temazcaltepec, Taxco, Teotlalco, and Zumpango also took their toll. The population decrease in Iguala, heavily affected by labor drafts, illustrates this trend: its number of tributaries decreased from 10,225 in 1548, to 840 circa 1579, and to 376 by 1643.[107] Although the decrease by 1643 to about 45 percent of the 1579 population is comparable to that of neighboring regions in the last quarter of the sixteenth century, the 1643 population represented only 8 percent of the 1548 tributary population. During the same period, the population of Chilapa, which contained Ruiz de Alarcón's parish, descended from 12,111 to 7,880,[108] and the population of Zumpahuacan south of the Toluca Valley decreased from 3,392 to 1,856.[109] These trends suggest that indigenous peoples in the Cohuixca and southern Toluca Valley regions were heavily affected, but not decimated, by epidemics between 1568 and 1595: on the whole, there was a reduction to between 41 and 65 percent of the 1568 population by 1595. Another indication of relative stability comes from the fact that Nahua ruling lineages still survived circa 1579 in four Cohuixca towns—Ohuapan, Huitzoco, Mayanala, and Tlachmalacac—but many other communities had lost their lineages by midcentury.[110]

Nonetheless, Ruiz de Alarcón's investigations coincided with a 66 percent decrease in population at Chilapa between 1600 and 1630.[111] This contrast between a sustained demographic decrease between 1568 and 1595 and a more devastating demographic decrease between 1600 and 1630 placed demographic and social pressures on Cohuixca and Tlalhuica Nahua communities that may have resulted in greater demand for ritual specialists in the hinterlands. This situation is illustrated by a 1636 letter from Jacinto de la Serna, then a member of Mexico's cathedral council, to Archbishop Francisco Manso y Zúñiga (1628–35). After the epidemics of 1631–33, the viceroy sent out a request in 1636 to all secular priests for suggestions on how to reduce indigenous mortality. De la Serna's response both noted that natives were fearful of leaving their homes to convalesce in a European-style hospital, and decried the proliferation of native healers:

These deceitful doctors exist in all parts and towns, and it is my opinion, because of the examination I have made of them, that they have an implicit and explicit pact with the Devil, or at least that they cure with superstitions. When they are asked how they cure, or who taught them, they answer that they inherited it from their parents, and that they were dead for a while, and that in the other life, their ancestors, or some venerable old men or saints showed them how to cure. . . . Thus, the Indians are persuaded that our medicines are not useful for them, and that they cannot heal if those who put a spell on them don't want it, and thus they don't use our medicines and die in misery.[112]

I would thus propose a hypothesis linking gendered dynamics in the nahualtocaitl and epidemic disease. The individually identifiable specialist sample that can be retrieved from the *Tratado*, de la Serna's *Manual*, and the 1584 Teotlalco trials suggests that female specialists tended to outnumber male specialists: twenty female and ten male specialists are listed in Tables 3.1–3.2, and Ruiz de Alarcón contended he was more likely to find women engaging in suspect ritual practices rather than men.[113] Given the steeper demographic decline in the Cohuixca-Tlalhuica region during the early seventeenth century, it may be plausible to believe that a larger number of female specialists reflected an increased local demand for practitioners due to an increased rate of illness and death.

If rising numbers of epidemic victims in this region motivated Nahua women to claim a specialization through ritual knowledge, one would expect to see gendered differences in the deployment of specialized ritual practices. Such a gender differentiation existed between male specialists (ten known individual cases) and female specialists (only four out of twenty) who verbally personified Nahua deities. This gap in the use of deity personification epithets could have been caused by two factors: either female specialists embraced ritual avocations, such as that of ticitl, that rarely called for the personification of deities, or many of the female specialists who entered the profession as a result of increased demand had differential access to the specialized linguistic knowledge recorded in the nahualtocaitl genre. In other words, they had a limited knowledge of the full range of Nahual Names an experienced specialist deployed during verbal personification. Even though they reflect distinct logics, both explanations are equally tantalizing, as they reflect a strong link between ritual knowledge and pragmatic aims: under the assault of epidemics, ancient knowledge became powerful once again.

JACINTO DE LA SERNA'S INQUIRIES INTO
NATIVE RITUAL PRACTICES

In spite of Ruiz de Alarcón's diligence as a crusader against the Nahual Names, neither his *Tratado* nor his activities contributed to the development of his ecclesiastical career; his work remained in manuscript form, and he remained a beneficiado at his distant curate until his death in the late 1630s or early 1640s. Ruiz de Alarcón's most influential reader was Jacinto de la Serna, who glossed most of the information compiled at Atenango and by reading Martín de León's 1611 *Camino al Cielo*, in his *Manual*, directed to future idolatry eradicators. In this work, de la Serna recounts a visit he made to Atenango in 1646, years after Ruiz de Alarcón's death. During this visit, de la Serna learned about the beneficiado's campaigns and came across a few Marian prayers he had composed in Nahuatl. Armed with "some loose papers on what [Ruiz de Alarcón] carried out in terms of superstitions and idolatries,"[114] de la Serna prepared his own work on native superstitions.

The gap between de la Serna's meteoric and Ruiz de Alarcón's modest ecclesiastical career suggests that an emphasis on idolatry eradication did not automatically advance one's prospects. Early in his career, de la Serna served as beneficiado of the parishes of Teotenango (1620–24), Tenantzinco (1625–30), and Xalatlaco (1630–34); the fact that Archbishop Manso y Zúñiga (1629–35) was a relative of his may have been a favorable factor. In September 1632, he received an honorary doctorate from the Royal University of Mexico; a few years later, he received a *ración*, or full conciliar appointment, as priest of the Sagrario in the cathedral of Mexico, a post he occupied almost without interruption from 1635 until his death in 1681. De la Serna also served three terms as rector of the Royal University and twice as rector of the Colegio de Nuestra Señora de Santos. In addition, he held the posts of visitador general, or diocesan inspector, and synodal examiner of the archbishopric under Manso y Zúñiga in 1632, under Archbishop Juan de Mañozca (1643–50) in 1646 and 1650, and under Archbishop Sagade Bugueiro (1655–62).[115]

The public display of diligence by secular parish priests acquired a broader political meaning in a debate that took place in the late 1620s and early 1630s in Mexico and Peru regarding the potential secularization of parishes held by regulars, and episcopal faculties regarding the appointment and examination of mendicants serving as priests. As noted in an October 1632 report written by Juan de Velásquez for the Council of the Indies, the debate between the two camps, Dominicans, Franciscans, Augustinians, Mercedarians, and Jesuits on the one hand and archbishops and cathedral chapters in Mexico and Peru on the other, concerned four major points: the possible secularization of mendicant parishes, the faculties archbishops held regarding the examination of mendicants, the removal of mendicants not fluent in their parishes' language, and whether the appointment of mendicants as parish priests in New Spain would follow the precedent set in Peru.[116] According to Velásquez, the mendicants sketched a bleak scenario if they were removed from their parishes: the natives, who had been taught the doctrine by regulars, would be scandalized, and since idolatry and superstition had not yet been eradicated, "the Indians would return to their ancient gentility," and it would be impossible to teach the doctrine in all those provinces with "difficult and obscure" languages.[117]

In this period, one of the most visible examples of anti-idolatry ardor in the secular priesthood was furnished by don Bartolomé de Alva's Nahuatl-Spanish confessional, printed in 1634. In this work, Alva, brother of the chronicler Fernando de Alva Ixtlilxóchitl and great-great-great-grandson of the Tetzcoca ruler Nezahualpilli, provided a detailed Nahuatl transcript that could be followed to the letter by inexperienced confessors. Alva, a mestizo fluent in Nahuatl educated at the Royal University who served as beneficiado of Chiapa de Mota and Zumpahuacan,[118] composed many piercing questions for Nahua believers. Confessants were asked whether they had believed in dreams, used peyote or ololiuhqui, worshipped images called *chalchiuhcoconeme*, "turquoise children," or *chalchiuhtamaçoltin*, "turquoise loads,[119] and told that their grandfathers were now in hell in the place once known as Mictlan, Atlecalocan, Apochquiahuayocan, "the Underworld, Place Without a Chimney, Place Without a Smoke Vent."[120] Although it is not known if Alva held any idolatry trials, some marginalia in this text noted two eradication exercises that other priests conducted in 1631: one in Pantitlan, where natives had been worshipping Tlaloc and Matlacueye, and another in Atlapulco, where residents followed traditional burial practices.[121] Since this work followed the conventions of the confessional genre, it provided a broad range of questions based on Alva's knowledge of Nahua cultural practices, but it offered much less detailed descriptions of indigenous devotion than those found in the works of Ponce de León, Ruiz de Alarcón, and de la Serna. In any case, this last author formally approved this confessional in his capacity as the diocese's visitador general.[122]

De la Serna's motivations for drafting his *Manual* were different from those that compelled Ruiz de Alarcón to produce his *Tratado*. De la Serna aimed to present a sweeping overview of native ritual practices for the benefit of an audience of novice priests with scant tutoring on the polymorphous ways of native ritual practices; he also had a limited interest in Nahuatl rhetoric. In a departure from Ruiz de Alarcón's linguistic focus, de la Serna compiled a knowledgeable description of the Nahua calendars, including illustrations that may have been copied from calendrical texts employed by Nahua ritual specialists. In fact, de la Serna's understanding of Nahua calendrical systems was deep enough to provide an accurate summary of the Nahua 260-day count. He also understood that the 365-day Nahua year was not equal to the 365.25-day Gregorian count, and that thus the former eventually fell out of step with the latter. His perspective on Nahua local beliefs is also informed by an appreciation of ecclesiastical administration policies virtually absent in the *Tratado*. In keeping with his ambitions as ecclesiastical administrator, de la Serna closed his work by proposing measures to be enacted during future campaigns. Moreover, the linguistic and ethnohistorical data in the *Manual* is more limited than that in the *Tratado*, as de la Serna rarely analyzes incantations.

Archbishop Juan de Mañozca, previously an inquisitor in Cartagena and Lima, shared de la Serna's zeal. In an August 1646 letter to the king, Mañozca indicates that, during his visit to the Toluca Valley in April 1646, he discovered "a great damage caused by superstition among the Indians, and I ordered the punishment of the teacher who was found guilty."[123] In a second letter, Mañozca promised to give the Council of Indies his report of an upcoming visita. He also emphasized the importance of empirical extirpation treatises in the struggle against idolatry by observing that, even many years after congregaciones, "the ashes and roots of their ancestors still live within them. . . . I am making arrangements to organize a treatise on this matter, which I will submit to the Supreme Council of the Inquisition, so that the diversity of cults these Gentiles had may be recognized and acknowledged, in order to extinguish any glimmer of those which have remained with them."[124] The manuscript copy of de la Serna's *Manual* now at the Biblioteca del Museo Nacional in Mexico City has traditionally been associated with a 1656 date, since de la Serna dedicated it to Archbishop Bugueiro and included an August 1656 letter from the Jesuit Marcos de Yrala, theology lecturer at the Colegio de San Pedro y San Pablo. However, Mañozca's reference to an idolatry treatise in 1646 suggests he may have encouraged de la Serna to work on his manuscript during the 1640s.

In the end, Ruiz de Alarcón and de la Serna's diligence had a limited impact on crusades against idolatry in the archbishopric of Mexico. Their works, which remained in manuscript form, may not have circulated beyond a small but powerful intellectual cycle that included Jesuit priests, episcopal authorities, and members of the Council of the Indies. Even though Lorenzo Boturini had a copy of de la Serna's *Manual* made for his manuscript collection,[125] no extant colonial works produced after 1656 refer to Ruiz de Alarcón's or de la Serna's treatises.

In fact, Ruiz de Alarcón's *Tratado* was providentially saved from destruction in at least one occasion. In 1847, historian José Fernando Ramírez reported that, after residing for many years in the holdings of the Jesuit Colegio de San Gregorio in Mexico City, this and other manuscripts were spared from certain destruction "through the diligence of [San Gregorio's] rector, Rodríguez Puebla, who rescued them from the fallen debris of a roofless room."[126] The Colegio de San Gregorio was the foremost Jesuit educational institution for native peoples in Central Mexico during colonial times: in its classrooms, several generations of Nahua students learned reading, writing, theology, and music. Furthermore, the Colegio served as an institutional anchor for the development of several Nahua sodalities.[127] Paradoxically, the first idolatry eradication manuals entirely based on the experiences of American ecclesiastics—Ponce de León's *Breve relación*, the *Tratado*, and the *Manual*—ended up collecting dust in the library of a Jesuit school devoted to indigenous education.[128]

CONVERSATIONS WITH, AND ABOUT, OLOLIUHQUI

The use of hallucinogenic plants as part of indigenous divinatory practices provided seventeenth-century idolatry extirpators with a far more concrete target than words or suspicious actions. In particular, Nahua specialists believed that these plants were in and of themselves powerful entities with fixed characteristics, names, and attributions in the natural world. This notion of embodiment contrasted markedly with a skeptical medical view that regarded native ritual practitioners as ignorant traditionalists and hallucinogenic plants as redoubtable but useful cogs in the wheel of the Galenic system, and also with an inconclusive set of ecclesiastical views, which ranged from tolerance to a portrayal of hallucinogens as demonic forces. These contrasting notions may be illustrated by focusing on one plant widely used in ritual contexts in Central Mexico: ololiuhqui, or *Turbina corymbosa*, a vine in the morning glory family also known as *Rivea Corymbosa* whose seeds were ingested by ritual specialists.[129]

Francisco Hernández, Philip II's *protomédico* and author of the most extensive treatise on New World plants completed in early colonial times, had a famously skeptical view of Nahua healers:

Among the Indians, men and women called titicih practice medicine indiscriminately. These [people] neither study the nature of the various diseases and their differences, nor do they prescribe medications after learning the reason for the disease, or its cause, and they follow no method for the illnesses they treat. They are mere *empíricos*, and they simply use for all manners of disease the herbs, minerals, or animal parts they received from their elders, as an inheritance that passes from hand to hand.[130]

The derisive term empíricos, or empiricists, allowed Hernández to replicate here Galen's attack on untutored medical practitioners' lack of theoretical foundations. In fact, as Osvaldo Pardo observed, since Nahua titicih relied on the transmission of traditional knowledge rather than on direct observation to arrive at universal causes, their approach ran against Hernández's attempts to arrive at a systematic account of the properties and proper medical use of New World plants.[131]

According to the received medical view of Spanish authors in early colonial times, indigenous healers were not only drones replicating a stagnant system of knowledge but also superstition's victims. They were also likely pawns of the devil, the first cause of all suspect native behavior. Thus, the hallucinogenic properties of *Turbina corymbosa* and the narcotic effects of *Nicotiana rustica*, an herbaceous form of tobacco known as *piciyetl* in Nahuatl, led some authors to state that knowledge about such plants could not come from nature itself. In his influential treatise on the medical properties of New World plants, the physician Nicolás Monardes proposed that the devil himself had taught the natives about the intoxicant properties of piciyetl, so that they would acquire erroneous beliefs through their artificial visions,[132] an opinion echoed by Alonso López de Hinojosos in his *Suma y recopilación de cirugía* of 1595. In spite of these conclusions, in his 1591 *Problemas y secretos maravillosos de las Indias*, Juan de Cárdenas could not decide whether piciyetl was "angelic medicine, or a remedy which demons had created."[133] Hernández noted, however, that ololiuhqui, also known as *coaxihuitl*, or "Serpent Herb,"[134] was associated with "wisdom and prudence."[135] Nevertheless, such wisdom was of a dubious origin, since it resulted from demonic visions facilitated by this hallucinogen. One of ololiuhqui's less controversial effects, according to both Hernández and Sahagún, was its restorative effects on the male libido.

Ecclesiastic authors could be tolerant about the ritual usage of certain plants by native specialists and did not espouse the wholesale demonization of such practices, but they usually drew a sharp boundary between licit and diabolical practices. As is well known, Sahagún rearranged the taxonomy of ritual specialists by splitting the Nahua term ticitl into two categories: the "good" ticitl, who performed healing activities that seemed to parallel European healing practices; and the "bad" ticitl, who, besides infringing Hippocratic mandates by giving overdoses and worsening ailments, was also "a shape-changing sorcerer, a diviner."[136] In fact, from a Galenic perspective, *Turbina corymbosa* possessed a number of natural qualities that could be redeployed within European medical practice in the New World. Thus, in his influential 1579 treatise on surgery and remedies for illnesses common in New Spain, Agustín Farfán prescribed the redoubtable ololiuhqui for strong stomachaches or for the extreme pain caused by gout. One would mix half an ounce of ground ololiuhqui seeds with rose oil, thicken and heat this mixture with candle wax, and apply it while warm on the aching joint, a prescription also echoed by Sahagún.[137]

Among Nahuas and Mazahuas, a number of ololiuhqui entities with diverse physical attributes embodied the wisdom that was being sought by the plant's users. Pedro Ponce de León, a parish priest from the Toluca Valley region of Nahua descent, affirmed that ololiuhqui users reported conferring with "a little black man," and even with Jesus Christ or with angels.[138] A Mazahua woman named Isabel Luisa reported that, after having given ololiuhqui to a client, he saw a "strange person" who spoke reassuring words about his illness. Furthermore, when administering an ololiuhqui-based remedy for fevers, Isabel Luisa addressed the ololiuhqui with the epithet Tlamacazqui Cecec, "Cold Priest."[139] Thus, Nahua users and keepers of ololiuhqui treated its seeds not merely as an herbal remedy, but as an immanent entity who existed beyond a ritual ingestion context. In his treatise, Ruiz de Alarcón reported that several Nahua male and female commoners had the custom of keeping a small basket decorated with handkerchiefs or dresses that contained a generous supply of ololiuhqui seeds and a cult effigy. It appears as if specific lineages in several towns—designated with the Nahua term *itlapial*, [basket's] "keepers"—passed these containers from one generation to another and kept them on household oratories designated by the hybrid term *santohcalli*, "saint's house."[140] The fear and respect the ololiuhqui keepers had for their baskets was so great that, when Ruiz de Alarcón scolded them for hiding them, each party responded that he had protected the ololiuhqui "so he will not hate me."[141]

Ruiz de Alarcón was convinced that the devil was both the necessary source of native knowledge about hallucinogenic and narcotic plants, and the ultimate explanation for the occasional successes of ritual practitioners. In his treatise, he characterized native use of ololiuhqui and peyote by *pahini*, healers, as follows:

Whether it is the doctor or another person in his place, in order to drink the [ololiuhqui] seed or peyote . . . , he closes himself up alone in a room, which usually is his oratory, where no one is to enter throughout all the time that the consultation lasts, which is for as long as the consultant is out of his mind, for then they believe the ololiuhqui or peyote is revealing them that which they want to know. As soon as the intoxication or deprivation of judgment passes from this person, he tells two thousand hoaxes, among which the devil usually includes some truths, so that he has them deceived or duped absolutely. . . . With these diabolical chimeras, fictions, and representations that the devil puts into their imagination, they make themselves esteemed as almost divine, leading people to believe that they have the grace of angels.[142]

Nahua specialists "drank" ololiuhqui, probably by grinding large amounts of *Turbina corymbosa* seeds and mixing them with water.[143] An alternative method, which brings to mind Farfán's gout remedy, was to rub large amounts of this mixture on one's skin.

Not only did Nahua specialists of either gender use ololiuhqui for several pragmatic aims, but many commoners with a basic knowledge of propitiatory techniques also partook of it. For example, during the afore-mentioned 1584 trial of Margarita Papalo, she stated that her own son, who was not a ritual specialist, drank ololiuhqui to find a remedy for an act of sorcery.[144] In 1625, fray Gerardo de Porras, prior of the Augustin-ian convent of Chiauhtla, punished an Indian "in the manner of the Holy Office" for drinking ololiuhqui.[145] Ruiz de Alarcón also mentioned a di-verse group of ololiuhqui drinkers: Agustín de Alvarado, a mulatto from Tepecuacuilco who discovered that a native official had bewitched him after consuming the hallucinogen in 1624;[146] a native of Nahuitochco in Tlaxcala who drank it in order to divine the whereabouts of his runaway wife;[147] and finally, Mariana, a healer whose sister used it to divine the proper cure for a wound.[148] Furthermore, Aguirre Beltrán discusses sev-eral Inquisition proceedings in which both natives and *castas*, people of mixed parentage, confessed to consuming ololiuhqui in order to establish the cause of a disease, discover who may be causing them harm and to divine future events, find a lost relative, and divine the location of ships in transit from the Philippines.[149]

Regardless of these pragmatic differences, Central Mexican indig-enous practitioners regarded the usage of *Turbina corymbosa* as a sys-tematic, calculated affair that resulted in the latent manifestation of an immanent presence in the natural world. Nahua ololiuhqui drinkers even incorporated Christian supernaturals into the realm of entities this seed summoned. In contrast with this view, colonial medical authorities re-garded this plant as a potentially dangerous element that had a limited range of pragmatic uses in Galenic medicine, and ecclesiastic authors remained uncertain as to whether such a redoubtable plant was supersti-tious or demonic. Paradoxically, this debate may have emphasized the renown of ololiuhqui, peyote, and piciyetl in a nebulous colonial realm: that of clandestine indigenous healing practices.

A RENEWED NAHUA ELECTIVE SPHERE

Given the painstaking attempts by Ponce de León, Ruiz de Alarcón, and de la Serna to record and analyze native ritual practices, it may seem that seventeenth-century secular extirpators possessed a greater degree of intellectual curiosity than their mendicant predecessors. It would be difficult to argue that Zumárraga and the Dominicans had no intrinsic interest in native ritual practices, since their trial records include information about deity names and ritual performances. What changed between 1571 and the mid-seventeenth century, however, was the pragmatic focus of extirpation attempts. Since the combined effect of epidemics, migrations, doctrinal education, and the substitution of local lineage rulers with elected officials had weakened or dissolved the preconquest collective ritual sphere in many Nahua communities before the early seventeenth century, what now emerged before the eyes of attentive seculars were the workings of the local elective spheres, which comprised private homes, life-cycle observances, and individual healing procedures. This was a world of symbols and practices about which the seculars knew little, and which bore limited overt parallels with canonical notions of idol worship and human sacrifice.

The contrast between collective and individual ritual spheres brings into focus a sharp distinction between the group of specialists prosecuted by Zumárraga and Tello de Sandoval, and that investigated by seventeenth-century extirpators. Between 1536 and 1547, a slight majority of prosecuted Nahua specialists were elite members or officeholders. After 1547, few Nahua specialists were accused of performing activities in the collective sphere; indeed, this realm was then being decimated by demographic change and the disappearance of local lineages.[150] With one or two exceptions, the elective sphere was the domain of choice for the specialists investigated by Ruiz de Alarcón and de la Serna, and for all other Nahua ritual specialists under investigation in 1571–1660.[151]

Nahua ritual specialists in the elective sphere absorbed and adapted European ritual practices and elements of doctrinal discourses that captured their imagination while their communities were reconstituted through demographic changes and the upheaval introduced by congregaciones. The end result was a rather diverse and ecumenical "black market" for ritual labor, in which specialists entered their profession drawn by an increased demand on the part of their peers, and by insatiable curiosity on the part of Spanish, criollo, and mestizo clients about native ritual prescriptions against a host of pragmatic concerns that included misfortune, sorcery, robbery, and sexual desire. In other words, the exchanges between native and nonnative elective spheres in both pueblos de indios and urban spaces conspired to bestow a degree of social value on Nahua ritual practices, regardless of their investment in certifiably ancient calendrical and linguistic knowledge.

In her work on nonindigenous specialists in Central Mexico, Laura Lewis suggested that native specialists were placed into two separate hierarchies by colonial society: a casta hierarchy, where they occupied a low rung; and a hierarchy of ritual knowledge, where they were placed in a higher position.[152] Nonetheless, the complexity of what constituted proper ritual knowledge, exemplified by my discussion of the Nahual Names above, the lack of any systematic measure of comparison among the various local individual ritual spheres, and the impossibility of measuring and comparing the pragmatic effectiveness of indigenous and nonindigenous ritual specialists argue against believing that colonial society as a whole assessed native practices as primordial, more desirable, or more effective. To be sure, native healing and divination practices were far from being the only clandestine ritual practices in the various local and regional individual spheres that proliferated in New Spain. Indeed, several inquisitorial proceedings attests to the existence of ritual practices of Judeo-Christian and Islamic origin that were reproduced by Spaniards, Creoles, and mestizos in clandestine spaces.[153]

Some ecclesiastics effectively validated clandestine native ritual practices by assigning them a role in the dynamic black market of colonial ritual labor. In a paradoxical account in his *Manual*, de la Serna reported consulting a female ticitl from Tenantzinco named Francisca in order to find out whether his servant Agustina had been bewitched by a Nahua specialist. This was a tacit avowal from an experienced extirpator of idolatries that the ontology of certain Nahua ritual practices was not in doubt. De la Serna's account closed with a triumphant appraisal of Christian fetishism, as opposed to native superstition: he reported that Agustina was healed through contact with a bone relic from Saint Gregorio López. This holy man's relics had been deposited in a church belonging to the Discalced Carmelite nuns of Saint Joseph in Mexico City by Pérez de la Serna before Manso y Zúñiga ordered their eventual transfer to the cathedral.[154] Moreover, Hernán Sánchez de Ordiales, the beneficiado of Cuacoman in Michoacán, was interrogated in 1624 for consulting an indigenous specialist with an excellent reputation in the locality, in order to find out whether he had been bewitched.[155]

In spite of the Galenic disdain with which Hernández and other authors viewed Nahua healing, seventeenth-century Nahua ritual practices were not dominated by ossified forms of ancestral ritual knowledge. The complexity of Nahua appropriations of Christian elements is best portrayed through three specialists investigated by Ruiz de Alarcón and de la Serna's informants, who reported having received incantations, instructions on ritual techniques, or knowledge about medicinal plants directly from Christian entities. After being confronted by Ruiz de Alarcón, Domingo Hernández, a very old ticitl from Tlaltizapan, recounted a vision he had as he lay near death. Two persons dressed in white robes swept him away and showed him two roads: a broad one for the condemned, and a narrow one for those who followed Christ. They told him to reflect upon this vision and to abstain from drinking pulque; then, they took him back to his house, where his relatives were already mourning him. Before he regained consciousness, the mysterious visitors told him, "Listen, you who are poor and wretched, you will see here the means by which you will have food and drink in the world," and then they taught him the incantations he would later use with great success. He also contended that he had been visited by three ladies dressed in white: the Virgin Mary, Saint Veronica, and a third one he did not recognize. The incantation he allegedly learned belonged to the nahualtocaitl genre: while featuring parallel epithets for each object and herb employed in the ritual performance, it also closed with the Latin formula *In nomine Patris et Filii et Spiritus Sancti.* With help from the local vicar, Ruiz de Alarcón pressured Domingo until he declared that his story was a fabrication, and that he had learned the incantation from another specialist.[156]

In his attempts to justify the transmission of Nahua ritual knowledge through conversations with Christian entities, Hernández was anything but an exception. Consider the case of Juan de la Cruz, a ticitl from Zacualpa prosecuted by Jacinto de la Serna who performed bloodletting and herbal cures. He appears to have received his specialist knowledge through a vision very similar to that of Hernández: as he lay in bed with a serious, unspecified illness, Archangels Gabriel and Michael came down to hand him a bloodletting needle. They also told him, "Our son, we come on behalf of Our Lord God to teach you the manner in which you shall let blood, so you may serve God, so you get up and bleed your mother, and everyone; and God commands that you shall be given two reales for every arm that you bleed." On another occasion that he was very ill, the Madonna came to him, bearing four medicinal herbs. Before him, they scolded an Indian woman in a blue *huipil*, or native tunic, a personification of his illness, and made her leave; at that time he also received an incantation to be used along with the medicinal herbs.[157]

At least one female specialist admitted to having Christian revelations. After her arrest by Ruiz de Alarcón in 1617, Mariana, a ticitl from Iguala, stated she had learned her ritual techniques from her sister. According to Mariana, her sister had drank ololiuhqui in order to heal a sick person; after curing her patient, a young man who may have been an angel—or the personification of the ololiuhqui itself—came to her and told her, "Behold, God gives you a favor and a gift because you live in poverty and much misery, so that with this favor you will have chili pepper and salt; . . . you will cure wounds by licking them, as well as rashes and smallpox. And if you do not respond to this, you will die."[158] Indeed, this angel was an eloquent speaker of Nahuatl, for he used a well-known couplet: *in chilli in iztatl*, "the chili pepper, the salt," a metonymical reference to quotidian sustenance.

In spite of their appropriation of Christian supernaturals and doctrinal discursive elements, these specialists were not attempting to reproduce the canonical Christian attitudes to healing or the Galenic suspicions surrounding some plants native to the Americas that were espoused by physicians, priests and missionaries. One may argue for the notion of individual revelation derived from Christianity that somehow triggered a hybrid native collective imaginary.[159] Nonetheless, in these episodes, Nahua cultural memory employs Christian revelation in highly pointed ways that may be lost when classified as just another example of indigenous cultural hybridity. First, Domingo and Mariana's sister claimed a direct connection with a Christian deity, which resulted in a claim to charismatic mediation between clients and Christian entities. Second, this claim was used to reproduce a form of ritual specialist knowledge that was not predominantly European in its choice of ritual techniques and medicinal herbs. Third, the appropriation of Christian deities to justify a native ritual practice was a common legitimating procedure in the indigenous elective sphere in colonial Spanish America. In seventeenth-century Peru, Juana Agustina, a widow accused of being a witch, attributed her recruitment into the career of ritual specialist to an angel who gave her "garlands of *catoto, chilcay* seeds, and an herb called *aminamin*; he told her that one bathes with these herbs and that [with them] she would have money to eat and dress."[160] Juana Agustina and Mariana apparently shared a similar attitude toward Christian supernatural entities. Even though it is impossible to determine their state of mind—that is, whether they truly believed they had a conversation with a Christian entity, the pragmatic intent that shaped their narratives is more accessible. Being aware of the clandestine origin of their ritual knowledge, they sought to legitimate it by alleging an individual rapport with a Christian entity.

Rather than conceiving the hybridity of the native elective sphere as a somehow uniform phenomenon, some of the data in this chapter allows us to engage in a relatively well-documented analysis of individual diversity. In other words, the choices made regarding ritual specialization and ritual knowledge by one specialist or a small group of specialists cannot be easily employed to characterize the Nahua elective sphere in its staggering diversity. Through the oral personification of Postclassic deities, some Nahua specialists were able to deploy Postclassic ritual practices; other Nahua specialists, by contrast, sought to incorporate doctrinal elements and Christian arguments into their practices; a few of them attempted both through highly mutable procedures. In fact, the complexity of the elective ritual sphere was rapidly compounded in the first decades of the seventeenth century by means of the unwitting European gift of alphabetic transcription to record incantations and calendrical information. This transformation gave rise to networks of literate specialists who would radically transform the inner workings of the indigenous elective and collective spheres in Central Mexico.

CHAPTER 4

Secular and Civil Campaigns Against Native Devotions in Oaxaca, 1571–1660

In Oaxaca, the transition from extirpation projects controlled by the Dominicans to the management of secular extirpators by episcopal authorities took place at the same time when secular extirpation attempts began in the see of Mexico: the last two decades of the sixteenth century. However, early secular extirpation attempts in Oaxaca occurred at more systematic intervals and in a broader range of linguistic and geographical contexts that in Mexico.[1] The designation of secular extirpators by episcopal authorities also became a more frequent policy in Oaxaca than in Mexico, at least for the transitional period between the late sixteenth and early seventeenth centuries. This chapter examines the extirpation policies that emerged in Oaxaca as secular priests took the lead in the legal and doctrinal confrontation of native ritual practices during a second cycle of extirpation attempts in Central Mexico (1571–1660). The writings of an influential anti-idolatry crusader, Gonzalo de Balsalobre, afford us a unique opportunity for an ethnohistorical inquiry into the social organization of indigenous practices in seventeenth-century Oaxaca, just as the work of Ruiz de Alarcón opens a comparable analytical perspective in Mexico.

TRANSITIONS TO SECULAR IDOLATRY ERADICATION UNDER LEDESMA AND BOHÓRQUEZ

The Dominican Bartolomé de Ledesma (1583–1604) assumed the episcopal seat at a time of momentous transformations in Oaxaca's ecclesiastical organization. A well-known author who had previously occupied the theology chair at the University of Lima and the bishopric of Panamá, Ledesma represented Oaxaca in the Third Mexican Church Council and presided over the efforts of the Dominicans to create the separate province of San Hipólito Mártir in Oaxaca in 1592–96. This province was carved out of the original Central Mexican Dominican province of Santiago, but not without controversy.[2] Moreover, during Ledesma's administration, the Jesuits gained an institutional foothold in Oaxaca City in spite of conflict with the Dominicans, and a generation of accomplished missionaries and linguists—Pedro de Feria, Jordán de Santa Catarina, and Juan de Córdova—passed away.

Ledesma's idolatry eradication policies were characterized by two developments: the granting of commissions against idolaters to parish priests, and the intervention of civil justices in cases of native sorcery and superstition. In fact, Ledesma's decision to enlist secular beneficiados in the struggle against idolatry predated by several years the rise of Francisco de Ávila as an extirpator in Lima under Archbishop Lobo Guerrero in 1605,[3] and Archbishop García Guerra's extirpation events in Toluca in 1610. Unlike Bishop Albuquerque, whose preference for granting Dominicans broad faculties against idolatry was articulated in his disputations with the Audiencia in the 1560s and 1570s, Ledesma's approach mirrored that of García Guerra: commissions against idolaters were granted one at a time and only to deserving ecclesiastical agents.

Ledesma's decision to hand appointments as *jueces* or *comisarios de idolatrías* to secular ministers fluent in native languages is attested as early as a September 1600 commission granted by the diocese's provisor and vicar general to Gregorio Castellanos, then the beneficiado of the Mazatec community of Ixcatlán in Teotila.[4] This commission empowered Castellanos to continue an ongoing idolatry inquest initiated by the beneficiado Pedro de Alabes in Tenango (called Gatiaá by its Mazatec inhabitants); as juez comisionado, Castellanos would conduct proceedings before an escribano and submit the trial transcript along with the defendants to Ledesma for sentencing. Four *relaciones de méritos*, or career summaries,[5] submitted by Castellanos to the real patronato yield further information about his eradication activities.[6] In the early 1600s, Castellanos served as beneficiado in the Mazatec communities of Ixcatlan and Xalapa. By 1605, the bishopric's visitador general reported that Castellanos, now beneficiado in the Cuicatec town of Cuicatlan in Teotitlán del Camino, was "very proficient in the Cuicatec language"; circa 1606, Castellanos was appointed to the Cuicatec jurisdiction of Atlatlauhca, where he prosecuted idolatries in Xalapa, Cuicatlan, and Atlatlauhca over the next fourteen years.

The transition to secular extirpation in Oaxaca was not begun without local resistance directed at the bishop's commissioners. In 1597–98, Doctor Alzorriz, the inquisitorial commissioner of Oaxaca, carried out a discrete investigation of the actions of Miguel de Cervantes, beneficiado of Miahuatlán, regarding an extirpation attempt carried out in 1596 in the Zapotec communities of San Miguel, Santiago, and Santa Ana Suchitepec. This investigation was encouraged by Bishop Ledesma due to evidence of wrongdoing against Cervantes presented by Gregorio de Monjaraz, encomendero of Miahuatlán. The accusations against Cervantes were substantial. Three natives of San Miguel Suchitepec— Luis Hernández, his brother Melchor Pérez, and his son Pedro Luis—accused Cervantes of instructing them and other natives not to surrender their idols to Pedro Ruiz de Rojas, who had been commissioned by Bishop Ledesma to lead an idolatry inquest in Miahuatlán. Furthermore, these and other witnesses testified that Cervantes circulated a damning letter in Nahuatl that instructed natives to favor Cervantes's allies in Suchitepec by "attempt[ing] to have the commissioner Cristóbal Gil recuse himself so he may not come as judge."[7] Even though Rojas did not succeed in obtaining further details from witnesses, Cervantes was not able to stop Gil from overseeing idolatry proceedings against Hernández, Pérez, Luis, and other residents of Suchitepec, who confessed to keeping idols and received sentences that included at least one year of exile. Alzorriz concluded that the three main native witnesses were not to be trusted, and that, even if Cervantes had pronounced some of the alleged warnings against Ledesma's commissioners, his record as an esteemed beneficiado called for a charitable sentence. In the end, this trial damaged Cervantes's reputation, since he was later removed from Miahuatlán by Ledesma.[8]

After the relatively brief tenures of Bishops Baltasar de Covarrubias (1605–8) and Juan de Cervantes (1611–14), the Dominican Juan Bartolomé de Bohórquez e Hinojosa (1617–33) expanded on Ledesma's projects against idolatry and undertook vigorous ecclesiastical reforms. Bishop Bohórquez, a former bishop of Venezuela,[9] was both a reformer who attempted to bring the powerful members of his own order into the fold of episcopal jurisdiction, and the eventual author of two no longer extant works on Zapotec.[10] Bohórquez's conflicts with the Dominicans of Oaxaca did not have a significant impact on his extirpation policies. Following Ledesma's lead, the Dominican appointed a number of secular priests as commissioned judges against idolatry. The only extant idolatry investigations under Bohórquez not linked to these commissions are a trial by Inquisitorial Commissioner fray Fernando de Porras of a Chiauhtla native who ingested ololiuhqui, and an accusation against

María de Montoya, wife of the alcalde mayor of Coatzacoalco, Lucas Soto, regarding the burning of copal before effigies called *iztac teteoh*, Nahuatl for "White Deities."[11]

The extent and scope of Bohórquez's campaigns are exemplified by the activities of three ministers: Pedro de Riano, Agustín de Espina Calderón, and Gerónimo Curiel. As beneficiado in the Amuzgo parish of Zacatepec, Riano destroyed idols and promoted doctrinal education between 1602 and the early 1620s. In 1622, Riano began serving as *vicario foráneo*, or adjunct vicar, and beneficiado of Xicayán de Nieto; soon afterward, he drafted a petition to the crown asking for a permanent appointment to this beneficio.[12] Espina y Calderón began his ecclesiastical career as beneficiado of the Cuicatec town of Papalotepac in the jurisdiction of Teotitlán del Camino in 1624. Bohórquez also named him as vicar general of Papalotepac. In April 1632, he was named visitador general of the entire bishopric, and in this capacity, Espina Calderón "discovered idols, and exiled the abuses and Gentile rites that Indians customarily practice."[13] Espina Calderón continued to prosper under Bishop Benavides: in 1639, Benavides aggregated the town of Cuicatlan to Espina's parish of Papalotepac, and in May 1642, Espina Calderón received a promotion that was occasionally bestowed on proficient extirpators: he was named commissioner of the Holy Office in Cuicatlan.[14]

Gerónimo Curiel's career, by contrast, provides a closer look at the activities of an extirpator with a strong command of an indigenous language. One of his most important campaigns involved a literate Amuzgo cacique from either Xochistlahuaca or Xicayán de Tovar who possessed ritual texts and who was tried in 1633 and sentenced to forced labor at the fort of Acapulco.[15] Curiel had been appointed as beneficiado of Xochistlahuaca and Xicayán de Tovar in the jurisdiction of Igualapa in September 1616, just before Bohórquez's arrival. Due to Curiel's experience and knowledge of Amuzgo, the bishop entrusted in him a series of increasingly substantial appointments. First, he aggregated the town of Cosaguiapa to Curiel's parish in 1621. The following year, he gave Curiel the unusually descriptive title of *juez general de idólatras hechiceros*, "general judge of idolaters and sorcerers," made him vicar *in capite* of the Igualapa-Xicayán (de Nieto) coastal region, and endorsed him as an efficient extirpator in a letter to the crown. In 1628, Curiel was appointed commissioner of Xochistlahuaca and Huatulco by the Holy Office, and in 1635, he obtained the beneficio of Teutila.[16] Only one idolatry case tried by Curiel is extant, and this proceeding survived only because he received a commission from the Holy Office in 1619 to investigate a mulatto—the fisherman Juan Ventura of Ometepec—in January 1620. Ventura was married to a native called Juana, who introduced her husband to don Tomás, an indigenous specialist who gave him a small effigy and instructed him to propitiate him in order to catch more fish. Nonetheless, there is no record of how the Holy Office punished Ventura.[17]

After the death of Bohórquez in 1633, the episcopal seat at Oaxaca remained vacant for all practical purposes during six years, until the arrival of Bishop Benavente y Benavides (1639–52) in 1639.[18] Few details are known about Benavides's engagement against idolatry. Besides the activities of Espina Calderón and Gonzalo de Balsalobre, discussed elsewhere, the Dominican chronicler Francisco de Burgoa sketched a confrontation with Zapotec idolaters at the end of Benavides's administration. Burgoa's account of an extirpation instance in San Francisco Caxonos embraces a style that joins the anecdotic to the hagiographic; still, his description of a specific observance is significant, since it suggests a strong parallel with Late Postclassic ceremonies.

Burgoa recounts that, during a 1652 visit he made to San Francisco, an elder principal from a neighboring town drew his attention among the native officials who had come to pay their respects. This unnamed elder was dressed in silk garments "in the manner of a Spaniard," and the accompanying officials paid him unusual deference. Before his departure, Burgoa asked the local vicar to investigate this elder's reputation; a few months later, his providential suspicions were corroborated when a Spanish deer hunter caught the elder performing a ritual sacrifice before a large native audience by a mountain near San Francisco. The vicar promptly visited the site and confiscated feathers, copal offerings, and a large plate made of woven leaves. The function of the plate was duly explained by the specialist and his concelebrants. Each participant would approach the plate to confess a transgression to an unnamed deity; each of their transgressions was represented by two small cornhusk strands tied together, which they would drop on the plate. The penitent would then draw blood and drip it over the cornhusk strands, and the priest would eventually take the plate and offer it to the unnamed deity.[19] A similar preconquest procedure was identified by Córdova in the sixteenth century; he noted that native confessants would place "an herb that they tied into a loop or rope," before a pigana, or Zapotec specialist, "in order to confess the sins of their choosing."[20] This herb's name, *tòla*, was also the noun the Dominicans had appropriated in the mid-sixteenth century to render the notion of sin into Zapotec. After this discovery, the vicar sought the alcalde mayor's support and had the main priest and other participants tried. Burgoa asserted they received an unspecified merciful punishment, acknowledging that the elderly priest died soon after the arrest.

Half a century later, another confrontation between Dominicans and specialists at San Francisco would result in a momentous revolt against ecclesiastic and civil power.

DOMINICAN DOMINANCE AND
ECCLESIASTICAL REFORM IN OAXACA

Throughout the sixteenth century and early seventeenth centuries, the Dominican order enjoyed unparalleled autonomy in Oaxaca. However, the 1620s and 1630s were characterized by a growing number of conflicts between mendicants and ecclesiastic authorities in New Spain. For instance, regulars fought the attempts made to reduce them to episcopal supervision in both Mexico and Rome, as evidenced by the spirited defense of regular privileges by fray Diego de Ibáñez, the former Franciscan guardian in Mexico City and the procurator general of the Franciscan province of Santo Evangelio, before the council of Propaganda Fide in the 1630s.[21] In Oaxaca, a protracted confrontation between Bohórquez and the Dominicans had its roots in the secularization of doctrinas administered by regulars and in previous attempts to reassert the authority of the bishop and the real patronato over mendicant influence. This conflict arose as a result of a May 1627 order from the Marqués de Cerralvo, then viceroy of New Spain, who dictated two radical reforms. First, in accordance with real patronato provisions from which the Dominicans had secured exceptions for decades, the order would now have to submit to the patronato three candidates for each vacant Dominican parish, instead of electing them internally. Secondly, each Dominican parish priest had to comply with the same procedures through which secular priests were appointed by the local bishop: they would receive their formal appointment to a parish from the bishop and would be subject to the usual episcopal examinations in order to administer the sacraments.[22]

Although the Dominicans agreed to appoint nonmendicant parish priests through the real patronato, they refused to submit to the bishop's authority in terms of licenses, examinations, and punishments. After a series of confrontations between Bohórquez and Dominican visitador Jacinto de Hoces, the bishop attempted to isolate the Dominicans and Franciscans in Oaxaca City by forbidding city residents to attend religious services at the temples of Santo Domingo and San Francisco under penalty of excommunication; as a result of this prohibition, throughout most of 1628 and 1629, city residents stayed away from these churches, as well as from the traditional Good Friday procession organized by the Dominicans, which went forward through deserted city streets. In

November 1629, in an attempt to mediate between Bohórquez and the Dominicans, the aforementioned Franciscan Ibáñez was named *juez conservador,* or specially appointed judge. The bishop questioned Ibáñez's jurisdiction over him and refused to come to his cell; Ibáñez responded by excommunicating Bohórquez and his supporters and publicly humbling them by listing them in the *tablillas,* or announcement boards, at the church of Santo Domingo, which listed all those not allowed to receive the sacraments. Bohórquez obtained a repeal from the Audiencia; by this time, however, Ibáñez had returned to Spain, and the Dominicans refused to comply, arguing that only Ibáñez could reverse this censure, relenting only when another juez conservador was named in 1631. Eventually, in August 1633, Bohórquez, who was gravely ill, decided to reconcile with the Dominicans and met with the provincial. To put an end to their disputes, the bishop turned over all the legal proceedings he initiated against the orders, and Provincial Requena had them burned before a notary.[23]

In the middle years of the seventeenth century, the episcopal and monastic establishment in Oaxaca underwent a slow but decisive transition that changed the dynamics of doctrinal administration throughout the bishopric. The first transformation was internal to all of the monastic orders in New Spain: the issue of *alternancia,* the election of the province's superiors from an alternating pool of Spaniard and criollo candidates every other chapter, was becoming a subject of contention.[24] The second transformation related to the growing tensions between the Dominicans of Oaxaca and episcopal authorities, as illustrated by the controversy with Bohórquez in the early 1630s, and by the difficulty in suppressing the political and financial benefits that many Dominican priests and officials extracted from their posts, which contradicted the order's emphasis on scholarship and poverty. The transgressions ranged from minor details, such as adopting "indecent dress" featuring embroidery,[25] to substantial abuses, such as living outside Dominican convents without permission,[26] or the buying and selling of posts.

The common practice of buying and selling civil appointments in the Spanish colonies is a well-documented form of corruption. The extent to which Dominicans participated in attempts to buy monastic posts and extract benefits from them in order to finance such bribes and further their careers was occasionally referenced by oblique terms at Dominican chapters in the mid-seventeenth century. Indeed, an unusually frank letter preserved in Rome's Dominican Archives demonstrates the degree of concern with which Dominican superiors regarded the scandalous activities of their order in Oaxaca. This letter, written by fray Vittorio Ricci in May 1647 after a visit to the Central Mexican Dominican provinces of

Santiago and San Hipólito, was a confidential report for the Dominican Vicar General Domenico de Marini. Ricci did not employ euphemisms when portraying the corruption among his brethren in New Spain. By citing and elaborating on a well-known passage from Paul (1 Timothy 6:10) on the roots of evil, this text discussed not only corrupt practices but also the debate over the secularization of doctrinas, and it concluded that this measure was the only cure for an order that had abandoned its monastic roots:

> Cupidity and money are the roots of all evil. All appointments can be bought. Whoever reaches a desired dignity increases [its price] well beyond the amount he paid for it, in order to proceed to a higher post; the position of provincial is worth several thousand *escudos*. . . . Finding himself in debt due to such purchase, a provincial makes a career out of fleecing his subjects, both in order to obtain another promotion, and to reach other objectives . . . , and he finds and acquires money using the same unorthodox procedures that the friars in the doctrinas employ with the Indians; his superiors, seeing that he fills up their own pockets, allow him to have a girlfriend and do not disturb him. . . . On some occasions, when I spoke to some seculars and ecclesiastics of no ordinary rank about the poverty of some doctrinas in these parts, they told me: "Your Reverence should not marvel at this, because the revenues are large, and perhaps more than sufficient, but the prelates of some convents steal in order to purchase the remaining higher posts later, and in order to become friends with the provinciales; this is how the provinciales usually extract between 25,000 and 30,000 reales from their posts."
> . . . Furthermore, the viceroys occasionally desire to intervene in the [monastic] elections. . . . Thus, in this New Spain, the authority a certain Viceroy claimed over a certain order because of the regulars themselves was so overwhelming, that even after a God-fearing provincial was chosen, it was necessary for him to give the Viceroy 30,000 reales, so that he would be allowed to name priors and other officials in his own order.
> One finds here some regulars—I do not know from which order—who move from one place to another in an almost public fashion with their girlfriends and children, as if they were married. Others ride on the same horse with their girlfriends in full daylight, as if with their own wives; and this happens in the doctrinas. Were it God's will that no order held doctrinas! . . . Those [regulars] who live in the doctrinas do not know the meaning of enclosure, of choirs, of learning, of regular discipline, of silence, of mortification. . . . Then, the doctrinas are the origin of all evil. . . . This is why it would be very useful for our order to surrender the doctrinas, after seeing the problems that they bring. . . . The seculars develop a greater attachment to their churches because of perpetuity, but the regulars are here today, and tomorrow elsewhere. . . . Thus, our order would receive a greater honor from forfeiting them, before they are ignominiously taken away throughout all the provinces in the Indies, because, if it is said that [New Spain] is . . . the most religious province in these parts, and such things as Your Reverence has heard occur here, what about all the other provinces?[27]

Ricci's sober critique did not result in a substantial transformation of Dominican administration of doctrinas in Oaxaca. Nevertheless, half a century later, a newly appointed bishop would employ a novel and more radical argument—the proliferation of idolatry in northern Oaxaca—to argue that Dominicans had to surrender many of their doctrinas to more conscientious secular ministers.

CIVIL EXTIRPATORS IN OAXACA BEFORE 1660

Four trials heard by Teposcolula alcaldes mayores between 1596 and 1652 provide an unusually detailed perspective on civil juridical policies against Mixtec indigenous healers and ritual specialists in the first half of the seventeenth century. Additionally, two of these trials illustrate the existence of local factionalism that motivated Mixtec officials to accuse their enemies of engaging in idolatry. In 1596, the civil authorities of Tilantongo and Teposcolula in the Mixteca Alta heard two cases against Mixtec men accused of causing or aggravating illness with herbal remedies. In the first instance, the inquest was motivated by suspicions against a local healer; in the second case, jealousy and resentment accounted for the accusations.[28] The former case was investigated by Tristán de Luna y Arellano, alcalde mayor of Teposcolula. In July 1596, a few hours after Gaspar Sánchez, a Mixtec healer from Atoyaquillo, administered a remedy known as *yuacisi* to Baltasar López, who had complained about abdominal pains, López died. This event compelled López's sister Inés de Luna and her husband Cristóbal to present a sorcery complaint against Sánchez. When three witnesses testified that Sánchez was regarded as a charitable local healer who held no animosity toward López, and that López's illness had preceded his death by several weeks, Inés Luna and her husband sought to withdraw their complaint. Unfazed by this development, Luna y Arellano pressed forward with the trial and called several defense witnesses, including the vicar of Tlacolula, who depicted Sánchez as a conscientious healer. Luna y Arellano held Sánchez responsible for the death of López, even if he could not be convicted as a sorcerer or malicious healer.[29]

In October 1596, Luis de Montesinos, Teposcolula's deputy alcalde mayor, heard an idolatry case against Gaspar Huertas, an itinerant Mixtec ritual specialist whose activities bring to mind the activities of Ocelotl and Mixcoatl sixty years earlier, since Huertas claimed to be a powerful mediator between humans and deities. Huertas arrived in the settlement of San Vicente near Chalcatongo along with his servant Domingo and announced to Domingo de la Cruz, Gaspar de la Cruz, and Juan López's wife that the great lord Tani Yoco, who resided in a nearby cave, had sent him to heal them. It is likely that Tani Yoco was a local name for Toyna Yoco, a merchant deity named in the 1544–47 trial of the lords of Yanhuitlan, and worshipped in the Mixteca Baja communities of Puctla and Mixtepec. Unlike Ocelotl or Mixcoatl, Huertas seemed to be in search of sacrificial victims. After Huertas applied various herbal remedies (*patles*, from the Nahuatl *pahtli*, "medicine") to his clients' bodies and extracted noxious substances from them, he asked them to give him a son or a daughter, or to offer themselves, to be led into "the Great Lord's cave." This phrase, which hinted at a human sacrifice, compelled the various clients to offer him candles and cash payments ranging from three to eight reales, which were more significant sums than the usual healing fee of two to three reales reported by Ruiz de Alarcón. When confronted by the civil judge, Huertas resorted to a routine trope that natives employed to excuse improper behavior: he claimed he was drunk when he performed the cures and spoke about Tani Yoco.[30]

Two civil idolatry trials provide limited but valuable details about political factionalism in Mixtec communities that resulted in the leveling of idolatry accusations. A January 1615 trial overseen by Captain Rodrigo Borge, alcalde mayor of Teposcolula, focused on sorcery accusations stemming from local political enmity.[31] During this trial, Cuquila native Francisco Larios accused his own gobernador, don Pablo de Santa María, of torturing him for suspicions of sorcery. Santa María admitted to torturing Larios, but he argued that he was seeking the restitution of communal funds that Larios had appropriated. After assessing the evidence, Borge ruled in Larios's favor by handing down a fine and a four-month exile against Santa María.

Another case heard in Teposcolula in 1652 brings to light the use of idolatry claims as part of a dispute between officeholders. In April 1652, don Pedro Portocarrero, alcalde mayor of Teposcolula, heard an idolatry case against four natives of the Mixtec community of Malinaltepec— Diego Palomares, Francisco Palomares, Diego García, and Gaspar Reyes—who stood accused of performing ritual practices before a deity effigy located in a nearby cave.[32] The case began with an accusation of idolatry in a nearby cave against the alcalde Diego Palomares, who had questioned a land sale to the Spaniard Juan García by his namesake, the gobernador don Diego Palomares, during a contentious communal meeting at Malinaltepec. Portocarrero sent an escribano and some native officials to inspect the cave, and they reported finding an idol, two candles, some copal, and a stone with an engraved checkerboard design. When the alcalde Palomares was brought before Portocarrero, he explained the gobernador's ill will against him by noting that, during the public meeting, he had demanded that the gobernador Palomares return the money he had received from selling the lands to Juan García because they were communal lands belonging to the town of Achiutla, and they could not be sold to a Spaniard. The alcalde Palomares contended that they were being framed by Gobernador Palomares, who had asked two men to place the idols found earlier by the notary. In fact, he argued, he had visited the cave with the idols four years earlier as part of an idol-seeking party led by the vicar of Yanhuitlan. This version of events was supported by Jacinto García, who declared that he had seen Gobernador Palomares place idols and offerings inside the cave earlier. García's account was supported by the testimony of a nephew of the defendant Diego de García. Gobernador Palomares denounced these testimonies, but still the alcalde mayor incarcerated him, tried him as a defendant, and ruled against him. Portocarrero's sentence included a substantial fine of fifty pesos—half for the civil justice, and half for litigation costs.[33]

BALSALOBRE'S CONFRONTATIONS
WITH DIEGO LUIS

The episcopal administration of the Benedictine friar Francisco Diego Díaz de Quintanilla de Hevia y Valdés lasted only about two and a half years from his arrival in Oaxaca City in early 1654 until his death in December 1656.[34] In spite of such a brief tenure, Hevia y Valdés's interest in idolatry extirpation campaigns and his policy of seeking assistance from the civil justice lent significant support to the best-documented extirpation campaign in the diocese of Oaxaca in the seventeenth century: the struggles of the secular Gonzalo de Balsalobre against native ritual practices in his beneficio of San Miguel Sola between 1635 and 1658. Hevia y Valdés had continued the preexisting policy of appointing especially qualified ministers, as he noted in his preface to Balsalobre's 1656 *Relación auténtica de las idolatrías, supersticiones y vanas observaciones de los indios del obispado de Oaxaca*:

Having heard after my arrival in this bishopric, about the pitiful ruinous state of Catholicism due to so much idolatry that propagates in hiding in the hearts of the natives, . . . I traveled this land, and along the more than 700 leagues that I covered, I discovered always greater abominations and misery, deserving of eternal lamentation, in spite of the zeal and fervor I witnessed in so many learned and pious ministers, in spite of so many churches and so many doctrinas. . . . In order to stop the propagation of such mortal poison, I created special ministers against idolaters, and instructed and passed sentences on many trials, which I placed in the hands of the . . . worthy viceroy of this New Spain.[35]

Whereas Hevia y Valdés seems to refer to several extirpators in this excerpt, the extant records provide evidence about the activities of only four of them: Balsalobre, the Mercedarian friar Pedro de Trujillo, who assisted Balsalobre in Sola, and the seculars Pedro de Torres Cortés and Bartolomé de Benavides. Not much is known about the activities of the latter two. In a March 1661 letter to the crown regarding worthy ministers, Bishop Cuevas Dávalos mentions that Hevia y Valdés offered Benavides, who held a poor, unnamed parish, a post in the cathedral, and the rectorship of Oaxaca City's Colegio de San Bartolomé; Benavides declined this offer and remained in his parish, working toward the extirpation of "loathsome idolatries."[36] Torres Cortés, beneficiado of Xalatlaco, a multilingual parish near Oaxaca City inhabited by Nahuas, Mixtecs, and Zapotecs,[37] was appointed by Hevia y Valdés as commissioned judge against idolatry in 1656. He led at least one superstition trial against María de la Cruz, an Indian woman accused of placing cacao grains as burial offerings.[38]

Although the activities of Balsalobre as extirpator were as significant as those of Hernando Ruiz de Alarcón and Jacinto de la Serna, little is known about his life. Balsalobre, a descendant of the conquerors Francisco de Almaraz and Pedro de Paredes, was born in Oaxaca City in the early seventeenth century and was ordained circa 1630.[39] He was granted the beneficio of San Miguel Sola in the early 1630s and presided over an idolatry trial against the ritual specialist Diego Luis in November and December 1635. In September 1642, during an interim period between the administration of two bishops, the Oaxaca cathedral chapter, which held temporary episcopal faculties in the absence or death of a bishop, offered to Balsalobre the post of provisor and vicar general. However, Balsalobre declined this post, alleging he was too ill to take it.[40] After overseeing an impressive number of idolatry trials in Sola between 1653 and 1658, first as vicario foráneo and then as commissioner general against idolatries, Balsalobre finally accepted an offer from Bishop Cueva y Dávalos to become provisor and vicar general and occupied this post from November 1659 until September 1664, thus bringing to an end a successful ecclesiastical career.[41]

Balsalobre's eradication activities in 1653–61 are known through a detailed set of trials.[42] His staging grounds were the various Zapotec towns in Sola, now known as Sola de Vega, one of the most important parishes in the far-flung jurisdiction of the Mines of Cimatlán and Chichicapa. Even though this jurisdiction experienced a substantial decline in the number of native tributaries, this descent was far more moderate than the one experienced by other jurisdictions near the Basin of Mexico: by 1600, the native population was 42.76 percent of the 1548 total,

and by 1623, it had decreased to about 31.57 percent of the 1548 estimate, or 7,600 native tributaries.[43] Since about 1570, there had been
a secular priest residing in the *cabecera*, or head town, of San Miguel
Sola, whose twelve original dependencies had been consolidated during
congregaciones in 1599–1601, yielding seven towns: San Miguel, Santa
Ana, Santa Inés, San Ildefonso, San Juan, Santa María, and Pueblo de
los Reyes.[44] Balsalobre's investigations of native ritual practices were
not circumscribed to the activities of specialists residing in these locations; through various testimonies, Balsalobre obtained knowledge
about specialists in the neighboring parishes of Lachixio and Ejutla,
both of which were located in the jurisdiction of Oaxaca. Another town
mentioned in these testimonies was Santo Domingo Teoxomulco, in
Teozacualco.

The idolatry trials conducted by Balsalobre in 1635 and 1653–58
contain an unusual amount of information about the circulation of
calendrical texts in Sola and in other neighboring Zapotec and Chatino
communities. In fact, Balsalobre's campaigns were a second act in an
unfolding cycle of extirpation attempts in the Sola region. According to
some testimonies collected in 1654–56, about nine ritual specialists were
tried and published in autos de fe by a secular priest who probably was
Balsalobre's predecessor as beneficiado of San Miguel Sola, the bachiller
Martín Fernández de Córdoba. Circa 1614, Córdoba investigated, in-
dicted, and disciplined four specialists in a customary exemplary parade
through San Miguel Sola: Alonso Pérez Huesee and Vicente from San
Ildefonso; Lorenzo Xuárez from Santa Ana; and a certain Gómez from
San Francisco.[45] At some point between 1614 and the early 1630s, before
Balsalobre's arrival, Córdoba punished at least five more specialists in
Sola: Diego Bayo of Loxicha and a resident of Xuchiatengo, Tomás Laa
of San Francisco, Lucas Pedro Huesechi and Alonso Huesechi of San
Juan, and Lorenzo Nachinaa of San Miguel.[46]

An understanding of Balsalobre's campaigns hinges on our assessment
of a single major witness, who often stood in person or through quoted
excerpts at the center of his proceedings. This man was Diego Luis, a
native of the neighborhood of Santa Ana in San Miguel Sola. According to the testimony he gave in 1654 through two interpreters, he was
among the oldest surviving ritual specialists in the region and claimed
to be eighty-eight years old; according to his testimony, he had been a
ritual specialist since about 1632.[47] This second and final confrontation
between Balsalobre and Diego Luis cannot be understood without an
assessment of their first confrontation, which took place in November
1635. At the time, Balsalobre was a novice beneficiado with some knowledge of Nahuatl but no apparent knowledge of Zapotec, a language that

he may never have mastered, as suggested by the fact that his interrogations of Sola witnesses were conducted through interpreters who spoke Nahuatl or Zapotec.

By contrast, Diego Luis was as educated a man as the local parameters allowed a native to be: he claimed to have been brought up in the Sola church and had been a church cantor, the town's escribano, and a *regidor*, or town councilman, of San Miguel Sola. He was also fully literate, and like other local native officials, he spoke both Zapotec and Nahuatl and in fact addressed some of Balsalobre's queries in Nahuatl. By 1635, Diego Luis was already an elderly resident of San Miguel Sola, about seventy years old, according to his own reckoning, and one of the town's regidores. Balsalobre was not even the first priest to hold suspicions about Diego Luis. In 1632, during one of Diego Luis's absences, the vicar of Sola, probably the aforementioned Córdoba, had found a suspicious manuscript containing calendrical information among Diego Luis's papers, as he was looking for the most recent tribute assessment drafted by Diego Luis as a town official.[48]

Balsalobre approached what probably was his very first idolatry trial with caution and only after securing the support of other colonial and native authorities. On November 21, 1635, as vicario foráneo of Sola, a title granted him by the cathedral chapter in the absence of a sitting bishop, Balsalobre asked Toribio Hernández and Domingo López, two Sola town officials fluent in Nahuatl, to assess the contents of a second manuscript book that had been taken away from Diego Luis; he also secured the judicial assistance of the corregidor of Sola. The officials gave a rather candid answer; they asserted the booklet in question was "a book from ancient times" for making divinations about illnesses and admitted it contained "the names of the devil, stone idols, sorcerers and sorceresses, and other things that they could not comprehend because the language in which it was written was mixed with the Chatino language."[49] Diego Luis admitted he had received the booklet from Félix de Alvarado, an official in the neighboring Chatino-speaking community of Santa Catarina Juquila, who had obtained it earlier from another town official called Lorenzo Martín. He also asserted that the book contained "the days of the year distributed into thirteen times," each of which was governed by a deity, and gave a list of thirteen deities, which was rendered by Balsalobre in a tentative manner in the 1635 trial records, without even recording each deity's Zapotec name. After consulting with the provisor and vicar general, on December 17, 1635, Balsalobre handed a particularly lenient sentence: Diego Luis was taken out in an auto de fe, which was carried out without corporal punishment in December 1635, and then he served for six months at the Franciscan convent at Oaxaca City.

He was also threatened with two hundred lashes and four years of forced labor if convicted of reincidence.[50]

Diego Luis asked his son Lorenzo Martín to make a transcription of the Chatino book from Juquila shortly before it was confiscated; after his return to Sola in late 1636, he continued to exercise his faculties as a renowned specialist and to hand out transcriptions of his text occasionally to interested parties, either for free or for fees of about one peso. In 1654, when Balsalobre confronted him with five different confiscated booklets, Diego Luis was able to identify three of them as his own: the first one was the recopied booklet; the second one was a transcript he had given to Melchor López circa 1635; and the third one was a transcript he had sold to the Sola fiscal Miguel de Quiroz for one peso circa 1652. He identified the two others as calendrical texts; one was written in the Zapotec dialect of the parish of Santa Cruz and had belonged to the specialist Francisco López; the other was a booklet that the specialist Luis López had passed on to his daughter, Gracia Margarita.

Nowhere in Diego Luis's 1654 trial does Balsalobre seem to threaten the elder specialist with corporal punishment or torture in an effort to extract a confession. A plausible conjecture is that Diego Luis assessed his status as a former idolatry convict, the incriminating testimony of several witnesses, and then he made a full confession for the sake of his inheritable property and his offspring, who stood to suffer the most from the consequences of Diego Luis's denials. In fact, as a precautionary measure, Balsalobre confiscated all of Diego Luis's earthly possessions before he began his interrogation—three small plots of land, twenty-two maguey plants, a small box with a lock whose contents were never disclosed in the trial, two load-bearing horses, and three small wattle-and-daub dwellings.

In any case, Diego Luis decided to make two damning statements early on in his trial; in the first one, given on February 4, 1654, he admitted to being a day keeper, provided a brief account of his activities and divination practices, and gave the names of several specialists and clients. Diego Luis's second deposition may be characterized as the breaking of an inner dam: during this declaration of February 22, 1654, he volunteered the names and personal circumstances of no less than seventy-three clients who had consulted him during his long career as the leading ritual specialist in the region, excused himself for not providing more names due to a faulty memory, and provided the names of all the other specialists known to him in neighboring communities, both dead and alive. In addition, in his declaration of July 6, 1654, Diego Luis identified the origin of the five calendrical booklets that Balsalobre had confiscated, and he also provided a more detailed list of the thirteen

Zapotec deities who, according to him, presided over the 260-day Zapotec divinatory count, called piyè in Valley Zapotec. The absence of an actual sentence handed out by Balsalobre, excluding the mention of an auto de fe that probably included Diego Luis and several clients in the 1656 *Relación auténtica*, does not allow us to assess whether Balsalobre offered the elderly specialist a more merciful sentence in return for his cooperation. We do know, unfortunately, that no ritual text confiscated by Balsalobre survived the flames of diocesan justice.

In contrast with the variety of avocations and performative roles assumed by Nahua ritual specialists in Cohuixca and Tlalhuica towns, the role of the ritual specialists in the Sola region investigated by Balsalobre was limited to the interpretation of the piyè. Ritual specialists worked from memory, consulted manuscript transcripts of the piyè day list, and cast maize grains in order to provide prognosis about diseases or about transgressions that would have caused the wrath of specific deities. In fact, the range of reported specialist titles reflected the relatively narrow scope of their specializations; in Zapotec, some of Sola's specialists were called *colaní*, or calendar specialists, and one of them, Esteban de Aquino, was called a *guechila*, "diviner," by an informant.[51] In Spanish, Balsalobre used the terms *letrado*, "solicitor," and *maestro*, "teacher, learned person." The first term was a native or ecclesiastical appropriation of the title that was usually given to legal representatives in colonial tribunals. The designation *maestro de idolatrías*, "teacher of idolatries," was a common ecclesiastical label for all manner of ritual specialists.

Both Balsalobre and his assistant fray Pedro Trujillo used Diego Luis's statements to prosecute a regional network of ritual-text owners and clients. The most multitudinous case involved thirty-six town officials of San Miguel and Santa María Sola, who were convicted and punished for performing propitiatory ritual practices for the goddess Nohuichana before fishing for trout in a nearby river.[52] Moreover, Balsalobre and Trujillo unabashedly employed deathbed confessions and extreme unction as a means of extracting confessions and thus cajoled many Sola residents into admitting to having consulted Diego Luis and other specialists as the last rites were being administered. Using this and other methods, Trujillo obtained confessions from forty-four clients of at least four local specialists between March and May 1654,[53] and from twenty-two other clients of about eight local maestros between August and November 1656.[54] By contrast, Balsalobre secured the confessions of thirty-two native clients of about sixteen local specialists between July 1657 and May 1658.[55] Not even the dead were exempted from such inquiries: on January 27, 1658, Balsalobre investigated the activities of

Felipe Encomendero, who had just died and was about to be buried, as a ritual-text owner and specialist client before allowing his body to be buried in sacred ground.[56]

TWO GENERATIONS OF ZAPOTEC

SPECIALISTS IN SOLA

The following section provides only a brief summary of the various ritual practices described in the Sola trials.[57] The ritual practices that Balsalobre uncovered in Sola belonged to the individual sphere. There is no evidence about sacrificios del común, the collective ceremonies abundantly attested in Villa Alta five decades later, if one regards the propitiation of Nohuichana before fishing for trout as relating to individual sustenance. In fact, one could characterize the scope of elective ritual activities in Sola by grouping them into four heuristic modes of symbolic action: life-cycle events (birth, baptism, marriage, and death), sustenance activities (primarily deer hunting, fishing, and household-scale agriculture), healing activities, and the propitiation of Christian and non-Christian entities to reach individual objectives. In contrast with the pragmatic goals of the Nahua practices recorded by Ruiz de Alarcón two decades earlier, most of the reported ritual activities in Sola relate to well-being and life-cycle events rather than to the curing of diseases. The residents of Sola associated a number of everyday, pragmatic aims with particular Zapotec deities. As it was the case for some Nahua ritual practices investigated by Ruiz de Alarcón, these beliefs coexisted without contradiction with the local cult and devotion of Christian entities. In fact, some practices highlighted some perceived rapports between Zapotec calendrical knowledge and Christian devotional practices. For example, a recurring preoccupation among some of Diego Luis's clients was establishing the most propitious date, according to the piyè, for burning candles before images of saints at the San Miguel Sola church in order to attain a miscellaneous range of individual objectives.

Even a cursory appraisal of the testimony of more than one hundred residents of Sola shows that there was a consensus of sorts among this group of clients about who were the leading ritual specialists in the region. In fact, given the prominence of Diego Luis as the eldest, most respected specialist in Sola, one could propose a grouping of all known local specialists into two generational groups: a group of ritual specialists who were contemporaneous to what appears to be Diego Luis's most active phase as a specialist (1632–54), and an earlier generation of specialists who were active during the first three decades of the seventeenth century. In 1654, the following were regarded as the most prominent ritual specialists in the area besides Diego Luis himself: Domingo Hernández Lalaa of Santa María, also known as "the Sorcerer," whose property was confiscated after he fled at the beginning of Balsalobre's inquest;[58] Gerónimo Sánchez, who fled his native Sola to seek refuge in the Loxicha area;[59] Felipe Guelalaa of Santa María;[60] Esteban de Aquino of San Juan, a follower of the respected specialist Luis López;[61] and Baltasar Martín of San Juan, who died circa 1645.[62] All of these specialists were said to own ritual texts.

The five specialists mentioned above were but a fraction of an entire generation of specialists active circa 1654 in the Sola area. Santa Inés had a specialist only known as Melchor; San Ildefonso had Luis Ximénez; in Lachixio, there were five maestros—Gabriel Coxo, Juan García, Marcos Ignacio, Nicolás El Ciego, and the better-known Marcos Xee; Santa Ana had Miguel Zorita, son of the dead maestro Diego Zorita; Santa María had Julián Osorio; San Sebastián had Baltasar Ramírez Xaa; San Vicente had Sebastián and Luis Martín; Teoxomulco had three specialists, Agustín, Diego Hernández, and Domingo Tiro; Xuchiatengo had Felipe del Puerto; and a maestro called Vicente resided in Yolotepec. There were only two female ritual specialists in this cohort; both resided in Santa María Sola, and both had kinship or marriage ties with male maestros. The more renowned one was Ana María, widow of the specialist Esteban de Aquino, who also inherited Aquino's ritual text along with his practice. The other female specialist was Gracia Margarita, the daughter of the respected specialist Luis López, who had also inherited a ritual text. Chapter 7 contains a detailed analysis of the relationship between literacy and ritual knowledge within this network of local specialists.

Diego Luis and other witnesses also identified a previous generation of local maestros who were active between the early seventeenth century and the early 1630s. The earliest specialist in this generation was Diego Quachila of Santa María, active circa 1604;[63] there was also a specialist called Inés, also of Santa María, who engaged in ritual activities around 1616.[64] Various witnesses gave accounts about the activities of three more specialists in the decade of the 1620s: Francisco Quilo Ramírez of San Ildefonso;[65] Bartolomé García of San Vicente in the parish of Ejutla, who owned a ritual text and had been recognized as a colaní since 1627;[66] and Melchor Xuárez the Elder of San Juan, another ritual-text user, and the previous husband of María, Diego Luis's wife in the 1650s.[67] Diego Luis also acknowledged the assistance of three specialists who helped him interpret the "book about the teachings of the thirteen gods."[68] First among them was Luis López, who, like Diego Luis, had also been a cantor at the church in San Miguel Sola and was the first husband of Diego Luis's wife María. Then, there was Diego Zorita, a member of a family of ritual specialists of Santa Ana that included his brother Mateo Zorita and his nephew Miguel Zorita; finally, there was Diego Yaguela, who helped Diego Luis decode the ritual text in the Chatino language that he obtained from Lorenzo Martín of Juquila in the early 1630s.

Both the calendrical system and the group of deities propitiated in Sola was part of a local compendium of ritual knowledge that may have differed from that of other Zapotec-speaking regions. Hence, Diego Luis pointed out that the piyè has a quadripartite division, a feature also attested in the Valley of Oaxaca, but his day list was divided into thirteen periods of twenty days, and each period was ruled by a particular deity.[69] In contrast with this division, the copies of the piyè confiscated in Villa Alta in 1704 were divided into a more canonical arrangement of twenty periods of thirteen days each. Furthermore, a comparison of the Sola pantheon with entries about Zapotec deities that appear in Córdova's 1578 *Vocabulario* shows a possible correspondence with several Pan-Zapotec deities, which received different names in Sola. These comparisons are discussed in detail in Chapter 7.

THE HOLY OFFICE AGAINST HEVIA Y VALDÉS

The ambitious reach of Balsalobre's extraordinary extirpation trials in Sola called for the support of both ecclesiastical and civil authorities. Balsalobre had the unqualified support of Bishop Hevia y Valdés, who promoted him from vicario foráneo of Sola to the post of commissioner general of the Ordinary Inquisition against idolatry on May 1, 1654. Additionally, between August and October 1654, he had an escribano record favorable testimony about his campaigns from at least ten Spaniards and several castas in Oaxaca City in order to justify his actions and defend himself from a suit against him brought by some Sola residents, who requested to have Balsalobre's idolatry proceedings inspected by the Audiencia of Mexico.[70] On October 4, 1654, this court ruled in favor of the natives and requested that the idolatry autos be brought before it. In a cautious political move, Balsalobre escorted his trial records to the Audiencia's Chancellery and may even have remained in Mexico City for eight months, as the Audiencia examined the case. On July 14, 1655, it issued a decision asserting that both the bishop and Balsalobre were proceeding correctly, and asking civil authorities in Oaxaca to assist them in their eradication efforts.[71]

The most serious challenge to the extirpation campaigns of Hevia y Valdés and Balsalobre came neither from the residents of Sola nor from the Audiencia, but from the Inquisition itself. In 1656, Balsalobre obtained the support of Hevia y Valdés in order to print and distribute his *Relación auténtica*, which would thus become the first Central Mexican extirpation treatise to be printed in New Spain. This succinct, twenty-two–folio publication included a laudatory preface by Hevia y Valdés, a summary of the trials conducted in Sola by Balsalobre, a transcription of the favorable Audiencia decisions, and a set of instructions outlining the legal procedures to be followed by vicarios foráneos and commissioned judges when presiding over native idolatry or superstition trials. In March 1659, a copy of the *Relación* drew the attention of the Holy Office in Mexico City. The inquisitors were greatly troubled by three violations of the Holy Office's protocol and jurisdiction. First, Bishop Hevia y Valdés called himself *inquisidor ordinario*, or "episcopal inquisitor," and designated Balsalobre as juez de comisión *de la inquisición ordinaria*. As argued above, even if Ruiz de Alarcón embraced the same erroneous designation, no inquisición ordinaria existed in New Spain: there was only the legitimate inquisition on the one hand, and the ordinario's ecclesiastical jurisdiction on the other. Second, the trial instructions in the *Relación* did not indicate that episcopal jurisdiction regarding idolatry and superstition applied only to natives. Third, as he rushed to publish the *Relación*, Balsalobre made public accusations against defendants whose trials were still in process, a violation of common ecclesiastical and inquisitorial procedure.[72]

Both the bishop and Balsalobre could not have chosen a worse time for incurring in procedural irregularities. Since 1654, the procedures and shortcomings of the Holy Office functionaries in Mexico City were being subject to a lengthy and demanding scrutiny by Visitador Pedro de Medina Rico, who was attempting to put an end to a series of institutional abuses and irregularities almost single-handedly.[73] Medina Rico was in fact the highest-ranking inquisitor who presided over the inquisitorial censure of the *Relación*, and he was among the officials who issued a March 1659 edict calling for the confiscation of Balsalobre's Sola autos, as well as every extant copy of the *Relación*. This proclamation was read in the cathedral of Oaxaca a day after Easter Sunday; by July 1659, the inquisitorial commissioner in Oaxaca reported having confiscated many copies of the *Relación*, as well as two bundles containing Balsalobre's trial records. On October 22, 1659, Medina Rico, Sáenz de Mañozca, and other inquisitors turned over the confiscated materials to the Jesuit fray Juan Ortiz de los Heros, *calificador* of the Holy Office, so he would make all necessary corrections before returning them to their owners in Oaxaca. An inspection of the extant Balsalobre proceedings shows that they were neither corrected by Ortiz de los Heros nor returned to Oaxaca.[74] Nevertheless, Balsalobre's ecclesiastical career was not permanently harmed by this controversy: the last available records about him indicate that he served as provisor and vicar general in Oaxaca under Bishop Cuevas Dávalos until at least 1664.

SECULAR CLERGY CAMPAIGNS IN OAXACA BEFORE 1660

From the standpoint of episcopal authorities, collecting information about native ritual practices in Oaxaca was a difficult proposition that was rendered especially laborious by the diversity of native languages and the geographical obstacles to travel. And yet, the bishops of Oaxaca confronted those challenges through the development of a systematic juridical routine. By appointing beneficiados with good knowledge of indigenous languages as commissioned judges, a legal net was cast into the forbidding sea of native ritual practices time after time, in an attempt to isolate and punish ritual specialists. Both ecclesiastics and the native officials understood that accusations about engaging in or covering up ritual practices were another procedural tool in the arsenal of legal measures, including *capítulos*, direct appeals to the crown or the Audiencia, and formal visitas of civil authorities, all of which could be used by individuals or factions to settle scores with their opponents. Thus, the accusations leveled by some native officials in Miahuatlán against Miguel de Cervantes in 1596, and the cycle of accusations and counteraccusations that pitted Mixtec official Diego de Palomares against his namesake in 1652 display the fragility of legal narratives about idolatry and showcase the interaction of local actors with complex political designs.

The unsystematic preservation of documents about extirpation campaigns in far-flung districts imposes another layer of complexity over a series of local, short-lived extirpation campaigns. Did Curiel confiscate a calendrical ritual text used by Amuzgo speakers, or was this text a compilation of incantations, or even a translation of doctrinal writings? How did an extirpator like Castellanos decide what was idolatrous and what was permissible regarding Mazatec ritual practices? Unfortunately, extant records are incapable of supporting a sustained inquiry into these questions.

Nonetheless, amidst this landscape of minimally described idolatry campaigns, the information furnished by an attentive reading of Balsalobre's trial records emerges as in invaluable description of the social stratification of clandestine ritual practices in one Zapotec township. This chapter focused less on the contents of these practices than on their social and generational contexts. A substantial motivation underlies this analytical choice. Balsalobre was not interested in the complexities of the Zapotec language or Zapotec local cosmologies, nor was he puzzled by the use of alphabetical writing to transcribe native ritual knowledge. Therefore, his proceedings are no match for the detailed description of ritual practices and incantations found in Ruiz de Alarcón's treatise. In fact, Balsalobre recorded a modest amount of ethnohistorical information regarding Diego Luis's ritual sphere, besides the names of Zapotec deities, broad descriptions of ritual observances in Sola, and these actions' pragmatic objectives.

Even though he burned one invaluable set of records, the "books of the thirteen gods" he seized in Sola, Balsalobre preserved unparalleled information about the social and kinship rapports within a local network of ritual-text interpreters and users. Furthermore, thanks to the testimony of Diego Luis, a historical narrative about the activities of two generations of specialists can be sketched. These data allow us to consider a type of ritual specialist whose intellectual curiosity, polymorphous literacy, and pragmatic orientation could only be regarded as the result of demonic perversity by their ecclesiastical enemies. This new breed of idolatry—literate, obstinate, eclectic—will be investigated in the following chapter.

CHAPTER 5

Literate Idolatries

Clandestine Nahua and Zapotec Ritual Texts in the Seventeenth Century

On December 22, 1704, Juan Mathías, a resident of the Bixanos Zapotec town of San Juan Malinaltepec near Choapa in northern Oaxaca, pointed at a small, well-thumbed booklet and before Juan Gracia Corona, the beneficiado of Yagavila, acknowledged it as his property.[1] His term for this booklet, *biyee que xotao xoci reo*, "the times of the ancestors and fathers of us all," which may seem hyperbolic or lyrical to our ears, was in fact painstakingly literal. Juan Mathías's father had given him the booklet seven years before, admonishing him to examine "that calendar which he was bestowing on him, for it was good for knowing the various times." These "various times," decidedly in the plural, were inscribed in a recursive count of 260 day names that had provided a temporal grid for many ritual and social practices in Proto-Zapotec and Zapotec-speaking communities during the previous 2,300 Gregorian years.[2]

Juan Mathías's calendar possessed a feature that set it apart from the dozens—or, perhaps, hundreds—of alphabetic copies of the Zapotec calendar in clandestine circulation at the time: it recorded the date of a 1691 solar eclipse and a 1693 lunar eclipse using both the Gregorian calendar and the Zapotec ritual count. We will never know whether Juan Mathías was struck with grief as he stole one last glance at his father's times—perhaps he had already made a copy of them, and hidden the text for safekeeping. In any case, since the absolution of his fellow townspeople hinged on the tenor and contents of his confession and of that of other local specialists, Juan Mathías made a statement that, truthful or euphemistic, was first of all eminently pragmatic: he told Gracia that, even though his father's teachings allowed him to tend to individual clients, he used this calendar infrequently and declared himself to be "young and modern."[3]

Juan Mathías's father's interest in eclipses was not exceptional among natives. From the mid-sixteenth century to the late eighteenth century, Nahua authors who cultivated the *altepetlacuilolli*, "altepetl records" genre in urban centers in the Basin of Mexico and the Puebla-Tlaxcala region generated hundreds of pages in which they recounted notable events—local political history, public festivities, miracles attributed to Christian saints, and eclipses and comet sightings. Their narrative was organized by Gregorian years that were often correlated with substantial or vestigial references to the Nahua year count. Thus, the midday solar eclipse of August 23, 1691, was recorded both by Juan Mathías's father in his isolated Zapotec village, and by an anonymous Nahua annalist from Puebla active in the last two or three decades of the seventeenth century, who eloquently described local reactions, noting, "it was as though people had lost their senses. Some ran to the church, some fell down in fright, and three simply died right away. . . . It was fearful what the lord of the near and the close, our lord God, did on that Thursday afternoon."[4]

Two important distinctions should be drawn between these two independent native reports of the eclipse. First, the Nahua author wrote from the vantage point of an acculturated citizen of an altepetl, with intimate knowledge of the ecclesiastic sphere and a vested interest in local struggles against residents regarded as mestizo meddlers.[5] Our Zapotec calendar specialist, by contrast, although a likely participant in his local political sphere, for his son was a fiscal in 1704, was relatively shielded from habitual contact with Spaniards and castas in his remote village. More importantly, the Puebla author regarded the eclipse as an extraordinary phenomenon wrought on humans by the Christian God, whom he designates, in an archaic turn of phrase, as *in tloque nahuaque*, "the lord of the near and the close." We do not know whether Juan Mathías attributed the eclipses he witnessed to Zapotec deities, but the close association of his report with a non-Christian calendar attests to the social currency this count still wielded in Northern Zapotec communities, which stands in stark contrast with the vestigial references to Nahua calendrical practices in late seventeenth-century Nahua annals.

This chapter examines the differential social articulation of alphabetic writing by native colonial authors who, like our man from Malinaltepec, occupied social spaces on the margin of urban centers in central New Spain, and who managed to turn the Spanish gift of alphabetic writing on its head, using it to perpetuate ritual genres and knowledge anchored in Postclassic social and symbolic practices and to recast devotional and astronomical knowledge of European origin into emerging native textual genres. Our two authors shared much in common as native colonial subjects and social actors within a legal system that carefully demarcated the rights and obligations as members of the república de indios. Nonetheless, the Zapotec author's intellectual efforts were inscribed within the logic of colonial clandestinity: in a colonial order that conflated authorship and ownership of proscribed texts by prosecuting anyone involved in their production or circulation, Juan Mathías's father was an aberration, an unwelcome result of the philological and lexicographic work of sixteenth-century Dominican authors and an example of the widespread dispersal of alphabetic literacy throughout rural landscapes in central New Spain. Although the archival record favors the study of historical narratives and mundane records produced by colonial indigenous authors,[6] our understanding of native responses to evangelization remains tentative without an examination of the clandestine convergence of alphabetic writing with ritual, devotional, and astronomical knowledge.

In order to assess this extraordinary merger, this chapter proposes four case studies that highlight Nahua and Zapotec clandestine intellectual labor in the seventeenth century: the interplay of the oral and written reproduction of ritual knowledge in Nahua communities in the Cohuixca-Tlalhuica region; the bold appropriation of a European almanac genre by Nahua translators; a network of users of Zapotec calendrical texts that emerged around a single household containing two generations of ritual specialists; and the production and circulation of dozens of Zapotec calendars and songbooks in forty northern Oaxacan villages.

FROM POSTCLASSIC LITERACY TO LITERATE IDOLATRY

A common observation could be made about the social specificity of writing in ancient Near Eastern, Mediterranean, and Mesoamerican societies: the circumscription of formal training in the interpretation and production of writing for elite groups and their close associates. Classicist Eric Havelock termed this condition "craft literacy,"[7] literacy being a specialized skill fully exercised only by a small segment of society, which, according to William V. Harris, comprised no more than 15 percent of the population even at peak literacy periods in Mediterranean antiquity.[8] As Stephen Houston has noted, a full understanding of the role of literacy in ancient societies, and in preconquest Mesoamerica in particular, should go well beyond estimates that may shift according to region, period, or methodology.[9] Houston argued for a variable definition of literacy within the parameters of specific scribal traditions, which placed an emphasis on the distinction between reading skills and writing competence, and which conceived writing systems as a means toward recitation and public performance, rather than as an end in itself. In the end, even though these writing systems may seem needlessly elaborate, they fulfilled discursive needs in their societies of origin with apt precision. This assessment, by necessity, opposes universalistic characterizations of the dynamics of literacy, epitomized by the depiction of alphabetic literacy as the nemesis of oral literacy.[10]

Writing and reading in preconquest Mesoamerican societies may be best regarded as a continuum of interlocking phenomena that reflected and reproduced social hierarchies and their narratives of origin. An education in nonalphabetic writing systems was reserved to specialists with ties to elite groups. Here, one may highlight appellations that distinguished between producers, such as *amatlacuilo* in Nahuatl and *huezée quíchi* or *huecàa yye* in Valley Zapotec, and interpreters or performers of texts, *amapohuani* and *tlamatini* in Nahuatl and *pèni huílla* and *péni huelàba yye* in Valley Zapotec. There also existed a distinction between records housed in temples and palaces containing the history and genealogy of ruling lineages, *xiuhpohualli* in Nahuatl and *quijchi tija* in Valley Zapotec, and public pictographic records in the architectural program of civil and religious buildings.[11] In Zapotec, the divinatory calendar and pictorial representation seem to be linked by a deep etymological tie: piyè, the routine designation for calendars, may be analyzed as consisting of the animacy marker *pi-* and the root *-yye*, "picture, letter, drawn or painted image."[12]

It is difficult to estimate the access of commoners to an education in nonalphabetic writing; still, some tantalizing observations suggest that literacy practices circulated beyond the social networks presided by rulers and priests. For instance, Itzcoatl (1428–40), the first Mexica emperor to extend Mexica-Tenochca hegemony beyond the Basin of Mexico, attempted to keep "the count of days, the paper of the years, the count of years, the paper of dreams" out of reach of commoners by burning them: "The Mexica rulers made an agreement; they said: 'It is not necessary that every man know the black, the red [*in tlilli, in tlapalli*]; what is carried, transported on one's back [political authority] will be debased, and this will only spread *nahuallotl* over the land.' With this, much falsehood was uprooted."[13] López Austin has proposed that Itzcoatl's attempt to curb the spread of pictorial writing—designated here as *in tlilli in tlapalli*, "the black, the red"—was a measure against the proliferation of "man-gods": ritual specialists who laid claim to ritual knowledge and its concomitant symbolic authority through their use of calendrical and historical records.[14] Even though Itzcoatl's attempts at censorship remain poorly understood, this passage conveys the pointed suggestion that the Mexica state did not exercise a monopoly over either literacy or ritual practices.

After the conquest, missionaries assessed Mesoamerican literacy practices in a variety of ways, often according to it the epistemic weight that alphabetic writing bore in European societies. In a much-quoted instance that was disseminated through fray Juan de Torquemada's 1615 *Monarquía Indiana*, fray Jerónimo de Mendieta noted the use of pictographic characters with phonetic values to record the *Pater Noster*,[15] and fray Diego Valadés argued that the natives of New Spain employed a species of what Aristotle called "artificial memory," exercised through the use of places and images, "in the elucidation of their affairs."[16]

In a cardinal passage written for a 1541 introduction to his historical narrative about Mexica society and the early postconquest period, fray Toribio Motolinia argued that the Mexica possessed five types of pictographic "books": of "years and times," of "the days and feasts they had throughout the year," of "the dreams, delusions, vanities and auguries they believed in," of "the baptism and names they gave to children," and of "rites, ceremonies, and auguries they had regarding marriage." In an interpretive move that epitomized the cautious ambivalence of subsequent generations, Motolinia declared that only the first kind of book was trustworthy, as it "speaks the truth, for, although barbarous and illiterate, they had a very orderly count of times, days, weeks, months, and years."[17] Motolinia did not explicitly include historical narratives in his classification, but his belief in their validity is vouchsafed by the rest of his work, which he claims is based on his understanding of native readings of the book of xiuhpohualli, "the count of [365-day] years."

Motolinia regards the native count of years as unassailable and everything else as doubtful. This eloquent characterization should be seen as a discursive pirouette that avoids passing judgment on the epistemic validity of genres that Spanish interpreters relied on in order to construct a coherent narrative of native societies.[18] Since native historical accounts weave through a past shot through with non-Christian deities, sacrifices, and offerings, how was a Spanish interpreter to discriminate between truth and demonic delusion? Motolinia does not answer this question directly, but his pragmatic response seems to be a recasting of Mexica historical narratives that emphasizes warfare, migration, and genealogical events. This approach prefigures subsequent solutions, which combined a serious regard for native literacy practices and a relatively high degree of confidence on the accuracy of native historical narratives with lasting suspicions about the demonic influence encoded in native accounts that touched on calendrical and ritual practices.

Certainly, this guarded but ambivalent attitude did not inhibit the production of native historical and genealogical records, as attested by the relatively large corpus of alphabetic texts in Nahuatl containing narrative or genealogical accounts of the ancient and recent past that were produced from the middle decades of the sixteenth century until the mid-nineteenth century, a trend that also existed in Zapotec-speaking communities in Oaxaca. These genres have been analyzed by several generations of scholars; three of them researched in recent times are land surveys and maps;[19] *títulos primordiales,* "primordial titles," or foundational historical narratives sometimes backdated to the early sixteenth century;[20] and pictorial narrative or alphabetic historical accounts.[21]

A more modest output of scholarly works about colonial Nahua and Zapotec ritual and devotional texts exists, but it includes the important pioneering work of López Austin, Andrews and Hassig, and Coe and Whittaker on the Nahua incantations transcribed by Ruiz de Alarcón, of Louise Burkhart on prayers, songs, and devotional texts independently produced by Nahua authors,[22] of Berlin on the "ancient beliefs" in Zapotec Sola,[23] and of Alcina Franch on Northern Zapotec calendars.[24] This chapter seeks to contribute to such efforts, bearing in mind that one moves into uncertain terrain, as clandestine native texts tend to be fragmentary and difficult to place within textual or performative contexts.[25] Thus, the four case studies below focus on the social spaces created and maintained through the circulation of these texts. This approach heeds Joanne Rappaport's call to define literacy within a clearly delineated context of social relations,[26] and dovetails with Roger Chartier's influential assessment of the diversity of literacy practices in Renaissance and baroque Europe.[27]

THE ORAL AND WRITTEN REPRODUCTION OF
NAHUA RITUAL KNOWLEDGE

There exist at least five references in Ruiz de Alarcón's *Tratado* to incantations independently transcribed by literate ritual specialists. The most egregious example is an incantation used for carrying loads and propitiating safe travel, discovered after one of his informants claimed to have chanced upon a copy of it. Francisco de Santiago, who was raised in Ruiz de Alarcón's home, found a text on a stretch of road and brought it to his benefactor, who had no difficulty in establishing its origin because it was signed by its owner, the deacon of Cuetlaxxochitla. When summoned, the deacon confessed that the original text had been lost, and that he had no information about its author.[28] This association between public office and clandestine text production would be a recurring one throughout the seventeenth century. Another independently produced text recorded an incantation to hunt deer with a snare. Most of the incantations recorded in this treatise have two to four sections, but this one is the longest, with twenty-two sections. This text was not a mere alphabetic transcription, as it also included metalinguistic comments. At the end of the incantation's seventeenth section, Ruiz de Alarcón reports that "it then says on the paper: *Otlamic: nauhcampa toyohuaz. Tic yehecoz*; [which means] that, once the incantation has finished, you shall shout very loudly toward the four directions."[29] Moreover, Ruiz de Alarcón quotes metalinguistic content in italics in his original manuscript: "If after this they have not come, they are ordered—*yoyohuaz coyotzaziz quitoz*—to howl repeatedly and to say *tahui*."[30]

The only literate ritual specialist Ruiz de Alarcón mentions by name was a woman called Petronilla; she was a healer from Tlayacapan who cured tertian fever with an incantation. Petronilla would prepare an infusion of the *coanenepilli* plant with rue and then utter an incantation. "According to the paper on which she had this incantation written," the extirpator affirmed, "it began with *ica motlatlauhtia in atl*, which in Spanish means 'With this prayer, one begs the water for something.'"[31] This incantation, only three sentences long, propitiated the water deity Chalchihuitl Icue. As noted by Lockhart,[32] its author employed tropes that occur frequently in Nahua doctrinal discourse: the patient was called *Dios itlachihualtzin*, "God's creature," and fever's pain became *in ilhuicac justicia*, "heavenly justice." The incorporation of Christian formulae memorized through the teaching of the doctrine recurs in a fourth incantation seized in written form. In an incantation to induce sleep in a victim in order to perform theft or sexual assault, an anonymous hypnotist,[33] after claiming to be Tezcatlipoca, Xolotl, and Xipe, prudently closes the spell with the formula *in nomine domini*, "In the name of the Lord . . ."[34]

A fifth and final written incantation may feature nonalphabetical signs inserted in the text. In order to transcribe an enigmatic incantation for bleeding that employs one or more epithets to name each of the participants in the performance—veins, hands, needle, blood, water, illness— Ruiz de Alarcón labeled each epithet with a letter. This incantation made a distinct impression on the experienced priest, since he analyzed it in detail in a lengthy letter to Archbishop Pérez de la Serna. When he comes to the epithet for the illness to be remedied by bleeding, Ruiz de Alarcón adds a description of a character that appeared in the original text:

Hark! Contain yourselves, gods of the wilderness, etc., [which is] where they place this character X, and they interpret it as the Enemy or Beelzebub, who may, as a being superior to those that are called gods of the wilderness or lesser [gods], drive them away from the place where they hurt the ill person. Thus, [the specialist] calls them "green ones," and then "green spiders," and he places another character there, which—since demons are called "spiders" and illnesses depicted as colors—seems to convey that these enemies cause the illness.[35]

In the original manuscript, the first character appears as an X; according to Ruiz de Alarcón, this icon represented a powerful entity that caused illness, embodied as green spiders, to scatter away. An unspecified character represented the illness-bearing spiders. Even if Ruiz de Alarcón copied this incantation from a text featuring actual nonalphabetic elements, this enigmatic graphic representation did not survive the transcription process.

How did the reproduction of ritual knowledge through oral means compare to its spread through transcriptions? A previous chapter outlined a key rhetorical trait of the Nahual Names genre: the use of epithets featuring morphological, syntactic, semantic, or syllabic parallelism to refer to entities propitiated in the course of the incantation. One of the epithets with the widest distribution in this corpus is that of piciyetl, *Nicotiana rustica*, an herbaceous species of tobacco used so often that Ruiz de Alarcón likened it to "the little dog who comes to all the wedding feasts."[36] The broad distribution of this epithet facilitates a circumscribed analysis of its reported use in incantations transcribed by Ruiz de Alarcón in a fifteen-year period (1614–29) in the Cohuixca and Tlalhuica communities.

The canonical form of the piciyetl epithet, as attested from seven variants drawn from six different incantations, can be defined as a two-part parallel template. The first part is a numerical form, *chiucnauh*, "Nine [Times],"[37] which occurs in both initial sections of the parallel epithet. The second part is a variable element referring to an item that has been pounded with a stone (*tlatetzohtzonalli*), slapped with a stone (*tlatecapanilli*), or crumbled by hand (*tlahtlamatelolli*). The epithet always contained two phrases referring to items that were acted upon in two different ways. For instance, the spell for trapping deer (*Tratado* II: 8) refers to piciyetl as *chiucnauh tlatetzohtzonalli, chiucnauh tlatecapanilli*, "Nine (times) Stone-Pounded One," "Nine (times) Stone-Slapped One," and uses a variant of this epithet that differs minimally from the first one. The remaining five variants (*Tratado* V: 1, VI: 3, VI: 4, VI: 24) are quite similar in morphological terms to the two written variants. In fact, setting aside the use of absolutive or honorific suffixes by different incantation authors (*-tli, -li, -tzin*, or none), it appears that the parallel epithet for the piciyetl is customarily constructed with only four verbal stems: *tzohtzon-* (pounding), *capan-* (slapping), *matelo-* (crumbling), and the more unusual *patlan-* (flying). A less canonical version of the piciyetl epithet, used

in only two instances, is rendered either as *xoxohuic tlatecapaniltzin,
xoxohuic tlatetzohtzonaltzin*, "Green Stone-Slapped One, Green Stone-
Pounded One" (Tratado II: 4), or *cozouhqui tlamacazqui, xoxouhqui
tlamacazqui*, "Yellow Priest, Green Priest" (Tratado V: 1).

In a sample of nine incantations collected by Ruiz de Alarcón from
literate users or through oral elicitation, this particular epithet possesses
a well-defined canonical form that was easily committed to memory due
to its repetitive structure. Excluding the two unusual epithet alluding to
color terms, the eight canonical variants show minor morphological and
semantic variability and a strong similarity in their syntactic structure.
This sample exhibits the constrained, slight modifications that one would
expect from a group of ritual specialists who repeated from memory an
epithet transmitted orally from one generation to another. Even in two
independent transcriptions, the deer-hunting incantation and the spell
for tertian fever, the piciyetl epithet partook of such morphological and
semantic variability.

It may be tempting to regard these results as merely confirming the
existence of a strong oral culture in the Cohuixca-Tlalhuica region; after
all, Ruiz de Alarcón identifies an incantation as transcribed by specialists only in five cases, or about 7 percent of the corpus. This example
suggests three distinct conclusions: first, that the ritual knowledge that
extirpators encountered in the Nahua hinterlands was linked to oral
transmission dynamics that survived nearly a century of political change,
demographic upheaval, and social engineering; second, that the control
and elicitation of oral performance, as shown by metalinguistic directions and the strong continuities between transcribed and oral expression in the piciyetl epithets, was a major concern behind the transcription
of incantations; and third, that oral and written transmission could coexist with ease in the social spaces where ritual specialists operated. The
third case study in this chapter expands on this last conclusion by examining the articulation of social spaces in which clandestine native authors
operated in Oaxaca.

A NAHUA ASTRONOMICAL AND DEVOTIONAL
MISCELLANY

Strict measures against the possession and circulation of unauthorized
manuscript copies of devotional works emerged from the First (1555)
and Third (1585) Mexican Church Councils, and these directives were
confirmed by the Council of Trent. Nonetheless, some indigenous intel-
lectuals avoided Tridentine scrutiny by circulating or sharing manuscript

copies in a clandestine manner among discreet circles of readers. Even though few extant examples exist of native devotional works that may have circulated in this manner, a brief glance at some of the known specimens is deeply revealing. In this section, I provide a brief overview of the Bibliothèque Nationale de France's Fonds Mexicain 381 (henceforth BNF-Mex 381), a manuscript Nahuatl miscellany of devotional and divinatory texts.[38] Two criteria render this unusual text relevant: first of all, it shows the broad range of genres and topics that clandestine Nahuatl texts could have addressed; second, since its production and usage is roughly contemporary with both the Ruiz de Alarcón incantations and the Sola divinatory texts, its contents reflect the intentions of a group of native readers whose interests contrasted with those of the ritual specialists represented in the other two case studies.

BNF-Mex 381 is a sixty-page manuscript that was once part of the collection of the eighteenth-century Italian scholar and historian Lorenzo Boturini. It is likely that it was bought in Mexico, along with other works owned by Boturini, by the French scholar Joseph-Marie Aubin, who took his priceless collection with him to Paris in 1840. While it is not absolutely certain that this miscellanea existed in its present form before joining Boturini's collection around the 1730s, the fact that it features several alternating hands, with Hand 1 being responsible for an initial section and the final section of the manuscript, suggests that this manuscript was copied by more than one literate native. A remarkable feature of BNF-Mex 381 is the diversity of genres it contains. The manuscript begins with a set of Nahuatl prayers for meditation, a Spanish prayer to the Virgin, a devotional enumeration of the thorns in Christ's crown, a *persignum crucis* in Nahuatl and Otomi, a Nahuatl translation of a Latin text about the life of Saint Nicholas Tolentino, a set of Latin prayers recorded in the equivocating transcription of a scribe who was a native speaker of Nahuatl, assorted prayers in Latin, Spanish, and Nahuatl, a correlation between the Gregorian months of April to December and the twenty Matlatzinca day signs written without numerical coefficients,[39] a list of holy days, and, most striking of all, a brief text on the signs of the Zodiac and on their correlation with the days and months of the Christian calendar. The manuscript closes with a short text about the Eucharist.

This miscellanea appears to have been in use from the early 1630s to the mid-1650s: on page 24, one finds a list of holy days with the annotation "a[n]nus 1633"; on page 45, there is a note about the feast of the Assumption in 1639; on the margins of the correlation between the Matlatzinca day sign count and the Gregorian calendar, a note indicates that a certain Caterina fled her home in 1654. Unfortunately, as is the case with other miscellaneous works, it is impossible to ascertain either the authors' identity or the exact location in which it was produced. Nahuatl predominates in the text, but the presence of Otomi and Matlatzinca terms suggests that the manuscript was produced by Nahuatl-speaking authors who lived close to speakers of Otomanguean languages in regions west and northwest of the Toluca Valley, in or near the jurisdictions of Querétaro, Metepec, or Temazcaltepec. This is precisely the area where two clergymen, Nahuatl-speaker Ponce de León and Matlatzinca-speaker Gutiérrez Bocanegra, conducted idolatry eradication efforts against literate specialists in 1610 and confiscated their devotional texts. Given the dates referring to the 1630s and the 1650s in BNF-Mex 381, the texts contained in this miscellaneous work were probably not collected in 1610, although a distant possibility is that some of the undated texts were indeed surrendered to Ponce de León.

The list of holidays on page 24, and the correlations between days of the week, planets, months, and signs of the zodiac on pages 47 to 54 suggest these sections were inspired by a *reportorio de los tiempos*. This early modern genre shared some traits with the book of hours and the almanac genre—a correlation between days of the months and days of the week indicated by the dominical letters *A* to *g*, a list of Christian holidays, and the canonical correlation between months and signs of the zodiac—but also included extensive information on the correlations among planets, months, days of the week, and signs of the zodiac, provided a characterization of personality types by zodiac signs, and usually included tables detailing moon phases for a particular time period (1495 to 1550, for example), and for a specific geographical location (such as Barcelona, Madrid, or Mexico City). Some reportorios even included instructions on common early modern healing practices, such as bleeding and cupping.

Among the most influential examples of printed reportorio editions, one could cite Bernat de Granollach's 1485 Catalan-language *Lunari*, Andrés de Li's 1495 *Reportorio de los tiempos*,[40] Jerónimo de Cháves's 1572 *Chronographia o Reportorio de los tiempos*, Bartolomé Hera y de la Varra's 1584 *Reportorio del mundo particular, de las spheras del cielo y orbes elementales*, and the most influential and perhaps most widely circulated *reportorio* in seventeenth-century New Spain, which was written with a regional readership in mind: Enrico Martínez's *Reportorio de los tiempos e historia natural de Nueva España*, printed in Mexico City in 1606.[41] Spanish reportorios circulated in Mexico City well before the appearance of Martínez's work: a lot of 341 books sold by bookseller Alonso Losa in July 1576 includes a *Chronografia o Repertorio* [sic], probably a copy of Cháves's text, and Irving Leonard observes that this work appears in the list of books inspected, but not necessarily confiscated, by inquisitors as they inspected ships arriving in New Spain from Europe.[42] In fact, during the expansion and reorganization of the Colegio de Santa Cruz in Tlatelolco in 1572 and 1573, the Franciscans Molina and Sahagún offered for sale several books from the school's collection in order to raise funds; among them, a *Reportorio*, valued at five pesos, is listed.[43]

Since these books circulated and were sold in Central Mexico without attracting great scrutiny, it is not surprising to find that Nahua readers studied and attempted to render reportorios and books of hours. The most salient example of the refashioning of a book of hours by Nahua authors is found in the first eight pages of the *Codex Mexicanus*.[44] In this text, each of these pages corresponds to a month in the Christian calendar, and the codex's surviving pages run from May to December. On each page, the days of the week are represented by letters, and important saints' days are spelled out in syllabograms.[45] This manuscript also includes a chart with the twelve signs of the zodiac.

Another Nahua attempt to interpret the European zodiac that presents a series of parallels with BNF-Mex 381 is an eight-page manuscript appended to a printed copy of Pedro de Gante's 1553 *Doctrina christiana en lengua mexicana*. This Nahuatl text, entitled *Reperdorio de los dienpos* [*sic*], was transcribed by an anonymous sixteenth-century hand. López Austin's translation and analysis of this *Reperdorio* allow a comparison with the contents of BNF-Mex 381.[46] Both texts contain predictions about agricultural practices, health, and well-being for each of the twelve months of the Latin calendar, which are paired with signs of the zodiac, and both offer the characterizations of personality types by signs of the zodiac that are a mainstay of the reportorio genre. Unlike the *Reperdorio*, BNF-Mex 381 offers predictions for each of the days of the week, contains calendrical lists, and shows a series of correlations among primordial elements, days, months, and zodiac signs.

Pages 47–54 of BNF-Mex 381 suggest that its Nahua author(s) adapted them from a reportorio, for they feature a brief text on the cardinal winds, a correlation among days of the week, signs of the zodiac, and primordial elements, and a correlation between months and zodiacal signs. Some elements in this Nahua appropriation imply that its author consulted a reportorio displaying canonical images for the twelve zodiac signs with no help or supervision from a nonindigenous reader. In the primarily visual reading of the signs of the zodiac by this anonymous Nahua interpreter, the eight signs represented by primarily iconographic signs (Aries, Taurus, Cancer, Leo, Virgo, Scorpio, Capricorn, Aquarius, Pisces) are given an accurate Nahuatl gloss. The icons for three signs are rendered equivocally in Nahuatl: the twins of Gemini become Wise

Men, or *tlamatinime*; Libra's scales are read as Merchant, or *pochtecatl*, and Sagittarius's centaur turns into Deer Man, or *tlacamaçatl*.[47] Surprisingly, there are faint echoes of this ambivalent reading in the zodiac-sign glosses provided by the Nahua annalist Chimalpahin. At the end of a manuscript section dedicated to the Mexica month count, Chimalpahin provided a Nahuatl translation for each zodiac sign that employed Spanish lexical items and Nahuatl glosses.[48] Thus, he translated Libra with the Spanish term *balanza*, and Sagittarius with both Spanish and Nahuatl terms—*centauro* and *tlacamaçatl*. As for Gemini, Chimalpahin wrote a lengthy explanation that referred in an indirect manner to twins: "The astrologers render it as two children who embrace each other. Thus, they say that, when the two are born, they therefore love each other much; they therefore never quarrel."[49]

The Nahuatl text about the signs of the Zodiac in BNF-Mex 381 is not a literal rendition of a Spanish reportorio; it rather seems that the authors browsed through a reportorio, making partial notes on its contents. Some lexical clues indicate that these Nahuatl students of the zodiac used a printed or manuscript version of Andrés de Li's popular *Reportorio de los tiempos*, first printed in Zaragoza in 1495. In Li's *Reportorio*, after a brief discussion of months, hours, and planets, there begins a section about the correlations between the nine heavens and the seven planets (Moon, Mercury, Venus, Sun, Mars, Jupiter, and Saturn). This section opens with the following words:

The planets are listed below.

On the first heaven and the seventh planet, **which is the moon, and which has its seat within it** [the first heaven].

The first heaven is where the moon has its seat; this is the lowest planet, the seventh one, which is located in the lowest circle of the [celestial] sphere; its circle is completed after eight years, and it is the lord of the seventh and last climate.[50]

On the other hand, after stating the correlations between months and zodiac signs with the Nahuatl glosses discussed above, a new section in BNF-Mex 381 begins with the following mixture of Nahuatl and Spanish words:

Sunday, **the planets are listed below.** First, the grammar. He is a lord, Monday. The second *mer*-heaven [*sic*] **planets, which is the moon, and which has its seat within it.** Sterile person. Tuesday, the third one, which is Mars. Third planets [*sic*] knight. Wednesday. The second heaven, which is Mercury, which is planets. He will become a doctor.[51]

It appears as if the Nahuatl authors incorporated the phrases "The planets are listed below" (*Siguense los planetas*) and "which is the moon, and which has its seat within it" (*que es la luna que tiene en el su asiento*), found verbatim in Li's *Reportorio*, into a jumble of notes in Spanish and Nahuatl. In any case, as amateur European astrologers, these writers attempted to grasp the correlations between signs of the zodiac, periods of time, and primordial elements—Earth, Wind, Fire, and Water—by consulting a reportorio that may have been based on Li's text. Nonetheless, the contents of BNF-Mex 381 do not provide a section-by-section parallel to Li's *Reportorio* and introduce topics that are not treated in this text. Since its Nahua author(s) were apparently not interested in a literal translation of the reportorio that was consulted, it would be difficult to link their work with a single printed or manuscript reportorio edition. However, the interest of Nahua writers in Li's publication is confirmed by the existence of a lengthier text produced by several copyists, some of whom worked on this text in the mid-eighteenth century: a 121-folio manuscript now preserved at the Tropenmuseum in the Netherlands, which provides a Nahuatl translation of most of the sections in Li's *Reportorio* and includes glosses from various other sources.[52]

The Nahuatl reportorio section in BNF-Mex 381 seems to follow its own peculiar logic. For example, a section on page 49 shows that each day of the week is related to one or two signs of the zodiac, to primordial elements, and to a particular archangel. In addition, an entire section is devoted to the following correlation between signs and elements (Spanish or Latin terms are shown in italics below):

First Planet. Every *sign* is counted here. During *Aries*, they are atop Fire; during *Leo*, they are in the middle; during *Sagittarius*, they are at the bottom of Fire, which lights up all the days. During *Taurus*, they are on top of Earth; during *Virgo*, they are in the middle of Earth; during *Capricorn*, they are at the bottom of Earth. During *Gemini*, they are on top of Wind; during *Libra*, they are in the middle of Wind; during *Aquarius*, they are at the bottom of Wind. During *Cancer*, they are on top of Water; during *Scorpio*, they are in the middle of Water; during *Pisces*, they are at the bottom of Water.[53]

The main section of this reportorio text contains seven paragraphs dedicated to the days of the week, beginning with Sunday. Each paragraph gives a brief discussion of the planet and zodiac sign born on that day, gives a forecast applicable to people born on that day, and points out whether illnesses may be easy or difficult to cure on that particular day. For example, the text's author(s) make the following remarks about Sunday:

Here it is written about all kinds of *planetas*, and all kinds of births. In the manner of the reportorio, the days are mentioned here. At dawn on *Sunday*, which is called *the first [prayer?]*, there the lords are born. The commoner will be born, and [this is] what his work is, what happens here on Earth when he is born: This child will then be summoned; since he knows his [reportorio], he will explain it to the people. This is how *Leo* comes to take he who is born under it: His body is a thing of wonder: precious stone, turquoise, emerald. His eyes are a frightening thing; his body is very red. Thus, he goes about on earth; he truly deserves to be feared, and has great renown. When he gets sick, he will get very wet; when he is given food, he will not let it go as soon as he comes to eat it. He will be coming in and out of his senses, he whose name is *Leo*. Then, he will die quickly; he who is of this birth will not heal.[54]

The characteristics and prognosis associated with people born under Leo may seem peculiar; nonetheless, the Nahua authors described here a recognizable cluster of traits that distinguished those born under this sign, according to early modern almanacs. Both this text and the afore-mentioned Nahuatl *Reperdorio* analyzed by López Austin agree on the characteristics of people born under Leo. In BNF-Mex 381, it is said that people born under Leo will live "deserving much respect, with much fame." The *Reperdorio* states the following about people born under Leo: "One bows before them; they are young men with a great heart, they are courageous."[55] In fact, the characterization of people born under Leo that appears in Enrico Martínez's 1606 *Reportorio* states that those born under Leo "are usually of good height, have blue eyes; they are bold by nature; . . . they will thrive in any manner of literary tasks, if they embrace them, and also in any exercise of wit; . . . they are usually some-what sad, prone to danger, and besieged by stomach pains."[56] Hence, BNF-Mex 381 and Martínez depict a somewhat convergent portrait of Leos. While the Spanish text assigns blue eyes to them, the Nahuatl text depicts their glance as "a frightening thing," which could be a Nahua misreading of *zarco*, "blue-eyed"; if the Spanish text emphasizes their literary prowess and wit, the Nahua text predicts those born on Leo will know how to explain the reportorio. The danger and stomach illnesses mentioned in passing by Martínez acquire a very specific set of predic-tions for illness from a Nahua perspective: people born on this day will eat like wild beasts, lapse in and out of their senses, and then die a quick death, with no possibility of being healed.

The appropriation of a Spanish reportorio and its adaptation to a Nahua cultural context bears witness to the great interest with which the authors and users of the Codex Mexicanus and the BNF-Mex 381 investigated European divinatory practices. The differences between the context of production of a reportorio and that of BNF-Mex 381 kept this act of appropriation from becoming a simple transfer of contents. In transcribing, glossing, and reinterpreting the contents of a Spanish reportorio, the anonymous Nahua writers had neither the possibility nor

the interest of replicating the encoded cultural assumptions that characterized the "horizon of expectations," to use Hans Robert Jauss's lucid
term,[57] of the reportorio genre. Paradoxically, such a selective appropriation of the European zodiac resulted in the emergence of a novel textual
genre, the Nahua reportorio, whose horizon of expectation was still in
the formative stages. This concern with the use of European ritual techniques seems to indicate a process of substitution of the tonalamatl, the
Nahua ritual calendar text, with a new textual genre based on Christian
divinatory techniques. In contrast with this tendency, other native cohorts of readers continued to produce and circulate copies of indigenous
calendars.

LITERACY AND CLANDESTINE DEVOTIONAL
SPHERES IN SOUTHERN OAXACA

In Oaxaca, the earliest evidence about the clandestine circulation of
ritual texts in seventeenth-century native villages comes from a rather
marginal area: two Amuzgo-speaking towns in the jurisdictions of
Igualapa and Xicayán (de Nieto), in the southwestern Oaxaca coastal
area. This incident took place in the early years of the ecclesiastical
career of Gerónimo Curiel, who served as beneficiado of the Amuzgo
towns of Xochistlahuaca and Xicayán de Tovar between 1616 and 1635,
and as beneficiado of Teotitlán del Camino from 1635 until at least the
early 1640s.[58] Curiel, who was fluent in Amuzgo, Mazatec, and Nahuatl,
claimed to have authored translations of the Christian doctrine into some
of these languages. From the perspective of Bishop Bohórquez, these
traits made Curiel an ideal extirpator, and thus he served the diocese
as a judge against idolaters for at least two decades after his appointment in 1622. In this capacity, he toured his parish "seizing idols, books,
characters, and other instruments of idolatry." In a brief discussion of his
career, Curiel highlighted his prosecution of an Amuzgo cacique, whom
he identifies as a sorcerer and as a proselytizer. In 1633, Curiel tried this
unnamed ruler, seized "the books, characters and instruments which he
employed," and sentenced him to hard labor at the fort of Acapulco.[59]

Two years after Curiel passed this notably harsh sentence, Gonzalo de
Balsalobre, a young secular priest residing in the town of San Miguel Sola
in south-central Oaxaca, had his first confrontation with Diego Luis, a
Zapotec literate specialist, as noted in Chapter 4 above. Diego Luis had
in his possession a calendrical text written in Chatino, a member of the
Proto-Zapotecan language family, which he had translated into Solteco,
the Zapotec variant spoken in Sola. Apparently, the original text had

come from Lorenzo Martín, a principal of the Chatino-speaking town
of Juquila, who had given it to Félix de Alvarado, who had passed it on
to Diego Luis. In 1635, Balsalobre brought Diego Luis to trial, confiscated the offending calendar, and had it burned before the door of Sola's
church, after parading Diego Luis through town as a penitent.[60]

This sentence would by no means end the circulation of ritual texts
in Sola. In February 1654, a surprised Balsalobre learned, as he interrogated Lorenzo Martín, one of Diego Luis's sons, that a copy of the text
had eluded the flames. Martín had made a transcription of his father's
text so he would learn to use it before the 1635 trial, and later he saw
the original burn during his father's auto. When Diego Luis returned
from exile, Martín presented him with the surviving copy of his text.[61]
Balsalobre began investigating Diego Luis for reincidence in idolatrous
practices in December 1653. Between 1653 and 1654, the beneficiado
uncovered extensive evidence about the clandestine circulation of ritual
texts and about one hundred clients who consulted him or had access to
his calendars.[62]

Berlin's study of the Balsalobre trial materials provides a substantial
description of the network of calendar authors, users, and owners in
Sola,[63] but the analysis presented here does not share one of Berlin's
crucial assumptions. In the Sola trials, native specialists were often but
unsystematically designated with the rather sarcastic designation of
letrado, a term referring to officials and clerks in Spanish civil courts
that Balsalobre used for literate ritual practitioners, perhaps in the same
ironic spirit that drove earlier chroniclers to transform *papauhqui*, a
term for Mexica priests, into *papa*, "pope." Even though Berlin assumed
that every identification of a specialist in the trial records as letrado indicated that he or she owned a ritual text, this assertion is often impossible
to corroborate, as no specific mention of text ownership is made in each
instance. However, if one uses the more stringent criterion of designating
a letrado as a text owner only if a mention of ownership is made in the
trial records, Berlin's group of sixty-one letrados is whittled down to a
list of thirty-eight ritual-text owners.

Paradoxically, these sources allow a detailed reconstruction of social
networks through which calendars were exchanged, but few insights into
the contents of these texts, which were destroyed by Balsalobre. The
texts contained the names of the thirteen gods in the local pantheon, and
they are sometimes referred to as "books of the thirteen gods." Diego
Luis's detailed testimony about the thirteen deities that governed the
Zapotec calendar, as discussed in the previous chapter, indicates that
the texts recorded calendrical information. Text descriptions are made
only incidentally, and few details about their format or contents are ad-

dressed. For example, Balsalobre proffers the following description of a text owned by Melchor López, an illiterate inhabitant of San Francisco Sola who obtained it from Diego Luis: "After comparing the said book with the other one found in Lorenzo Martín's possession, it appears to be one and the same, except for some symbols or characters which the second book bears on its last pages."[64] These trial records, however, do not mention incantations, spells, or songs.

The Sola texts were kept within the immediate family of their authors or owners and passed on as treasured possessions from one generation to another. According to Marcial Ramírez, a semiliterate cantor in the town of Los Reyes near Sola, Diego Luis made a copy of a ritual text for his father Cristóbal Ramírez, which he had inherited after his father's death, along with all of his papers. Marcial asserted that he had burned this book after "seeing that it was an evil thing," but no other witness corroborated this act.[65] Other Sola residents who inherited calendars avowed keeping them, even if they were illiterate or made little use of their texts. At the trial of the illiterate specialist Gracia Margarita, who did not use texts as a ritual practitioner, and her husband Miguel Martín, who was literate, but did not work as a ritual specialist, Miguel recounted how the book of his dead father-in-law, the letrado Luis López, was kept in the family long after his death, until it was seized by Balsalobre's agents in April 1654:

Through the interpreter, [Miguel Martín] declared that about seven years ago, when Diego Luis was in his home—in which [Diego Luis] lived because he had married [María], his mother-in-law and the mother of his wife—his wife opened a box and took out a small book written entirely by hand. She showed it to said Diego Luis, saying that it was the book of the devil that his father Luis López had left them, and which her foster father Melchor Xuárez had used, for after the death of said Luis López [Melchor] had married her mother, and he was also a letrado and gave consultations to the Indians. Then, Diego Luis leafed through said book and recognized the handwriting, and said it belonged to Luis López, and was just like one he used himself.[66]

This passage uncovers an interesting but still enigmatic axis of kinship relations through which ritual knowledge was passed on among specialists associated with the same household, as shown in Figure 5.1. This household was established by Luis López, a literate specialist from San Juan Sola, who married a woman known only as María, and fathered Gracia Margarita. Luis López passed on ritual knowledge and a book containing "the thirteen gods of the Gentiles"[67] to his neighbor, Esteban de Aquino, and a copy of one of his texts ended up in the hands of Diego Luis. Diego Luis had in turn given or sold copies of ritual texts to at least seven clients in Sola. In spite of the fact that María was not identified as

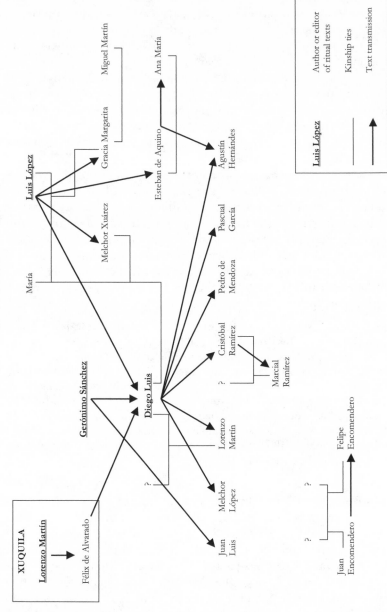

PARISH OF SOLA

XUQUILA

Lorenzo Martín

Félix de Alvarado

Gerónimo Sánchez

Diego Luis

Luis López

María

Melchor Xuárez

Gracia Margarita

Miguel Martín

Esteban de Aquino

Ana María

Agustín
Hernándes

Pascual
García

Pedro de
Mendoza

Cristóbal
Ramírez

Marcial
Ramírez

Lorenzo
Martín

Melchor
López

Juan
Luis

Juan
Encomendero

Felipe
Encomendero

Luis López

Author or editor
of ritual texts

Kinship ties

Text transmission

FIGURE 5.1   Clandestine Circulation Network for Ritual Texts in Sola (Oaxaca), 1629–1654.
SOURCE: AGN-Inq

either a specialist or an author of ritual texts, three of the most influential literate specialists in Sola lived in her household. After the death of Luis López circa 1629, María was remarried to Melchor Xuárez; Aquino began to work as a ritual specialist and passed on ritual knowledge to his wife Ana, who was also consulted for divination occasionally, when Aquino was drunk or unavailable.[68] Melchor Xuárez not only inherited Luis López's widow but also his ritual text, which he used for divination purposes. At some point between 1629 and 1647, Melchor Xuárez died or left María, and she married a ritual specialist for the third time, Diego Luis, who came to live in her house. After Esteban de Aquino's death circa 1652, his widow Ana inherited the ritual text that Aquino had obtained from Luis López.

The Sola ritual texts not only circulated among specialists and clients linked by kinship or friendship ties, but were also copied for a reasonable fee. According to one of Diego Luis's depositions, Diego Luis made a copy of the "book of thirteen gods" for one of his clients, the letrado Pedro Mendoza, and charged him one peso as payment for his work. Fifteen days after this purchase, Diego Luis gave him a lesson on the usage of calendars. After the following fifteen days, he went back to Pedro's house, gave him a copy, and "taught him the manner in which [Pedro] would use it, because said witness knows how to read and write. Upon receipt of said book, [Pedro] paid him one peso for his work; three or four months later, [Diego Luis] went back to Pedro's house upon his request so he would teach him again how to use such book, and this witness taught him. However, since this is difficult, he thinks that [Pedro] was not able to learn it."[69]

This testimony suggests that being able to elicit information from and interpreting the ritual texts authored by Diego Luis was a skill that went beyond simple literacy. In the example above, Pedro Mendoza happens to have been fully literate, but still he took lessons from Diego Luis in order to learn to interpret the calendars, but failed in this attempt. Some less experienced specialists valued ritual texts enough to have owned a copy, even if they were not fully capable of interpreting them. Similarly, an illiterate student of Diego Luis, Melchor López, admitted in his declaration that he had not been able to comprehend all the contents of his book. Although he was skilled enough to divine an appropriate day for the harvesting the first ears of corn and for the offering of alms at the church, more difficult cases called for consultations with Diego Luis.[70] Sometime around 1634, Diego Luis made a copy of a ritual text for the letrado Cristóbal Ramírez. After owning this copy for fourteen years, Cristóbal confessed to his son Marcial that he had not been able to fully understand the manner in which the text should be interpreted. Cristóbal did not pass on even his limited understanding of the text to his son, but he did bestow it as part of his inheritance.[71] Hence, the preservation and copying of calendars did not hinge on their owners' degree of ritual knowledge, or even their literacy status.

THE TIME COUNT OF THE GRANDFATHERS
AND FATHERS OF US ALL

Linguistic and residential compartmentalization are important factors in the social history of Villa Alta, a vast jurisdiction to the northeast of Oaxaca City inhabited by speakers of Chinantec, Mixe, and Zapotec. This region's geography is dominated by a mountainous landscape, and human settlements have traditionally been dispersed throughout valleys, mountaintops, and piedmonts. Such a landscape placed substantial restrictions on travel and communication among the various Zapotec communities of Villa Alta, and between them and the Valley of Oaxaca. Even though each Northern Zapotec town in Villa Alta employed a local speech variant, colonial administrative and linguistic categories emphasized a preexisting ethnic distinction among three Northern Zapotec groups: Caxonos or *bene xhon* in the south; Bixanos or *bene xan* in the north and east; and Nexitzo or *bene xidza* in the northwest reaches of this district.[72]

Still, geographical intricacies were not an obstacle to the dissemination of alphabetic literacy throughout the region. More than 460 documents in Zapotec from Caxonos, Bixanos, and Nexitzo communities now extant at the Archivo Histórico Judicial de Oaxaca (AHJO) and the Archivo General de la Nación (AGN) attest to the importance that written texts held for social and political arrangements within and beyond town boundaries. Between the 1590s and the 1820s, Northern Zapotec villagers produced short texts in a variety of genres. While more than one-third of those extant were testaments, the most popular genres included *memorias* or formal legal statements, bills of sale, testimonies, petitions, and letters. Between 1676 and 1700, a period that corresponds to the probable date of production of the texts discussed below, Zapotec notaries and other literate specialists produced about one-sixth of the corpus of nonclandestine colonial Northern Zapotec texts. Given the extent and diversity of this corpus, which allowed individual villagers or entire communities to defend their interests within the documentary framework of colonial jurisprudence,[73] it is not surprising to find that the number of clandestine Northern Zapotec ritual texts was relatively large.[74]

A collection of booklets copied by Northern Zapotec specialists in the last two decades of the seventeenth century grants us an exceptional opportunity to assess the clandestine production and circulation of ritual texts in Villa Alta. In 1704 and 1705, Oaxaca bishop fray Ángel Maldonado conducted the most ambitious extirpation campaign ever conducted in New Spain. As a result of this initiative, the authorities of forty communities surrendered 107 separate textual units containing alphabetic ritual texts in Bixanos, Caxonos, and Nexitzo Zapotec. Four of these documents, designated as Booklets 100, 101, 102, and 103 by the Archivo General de Indias (AGI), consist of four collections of transcribed ritual songs. The remaining 103 units are copies of the 260-day Zapotec ritual calendar, bound into ninety-nine separate booklets.[75] This calendrical corpus encompasses ninety-one complete calendars, seven calendars with at least 75 percent of the 260 day names, and three calendar fragments, as well as two calendars with aberrant day orders.[76] These texts, along with the better-known Maya books of Chilam Balam, are the two largest extant corpuses of clandestine ritual texts authored by native authors in colonial Spanish America.

These materials received no scholarly attention before the pioneering work of Cristina Zilbermann and José Alcina Franch.[77] Alcina Franch's 1993 monograph examined, except for the four collections of ritual songs, the entire calendrical corpus from Villa Alta. This work retains its status as an overarching summary of some details that appear in the collective confessions, particularly regarding the timing of collective rituals, the items offered, the names of sacred sites, the foodstuffs consumed during rituals, and the pragmatic goals of individual practices. This work also proposes a generally accurate characterization of the two distinct elements of each day form—a prefix or augment, and a root—and contains several calendar transcriptions and reproductions. Alcina Franch and his collaborators, however, had little knowledge about Zapotec languages; therefore, their discussion of linguistic evidence other than calendrical day forms should be regarded as tentative. The section below examines three paramount issues that Alcina Franch's team did not address, given their philological limitations: linguistic and textual evidence regarding the provenance of the booklets; evidence about correlation statements in the calendars; and the social context of production of these texts.

Alcina Franch identifies each calendar he published by place of origin based on the contemporary order of binding of collective confessions and calendars of *legajo*, or archival unit, Audiencia de México 882 at the AGI. Nonetheless, linguistic criteria and annotations found in the calendars strongly suggest that place of origin cannot be assigned by binding order alone. In fact, the order of the collective confessions, collective petitions, lists of absolved individuals, assorted ecclesiastical documents, and of the ninety-nine booklets containing 103 separate calendrical texts and four collections of ritual songs was modified between the early eighteenth century and the 1960s, when the booklets were numbered and an unsystematic pagination was given to the entire legajo.[78] Therefore, extreme caution should be employed before attributing particular booklets to specific communities, since most of them bear no annotations that may link them to their owners.

The Villa Alta calendars demonstrate that, in the last two decades of the seventeenth century, a 260-day divinatory count, or piyè, dating back to 600 BCE was in use in at least forty Zapotec communities along with the *yza*, a vague solar year count of 365 days of preconquest origin. The piyè possessed the same structure reported by Córdova for the Valley of Oaxaca.[79] It consisted of two independent cycles: a group of prefixes that stand for a count from one to thirteen; and twenty nominal roots referring to plants, animals, or forces of nature. The combination of these counts thus provided a unique designation for each of 260 days.[80] This count, called biyé in Northern Zapotec variants, had four major subdivisions of sixty-five days, each composed of five thirteen-day periods.[81]

Since the 260-day count is endless—Day 260, *quecellao* (13-Face), is followed by Day 1, *Yagchila* (1-Cayman), and by the rest of the cycle—the correlation of the colonial Zapotec calendar with the Julian and Gregorian counts can be established only if there exist several internally consistent instances of Gregorian days for which we know the corresponding day in the piyè. Felicitously, Booklet 27, composed by Nexitzo or Bixanos Zapotec speakers, bears such statements and aligned its day count with the dominical letter system.[82] This method was used to label days of the week using the letters *a* through *g* in both European almanacs and colonial Mesoamerican calendars, such as the Q'eqchi Maya calendar from Lanquín,[83] the Codex Mexicanus, and the Matlatzinca calendar included in BNF-Mex 381. Thus, Booklet 27, which bears no indication of a Gregorian year, aligns several separate piyè dates—9-Water (*yologniça*) and the letter *d* with February 1, 11-Earthquake (*laxoo*) and the letter *d* with March 1, and 3-Rabbit (*quiolaba*) and the letter *g* with April 1. Moreover, the statement *naa tza tomiigo 19 lao beo brero*, "now the day is Sunday, 19 of the month of [Fe]bruary," is aligned with 1-Deer (*qagchina*) and the letter *A*. These statements, penned in a hand different from that which composed the day count, are mutually consistent and may be used to identify their year of composition as 1690.[84]

It would be erroneous to regard each of these booklets as standardized copies of the same template. There is, indeed, a core of textual contents—the ordered list of the 260 day names, four major subdivisions and divisions by *trecena*, and the names of the fifty-two Zapotec 365-

day years—but each text was composed of different authorial layers. The first one, which often contained all of the aforementioned core elements, was in all likelihood provided by the primary author or authors of the text. Other owners or readers of the text provided supplementary layers, which contained a miscellaneous range of annotations: specific auguries or cardinal orientations for each day, cosmological diagrams, brief excerpts from larger cosmological or historical narratives, correlation statements regarding Christian holidays. They were, therefore, open-ended texts created through pluralistic authorial practices. Figure 5.2 provides an example of the supplementary annotations made by a primary or secondary author in Booklet 81. Furthermore, this document displays an unusually specific reference to eclipses in the corpus of Mesoamerican colonial texts—an astronomical phenomenon also employed as a point of reference by the authors of hieroglyphic inscriptions in Monte Albán fifteen centuries earlier.[85]

This calendar, first introduced at the beginning of the chapter, was turned in by Juan Mathías of San Juan Malinaltepec, who stated his father gave it to him circa 1697.[86] Mathías's father or one of his associates had a keen interest on eclipses, as shown by two annotations made by the calendar's author sometime after the main text was finished. The first note is aligned with the day 2-Jaguar (*yolatzi*) and reads *miercole tza niga bitago beoo bisabini 21 enero año de 1693*, "On this day Wednesday, the moon got eaten (was eclipsed); it floated in the air, on January 21, 1693."[87] The second note right below, placed besides 5-Earthquake (*yoxoo*) is equally succinct: *tza Jueve goqueaqui gobitza sanero 23 agosto año de 1692*, "Earlier, on the day Thursday, the sun burned, on August 23, 1692."[88] Contemporary astronomical data shows that both dates correspond to known eclipses. On Thursday, August 23, 1691, a total eclipse of the sun would have been seen throughout central New Spain, as suggested by the Nahua annalist's report quoted above. In Booklet 81, the scribe recorded the European year's last digit as 1692, rather than 1691. On the evening of January 21, 1693, a total eclipse of the moon was indeed visible in central New Spain.[89] Furthermore, these annotations are fully consistent with the correlation established in Booklet 27; in other words, the authors of both texts independently agreed on their reckoning of days.

The 260-day piyè and the 365-day yza were parallel counts that allowed calendar specialists to provide a unique identification for a day within a range of fifty-two years of 365 days. For structural reasons, the first day of each of these vague solar years always fell within a series of four of twenty day signs. Since fifty-four of the Villa Alta calendars provide an either partial or complete list of the fifty-two yza, each

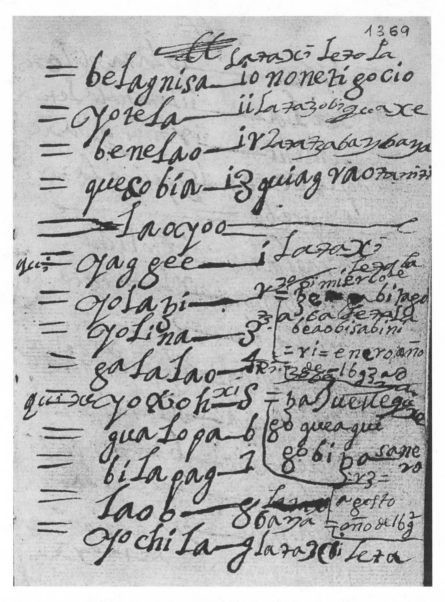

FIGURE 5.2   Eclipse Annotations in Booklet 81.

SOURCE: Gobierno de España. Ministerio de Cultura. Archivo General de Indias, México 882, 1369r

named after the piyè date on which it began, we know that the four day signs serving as year bearers were Earthquake, Wind, Deer, and Soaproot.[90] These elements of time reckoning were anything but esoteric, since several communities fasted or made offerings at the beginning of the Zapotec year. Most Zapotec Villa Alta communities reported special commemorations held "close to the New Year," an ambivalent designation; less ambiguously, eight Nexitzo towns located near or in the parish of Yagavila specified that the first major offering of the year was made in February,[91] and five of these towns specifically mentioned Saint Matthias's day. Zoogochi's cabildo avowed that male town residents bathed in cold water on three consecutive mornings and refrained from sleeping with their wives for three nights on the feast of Saint Matthias, commemorated on February 24 on nonleap years and a day later on leap years, according to the instructions of Juan Pacheco, a specialist from nearby Yaxila.[92] Four neighboring communities concurred with Zoogochi. The people of San Pedro Yagneri and San Pedro Yavago confirmed having observed bathing and sexual fasts on Saint Matthias's day,[93] Xosa's town officials offered candles at their church on the same holiday,[94] and Santa Cruz Xuquila residents confided they had two major sacrificial offerings per year, "one around [the feast of] Saint Matthias, and another at the time that corn fields are prepared for sowing."[95]

What was the local significance of this Christian holiday? These devotional acts were driven by an elegant and eminently pragmatic solution to the correlation problem: between 1689 and 1704, the first day of the 365-day Zapotec count fell either on February 24, 23, or 22—thus, the feast of Saint Matthias was in exact or almost exact synchrony with the beginning of the Zapotec year in the fifteen-year period that preceded Maldonado's campaign. This correlation is corroborated by yet another exceptional document: the first calendar bound within Booklet 85 (henceforth, Calendar 85a). Calendar 85a was among a group of three calendars surrendered by three maestros from Nexitzo-speaking San Miguel Tiltepec: Miguel Hernándes, Juan de Luna, and Juan Velasco. The front cover of Calendar 85a depicts a table, shown in Figure 5.3, containing the only extant list of the names of the subdivisions of the Zapotec 365-day count. This folio also shows that the structure of the Zapotec yza closely resembled that of the Nahua xihuitl: both counts had a five-day period at the end of the year. In Nahuatl, this period was called *nemontemi*, "one lives in vain." In Northern Zapotec, this interval is described with two obscure terms, *quicholla* and *queai nij*; another calendar from the same region and period states that during these days, "one is incapacitated, one is angry."[96]

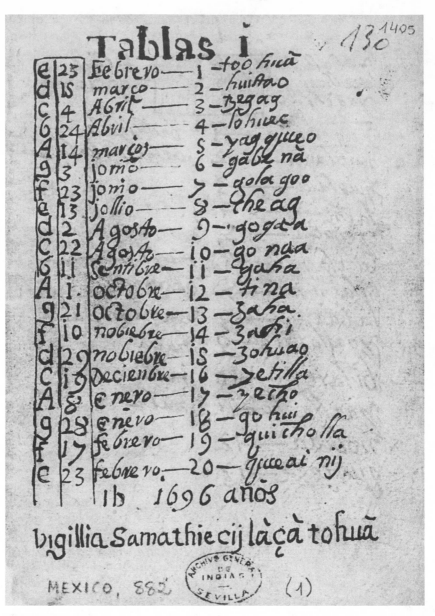

FIGURE 5.3 The Zapotec 365-day Year in Booklet 85a and its Correlation with a Christian Feast in 1696.

SOURCE: Gobierno de España. Ministerio de Cultura. Archivo General de Indias, México 882, 1405r

This document also establishes a correlation with dates and days of the week in two consecutive Gregorian years, February 1695 to February 1696. Here, the first and the last days of the Zapotec year are both identified as February 23; this is consistent with the custom of counting days from noon to noon, rather than from midnight to midnight. The correlation from Booklets 27 and 81 establishes that February 23, 1695 fell on 11-Earthquake and February 23, 1696 on 12-Wind; these two days provided the name for two consecutive Zapotec 365-day years. The note under the table could not be more explicit: it reads *vigillia Samathie cij làçà tohuâ*, "the eve of Saint Matthias receives the turn [beginning] of *tohuâ*," *tohuâ* being the name of the first subdivision of the Zapotec year. This concise statement rendered a rather complicated correlation issue readily accessible to any reader of this text.

THE SOCIAL LIFE OF A ZAPOTEC
ANCESTRAL COUNT

These calendars circulated in a collective sphere that operated in relative clandestinity and encompassed several Northern Zapotec towns. It is clear that calendar authors regarded the production of these texts as a public but illicit practice that had to be carefully compartmentalized from a broader textual sphere. Several calendar owners reported having buried these texts for safekeeping; others inserted a title page that contained the beginning of a document in Zapotec directed to civil or ecclesiastic authorities, or a page with several polite formulas written out as if to practice one's letter-writing skills. The most ingeniously misleading title page in this category, which appeared at the beginning of Booklet 39, contains several lines from the Latin hymn *Iam Luces Orto Sidere*, "Now That the [Day] Star Shines," commonly attributed to Saint Ambrose. Such a device would have allowed a day keeper to hide a text in plain sight and suggests a close relationship among literacy, service in church as a singer, and traditional ritual knowledge.

Many calendars began with a formula that indicated the contents and genre of these texts for any literate Zapotec reader. The formula was variable, but it often included the clauses *niga betapa yaga biyee*, "here are the four time counts," which refers to the four 65-day subdivisions of the 260-day calendar, and/or *lani que xotao xoçi reo*, "the holidays of the ancestors and fathers of us all." In total, about twenty calendars contained a version of this formula,[97] and four calendars contained the first phrases of a cosmological narrative regarding the most recent creation of the world.[98] The fact that this narrative ended with the words "et cetera" in two instances implies that its implied audience were literate readers who had access to the narrative's full version, perhaps in oral form. Surprisingly, the authors of seven calendars used the Spanish word *tiempo*, "time,"[99] to refer to the 260-day count, rather than *biyee*, the standard term employed elsewhere. In fact, the unusual label *calentario de los yntio* [*sic*], "calendar of the Indians," appears in Booklet 82. The use of these terms suggests that, by the late seventeenth century, literate specialists found it useful to employ Spanish terms with a broad circulation in a multilingual public sphere, in order to convey the significance of these calendrical texts to Zapotec readers.

The collective confessions highlight the activities of several ritual specialists who, as Diego Luis had done in Sola half a century earlier, distributed calendars to specialists and apprentices in various communities, either as a gift or for a fee. Two would-be day counters from Cacalotepec, Sebastian Hernándes and Juan Marcial, testified that Gabriel López, a well-known specialist from the neighboring town of Yavechi, had sold them one booklet each for six reales—about two to three days' wages for a skilled laborer—and told them "that if they began learning, they would know [the count], and he gave them one lesson, explaining those papers for them." Although Hernándes and Marcial did not fully master the day count, López found a more proficient student in Nicolás Ruis of Lachichina, who told the magistrate that he had paid López 3 reales for "one of the booklets they call books of ancient times," a Spanish formula that probably translated the Valley Zapotec term *quijchi tija colàça*, "lineage book of ancient times."[100] Questioned further, Ruis said that he bought the text around 1698, using it to learn "the appropriate days for superstitious observations," apparently for his own individual needs, since "he had not indicated [the days] to others."[101] López, an apparently modest man who offered his services as the sole resident specialist in Yavechi on a sliding scale—"half a real, a real, and he does not collect a thing from the poor"—composed at least four booklets, according to the Villa Alta confessions: a booklet he owned, the two booklets he sold to Hernándes and Marcial, and Ruis's calendar.[102] This was the largest number of surrendered booklets from the same author. Hence, he is a prime candidate for the authorship of a series of seven calendars that were copied from a single source, given their internal structure—Booklets 45, 46, 48, 50, 52, 71, and 77.

The booklet trade in which Francisco Morales engaged was facilitated by his training and geographical location. Besides being the escribano of the Bixanos town of Yetzelálag in 1704,[103] his home community was located on Villa Alta's main northbound trade route, which connected San Ildefonso, Villa Alta's cabecera, with Guaspaltepec, a terminus with riverine access to Veracruz.[104] Lópes's text circulated primarily in Nexitzo communities and could be regarded as affordable; Morales's range was broader, and his prices were higher. One of his clients, Joseph Velasco from Yagayo, declared that he bought a calendrical booklet from Morales for the relatively high amount of twelve reales, but the interval during which he held the booklet before surrendering it, five months, did not allow him to learn its proper use.[105] In fact, learning to read and interpret the piyè could take years; thus, Pedro de Asevedo of Tagui avowed that, after buying a booklet from Morales and attempting to learn its proper use for a year, he relented, selling it to Francisco de Chaves of Talea. The social trajectory of this text, which was produced by a Bixanos specialist and sold to a Nexitzo speaker, who transferred it to a Caxonos speaker, suggests that linguistic and ethnic differences did not hinder the dispersal of calendrical information. Indeed, Morales's renown as a specialist cut a broad swath through Villa Alta, since witnesses from Camotlán, Temascalapa, Yatzona, and Yelago knew him as a respected "teacher of idolatries."

The relative ease with which booklets traveled across Villa Alta is illustrated by two further examples. In Reagui, Juan Gerónimo, one of the four local maestros, became an important link in a tripartite exchange of booklets, reales, and ritual implements. Local resident Cristóbal Hernándes bought a calendar from Gerónimo, as well as six reales worth of parrots' feathers—a commodity used in various ritual practices that could come from as far away as Chiapas—from Yaee resident Nicolás Tarifa, who acquired a transcription of Gerónimo's booklet.[106] Calendars were also occasionally given as gifts, as shown by the transfer of texts from three maestros at the Nexitzo village of Teotlaxco. Gaspar Gómez and escribano Juan Santiago gave copies of their texts to their fellow maestro and principal Domingo Morales of Zoogochi;[107] Baltasar Santiago gave a calendar as a gift to a young apprentice from the Caxonos town of La Oya, Joseph Mendez.

How did this broad pattern of text dispersion influence the oral reproduction of ritual knowledge? Three further examples challenge the assumption that literate calendar specialists simply replaced their illiterate forebears due to the advantage conferred upon them by European letters. Although the aforementioned Joseph Mendez of La Oya obtained a calendar from Teotlaxco, town officials emphatically denied on two separate instances that they could employ Mendez as the organizer of communal rituals solely on the basis of calendar ownership, declaring instead that "since he was a young man, we employed and consulted Juan Baptista and Gerónimo Flores from the town of Lalopa, who were also consulted by individuals."[108] Moreover, Pedro de Aquino of San Juan Malinaltepec implied that even experienced calendar owners regarded public divination as a competitive and difficult endeavor. Aquino declared that, even after having possessed a calendar for twenty years, he employed it for individual practices and would not use it "in public," even though he wished to do so, since "he was afraid of other, more expert maestros."[109]

An apparent division of labor between correlation and calendar specialists existed in Yavago, where specialists who did not own alphabetic calendars informed town residents when they should observe Saint Matthias's holiday—a proxy, as argued above, for the beginning of the Zapotec year. Even if four Yavago specialists—Juan de Santiago, Juan de Luna, Juan Sánches, and Balthasar Martín—owned and used Booklets 94, 95, and 96, the town consulted these maestros primarily to plan observances associated with the inauguration of town officials, while the maestros Juan Francisco and Juan Martín told them when to celebrate the holidays of Saint Matthias and the town's patron saint, Saint Peter, for they knew this correlation, and thus its likely ritual implications, "by heart."[110] This is a remarkable display of preference for illiterate specialists, especially since an annotation in Booklet 94 shows that its author knew the correct Gregorian month and day on which a Zapotec year 5-Earthquake began.

The statements made during the collective confessions did not reveal substantial status distinctions between literate and illiterate specialists; in some cases, maestros stated they have no text to surrender, either because they knew the day count by heart or because they could not read. None of the confession's narrative vignettes provide an indication of a pitched contest between text and memory users. However, some examples suggest that illiterate apprentices could expect to receive assistance from calendar owners. For instance, in Lachixila, an enterprising but illiterate apprentice called Miguel López confided "sharing" a calendar with the literate maestro Francisco de Mendoza, a curious term that conveys Miguel's broad understanding of literacy. López also benefited from consultations with the two other calendar owners in his village, Juan de Bargas and Agustín Pérez. Apparently López yearned for cosmological knowledge, since he questioned four other specialists from Chinantec communities about the "things of his ancestors": Tomás de Aquino in Petlapa, don Juan Mansano of Jocotepeque, Andrés de Medina of Lobani, and a certain Simon from Tepinapa.[111]

However, there existed a correlation between calendrical literacy and the geographical scope of a specialist's network of clients. Evidence from fifteen Villa Alta villages implies that calendar ownership and one's reputation as a specialist beyond hometown boundaries were closely linked. Table 5.1 provides the names of twenty-one specialists whose services were requested either by town officials for collective observances, or by individuals. The towns that made the most frequent requests tended to be small; for instance, Lachichina, La Oya, and Yalahui had estimated populations of 205 or less in 1703. A majority of the specialists who had clients outside their own communities were texts owners—twelve out of sixteen specialists whose status as calendar owners is known. These patterns imply that literate specialists were located within regional social networks that did not necessarily exclude or compete with those surrounding illiterate maestros. Moreover, a handful of specialists could cover a relatively

TABLE 5.1　*Villa Alta Calendar Specialists*
with Clients Outside Their Home Communities

Hometown	Specialist	Ritual-text owner?	Towns where clients resided
S Juan Juquila	Yllescas, Gabriel	Yes	Lachichina
Lachirioag	Alonso, Joseph	Booklet 2	La Oya
Lachixila	Vargas, Juan de	Booklet 31, 32, or 33	Yovego
Lalopa	Bautista, Juan	Yes	La Oya, Lachichina
	Flores, Gerónimo	Yes	La Oya
Laxopa	Nicolás, Fabián	Not known	Yahuio, Yelaxi
	Nicolás, Martín	Not known	Yahuio, Yelaxi
Tabegua	Martín, Diego	No	Yaglina, Zoochina
Tagui	Gonzalo, Juan	Not known	Yalahui
	Marcos, Juan	Not known	Yalahui
	Vargas, Miguel	Not known	Yalahui
Teotlaxco	Gómez, Gaspar	Yes	Xogochi
Yaa	Bautista, Joseph	Yes	Yatee
Yaee	Yllescas, Pedro	Not known	Lachichina
Yagayo/ Tiltepec	Martín, Joseph	No	Lachichina
Yatoni	Hernández, Francisco	Yes	La Oya
Yatzona	Vargas, don Gaspar	Booklet 24 or 25	Camotlan
Yaxila	Pablo, Gabriel	Yes	S Juan Juquila
	Pacheco, Juan	No	S Juan Juquila, Xogochi, Yagavila
	Santiago, Bernabé	No	Tepanzacualco
Yetzelálag	Morales, Francisco	Yes; distributed 3 booklets	Camotlán

SOURCE: AGI-Mex 882

large geographical scope—a mere twenty-one specialists operated in twenty-nine out of about eighty-three Zapotec communities in Villa Alta. This fact suggests that these client networks may have survived periodic eradication efforts due to the fact that even a single specialist could serve a substantial number of linguistic, ethnic, and social domains.[112]

Furthermore, specialists from certain communities were regarded as optimal sources for rare textual genres, as it was the case for transcriptions of ritual songs. There are only five reports about the existence of these songbooks, and specialists from Betaza were the sources for two of them. Hence, Fernando Lópes of Lachirioag avowed having purchased Booklet 100 from the renowned specialist Pedro de Vargas of Betaza, even though at least another collection of songs was produced locally in Lachirioag. Additionally, two performers of ritual songs from Yoeche confided that the songbook they used had been bought by town officials from another Betaza maestro, don Juan Martín.[113]

CLANDESTINE RITUAL TEXTS AND THEIR READERS IN SEVENTEENTH-CENTURY CENTRAL MEXICO

These four case studies afford us an overview of clandestine writing and reading practices in various Nahua and Zapotec communities in the seventeenth century. The contrast between the scarcity of clandestine ritual texts in the communities investigated by Ruiz de Alarcón before 1629 and the relative abundance of such texts in Sola twenty years later does not necessarily suggest an increase in the influence of literacy in indigenous communities, but a crucial difference in the cultural adaptation of Nahua and Zapotec communities to Spanish literacy which merits further study. Some clandestine texts were produced in locations that had been under the influence of secular priests or regulars for several decades. Petronilla, the literate healer from Tlayacapan, lived in the shadow of the Dominican convent of Tepoztlan, established by 1556;[114] in the Sola region, there had been resident secular priests at Exutla and at San Miguel Sola since about 1570.[115] Although the diffusion of ritual texts confiscated by Ruiz de Alarcón and Gonzalo Curiel between 1613 and 1633 may be regarded as an initial period in the spread of literacy to remote indigenous communities, only detailed research on the spread of literacy in both isolated and integrated native communities in Central Mexico during the latter half of the sixteenth century may lead to a more definitive conclusion.[116] This evidence suggests that the first decades of the seventeenth century was a crucial period in the native use of writing for clandestine devotional purposes.

In terms of the rapport between social status and production of clandestine ritual texts, there were some correlations between membership in the upper tiers of local political hierarchies and ownership of ritual texts. In the Nahua Cohuixca area, it was the deacon of Cuetlaxxochitla who signed his name on his transcribed incantation; in Sola, at least five church cantors, one principal, and a former *alcalde*, or local magistrate, and cantor could be counted among thirty-eight owners of ritual texts mentioned in Balsalobre's proceedings. In fact, just like some of their contemporaries, the Yucatec Maya *maestros cantores*,[117] or church cantors, these specialists appear to have led a dual existence as leading members of the public Christian sphere and as owners and readers of clandestine calendrical and divination texts of Postclassic origin. Both in Cuetlaxxochitla and in Sola, the activities of these literate native officials linked the public sphere of orthodox Christian practices with marginal social spheres, located in a social space that went beyond the domestic sphere and merged with a local public sphere, in which various forms of ritual knowledge, Christian or not, circulated clandestinely through texts.

What was the effect of literacy on the content of native ritual practices, and on its oral dimensions? The case studies presented here depict a plurality of interactions between literacy and "idolatries" that suggests the impossibility of committing to a monolithic answer, or adhering to a purely epistemological analysis. Even if some analysts have presented the impact of literacy and evangelization on native populations colonized by the Spanish as a dramatic epistemic confrontation between Western writing and native practices of orality and writing,[118] my analysis leads to two conclusions that go beyond well-known assessments about the phonetic ideologies embedded in Greco-Latin writing systems.[119] First, as shown by the circulation of calendrical texts in Sola and Villa Alta, the particular features and assumptions of genres of Postclassic origin closely guided the native appropriation of the Latin alphabet. Second, as shown by the transcription of the Nahuatl epithets for the piciyetl, some Nahua ritual specialists employed the Latin alphabet as a powerful vehicle for the inscription of a latent oral performance. This notion of orality was not limited to the yoking of specific sounds to graphic symbols, as Derrida would argue, but included an inherent calculation about parallel syllabic and morphological structures in rhetorical practice. In other words, the transcription of these epithets by Nahua specialists in that particular social context reinforced, rather than effaced, a broad performative (and not merely phonetic) dimension that alphabetic transcription indexed only in a weak way. The simultaneous reproduction of a ritual oral genre, the nahualtocaitl, through written and oral means demonstrates that the transcription of ritual knowledge did not result in the sudden demise of orality.

In his discussion of reading practices in early modern and Renaissance Europe, Chartier emphasizes the differences in reading practices among different groups of readers based on degree of literacy. He also suggests that oral elicitation of the written text could play a significant role in different readings of it.[120] One could arrive at a similar conclusion when considering the diversity of reading practices in early seventeenth-century Nahua and Zapotec communities, for both alphabetic and non-alphabetic literacy modes coexisted in the same social spheres without contradiction. This diversity was not unique to Central Mexico; in Elizabethan England and in Golden-Age Spain,[121] the owners of and audience for printed books included readers who supported their interpretation through a perusal of the illustrations that accompanied the text. According to Michel de Certeau's eloquent evocation, these readings implied an intense oral and physical interaction with a sacred or devotional text that led to its bodily appropriation: "Only over the last three centuries has reading become an ocular gesture. . . . In earlier times, the reader interiorized the text; he made his voice the body of the other; he was its actor."[122] Thus, the Manichean vision of oral versus literate cultures rests on an aprioristic analysis that does not reflect the complex rapports between orality and textuality in Europe and New Spain in the seventeenth century.[123] In both terrains, two similar elements governed both reading practices: the act of interpreting a text orally, and the inevitable variation in the interpretation of a text by individuals with varying competence.

The clandestine circulation of ritual and devotional texts fostered the emergence of Nahua and Zapotec cohorts of readers. The exchanges of texts chronicled here suggest that, much like the groups of readers created by the circulation of *pliegos sueltos* in Spain, chapbooks in England, and the *Bibliothèque bleue* in France, such communities of native readers and manuscript authors were diverse in terms of sociocultural background, literacy skills, and modes of appropriation of the text.[124] These groups of readers maintained a certain integrity through the circulation of texts in a social space defined by the absence of the licencia del ordinario, the measures of control prescribed by the Mexican councils and the Council of Trent, and the periodic extirpatory interests of friars and secular priests. Located as they were at the margin of public Christian native practices, the clandestine ritual manuscripts provided an essential textual core for the reproduction of a common clandestine social space in which native cohorts of readers transcribed and transmitted divinatory practices of Postclassic origin. In spite of various eradication efforts, in the seventeenth century, literate idolatries prospered through the work of Protean writers, obstinate readers, and driven translators.

CHAPTER 6

After 1660

Punitive Experiments Against Idolatry

The thesis that a momentous transformation in the attitudes of indigenous peoples toward Christianity in New Spain and Peru occurred in the middle decades of the seventeenth century is a an idea both received and seductive. As noted by Kenneth Mills, in an influential 1946 essay, George Kubler identified the 1660s as a period in which Christian teachings finally prevailed among Quechua populations.[1] As for Central Mexico, Hugo Nutini characterized the 1650s as a period when the "crystallization" of Nahua and Christian forms of devotion took place, setting the stage for the development of native syncretism, which he analyzed in central Tlaxcala.[2]

However, the timing and substance of such a change of heart in colonial indigenous devotions remains open to debate. With regard to Peru, Mills argued that the changes in terminology and rhetoric in the 1660s did not correspond to a shift in actual extirpation policies; he also contended that the archival record suggests an uneven adoption and understanding of Christian practices in many Quechua communities in the archbishopric of Lima.[3] For Central Mexico, the pioneering work of Aguirre Beltrán on unorthodox colonial healing practices, Alberro's concise assessment of clandestine native healers, and Gruzinski's inquiries into multiple, hybrid Christianities have illustrated the difficulty of enshrining a particular period in the seventeenth century as an absolute turning point in the native reception of Christianity.[4]

This chapter contends that what demonstrably took place in the 1660s in the dioceses of Mexico and Oaxaca was not a tidal change in native devotional practices, but a decisive shift to more systematic measures against idolatry, and toward a more violent punitive calculus directed at native bodies and minds. In Mexico, the period between 1660 and

the first decade of the eighteenth century is marked by renewed episcopal interest in extirpation attempts and by the concentration of routine
decisions regarding the punishment of natives for matters of faith in the
hands of the provisor de indios. In Oaxaca, the midcentury Balsalobre
campaigns were the culmination of anti-idolatry secular zeal during a
second cycle of extirpation attempts. These campaigns also ushered in
a third cycle in eradication efforts characterized by an increase in idolatry trials held by civil justices, and by the development of a novel disciplinary institution: a prison that would isolate recidivist "teachers of
idolaters" from the general population. Although by 1668 the bishop
of Quito, Alonso de la Peña Montenegro, was willing to discern between
grave or "false," and less serious or "superfluous" types of idolatry in
his influential 1668 *Itinerario para párrocos de indios*,[5] the punitive
measures embraced by the bishops of Oaxaca and their provisores after
1660 demonstrated that they regarded all forms of this transgression as
equally intolerable.

Chapter 2 of this work reviewed ecclesiastical policies that characterized a first cycle of confrontations between native ritual practitioners
and the regular clergy between 1537 and 1571; Chapters 3 and 4 investigated extirpation campaigns led by seculars during a second cycle of
extirpation campaigns between 1571 and the early 1660s. This chapter outlines the major transformations in extirpation policies in Mexico
and Oaxaca, with a few strategic incursions into the see of Tlaxcala,
during the first period of a third cycle in extirpation attempts in Central Mexico. It begins with an examination of the 1660s, a transitional
period both in Oaxaca and Mexico, and extends its consideration of
extirpation campaigns into the early eighteenth century, providing an
institutional context for the analysis of native responses to extirpation
events in Chapter 7.

ECCLESIASTICAL TRANSITIONS IN MEXICO
AND TLAXCALA IN THE 1660S

The period between 1662 and 1668 was a transitional one in the archbishopric of Mexico, since a succession of events blocked the lasting appointment of an archbishop.[6] In 1662, Archbishop Mateo de Sagade Bugueiro,
who began his tenure in 1655, was given three appointments in rapid
succession: the episcopal seats at Cádiz, León, and Cartagena (Spain); he
left Mexico City and began his tenure as bishop of Cartagena in 1663. In
1664, Diego de Osorio de Escobar y Llamas, formerly bishop of Puebla,
was elected viceroy of New Spain. Even though the crown gave him a

joint appointment as viceroy and archbishop of Mexico, he declined the archiepiscopal seat and accepted to oversee the diocese until a new archbishop was elected. The crown then turned to the bishop of Oaxaca, Alonso de Cuevas Dávalos, who was held in great esteem due to his role as mediator between indigenous rebels and civil authorities during the 1660 Tehuantepec rebellion, and named him archbishop of Mexico, but he died in October 1664 without taking office. The Franciscan fray Marcos Ramírez de Prado, former bishop of Chiapas and Michoacán, was subsequently named as archbishop of Mexico in 1666, but he died in 1667 without taking his appointment. Such a lengthy vacancy was finally solved by the 1668 appointment of the Augustinian fray Payo Enríquez de Rivera, a former bishop of Guatemala and Michoacán. Enríquez de Rivera proved to be an able administrator of ecclesiastical affairs and was subsequently named viceroy of New Spain in December 1673. His tenure as archbishop lasted until 1681, when he was named to the bishopric of Cuenca.

Two of the most noteworthy idolatry and superstition trials heard in this transitional period were those of Gregorio Juan (1660) and Juan Coatl (1665), both of whom resided in the episcopal jurisdiction of Tlaxcala. Since Gruzinski examined both cases in detail, only a brief appraisal is offered here.[7] In November 1659, Gregorio Juan, a Nahua resident of Xicotepec in the Sierra of Puebla and also fluent in Totonac, was arrested by the ecclesiastical authorities of Huauchinango after its fiscal mayor Juan Francisco heard some allegations of superstitious practices. The testimony in the case indicated that at least two couples from the town of Ayohuizcuauhtla participated in a ritual performance in which, after a concelebrant played the teponaztli drum, Gregorio Juan personified a powerful deity from within a tentlike enclosure. This mysterious deity, who claimed to be the Creator, boasted of enjoying the allegiance of the Twelve Apostles and referred to Jews as being the executors of his will, spoke through Gregorio Juan in Nahuatl and Totonac, promised well-being to his followers, and threatened nonbelievers with destruction. When Juan was interrogated at the convent of Huauchinango, he revealed that another Indian called Pedro introduced him to the cult of this deity, designated in the trial records as "Goat" and "Star." The deity appeared in the guise of a child with dark blue skin, a white face, and saffron-colored hair. From this scant evidence, it appears as if Gregorio Juan promoted the cult of a local entity with substantial Christian influences, but his neighbors rejected his attempts to secure a following for it and bore witness against him at Huauchinango.

One day after Easter Sunday of 1665, around eleven in the morning, the guard at the ecclesiastical jail in Puebla made a terrible discovery: an

Otomi by the name of Juan Coatl had managed to hang himself in his cell by manufacturing a thin cord with straw from an old broom.[8] Coatl was the main defendant in an idolatry inquest led by don Diego Osorio de Escobar y Llamas, bishop of Puebla, after an ecclesiastical visit to the dependencies of Huamantla had turned up accusations against him. Paradoxically, Coatl's suicide resulted in the production of documents that guaranteed his survival in the historical record. Immediately after Coatl's death, Bishop Osorio de Escobar sent several letters and copies of the original proceedings to the Council of Indies, stressing that the defendants in ecclesiastical trials occasionally chose to end their lives. Coatl's suicide was also an indirect trigger for a jurisdictional dispute. During his testimony, and in private conversations with his interpreter, Coatl reported the existence of a cave filled with valuable offerings that had been placed there "since ancient times" by the adherents of a cult he now directed. Therefore, the Audiencia's prosecutor issued an opinion urging the ecclesiastical judge to yield to civil justice in future proceedings, and stating that the case and its prized offerings, when they were located, belonged to the royal jurisdiction.[9]

What cult did Juan Coatl preside over? According to his testimony, he had taken part in the cult of a female supernatural known as Soapile, a modification of the Nahuatl term *cihuapilli*, "noble lady," represented by a female effigy kept in a cave whose dress and shoes Coatl had inherited from his grandfather. Soapile was a manifestation of La Malinche, the volcano that dominates the landscape of southern Tlaxcala; according to Coatl, people from eight towns used to come to pay their respects at Soapile's cave, bearing contributions according to their status: two reales for married couples, one real for the unmarried, and half a real for young boys. On Christmas, they would also bring the Soapile image clothes for her wardrobe. Coatl declared that the cave contained those offerings, as well as wax, and "the feathers of ancient times with which our ancestors danced." According to other cult participants, the cave also contained four paintings—one representing Soapile, another depicting an Indian with a staff, a depiction of four snakes, and another one representing a coiled snake. Coatl was also said to have a text, which he used to give calendrical names to local children. Coatl's decision to kill himself might even have been a self-fulfilling prophecy: during his deposition, he stated that he expected to die after exposing this cult to the ecclesiastical authorities.

In spite of such tantalizing descriptions, no document reports an actual inspection of Soapile's cave. Gruzinski emphasized the parallels between hybrid Christian supernaturals such as the Virgin of Ocotlán in Tlaxcala City or Our Lady of Huamantla, and a Soapile who, even if she represented a local deity or deified landscape element, also depicted a very crude form of Mariolatry. She was, after all, a female image with Spanish dress and shoes and an ever-changing wardrobe provided by her devotees who provided well-being to her followers.[10] The cult appears to have gone from an element in a collective ritual sphere encompassing eight towns earlier in the century to a clandestine observance in a reduced elective sphere over which Coatl presided. An ecclesiastical theory about this cult's origin was advanced nineteen years after Coatl's suicide in a letter from the bishop of Puebla, Manuel Fernández de Santa Cruz, to the viceroy. According to the bishop, Coatl's disregard for the Christian faith was a result of the poor doctrinal education natives received from the Franciscans of Huamantla, for these mendicants visited Ixtenco only to say mass and had no Otomi. In fact, Coatl's associates barely knew how to bless themselves in their language and could recite only one or two prayers in bastardized Latin. Fernández de Santa Cruz noted with satisfaction that there had been no further idolatry reports after an Otomi-speaking minister was appointed to Ixtenco and recommended similar appointments of linguistically capable priests in Tlapa, a region that was at the time regarded as prone to idolatries.[11]

Two proceedings from the alcaldías mayores of Tlapa and Igualapa in the diocese of Tlaxcala provide evidence for an active idolatry extirpation program during the 1662–68 transitional period and showcase local political tensions that may have motivated idolatry accusations. The most peculiar case concerns don Juan de Santiago, a principal from the town of Ayutla in the jurisdiction of Igualapa. In late 1665, Santiago was imprisoned in the head town of Cuilotla due to unspecified idolatry charges by Nicolás Soltero y Castañeda, beneficiado of Acatlan, and commissioned judge against idolatry under the bishop of Puebla, Osorio de Escobar. After his imprisonment, Francisco Bravo de Lagunas, beneficiado of Ayutla, began a second ecclesiastical proceeding against him for propositions against the faith. This second case emerged from an altercation between Santiago and Francisco Juan, Ayutla's fiscal. According to Juan, Santiago beat him with a stick, protesting that Juan had no authority to teach him the doctrine because, unlike Juan, Santiago had "truly come from Castile in order to teach it." Juan's accusation was corroborated by Ayutla's alguacil mayor.[12]

In spite of his political and theological difficulties with native officials and two beneficiados, Santiago had a bold local ally: the Spaniard Francisco Durán, who owned a fish market. In December 1665, Durán came to the prison of Cuilotla with some associates shortly after midnight bearing an harquebus and a copy of the key to the prison gate. In a daring move, Durán opened the door for Santiago and cut his fetters with a machete. After Santiago was freed, Durán, Santiago, and some armed Indians took to the road, announcing to some onlookers that they would begin litigation procedures in Puebla. The focus of this suit is not mentioned in extant reports, but some of the testimony points to tensions between beneficiado Bravo de Lagunas and Durán. In March 1666, after the Holy Office commissioner of Tlapa began to collect testimonies about Santiago's escape, Durán's brother-in-law stepped forward to report that the beneficiado Soltero y Castañeda advised him to avoid giving testimony if an ecclesiastical judge came to Ayutla to collect testimonies about the escape or Lagunas's misdeeds. Lagunas requested that the Holy Office punish Durán for aiding idolaters, but the outcome of this confrontation is not extant.

The second case concerns idolatry accusations against don Francisco de Alvarado, cacique of Tlapa. By late 1666, Alvarado had been tried by an ecclesiastical judge, found guilty of idolatrous practices, and sentenced to receive one hundred lashes and a ten-year exile from Tlapa. These penalties did not seem stern enough for don Alonso García, Tlapa's gobernador, who managed to obtain an edict from Viceroy Marquis of Mancera barring Alvarado from ever again holding elective office in Tlapa. In order to prevent any political maneuvers from Alvarado, García had the edict sent to the alcalde mayor of Tlapa and other officials.[13] In fact, Tlapa was regarded as a region rife with idolaters in the late 1660s and early 1670s. Citing several idolatry cases heard by several ecclesiastical judges in Tlapa circa 1655 as precedent, a June 1673 order from Viceroy Marquis of Mancera instructed the alcalde mayor of Tlapa to conduct a personal inspection of the towns, reporting their population levels, geographical location, and distance from each other. This information was later used by the bishop of Puebla to investigate allegations of idolatry in the region.[14]

EXTIRPATION POLICIES IN MEXICO IN THE LATE SEVENTEENTH CENTURY

Payo Enríquez de Rivera's appointment as archbishop in 1668 put an end to institutional uncertainties about ecclesiastic administration. Two cases regarding Nahua ritual practices highlight the active role that the provisorato took in terms of idolatry accusations during Archbishop Enríquez's tenure. A third case shows that, as in Oaxaca, Mexican civil authorities occasionally tried natives accused of sorcery, given that malicious damage attributable to it was also the province of civil justice. In the first case, in early 1677, the Franciscan fray Juan de Molina, minister of San Miguel Totocuitlapilco in Toluca, heard a case against the alcalde Juan de los Ángeles and some of his associates for keeping an effigy described as "an image of Death" on an altar and for collecting money for masses to be said before the image. Following the usual steps, Molina incarcerated the defendants in Toluca and in Metepec and had their property seized. However, in September 1677, Ángeles's defense lawyer wrote to the Franciscan superiors, questioning Molina's authority to proceed in such a case. As a result of a subsequent review, it was confirmed that Molina, who tried this case with the provisorato's consent, had acted according to procedure, for he held the proceedings on behalf of Provisor of Indians Diego de la Sierra and forwarded the trial records to the indigenous ecclesiastical tribunal in Mexico City.[15]

A second case throws light on the jurisdictional crossroads at which some extirpators operated in this period. In July 1680, the principales don Pablo Gabriel and don Felipe Gabriel complained to the Audiencia that the Franciscan fray Gaspar de Lara, minister of their town of Santiago Tlazala in Toluca, went to their house one evening in order to arrest their parents don Miguel Diego and Inés Catalina for suspicions of idolatry, also claiming that "they did not go to mass." The Franciscan also seized three thousand pesos the suspects kept in a locked box. This complaint motivated the Audiencia to step in, invoking the 1576 edict discussed in Chapter 3, by which this court had ordered the Dominicans of Oaxaca to refrain from confiscating precious items from natives accused of idolatry.[16] The fact that jurisdiction over valuable confiscated property was in question motivated the prompt intervention of all concerned juridical authorities. Don Lope Cornejo, provisor de indios, appeared before the Audiencia and condemned with harsh words their attempts to intervene in matters of ecclesiastical justice. Eventually, the case reached the crown, and a Madrid memorial drafted in September 1682 commanded the Audiencia in energetic terms to yield to ecclesiastical jurisdiction and cease its intervention.[17]

A third case heard under Archbishop Enríquez demonstrates that sorcery accusations not only pitted natives against each other but also entire communities against a single individual. A broad range of physical ailments and misfortunes could be attributed to suspicions of sorcery in colonial Nahua communities. Mesoamerican ritual practices also emphasized the importance of individual actions that could trigger an ailment due to pollution or to acts that offended a specific deity.[18] A telling glimpse of the collective dynamics of sorcery accusations is provided by the 1681 trial of Pedro de Juárez, a resident of Tlachmalacac in the jurisdiction of Iguala, a region that had been scoured for idolaters by

Ruiz de Alarcón fifty years earlier.[19] Pedro de Juárez was reputed to be a *tetlachihuiani*; this Nahua term for malevolent specialists, which meant literally "one who does things to people," was translated by Sahagún as "sorcerer" and "soothsayer."[20] He had been punished earlier by the beneficiado don Juan de Soto, who burned some *amatl ahmo cualli*, "bad papers," found in Juárez's house, along with human bones used as ritual implements. Juárez's status as a literate tetlachihuiani was confirmed in a declaration stating his innocence, which he signed. In spite of his protestations, the entire town of Tlachmalacac seemed to have a complaint against him. He was accused of using sorcery to cause the death of seven people, including two women with whom he had had affairs. Consequently, small mobs had attempted to kill him in public on four different occasions, and Juárez defended himself by demanding to be brought before a competent court.

If the people of Tlachmalacac had held fast to the notion that their ills were caused by Juárez's sorcery, a trial may have been unnecessary, and Juárez may well have been lynched by his own neighbors. Instead, in August 1681, Tlachmalacac's native officials drafted a Nahuatl document stating their case against Juárez and turned over the defendant to a competent authority, the alcalde mayor of Tlapa don Juan de Berver Machuca y Miranda. This decision suggests that, even if the town officials did regard Juárez as a sorcerer, they had decided not to let town residents take justice by their own hand. Instead, they decided to defer to civil justice in the case, with the presupposition that Juárez would probably be found guilty and punished. The extant documentation ends *in medias res* in September 1681, just as Juárez's testimony begins, and this detailed depiction of sorcery accusations fades from view.

In 1681, after serving as archbishop of Mexico since 1668 and as viceroy in 1673–80, Enríquez de Rivera left his diocese to be installed as bishop of Cuenca in Spain. The crown appointed to this vacancy don Manuel Fernández de Santa Cruz y Sahagún, who had been bishop of Puebla since 1677, but he declined both the archiepiscopate and the viceroyalty, choosing to remain in his see. The next appointee was don Francisco de Aguiar y Seijas (1680–98), a former canon at Astorga's cathedral who briefly served as bishop of Michoacán before coming to the see of Mexico. In spite of having limited experience in episcopal administration, Aguiar y Seijas tackled the complex ecclesiastical affairs of Mexico with energy, laying the first stone for a new church dedicated to Guadalupe in Tepeyacac and favoring the establishment of pious enterprises, such as the Colegio de Niñas de Belén and the Casa de Ormigos, a refuge for women deemed insane. He would become a candidate for beatification in the eighteenth century.[21] Extirpation activities under Aguiar y

Seijas are attested by a few brief, routine examples: a 1689 accusation against two mestizos for participating in native ritual practices in a cave near Acolman;[22] an incomplete sorcery trial against two natives of Palula in the jurisdiction of Tepecuacuilco in 1689 who were counseled by the escribano of record to claim drunkenness as an excuse for having engaged in acts of sorcery;[23] and a 1695 accusation against a native healer and diviner employed by a Spaniard from Real del Monte (Pachuca). This last case was eventually turned over by the provisor of Indians to the Holy Office. Finally, in 1698, nine Tepepan natives were surprised by native alguaciles as they tended to *pipiltzintzintli*—a term referring to a plant with psychoactive properties, possibly *Salvia divinorum*. The alguaciles extorted thirty-five pesos from them, but the alcalde mayor of Xochimilco ordered that the fine be turned over to him.[24] Whereas Aguiar y Seijas was quite interested in the possibility of appointing visitadores to the diocese, as attested by a December 1682 letter to the crown,[25] there is no extant evidence that he used visitadores to extirpate idolatries, as his predecessors Manso y Zúñiga and Mañozca had done before him.

After the death of Aguiar y Seijas in August 1698, the see of Mexico remained vacant until the election of Juan Ortega y Montañés in 1699. This prelate, who had been bishop of Durango, Guatemala, and Michoacán, also served as interim viceroy of New Spain. In contrast with the frenetic pace of extirpation activities in Oaxaca in the first decade of the eighteenth century, there is a documentary vacuum regarding idolatry or native superstition trials that extends throughout most of Ortega y Montañés's tenure. In fact, one has to look to other jurisdictions to find evidence of extirpation activity in this period: the controversy about the actions of don Onofre del Castillo, Holy Office commissioner in Puebla, during local Holy Week celebrations in 1700. Castillo was scandalized by a Shrove Tuesday procession in some of Puebla's indigenous neighborhoods. This pageant featured a "doll-like" human effigy, which the Indians shook about in their festive dances. Consequently, Castillo took away the effigy and began a proceeding against some of those indigenous revelers. Since he had no jurisdiction over Indians as Holy Office commissioner, the ecclesiastical council sent two notaries to collect Castillo's trial records. Nonetheless, Castillo took the records away and locked up the notaries. At this point, civil and ecclesiastical authorities contacted the Holy Office, asking that Castillo turn in the documents. The controversy over Castillo's actions continued until 1702. It would not be until January 1709, only months after Ortega y Montañés's death, that the cathedral chapter named Juan Ignacio de Castorena y Urzúa, a former cathedral chapter member and rector of the Royal University, to the post of provisor of Indians in the archbishopric of Mexico.[26] As discussed in Chapter 8 below, Mexico's *provisorato* would acquire renewed juridical strength under this ambitious extirpator.

AFTER 1660:
THE THIRD EXTIRPATORY CYCLE IN OAXACA

In a pastoral letter that opened Balsalobre's 1656 *Relación auténtica*, Bishop Hevia y Valdés issued a powerful symbolic battle cry against idolatry. Hevia y Valdés compared this enterprise to the early struggles against paganism in Castile and depicted the nature of this confrontation by appropriating and glossing a celebrated passage from Paul's Sixth Epistle to the Ephesians:

As good soldiers . . . , we should arm ourselves with God against the common enemy, who will renew his strength upon seeing us prepared, self-contained, and fervent, for he wages great resistance against the Church, fortified as he is in the hearts of natives. For this invisible war, may the chastity belt be *cingite lumbos vestros* [have your loins girt about (with truth)]; may the coat of mail of justice be *induite loricam iustitiae* [put on the breastplate of righteousness]; may the shield of faith be *sumentes scutum fidei* [taking the shield of faith]; may the sallet of hope be *galeam s*[a]*lutis assumite* [put on the helmet of salvation]; may the spirit's sword be *gladium spirit*[orum], *quod est verbum Dei* [the sword of the Spirit, which is the word of God], that is, the preaching of the divine word, and, above all, prayer and vigilance.[27]

Hevia y Valdés's successors seem to have taken these words to heart as they waged a series of increasingly violent campaigns against native idolatry and superstition between 1660 and 1735. This period, a third cycle in the development of ecclesiastical projects against native traditional devotions since the 1530s, resulted in multiple punitive pageants in which natives were disciplined with the lash and the spectacle of public scorn, in the summary execution of rebels who attempted to strike back at native informers, in idolatry accusations and counteraccusations motivated by local enmities, and in a most peculiar punitive enterprise: an ecclesiastical jail in Oaxaca City reserved for the permanent imprisonment of "teachers of idolatry" from all corners of the diocese. The reminder of this chapter is devoted to a discussion of the extirpation policies adopted by four Oaxacan bishops between 1665 and 1696—Alonso de Cuevas Dávalos, fray Tomás de Monterroso, Nicolás del Puerto, and Isidro Sariñana—whose actions set in motion a third cycle in idolatry extirpation projects. A renewed interest in idolatry in the late seventeenth century was not exclusive to Oaxaca. For instance, in Chiapas, Bishops

Marcos de la Serna and Francisco Núñez de la Vega conducted pastoral visits and intensified their prosecution of indigenous idolaters between the 1670s and the early eighteenth century.[28]

The complex military, political, and bureaucratic responses to the indigenous rebellion of Tehuantepec in 1660 serves as an important signpost in the redefinition of alliances and enmities between native communities and ecclesiastical and civil authorities in Oaxaca. On March 22, 1660, at the beginning of Holy Week, about six thousand Zapotecs in the town of Tehuantepec rose up in anger at the punitive way in which their alcalde mayor Juan de Avellán had recently applied the *repartimiento de efectos* as it pertained to cotton cloth. Repartimiento policies, which imposed the sale of goods in native communities at high prices that favored speculation by alcaldes mayores, sought the forced integration of natives into the colonial cash economy. The rebels stormed the royal houses in the center of town, set the royal stables on fire, and in the confusion Avellán was killed, along with three of his associates.[29] Two months after these events, on Corpus Christi Day, the Zapotecs of Nejapa also took up arms against colonial authorities, forcing a military standoff that was resolved only through the mediation of Bishop Cuevas Dávalos.

A collection of essays about the rebellion offers two complementary analyses of the motivations and dynamics of this movement.[30] In this work, Díaz-Polanco, Burguete, and Sánchez rehearse a cumulative theory of sorts: taxation abuses, followed by punishment and humiliation for recalcitrant native elites, may have provided a spark for the Tehuantepec rebellion. In their view, the colonial rulers eventually achieved their goal, a return to the administrative status quo before the rebellion, through appeasement and coercion, thus stalling the indigenous objective—peace with reform. By contrast, Carmagnani stressed the symbolic use of social space by native rebels and colonial officials and emphasized the great divergences in participation by different native actors at various stages in the rebellion. In his view, rather than a rebellion with clearly stated political goals, this movement was a struggle against the expanding political role of alcaldes mayores, which collided with the reformulation of communal identity in seventeenth-century Oaxaca.

The Tehuantepec rebellion occupies a unique place in the historiography of colonial Mexico due to its putatively multiethnic character and expansion over a large territory, which would stand in contrast with the localized scope of other colonial indigenous rebellions.[31] Three of this insurrection's elements figured prominently in discussions about these events among colonial officials: the motivation for the murder of an alcalde mayor by his subjects; the defiance shown by the rebels as they appointed new local authorities and held control over their localities in the following year; and the extent to which communities near Tehuantepec and Nejapa supported the rebels. According to the simile chosen by the rebellion's chroniclers, in 1660 and 1661 the insurrection spread "like wildfire" through several indigenous communities. Nevertheless, as Judith Zeitlin argued in an incisive analysis of the Tehuantepec rebellion, its regional scope and the rebel's political objectives were misrepresented by the oidor Juan de Montemayor y Cuenca, who was sent to Oaxaca in February 1661 by the newly appointed Viceroy Conde de Baños to investigate the insurrection. Montemayor's first audacious move was to arrest the entire rebel Tehuantepec cabildo when they attended the installation of the new alcalde mayor, thus avoiding a large-scale military campaign. The oidor then exacted unusually harsh punishments: one cabildo member and four other rebels were put to death, and twenty-eight insurgents received a combination of whipping and exile penalties.

According to Zeitlin, once Montemayor regained his authority over the region's cabildos, he wrested control of the rebellion's narrative by fostering the writing of two accounts about insurrections in Tehuantepec and other Oaxaca localities by two of his closest collaborators, Cristóbal Manso de Contreras, and Juan de Torres Castillo. Besides the fact that a flattering portrayal of Montemayor's role in the rebellion favored his political ambitions, two elements cast a shadow of doubt on these chronicles. First, although the Council of the Indies repeatedly asked for sworn testimony about claims that the rebels referred to their new gobernador as king and wrote letters to neighboring villages urging them to revolt, and about allegations that natives throughout the region were waging war against the Spaniards, no such proof was ever furnished by Montemayor and the viceroy. Second, in a December 1662 letter to the king, ten indigenous caciques and principales contended that the revolts had been limited to Tehuantepec and Nejapa, and that Montemayor had exaggerated the scope of the movement due to his desire to replace administrators in these localities and in Villa Alta with his cronies.[32]

Bishop Cuevas Dávalos, who served the see of Oaxaca between 1658 and 1664, acted as a successful mediator between rebels and civil authorities during and after the Tehuantepec rebellion. Once this insurrection was quashed, this bishop chose not to engage in extirpation campaigns in a direct manner. Nevertheless, his two immediate successors, fray Tomás de Monterroso (1664–78) and Nicolás del Puerto (1678–81), took decisive and unprecedented measures against idolatry through personal visits and with the assistance of alcaldes mayores.

Monterroso's concern for the idolatrous tendencies of his native parishioners was such that he wrote a Latin epistle to Pope Clement X in 1676 depicting some of their forbidden practices. Since ecclesiastical authorities in Oaxaca and Mexico seldom used the formalized conduit of a letter to the pontiff to discuss idolatry campaigns, this document stands out for its vivid style. In his letter, Monterroso begins by asking what remedy could exist for his parishioners, who persisted in erecting and adoring graven images of "fruits of the land, and snakes," revering stone images of the "god of storm and thunder"—a likely reference to Zapotec deity Cocijo, and burying their dead with effigies of this deity. He then briefly mentioned calendrical divination practices, using, paradoxically, the Nahuatl terms *tonal* (day, fate) and nahual, and mentioned the ritual beheading of turkeys and the burning of copal that took place as celebrants asked favors of their stone images. At this point, Monterroso made a singular request: He asked Clement X to grant him the faculty to punish recidivist idolaters severely, whipping them to the point of death, if necessary. Monterroso's report of his attempts to separate "those miserable ones" from their idolatrous practices through the whip during several campaigns in 1665 culminated with a boastful announcement about the confiscation of "fifty thousand" cult effigies and ritual implements, a hyperbole impossible to corroborate.[33] Finally, in a second letter dated a week later, Monterroso described the popular devotion to the Virgin of Guadalupe and noted his belief that indigenous people would turn away from idolatry through her intercession.[34]

During Nicolás del Puerto's brief tenure as bishop of Oaxaca (1679–81), the six towns in the Caxonos region—San Francisco, San Mateo, San Pedro, Santo Domingo, San Pablo, and San Miguel—loomed large as strongholds of idolatry in the consciousness of the extirpators. In a 1679 letter to the crown,[35] del Puerto reported the discovery of a "high priest" who, along with four others, exercised a parallel ministry in some of the aforementioned six towns. This man and his attendants were treated as if they were Christian priests, heard confessions, and admonished their followers not to confess with the Dominicans. Following an unusual punitive procedure that would later become the centerpiece of idolatry eradication in the diocese, del Puerto had these priests and some of their followers arrested and imprisoned in the royal jail of Oaxaca City, intending to turn the absence of these priests into a permanent exile from their native communities.[36] After these specialists were imprisoned, all the parishioners of San Francisco Caxonos came into the church and implored their vicar's pardon, declaring that they never had had a "true confession." In the light of later confrontations between the residents of San Francisco and their ministers, this maneuver seems an attempt to preempt further judicial actions against native specialists through a public, symbolic embrace of Christian devotion.

Bishop del Puerto's leading extirpator in Caxonos and other Villa Alta towns during this campaign was fray Bartolomé de Alcántara, an ecclesiastical judge with lengthy experience with idolatry trials who was also a renowned preacher in both Valley and Sierra Zapotec. In a June 1683 request for a promotion to the Dominican headquarters in Rome, Alcántara boasted about his punishment of some "idolaters and sorcerers whom I dragged out of the most rugged mountains of the sierra and frightful gullies, with great risk to life and limb." In an August 1683 letter of support, fray Joseph López, the Dominican provincial in Oaxaca, stated that Alcántara deserved this promotion due to the campaigns he led during López's four-year tenure, which resulted in the capture of more than fifty idolaters.[37] No further details of Alcántara's campaigns are extant, but a 1706 attestation drawn by the Dominicans before the escribano Díaz Romero specifies at least three proceedings instructed by Alcántara in the last decades of the seventeenth century: the trial of Yaxila and someone known as *Matavenados*, "Deer Killer" in San Ildefonso; the trial of Nicolás de Acevedo and his associates in Lachirioag; and the trial of don Juan Martín and don Bartolomé, caciques of Betaza.[38] Both of these Zapotec queche would continue to attract scrutiny from civil and ecclesiastical extirpators between the 1680s and the early eighteenth century.

ALCALDES MAYORES AGAINST IDOLATRY
IN VILLA ALTA

In a development that confirms Carmagnani's observations about the expanding powers of alcaldes mayores in Oaxaca in the late seventeenth century, between 1665 and 1736 the alcaldes mayores of Villa Alta presided over at least a dozen trials against Indians accused of engaging in idolatry or sorcery.[39] Although civil attempts to try native defendants of crimes against the faith could be regarded as a violation of ecclesiastical jurisdiction, trials preserved in the judicial archives of two alcaldías mayores in Oaxaca, Villa Alta and Teposcolula, demonstrate that, besides marking a transition in episcopal policies toward idolatry, the decade of the 1660s was also characterized by a vigorous civil prosecution of native idolatry. Even if the extant documents in these two archives are not an exhaustive record of all seventeenth-century trials carried out in these jurisdictions, they still are the most complete set of colonial judicial archive collections in Oaxaca.

During the 1660s, there was at least one idolatry trial initiated by Juan de Baena, escribano and deputy alcalde mayor in Teposcolula: a case against Catalina Mendoza and Melchor Hernández of Tamazulapa, accused of performing "idolatrous" practices in order to murder the local alcalde Domingo de Ayala in 1662.[40] By contrast, Diego de Villegas y Sandoval Castro, alcalde mayor of Villa Alta in 1653–55 and again from late 1665 until late 1667,[41] was an especially active civil extirpator of idolatries under the aegis of Bishop Monterroso (1665–78), for he presided over at least three idolatry cases in 1665 and 1666: the trial of Luis de Vargas of Yojovi,[42] and the related trial of his murderer, Lucas de los Reyes in 1665;[43] the trial of Juan Gonzalo and Pedro de Viloria of Lachirioag in 1666;[44] and finally, the multitudinous trial of eleven residents of Lachirioag in 1666.[45] Except for an *aperçu* in Chance and a brief discussion by de la Fuente,[46] these idolatry trials have received little attention.

At least three of Villegas y Sandoval's successors heard idolatry trials in Villa Alta. For instance, don Fernando de Velasco y Castilla, count of Santiago and Calimaya, presided over a brief trial in 1668.[47] Moreover, Captain Cristóbal del Castillo Mondragón, alcalde mayor of Villa Alta between 1677 and 1683, assisted Bishop Nicolás del Puerto (1679–81) during the extirpation attempts carried out by the Dominican Alcántara and others,[48] but left no extant trial records. The section below focuses on three Villa Alta civil idolatry trials heard in 1665–66.

Political and personal enmity, as well as profit derived from the seizure of a defendant's property, have routinely been identified as some of the most common causes for the accusations leveled against defendants at the onset of some inquisitorial procedures.[49] To this repertoire of biases, one should add instances of blackmail against natives caught *in medias res* by non-Indians, and even by fellow natives. The dynamics of blackmail in Villa Alta Zapotec communities are illustrated in unusual detail by two 1665 cases: the blackmailing of Luis de Vargas by Lucas de los Reyes, and Joseph Gómez's attempt to blackmail two of his neighbors.[50]

Luis de Vargas's case involved a blackmailer who decided to go back on his promise to keep silent, perhaps in order to deflect any impending accusations about his actions. In October 1665, the mestizo Lucas de los Reyes, appeared before Villegas y Sandoval in order to denounce a conflictive encounter he had had with Luis de Vargas of Yojovi. This conflict cut across ethnic and social divides: not only was Reyes mestizo and Vargas Zapotec, but Reyes had been born in Analco, a *barrio*, or neighborhood, established by indigenous migrants who assisted the Spanish in the conquest of Villa Alta. Early on the morning of August 4 of that year, Reyes came across Vargas near Yojovi, a town near Tabaá, as he looked after some mules belonging to the Analco cacique Luis de la Cruz. Vargas ran away suspiciously, so Reyes pursued and tackled him. As Vargas lay on the ground, Reyes noticed he was carrying two plucked and beheaded turkeys, two pieces of the tree-bark paper called *yaguichi*, and two uncooked maize tortillas. These objects were a sign of recent Zapotec ritual sacrifices; therefore, Vargas told Reyes, "You have caught me in my sin," and asked him to come down to Yojovi so he could bribe him.

At this point, the narrative diverged into three different versions of the events, as told by Reyes, Vargas, and an alcalde of Yojovi. Reyes admitted coming down with Vargas to Yojovi and receiving a mule and nine pesos, which he had taken "fearing that either he would be killed or [Vargas] would run away." When Vargas was first brought before the alcalde mayor, he denied Reyes's testimony and asserted that he had paid Reyes in order to settle a debt. After being counseled by his defense attorney, Vargas admitted having been caught by Reyes shortly after an individual sacrifice on behalf of his crops,[51] and he stated he had given Reyes a mule and not nine, but eleven pesos in exchange for his silence. In order to disguise this payment, Vargas asked an alcalde of Yojovi to draft a note in Zapotec stating that, on August 4, 1665, Vargas had given Reyes a mule in order to settle a debt of fourteen pesos.[52] Reyes showed this note to the cacique Luis de la Cruz in order to account for his new mule and gave one peso to his fellow muleteer Francisco.

Due to Reyes's testimony, Juan de la Cruz, one of Yojovi's alcaldes, was also imprisoned and brought before Villegas y Sandoval. His account provided a midpoint of sorts between Reyes's and Vargas's carefully amended avowals. Cruz declared that after he was called to Yojovi's main square by a *topil*, or minor town official, Reyes told him he had caught Vargas "practicing idolatry on the mountain." Depicting himself as a Christian cabildo official in the courtroom, Cruz testified that he had promptly had Vargas tied to the pillory to be given fifty lashes, after which he would be turned over to the authorities. However, Reyes asserted he was only interested in collecting a debt from Vargas, so Cruz untied Vargas and left. According to Vargas, both men then went into a maize plot to negotiate; reportedly, Reyes asked Vargas to give him fifty pesos, an amount which "a Mixe whom I caught in the same sin" had allegedly paid, but Vargas brought him down to half this amount: one mule worth about fourteen pesos, and eleven pesos in cash.

In the end, Villegas y Sandoval ruled that Vargas would be punished in an auto in which he wore a beheaded turkey on his chest, and he would receive two hundred lashes. Vargas was also sentenced to one year's service at the church of Villa Alta and required to pay a fine of eighteen pesos, sixteen for legal costs, and two for lamp oil for the church.[53] Reyes, however, was only sentenced to return the mule and the nine pesos to the civil justice, and de la Cruz received a conditional absolution. This decision did not end the dispute between Reyes and Vargas. On Christmas Day 1665, Luis de Vargas, who was completing his one-year service at the church of San Ildefonso, left Villa Alta with two friends to drink pulque at the home of Cristóbal de Xuárez of Lachirioag. While in Xuárez's home, he ran into Lucas de los Reyes, who tried to fight with Vargas, so he was thrown out. The morning after, Reyes told Xuárez's wife that he had fought Vargas outside Lachirioag. Vargas's corpse was found later, but by that time Reyes had fled the region.[54]

The case involving Joseph Gómez, Juan Gonzalo and don Pedro de Viloria portrays a more complex set of social dynamics, since it pitted indigenous informants against specialists and a native extortionist in a small community. In March 1666, Simón de Bautista of Lachirioag appeared before Villegas y Sandoval and reported his daughter had told him about a troubling rumor regarding don Pedro de Viloria, gobernador of the neighboring town of Yatee, and Juan Gonzalo, one of don Pedro's associates. Apparently, the two men bribed Joseph Gómez with forty pesos after he had caught them beheading two newborn puppies around Lent of 1665. When Villegas y Sandoval asked Bautista why he had waited so long to denounce this, he replied that Nicolás de Vargas, the official interpreter of Villa Alta's civil court throughout the administration of several alcaldes mayores,[55] had asked him to report to him any suspicious meetings in his town; in other words, he was a native who had agreed to be an informant. Later, Joseph Gómez was imprisoned and taken to court, and he admitted that, about a year before, he had caught Viloria and Gonzalo on a clearing outside Yatee around three in the morning as they were beheading a newborn puppy. Gómez contended that he only received twenty rather than forty pesos: about fourteen pesos in coins, an old horse valued at five pesos, and the rest in turkeys and chickens. To pay this bribe, Gonzalo was forced to sell his team of oxen; Gómez apparently used this money to set up a business buying and selling pigs in the region.

Viloria, Yatee's gobernador, initially denied the accusations, and his own wife argued that she had no part in the matter, since it had been settled among men. Nonetheless, after conferring with his defense attorney, Viloria made a full confession. As he embraced a crucifix he had requested "so the devil would not disturb him," Viloria declared that Juan Gonzalo came to see him at night and invited him to make a sacrifice "to the devil" in order to ask for a good harvest, in the manner of "our fathers and grandfathers." Viloria claimed to have little knowledge about the meaning of this sacrifice. He would only identified the sacrifice's recipient as "the devil;" when pressed for details, he stated that the devil, a prideful angel whom God had banished to the underworld, had deceived him into performing such a ceremony.[56] Since Gonzalo, the instigator of the sacrifice, had fled Yatee with his entire family, he was not interrogated, but his property was seized, and he was sentenced in absentia to the same punishment as Viloria: two hundred lashes and one-third of the legal costs. Furthermore, Viloria was removed from his post as gobernador and forbidden to serve in public office. In April 1666, Gonzalo returned to Yatee and presented himself in court with an attorney; at this time, he received his two hundred lashes and was sentenced to four months of service at Tabaá's church. Unlike Reyes the mestizo extortionist, who was not given a corporal punishment, Gómez was sentenced to one hundred lashes and ordered to return the twenty pesos he had received to the civil justice. In a symbolic twist, this amount financed the manufacture of an effigy of Christ in the cross for the church of Yatee by local sculptor Juan de los Reyes.[57]

In both civil and ecclesiastic courts, the architecture of an idolatry trial rested on a keystone that held the entire procedure in place: the assumption that a series of acts, or a string of words, constituted an act of devotion directed toward a non-Christian entity. If the judge was particularly knowledgeable about certain practices, this assumption was relatively easy to uphold: so long as witnesses provided the court with a credible narrative or physical evidence about suspect actions or objects—such as sacrificed animals, censers, or food—an idolatry conviction could be handed down. Legal narratives about idolatry called in fact for a received dénouement: the defendants' acknowledgment that the suspect acts they had engaged in were part of a deliberate act of idolatry. An overwhelming proportion of the determinations of guilt in the idolatry trials discussed in this work depended primarily on an act of confession by the accused. Hence, native defendants in an idolatry trial were under constant pressure to fulfill a heavily scripted role in a legal narrative.

Only in a few cases was this narrative called into question. The trial of eleven idolatry suspects from Lachirioag between February and April 1666 by Villegas y Sandoval provides a revealing glimpse at the dynamics of proof in a faltering idolatry trial. This intricate case involved two local factions, racial tensions among an African slave, non-Indians, and indigenous people, and nagging questions about credibility that poisoned what initially seemed an exemplary narrative about nocturnal idolatries. Villegas y Sandoval had asked Antonio de Cabrera, a black slave belonging to don Gaspar Calderón, encomendero of Lachirioag, to keep a watchful eye on any suspect activities in town as he and his owner visited Lachirioag in April and May 1665 to collect tributes.

On May 2, 1665, Cabrera went back to the alcalde mayor with a detailed narrative of two events he witnessed. On April 18, he saw some natives enter the house of Gerónimo López late at night and gather around two large pots containing deer meat. A week later, Cabrera caught López and many residents of Lachirioag as they were coming down the hill of Yaguisi toward the town early at night, and once again he saw natives cooking deer meat in López's dwelling. Neither Cabrera nor the civil authorities had a clear idea about the meaning of these gatherings, but they seemed suspiciously similar to received narratives about nocturnal idolatrous sacrifices. Villegas y Sandoval and the alguacil Martínez de la Sierra waited for several months to gather evidence and asked Lachirioag resident Diego de Alcántara to spy on his neighbors, to no avail. It was not until February 1666 that they moved to arrest six of the presumed idolaters: Lachirioag cacique and gobernador don Juan Martín and his wife María Ana; alcalde Juan González; alguacil Joseph Gonzalo; former maestro de doctrina Gerónimo López; and regidor Juan Contreras. Later in the trial, four other presumed idolaters were also imprisoned. As the trial began, something uncanny occurred: none of the accused admitted having participated in the meetings described by Cabrera; in fact, they only admitted to coming across Cabrera by chance, but never under suspicious circumstances. Some even admitted that parceling out deer meat after a hunt was a common practice, but they stressed this was always done in full daylight.

At this point, the informant Diego de Alcántara brought to the court's attention the involvement of two men who belonged to a rival political faction. One of them was the cacique don Diego Martín, a prominent Lachirioag resident who had kinship ties to two officials who had been arrested: he was Gerónimo López's nephew, and a second cousin to don Juan Martín. Don Diego Martín declared that the slave Cabrera had come to his house after midnight on two separate occasions in April 1665 to warn him that the townspeople were holding suspicious gatherings. He also stated that he and the cacique don Francisco Gutiérrez were despised by the commoners, "because they take away their pulque and their drunkenness."[58] In fact, Lachirioag was riven into two political factions: one led by Gerónimo López and don Juan Martín, who stood accused of organizing suspicious gatherings at night, and another led by don Francisco Gutiérrez and don Diego Martín, who presented themselves as opposing drunkenness and idolatry.

This rivalry was confirmed by a breakthrough in incriminatory information. About two weeks after don Diego Martín's first deposition, Luis de la Cruz, the Analco alcalde whose employee Lucas Reyes had murdered Luis Vargas, reported a confidential conversation he had just had with don Diego Martín. On the strength of this revelation, the alcalde mayor called don Diego to make a second deposition. This time, don Diego provided various details he had not volunteered before out of fear of reprisals. First, don Diego asserted that it was he who had led the slave Cabrera to spy on the two nocturnal meetings of his fellow residents. Secondly, he reported that Juan Bautista, Gerónimo López's son and his own cousin, had told him that López was an idolater who "beheaded the deer, poured their blood in a tube, took it to the hill of Yaguisi, and poured it into a hole by a cross atop the hill in order to summon the devil."[59]

Bautista also told him that López was a specialist who heard confessions from the townspeople and who baptized newborns with Zapotec names before their priest gave them Christian ones.[60] Don Diego also declared he had confronted López directly by telling him, "Turn away from those fiendish things that belong to the devil!" López retorted, "Go away, you who lick the Spaniards's dishes [*lambeplatos de los españoles*]; you are no longer my nephew!"[61] When Juan Bautista was brought in to respond to don Diego's accusations, he denied everything and asked to be brought before his accusers. An unpleasant surprise awaited the court officials: a day after his second deposition, don Diego was reported to have taken his horse and galloped away. Some Zoogocho residents claimed don Diego told them he was going to Oaxaca because of the dispute in Lachirioag. In any case, the prosecution had lost its most valuable witness.

A week after don Diego's flight or suspicious disappearance, the slave Cabrera arrived in San Ildefonso in order to face the defendants. Cabrera, an old man in poor health, had been brought on a hammock from Oaxaca and testified in Nahuatl or Zapotec, even though he had a good knowledge of Spanish. Cabrera reiterated the narrative about the two nighttime meetings when confronted with don Juan Martín, but don Juan confronted him by stating repeatedly, "It was not so," and "You lie, black man!"

Don Juan also questioned Cabrera's credibility by raising the specter of African lust:

I scolded you [Cabrera] because you used to let yourself into the commoners' houses. There are some women who came to me asking for justice because you forced them into fornication: Pedro Sánchez's wife, Simón Bautista's wife, and Juan Aldas's widow, whom you also assaulted; there is also the wife of the cacique Mateo Martín, from whom you stole a chicken. You also left your trousers in [our] town so they would keep quiet, so they would not tell your owner about it.[62]

It is difficult to assess the credibility of native claims about Cabrera's sexual drive. On the one hand, their accusations cast a pall over Cabrera's motivations: almost every defendant who was confronted with Cabrera reiterated the names of the assaulted women and stated that Cabrera had left his trousers behind; some even stated that Cabrera avoided receiving fifty lashes as punishment for his assaults on women after he dropped to his knees and begged don Juan for mercy. Cabrera never attempted to deny these accusations, therefore raising questions about his credibility. On the other hand, no woman came forward to accuse him of assault or robbery.[63]

The alcalde mayor approached this impasse by calling character witness. On the side of the defendants, Simón Bautista, the husband of one of Cabrera's purported victims, Cristóbal de Mereles, and Juan Mateo declared that Cabrera drank pulque often and had attempted to assault several indigenous women. On the side of the absent don Diego, two non-Indian residents of San Ildefonso came forward to attest to his reputation as a good Christian. On April 15, 1666, Villegas y Sandoval handed down a sentence that reflected his misgivings about a narrative of idolatrous acts that had failed to crystallize during the proceedings:

Bearing in mind that, in spite of the exacting and detailed proceedings made on behalf of this case, it has not been possible to prove and examine the contents of the initial accusation—and even this accusation was not legitimate and truthful as far as it involved the deposition of don Diego Martín, now absent—I must absolve, and I do absolve all the defendants in this trial, reserving to the Royal Justice the right to initiate further proceedings against them and to continue to search for don Diego Martín, so he may ratify his deposition.[64]

Paradoxically, 2-Jaguar, the piyè date when Cabrera spied on the deer eaters of Lachirioag, continues to be an enigmatic cosmological choice, if their consumption of deer meat was indeed tied to a celebration. A somewhat distant possibility is that Lachirioag's ritual specialists may have known that 2-Jaguar was a piyè date associated with eclipse events, as suggested by the 1693 annotation regarding a solar eclipse in Villa Alta's Booklet 81 discussed in Chapter 5. In any case, at the end of this trial, a faction that may have performed communal ceremonies and held stern views regarding the meddling of outsiders had successfully challenged the testimony of a slave and forced a local elite member into temporary exile. A generation later, the stakes had grown: this time, the lives of Dominicans, Spaniards, and native allies would all be at play.

VILLAVICENCIO'S CAMPAIGNS
IN TLAXCALA AND OAXACA

Diego Jaimes Ricardo Villavicencio was one of the most zealous secular ministers who engaged in idolatry eradication in the late seventeenth century. Bishop Fernández de Santa Cruz of Tlaxcala appointed Villavicencio as commissioned judge of idolatry,[65] and he later enjoyed the support of Bishop Sariñana of Oaxaca. Villavicencio's activities in Popoloca-speaking areas to the southeast of Puebla, documented by two surviving proceedings and a 1692 publication, epitomize secular attempts to eradicate native ritual practices in Oaxaca at the close of the seventeenth century. Villavicencio began his ecclesiastical career as beneficiado and vicar of Teotitlán del Camino, a Mazatec-speaking parish with eleven dependencies in the diocese of Oaxaca.[66] In 1674, as commissioned judge against idolatry under Bishop Monterroso, Villavicencio confiscated several idols in San Francisco de la Sierra and forwarded them to Monterroso.[67]

It was during this period that Villavicencio apparently acquired a good knowledge of Popoloca (sometimes called "Chocho" in colonial records), a skill he would put to use during his interrogation of native specialists. By 1688, Villavicencio was named beneficiado and ecclesiastic judge of Santa Cruz Tlacotepec, a Popoloca-speaking parish sixteen leagues to the southeast of Puebla. He had also received a commission against native idolaters from the provisor of Indians in Puebla in July 1688.[68] Villavicencio wasted no time in exercising these faculties; shortly after this appointment, he heard testimony about the activities of Diego Hernández, an elder Popoloca ritual specialist from San Luis Tlacotepec. Through various witnesses, a case was built against Hernández, Agustín Francisco, and the local deacon and bugle player Cristóbal Salvador, who were accused of making ritual sacrifices. Since these accusers were regarded as natives, Villavicencio was able to convict and incarcerate them in the ecclesiastical prison of Tlacotepec, which he called "prison of idolaters," inspired by the much larger prison that Bishop Sariñana had begun building in Oaxaca City in that year.

Villavicencio discovered that Hernández was a well-known specialist within the local elective sphere. One of his main clients was Nicolasa Juana, a woman regarded as mulatto because of her skin color and parentage who had married the Popoloca Juan Mateo. In order to stop Nicolasa from fleeing, Villavicencio had her incarcerated in the Tlacotepec jail in September 1688. Since Villavicencio had no jurisdiction over non-Indians, he submitted information on the case to the provisor de indios in Puebla, who turned it over to the local prosecutor of the Holy Office. In October 1688, the prosecutor granted him a commission to inquire about the ceremonies Hernández performed on Nicolasa's behalf; in December of that year, Villavicencio interrogated Cristóbal Salvador and Diego Hernández.

Salvador declared that Nicolasa called him to offer chicken and turkey blood to three idols that she owned—a white one with a red ribbon, a green one, and a brown one—to secure good health, the well-being of her livestock, or a bountiful harvest; after these sacrifices, Nicolasa abstained from sexual intercourse during four days. Salvador also admitted to curing a swelling on Nicolasa's neck by sucking on it and reciting an incantation. Hernández also admitted to performing similar sacrifices for Nicolasa and stated that he had presided over a group composed of Nicolasa, her husband Juan Mateo, her son Pedro Hernández, and her daughter Pascuala María as they pierced their tongues to offer blood sacrifices to their effigies. Additionally, Hernández described a Popoloca ceremony for naming newborns:

In order to impose the symbols and names of the devil upon the daughters and granddaughters of [Nicolasa], who consulted him to baptize eight or nine children before they were christened at the church, he would tie their arms and legs with cotton thread, and pour water on their hands, feet, and head, calling forth the devil so he would give them health. When he poured the water, he said *chacui inchengi nthenguicna nchana*, which means "Come forth, devil, help this child" [Come, Human Owl, help this child]. He imposed the following names on them; the first child was called *tohondahá*, the second one *sxrondahá*, the third one *nthonda*, the fourth one *sxrachagó*, the fifth one *sxroguichró*, the sixth one *sxrachagó*, the seventh one *sxronchagó*, the eighth one *sxintchihá*, and the ninth one *rohachagó*, and he gave these symbols and names to those children by request of [Nicolasa] and her husband. When this witness was asked what these names meant, and what had happened to the three idols to whom [Nicolasa] offered sacrifices, he said they were the devil's names.[69]

The children's names above appear to be garbled versions of Chocho-Popoloca calendrical names.[70] Hernández also referred to a previous set of idolatry proceedings, conducted by either Villavicencio or his predecessor, after which Juan Mateo had been incarcerated and punished.

In November 1688, Villavicencio also heard a case against Juan Pascual and his wife María Flores, two mestizos who owned a sheep ranch near Tehuacán. As in Nicolasa's case, the proceeding stemmed from a native idolatry trial: the one against Popoloca specialist Francisco Lucas, who also looked after Pascual's sheep. In addition to his services as a shepherd, Lucas was asked to perform several propitiatory sacrifices in behalf of Pascual's health and livestock and to ensure rainfall. For these sacrifices, Pascual and his wife would bring out two carved stones, one blue, the other white, pierced through with a rope and kept in a locked pine box. Lucas would then burn copal and behead chickens or turkeys in order to offer their blood to the effigies. On certain occasions, Lucas would ask Pascual to pierce his tongue over a piece of paper in order to offer his blood to these unnamed, mysterious entities.[71] In other words, both Nicolasa and Pascual owned effigies and ritual implements and had a general knowledge of Popoloca ritual practices. What they lacked was

specialized knowledge of canonical procedures for ritual sacrifice and
the appropriate incantations.

In January 1689, the inquisitorial prosecutor of Puebla granted Villavicencio a commission to interrogate the two mestizos and the mulata
"in the manner of the Holy Office" and asked him to collect testimony
about the defendants' ethnic status. The proceedings against Juan Pascual are no longer extant, but the inquiry into Nicolasa Juana's eth-
nicity yielded fascinating results. Villavicencio sent Nicolasa to the
ecclesiastical jail in Puebla and then interrogated three witnesses about
Nicolasa's parentage. All of the witnesses agreed that Nicolasa was
known and addressed locally as a mulata, commented on her light com-
plexion, and noted that her father Lucas Hernández was a mestizo and
her mother Gerónima María a mulata.

Following a time-honored strategy, when Nicolasa realized that she
was about to be handed over to the Holy Office, she had a petition
drafted in which she stated she was a "legitimate Indian," a development that forced the Holy Office to request information about the eth-
nicity of her grandparents. The results of these proceedings were rather
surprising: even if Nicolasa's parents were found to be non-Indians, the
Holy Office of Puebla ruled that, on account of the fact that both Nicolasa, her husband, and son spoke exclusively Popoloca, she would have
to be regarded as an Indian in jurisdictional terms, even if she "had
some blood that did not come from an Indian" in her lineage. In other
words, the Holy Office was recognizing a de facto reality: as a result of
the intermarriage of natives with resident castas in native communities,
their offspring were quickly acculturated into native society and the local
language. In such cases, the received conception of *sangre*, a rudimentary
notion of genetic heritage, was overruled by a cultural factor: one's membership in a community of native speakers of an indigenous language.[72]

With the sponsorship and support of Bishop Sariñana, in 1692 Villavicencio published a treatise on native superstition and idolatry entitled
Luz y méthodo de confesar idólatras. Since Balsalobre's 1656 extirpation manual had been confiscated by the Holy Office in 1659, Villavicencio's 1692 imprint may be regarded as the first instruction manual
for novice extirpators that circulated without censure in the dioceses of
Mexico, Tlaxcala, and Oaxaca. Villavicencio's scope was much broader
than that of the treatises written by Ponce de León, Ruiz de Alarcón,
or de la Serna. Instead of focusing on specific data about the ritual
practices of a linguistic group whose language he had mastered, Villavicencio attempted a general description of the phenomenon of idolatry,
beginning with examples from classical antiquity and working his way
through the Mexica ritual practices reported in Torquemada, López de

Gómara, León, Bautista, and other sources. The intent of this work was eminently didactic. Like Balsalobre's *Relación auténtica*, Villavicencio's *Luz y méthodo* was conceived as a manual for newfangled extirpators in isolated native communities; unlike Balsalobre's work, *Luz y méthodo* did not focus on legal procedure and on the various stages in the compilation of accusations and testimony, choosing instead to emphasize the manner of interrogating idolatry suspects in order to ensure their conviction. Villavicencio went so far as to propose eighteen generic types of ritual sacrifice and nine categories of ritual observances that did not involve sacrifices, in order to offer a broad perspective on native practices for the benefit of amateur extirpators.[73]

In spite of the vivid portrayals of native devotions that Villavicencio elicited from witnesses in his trials, his description of such practices in *Luz y méthodo* is rather flat and undifferentiated. Villavicencio's accidental ethnography was deeply rooted in a genre that privileged the recounting of anecdotes or narrative vignettes over the detailed and systematic description of specific instances of ritual performance.[74] In contrast with the accounts of Ruiz de Alarcón, Balsalobre, and de la Serna, Villavicencio diluted the social and biographical information of ritual practitioners, favoring a general account in which a Popoloca ritual practice may easily be replaced with a Nahua observance. Even though Villavicencio spoke Popoloca, he chose not to discuss any of the incantations he recorded during his idolatry trials. More importantly, in a rhetorical move that resembles Olmos's description of Mexica religion as an antipodal version of Christianity in his *Tratado de hechicerías*, Villavicencio regarded the devil as the prime mover for these practices. In spite of these limitations, Villavicencio organized his formulaic interrogations—a series of questions to be asked of natives at the confessional—around a default social categorization of idolaters. Perhaps influenced by his investigation of specialists' clients Nicolasa Juana and Juan Pascual, Villavicencio distinguished between two groups: *sacrificadores*, or ritual practitioners; and *alquilantes*, or clients, who had some knowledge of ritual practices, but who allowed sacrificadores to take the lead in performing them.

SARIÑANA'S PERPETUAL PRISON
FOR IDOLATERS

Isidro Sariñana (1683–96), del Puerto's successor, arrived at Oaxaca's episcopal seat after a remarkably successful ecclesiastical career: not only had he been a member of Mexico's cathedral council, held a lectureship

in theology at the Royal University, and served as *calificador* for the
Holy Office, but he was also a much celebrated preacher and author.
Among his best-known works, one may cite his *Llanto del Occidente*,
a lavishly illustrated eulogy that chronicled the funeral commemoration held for Philip IV in Mexico City by Viceroy Marquis of Mancera
in 1666;[75] his oration at the dedication of the cathedral of Mexico in
1668;[76] and his oration at the funeral of twenty-one Franciscans who
died during the 1680 Pueblo rebellion in New Mexico.

These works afford us some revelatory glimpses at Sariñana's rhetorical engagement with idolatry before becoming an active eradicator. In
Llanto del Occidente, Sariñana portrayed Philip IV as a devout Marianist who defended Christianity with the ferocity of a besieged ermine—a
simile that hinged on the royal appearance of the ermine's white fur.[77]
Most importantly, in his funeral oration for the Franciscans of New
Mexico, Sariñana employed a suggestive image, the arrows with which
Pueblo natives mortally wounded the mendicants, to illustrate native
duplicity:

The instruments the Indians employed are the most suitable glyphs of their concealed and treacherous deceit. The quiver where arrows may be hidden is the symbol of the deceit which conceals treason. [...] In Chapter Three of the *Threnos*,
Jeremiah referred to arrows as "the children of the quiver." [...] Hence, these
foretelling quivers were glyphs of the betrayal concealed within, for just as the
quiver hides an arrow until one's impulse brings it out at the right moment, the
betrayal conceived by the Indians' depraved spirits was hidden until the appointed
day when fury gave birth to it with sudden quickness.[78]

Sariñana's depiction of the duplicity of the Pueblos fulfilled two objectives. First, as a Baroque sermon by an illustrious preacher, it struck the
right emotional cord with his illustrious audience at Mexico's cathedral
by linking Franciscan martyrdom with an impeachable Old Testament
source—Jeremiah's *Threnos*, or Lamentations. Second, he explained the
surprising nature of the Pueblo rebellion by presenting native resolve as
a "glyph of betrayal" easily hidden, as an arrow inside a quiver. In addition, Sariñana denounced the "appearance of humility" as part of the
treacherous nature of natives, who hid their true designs beneath "obsequiousness." Lastly, Sariñana used a vivid organic simile to depict the
fight against heterodoxy: "the Holy Church is such a majestic tree, that
it thrusts its branches across the entire earthly realm. As a mother, however, it suffers the damage heresy or apostasy inflict on any branch, and
this Religion laments the branches broken by each lost Christianity."[79]

Sariñana's determination to confront indigenous apostates served as
a basis for a punitive experiment in Oaxaca City as innovative as it was
redoubtable: a prison devoted to the permanent seclusion of "teachers of

idolatries" and recidivist idolaters that would be known as the *prisión perpetua de idólatras*. He was probably inspired by inquisitorial precedent. In Mexico City, in the early seventeenth century the Holy Office erected a *prisión perpetua* for proselytizing Jews and for heretics who could not be trusted to return in peace to their local surroundings.[80] In the archbishopric of Lima, a prison for idolaters called the Casa de Santa Cruz was finished in 1618 and ceased to exist before 1639; its inmates remained imprisoned for unspecified periods, earning their keep by weaving textiles.[81]

Sariñana's ambitious project against native idolatry required the intervention of a small army of secular priests with proficiency in native languages and a particular vocation for inquisitorial tasks. Six of Sariñana's secular soldiers—Basques de Hinostrosa, Heras y Torres, Ortiz de Acuña, Ramírez de Aguilar, Morales Altamirano, and Aragón y Alcántara—briefly noted their eradication activities in their career summaries, thus providing an invaluable glance at policies against idolatry in this period. Don Antonio Basques de Hinostrosa became beneficiado of Coatlan in Miahuatlán in 1684 and began his career as extirpator there in 1686, after receiving from Sariñana faculties to preside over idolatry trials. In 1688, he obtained the beneficio of San Agustín Mixtepec in Nejapa, and during the early 1690s, he served as synodal examiner in the Coatlan, Valley, and Sierra variants of Zapotec. In 1700, Basques de Hinostrosa was named commissioner of the Holy Office in Mixtepec; since the bishopric's seat was then vacant, he used this title to prosecute natives, "arresting the dogmatizers and submitting them to the prison of idolaters in Oaxaca City, taking away from some Indians the various idols they worshipped, and the manuscript books of their sects and evil doings." He later continued his extirpation activities as vicario foráneo and ecclesiastical judge of Mixtepec, a title granted him by Bishop Maldonado in 1706.[82] Diego de las Heras y Torres was another secular priest proficient in native languages, for he was licensed to preach in coastal and highland Mixtec variants. After serving as vicar of Guajolotitlán, Chalcatongo, and Pinotepa del Rey between 1691 and 1693, Heras y Torres received the beneficio of Tototepec, as well as faculties to conduct idolatry trials. He later became vicario foráneo and ecclesiastical judge of both Tototepec and Xamiltepec.[83] Don Rodrigo Ortiz de Acuña served as vicar in the parishes of Ejutla, Amatlan, Loxicha, and Miahuatlán between 1680–92 and received from Sariñana the faculty to act against idolaters as beneficiado of Teozacualco in 1695. However, his resumé emphasized his role as a synodal examiner in Mixtec and Zapotec, rather than specific extirpation campaigns.[84]

Another extirpator in remote parts was don Antonio Ramírez de Aguilar, who was proficient in Mazatec and Nahuatl. After serving in Teotitlán del Camino between 1679 and 1681, only a few years after Villavicencio, Ramírez de Aguilar became vicar of the parish of Chacaltianguis. In January 1685, Sariñana gave him faculties to try idolaters in Chacaltianguis and also named him vicar of Xalapa; in fact, Sariñana praised his work as extirpator and asked him to preach sermons about the Christian doctrine "in a clear style" to his parishioners. Due to these merits, he was named beneficiado and vicar of Tuxtla and San Andrés in 1686.[85] Diego de Morales Altamirano was another extirpator in a remote corner of the diocese: appointed in 1680 as beneficiado of Chinameca, a Coatzacoalco doctrina near the Gulf of Mexico, he was named vicario foráneo in June 1680 and again in March 1684. Sometime between 1684 and 1687, Sariñana gave him a commission to extirpate idolatries in the region, and Morales Altamirano subsequently obtained posts in Miahuatlán and Oaxaca City after 1688.[86] In addition to delegating faculties to these ministers, Sariñana also retained some legal experts—such as Gaspar Calderón y Mendoza, a magistrate in the highest criminal court in Mexico City, the Sala del Crimen—to elucidate any procedural doubts during idolatry proceedings.[87]

The rising star in this cohort of secular extirpators was undoubtedly Joseph de Aragón y Alcántara, a priest who accumulated an impressive curriculum as Sariñana's right arm in Juquila, Miahuatlán, and Ejutla. He initiated his career as extirpator after being named in 1688 as beneficiado of Santa Catarina Juquila, the Chatino-speaking town from which Diego Luis of Sola obtained a ritual text in 1635. By February 1690, he had arrested and tried twenty-six specialists from the eighteen dependencies of Juquila and had dispatched them to Oaxaca City in order to incarcerate them in Bishop Sariñana's prison; later, he participated in their formal absolution during Lent of that year. All in all, Aragón y Alcántara spent more than two years trying the idolaters of Juquila and resorted to his personal funds—since he allegedly refused to charge the legal costs to the defendants—to convict a total of forty-six maestros. Aragón y Alcántara then served as beneficiado of Yagavila in Villa Alta between 1692 and early 1694, but he did not pursue idolaters during that time. After obtaining the beneficio of Ejutla in February 1694, he led an intensive campaign against idolaters in sixteen towns in the Sierra de Ocelotepec in Miahuatlán, as well as in the Ejutla estancia of San Vicente, securing the conviction of forty-four maestros who ended their days in Sariñana's prison.[88] Bishop Maldonado profited from Aragón y Alcántara's expertise, and under Maldonado he became visitador general and provisor y vicario general de indios.

In 1686, Sariñana presented a striking rationale for erecting a prison for idolaters in Oaxaca City in a letter to the crown. After experimenting with whipping, autos de fe, and other means of punishment, Sariñana favored a newfangled punitive project

because punishing them by whipping and parading them in public does not have a significant effect. On the other hand, it is not possible to release them to the secular authorities for capital punishment, since their status as neophytes, which they still enjoy due to their very limited capabilities, renders them exempt from such punishment. . . . Therefore, my Lord, the most adequate punishment would be to remove them from their towns and houses because the great love they have for the misery of their localities is in direct proportion to the grief that such separation would cause. Leaving these teachers [of idolatry] in their towns would be as leaving in them the contagion of mange; moving them elsewhere would run the risk of having them infect the sane ones.[89]

The crown moved swiftly to honor Sariñana's ambitious request of three thousand pesos de oro for the project, issuing a cédula in February 1688 that granted this amount in two installments. Sariñana then began building the prison in the very center of Oaxaca City, only a few streets southwest of the cathedral, on land ceded by Antonio del Grado, beneficiado of Xicayán and collector of tithes for the bishopric.[90] Sariñana received the second installment of royal funds by February 1690, and at this time he reported to the crown his plans to inaugurate the prison formally by bringing Aragón y Alcántara's twenty-six "teachers of idolatry" from the Sierra of Juquila. Joining public penitence to exemplary praise, Sariñana nominated Juan Mendoza, the only native in Santa Catarina Juquila not guilty of engaging in collective ritual practices, as gobernador.[91] Since Mendoza died before receiving his reward, Sariñana arranged for his widow to receive a lifelong pension. In his letter to the crown, Sariñana provided us with the most detailed extant portrayal of his prison's daily routine:

I have brought with me to [Oaxaca City] twenty-six maestros, whom I will grant a public and solemn absolution . . . at the cathedral in the second or third week of Lent this year. . . . I will then transfer them to the perpetual prison, which is so close to being completed, that its last works may be finished in this interval. Among other prison rooms, I have erected an ample passage with seven brick arches, where [prisoners] will work in order to contribute toward their keep; there is also a chapel on a higher level away from the common spaces, where I have placed an altarpiece with the images of Our Lady of Guadalupe, who will be their patron, and Saint Peter Apostle, Saint Peter of Arbuez, and Saint Peter Martyr. . . . There, they will hear Mass, say the Rosary every day, and they will constantly be instructed on the mysteries of our holy faith.[92]

Like his predecessor Tomás de Monterroso, Sariñana expected that Guadalupe would hold special significance for lapsed indigenous Christians.
His choice of Arbuez, however, celebrated inquisitorial resolve, for the
received narrative about him, the first inquisitor of Aragón, held that he
was stabbed to death by order of several Jews who were under inquisitorial scrutiny.

In a December 1692 letter to the crown, Sariñana announced the
completion of the prison, which now had its own drinking well and a full
range of liturgical implements for its chapel. The prison ended up costing
the princely sum of 5,286 pesos and 2.5 reales; 3,000 pesos had come
from the crown, 1,000 pesos from Grado's land grant, and 1,286 pesos,
2.5 reales from funds raised independently. Paradoxically, Sariñana's
radical punitive experiment lasted only a few years, due to two crip-
pling events that took place in 1696. First, on August 23, an earthquake
devastated many buildings in the center of Oaxaca City, including the
churches of San Pablo, San Francisco, La Merced, the cathedral, and
Santo Domingo el Grande,[93] as well as the new prison of idolaters; then,
in November 1696, Sariñana died, leaving the prison's finances in a state
of uncertainty.

The difficulty of this situation led the cathedral chapter of Oaxaca City,
which acted in lieu of the bishop while a new prelate was elected, to appropriate the income from vacant beneficios for the preservation of the prison
of idolaters and other pious works in February 1697. Nonetheless, these
funds were not sufficient to alleviate the rapidly deteriorating situation of
the prison inmates, so a month later, Manuel Hidalgo,[94] the ecclesiastical
prosecutor and chaplain of the prisión perpetua, made a desperate plea
before the cathedral chapter. Hidalgo's request for help touched on the
economic and social indignities that convicted idolaters suffered:

In this perpetual prison, there have been, and there usually are, many Indians
imprisoned for idolatry crimes brought from several districts in this bishopric.
Since they customarily are of advanced age, . . . they are left without the support
of their towns, relatives, and acquaintances, and since the death of Bishop Sariñana, there has been no one in this city who takes pity on these miserable people,
no one who looks upon them with merciful eyes. Their sustenance has been so
scarce that . . . , those who took ill have perished due to hunger, helplessness, and
lack of medicines, rather than because of the illness that began afflicting them. . . .
Since as a nation they are so frail, so bashful, so lacking in mutual charity, and so
lacking in good stewardship, . . . every prisoner who comes into this jail perishes
if he does not have any outside support, and this is an everyday occurrence, as it
can be certified by the priests of this holy church, who bury them.[95]

Hidalgo also mentioned the devastation that the recent earthquake had
wrecked on the prison building and asked that the income from vacant

beneficios be spent in repairs. His pleas for help moved the cathedral chapter to pledge funds out of their own pockets for a total of fifty pesos for each year that the bishopric's seat remained vacant, plus a gift of ninety *fanegas* of maize to succor the famished inmates.[96] Noting the importance of keeping "teachers of idolatry" away from their local communities, the chapter also destined more funds from the income of vacant parishes and made a general request for alms from all curates.

Sariñana's prison was so devastated by the earthquake and the subsequent lack of funds that it was abandoned for a new building in a different location. After the fleeting four-month tenure of fray Manuel de Quiroz, Sariñana's successor, fray Ángel Maldonado (1700–28) inherited Sariñana's punitive project and turned it into one of the supporting pillars of the exacting extirpation campaigns he carried out in Villa Alta between 1702 and 1704. Before he began his successful campaign to secularize ten Dominican doctrinas, which he regarded as ill-administered and idolatrous as a result of the order's neglect, Maldonado obtained a concession from the Dominicans for his new prison for idolaters. In August 1702, fray Baltasar Asencio, procurator general of the Dominicans of Oaxaca, granted Maldonado a plot of land adjoining the orchard of the convent of Santo Domingo el Grande, with the proviso that this bequest would revert to his order if it were no longer used for this prison. Since this orchard was located in the northeastern corner of the convent's ample land holdings, this meant that the new prison of idolaters was built several blocks north of the cathedral square, in an area of Oaxaca City that contained mostly orchards and agricultural land and at some distance from the densely populated city center.[97] Maldonado would put to use this new prison of idolaters during a stunningly innovative war against idolatry in Villa Alta.

NOVEL DISCIPLINARY DYNAMICS IN OAXACA AND MEXICO

The developments in idolatry extirpation policies in the dioceses of Mexico and Oaxaca that took place in the latter half of the seventeenth century could be characterized by a drive toward institutionalized and centralized procedures for uncovering, confronting, and punishing native ritual practices. In an early cycle of extirpation campaigns that unfolded between 1571 and the 1660s, extirpators had often been appointed on a piecemeal basis by episcopal authorities, especially in the archbishopric of Mexico. From the 1660s onward, these procedures were no longer sufficient for investigating and containing unorthodox native ritual and devotional practices. In Mexico, the drive toward institutionalization resulted in an emphasis in the managerial and juridical abilities of the provisor de indios; in Oaxaca, this policy yielded the establishment of a central punitive repository for influential local ritual specialists, a prison devoted exclusively to idolaters, which constituted a unique judicial experiment in New Spain. Furthermore, episcopal authorities such as Sariñana in Oaxaca and Santa Cruz in Tlaxcala realized that extirpation attempts would have to go hand in hand with the appointment of linguistically able ministers in small, isolated native communities whose ecclesiastical administration had been overlooked during the congregaciones period in the early seventeenth century.

A substantial number of trials from the late seventeenth century reveal a change in the received narratives about native devotions created through legal proceedings. On the one hand, the practices in the elective sphere seem to have continued more or less unabated, with the occasional complication of bribing and blackmail as a factor in idolatry accusations. On the other, reports about clandestine communal ritual practices—which took place in caves, in private homes, in the fields, or at sacred landmarks associated with local cosmologies—rose slightly. In the case of Popoloca specialists and their mestizo clients, an interethnic complicity of sorts seems to have transformed earlier specialist-client relationships. Nonnatives no longer consulted native specialists only in cases of suspected sorcery, or to make divinations about lost objects and future events: some of these clients now had their own ritual implements and actively participated in the practices of an elective ritual sphere that was perhaps becoming even more inclusive.

The preservation of substantial trial records for idolatry cases in Zapotec towns in Villa Alta and Popoloca communities in southeastern Puebla allow for a more detailed consideration of legal and sociopolitical dynamics. At least one landmark case, the trial of the deer eaters of Lachirioag, exposes the difficulty of eliciting a plausible narrative about acts that could be regarded as idolatrous without a confession, or without the cooperation of experienced observers of native ritual practices. Did cooking and carving a deer in a private home in the middle of the night constitute a veritable act of idolatry? The answer to this question rested, of course, on an assessment of the beliefs instantiated by such an act. Once the defendants presented a united front and avoided yielding insights into their state of mind as the deer cooked, the accusation of idolatry became untenable. Paradoxically, such an episode suggests that native complicity was an integral factor in the conviction of idolaters. In other words, ritual specialists had a particularly well-developed consciousness about their acts, the clandestine spaces in which they were performed, and the local social dynamics that allowed for the carefully managed reproduction of orthodox and unorthodox practices side by side. The next chapter provides a narrow but unusually well-documented perspective on the development and destruction of a space of dissent in which Zapotec communities performed ancestral devotions in southern Villa Alta, a region that would regain its reputation as a focal point for rebellion and idolatry in the early eighteenth century.

CHAPTER 7

In the Care of God the Father

Northern Zapotec Ancestral Observances,
1691–1706

On Wednesday, September 15, 1700, don Juan Bautista and Jacinto de los Ángeles, two Zapotec men who would be beatified by the Catholic Church three centuries later, huddled in the back rooms of the Dominican house of San Francisco Caxonos, hours away from their deaths at the hand of their fellow townspeople. Something had gone very wrong the night before in this town, located in the southern reaches of the jurisdiction of Villa Alta. It was too late for compromises: a throng surrounded the church as they beat on wooden boxes shouting, "You cuckolds! You friars! You will die right here!" Also trapped inside were the Dominican friars Alonso de Vargas and Gaspar de los Reyes, eleven Spaniards and mestizos, and about twenty native allies from four neighboring towns. Don Juan and Jacinto had triggered the riot after alerting Reyes to an unorthodox ceremony held the night before at the home of José Flores, the *mayordomo*, or chief official, of the local confraternity of Saint Joseph. The mob threw stones at the group under siege, wounding a native ally; its defenders, four of which had harquebuses, shot into the air first and then into the crowd, killing a rebel from San Pedro Caxonos. When the Spaniards ran out of gunpowder, a desperate negotiation ensued. The rioters were not appeased when their vicar showed them an image of the Virgin; they refused an offer of money and stated that, unless the two informants were turned over, they would burn the church and its defenders and flee to the mountains. In fact, they had already set one of don Juan's houses on fire and attempted to destroy another belonging to his wife.[1]

In the end, the besieged Spaniards surrendered the two wanted men over the friars' protests. After the informants were handed over, they were taunted, whipped, and executed. Reportedly, some of the rebels drank from their blood; their corpses were disposed of in such an effective manner that no traces of them were ever found. The informants' fate would not be corroborated for several months; in fact, two days after the riot, the residents of San Francisco asked for the Dominicans' pardon and received an absolution on their knees. Afterward, Juan Antonio de Mier del Tojo, who served as alcalde mayor of Villa Alta since 1697,[2] began an investigation into the fate of don Juan and Jacinto. Initially, it was claimed they had fled the area, but after the imprisonment of thirty-four rebels, the alcalde mayor obtained a full confession. After a protracted trial, the alcalde mayor handed down a draconian punishment. On January 11, 1702, fifteen of the Caxonos rebels were hanged and quartered, and their remains were displayed along the main road between San Francisco and Oaxaca City.[3]

A full understanding of this riot and a subsequent extirpatory exercise in 1702–6 calls for an analytical stance that approaches indigenous local devotions as independent social and symbolic phenomena that interdigitated with colonial rule in myriad ways. Such a stance is inspired in part by William Christian's insistence on studying specific peasant religious practices as "local religion." However, rather than assuming that Spanish peasants and Zapotec villagers shared a theological and pragmatic bedrock in their rapport with the sacred, this chapter investigates indigenous beliefs in Villa Alta in terms of collective and elective devotional practices. Hence, I offer below a detailed, microsociological consideration of the actors involved in the defense and destruction of local Northern Zapotec observances. This approach is indebted to Pierre Bourdieu's notion of the religious field of practice, an ever-expanding or contracting social and symbolic sphere that regulates itself through the interested interaction of its participants.[4] In his analysis, Bourdieu stressed two properties of this field: the inherently dialectical nature of religious production, and the limits placed by the logic of the field on the nature and type of discourse that its participants deploy. In other words, I propose below that the logic of the Northern Zapotec fields of devotional practice involved the preservation of ancestor worship, local autonomy aspirations, and a defense of cosmological beliefs that were central to the identity of Northern Zapotec communities, or queche.

This chapter focuses on four cases that encapsulate distinct local attitudes toward traditional and Christian ritual practices in four communities: the Caxonos Zapotec queche of San Francisco Caxonos, Lachirioag, and Betaza; and the Nexitzo Zapotec queche of Yalahui. This is not an exhaustive examination of all the data regarding Zapotec devotions collected by Oaxacan Bishop fray Ángel Maldonado between 1702 and 1705, the most ambitious idolatry extirpation campaign in New Spain

for which we have surviving records.[5] Rather, I present here an overview of these observances, along with ecclesiastical and civil measures
that sought to destroy them at the close of the seventeenth century. My
discussion is grounded in an overview of two collections of ritual songs,
which reflected both the local cosmologies of Lachirioag and Betaza,
the worship of foundational ancestors, and pan-Zapotec cosmological
theories. I also examine several songs from Yalahui that appropriated a
traditional Zapotec ritual genre for evangelization purposes. The Caxonos revolt provides an important framing device for understanding the
failed defense of a local system of Christian and traditional devotions.
The chapter closes with an assessment of Maldonado's inventive extirpation experiment in Villa Alta.

THE NICACHI SONGS OF VILLA ALTA

A highly promising line of evidence regarding colonial Zapotec ritual
practices is contained in two distinct ritual genres transcribed by literate
devotional specialists in northern Oaxaca in the seventeenth century:
calendrical texts and ritual songs. Chapter 5 discussed the extant Zapotec calendars from Villa Alta; this section turns to a characterization
of the four collections of ritual songs preserved at the Archivo General
de Indias, legajo México 882, as Booklets 100, 101, 102, and 103.[6] This
song corpus from Villa Alta song contains two distinct ritual genres: *dij
dola* and *libana*. In Booklet 100, songs performed by ritual singers are
termed *dij dola*, a term that may be translated as "song."[7] This label
may be applied to the twenty-two songs contained in Booklets 100 and
101, which are written in Caxonos Zapotec and make no overt reference
to Christian entities. By contrast, *libana*, a word whose Valley Zapotec
equivalent, *lipàana*, is glossed as "elegant dialogue," and "sermon" by
Córdova,[8] is an explicit title for three of the fifteen songs in Booklets
102 and 103. These compositions, written in Nexitzo Zapotec, present
memorable portrayals of Christian entities such as Christ, the Virgin
Mary, Saint Francis, Saint Dominic, and the Magi.[9]

Many of the Villa Alta testimonies refer to a split between a collective and an elective ritual sphere. Witnesses made a distinction between
sacrificios de particulares, personal observances performed with the
assistance of ritual practitioners, and sacrificios del común, or communal sacrifices. An important celebration in the communal sphere was
the performance of songs identified as *cantos de teponastle*, "teponaztli songs," performed before the community by singers and musicians
called *belao*. For instance, in November 1704, the diviners Fabián and

Martín Nicolás described communal ritual practices in their queche, Santiago Laxopa, as follows: "After having engaged in idolatry, we all went to play the teponaztli drum, which is called *nicachis* [*sic*] in our Zapotec language; while people got drunk, some of us sang and played rattles, and everyone danced to the beat of a turtle shell—men and women both, as it always has been and still is done in all this jurisdiction and in other provinces."[10] The cylindrical drum, the rattles, and the tortoise shell, along with the standing drum and the whistles are all traditional Mesoamerican musical instruments associated with communal ritual singing and dancing, as recorded by Diego de Landa and Sánchez de Aguilar in Yucatán, and by Acosta, Motolinia, Pérez de Ribas, and other authors among the Nahua.[11] Some of these songs were intoned to the beat of the cylindrical drum, called *nicachi* in Zapotec, teponaztli in Nahuatl, and *tunkul* in Yucatec Maya, and carried a label derived from the generic term for "song," *cuicatl* in Nahuatl, and *kay* in Yucatec Maya. Beyond Maldonado's records, there exist few references to the social contexts in which Zapotec dij dola were performed. One exception is Burgoa's description of the wedding ceremony held for one of Yanhuitlan's noble ladies; during this occasion, this chronicler notes, Mixtec and Zapotec lords "came out performing the dance of the teponaztli."[12]

The dij dola in Booklets 100 and 101 have the best-documented context of production. Booklet 100 bears the annotation "From Fernando Lópes of Lachirioag, who bought it from Pedro Vargas of Betaza." This is the text surrendered on November 19, 1704, to juez visitador Aragón y Alcántara by Fernando Lópes, along with thirteen bean halves used for divination.[13] On the same date, Pedro Gonzalo of Lachirioag surrendered "a notebook with eight folios, which he said was for teponaztli songs." This description matches the physical appearance and contents of Booklet 101. There is little biographical information about Pedro Gonzalo, but some information has survived about Fernando Lópes and Pedro de Vargas, owners of Booklet 100. A collective confession identified Fernando Lópes as one of the three leading "teachers of idolatries" in the queche of Lachirioag, and Lópes stated he had bought his songbook from Pedro de Vargas, who also served as regidor of Betaza circa 1695.[14] Other testimony established Pedro de Vargas's status as a renowned specialist. According to Pedro's son Fabián de Vargas, a ritual specialist who served in the Betaza town council in 1703, his father refused to teach him about divination practices, arguing he was afraid of prosecution, and decided instead to pass on his knowledge to Fabian's oldest brother. Fabián claimed one of his father's texts after his death and received instruction from other specialists.

Fabián also gave the following overview of Betaza's collective sphere, which depicts the local cabildo at work orchestrating ritual action, extracting individual contributions, and incorporating the cult of Christian entities into the celebrations:

During the communal idolatries [the specialists] sacrifice two or three deer, and many turkeys and puppies, and they make the men fast and avoid their wives for thirteen days, and during this time, rather than going to the steam baths, they bathe in the river at the cock's first or second crow. They confess with the priests before the sacrifices, bringing each a real or a real and a half. In order to receive these reales, the regidores are present there, and the amount they should bring is determined beforehand by the town council, the escribano, and the other priests. They also bring four young boys to these communal sacrifices; . . . these boys behead the turkeys and the dogs, and open the deers' chests as the priests hold down these animals. . . . In a piece of paper made from tree bark, they pour [the animals'] blood; then, everyone comes in, gets on their knees, and over the bloodied paper, they toss a bit of ground tobacco called [piciyetl]. . . . After making those sacrifices, the alcaldes purchase some thin candles from the money that remains and place them on the altars at the church, and then they order people to sing a litany. A large feather that adorns the images of Our Lady is taken to the sacrifices, and the person who plays the teponaztli drum and sings diabolic songs wears it on his head. . . . During the sacrifices, they post guards in various places, so they may give a warning if they see a Spaniard or any suspicious person.[15]

Although this testimony provides only a fragmentary depiction of cosmological beliefs mediated through Spanish legal discourse, the calendars confiscated in Villa Alta afford us a view into specialized Zapotec knowledge about the universe. Mesoamerican ritual specialists envisioned the cosmos and the 260-day ritual calendar as deeply interrelated structures. In Postclassic times, one of the most succinct depictions of this interdigitation of space and time is perhaps the cover page of the Codex Fejérváry-Mayer, which shows Xiuhteuctli at the center of a diagram that contains the four cardinal directions along with associated deity pairs, colors, trees and birds, and a dismembered Tezcatlipoca; two separate cycles in this illustration show the progression of the 260-day calendar, which thus becomes intertwined with cosmological spaces.[16]

The best graphic representation of the Zapotec cosmos, as understood by colonial specialists, appears as a simplified sketch drawn by the anonymous author(s) of Booklet 11 of Villa Alta, shown in Figure 7.1.[17] This drawing depicts the universe as a structure with nine levels above Earth and nine levels below. Eight levels, represented by circles, existed between the House of the Underworld (*yoo gabila*) and the House of Earth (*yoo yeche layo*; literally, "House of the Town on Earth"), and

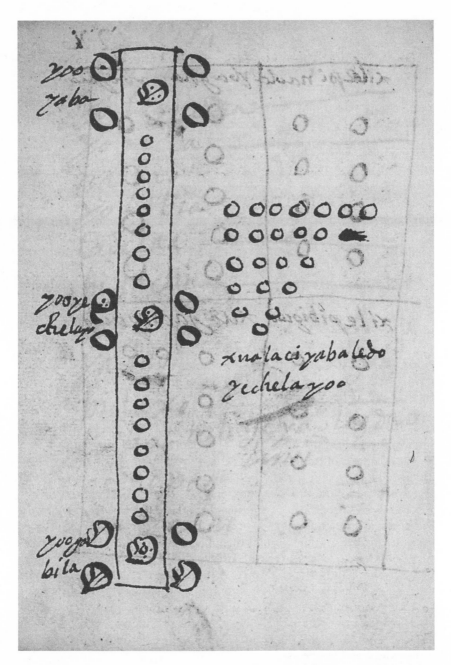

FIGURE 7.1   A Late Seventeenth-Century Depiction of the Zapotec Cosmos in Booklet 11.

SOURCE: Gobierno de España. Ministerio de Cultura. Archivo General de Indias, México 882, 384v

there were eight more levels between the House of Earth and the House of the Sky (*yoo yaba*). Four circles, which may represent cosmological supports or cardinal directions, surround each of these three houses. On the right side, a diagram containing twenty-three circles grouped into six levels, with one circle crossed out, bears the label *xua laci yaba ledo yeche layoo*, which may tentatively be glossed as "The lords of the turn of Heaven, ending at Earth."[18]

The Villa Alta calendrical corpus depicted a complex spatio-temporal continuum in which time was closely related with cosmological space. As noted above, the Zapotec 260-day count, or piyè, divided into twenty periods of thirteen days each. Several Villa Alta calendars stated that each of the twenty trecenas in the piyè originated in each of the three main cosmological levels, following a set rotation around Earth, Sky, and Underworld: for instance, in Booklet 85a, Trecena 1 was associated with the House of Earth, Trecena 2 with the House of the Sky, Trecena 3 with the House of Earth, Trecena 4 with the House of the Underworld, Trecena 5 with the House of Earth, and so on until Trecena 20, yielding ten trecenas associated with Earth, and two groups of five trecenas each linked to either Sky or Underworld.[19] As an example of the relationship between time periods and cosmological realms, Figure 7.2 shows a depiction of the first trecena in Booklet 85a: the gloss on either side of the house drawn atop the list of the first thirteen days in the count (*yagchilla*, 1-Cayman, to *queçee*, 13-Reed) states that the trecena, called *coçij* in Valley Zapotec and *llanij* in Villa Alta, is associated with the House of Earth (*yoho lleo*) and that this house "receives the turn" (*ricij laza*) of the first of four 65-day divisions (*goçio i*) in the calendar.

The structure of Booklets 100 and 101 suggests they contain two separate song cycles that traverse, in a symbolic fashion, the cosmological layers depicted in Figure 7.1. Booklet 100 contains thirteen songs. The first nine songs have variable lengths: the longest has twenty-six stanzas; the shortest, five stanzas. The song cycle ends with four shorter songs, each one to five stanzas in length, which are numbered one through four. Booklet 101 contains a cycle of nine songs whose length fluctuates between three and fifteen stanzas. A possible interpretation of this arrangement is that both Booklet 100 and 101 contain a nine-song cycle in which each song is associated with a specific range of cosmological levels between the House of the Underworld and the House of Earth, or the House of Earth and the House of the Sky. The four remaining songs in Booklet 100 may be associated with the four cosmological supports, shown as circular elements in each of the three levels in Figure 7.1, that hold up one of these three houses.

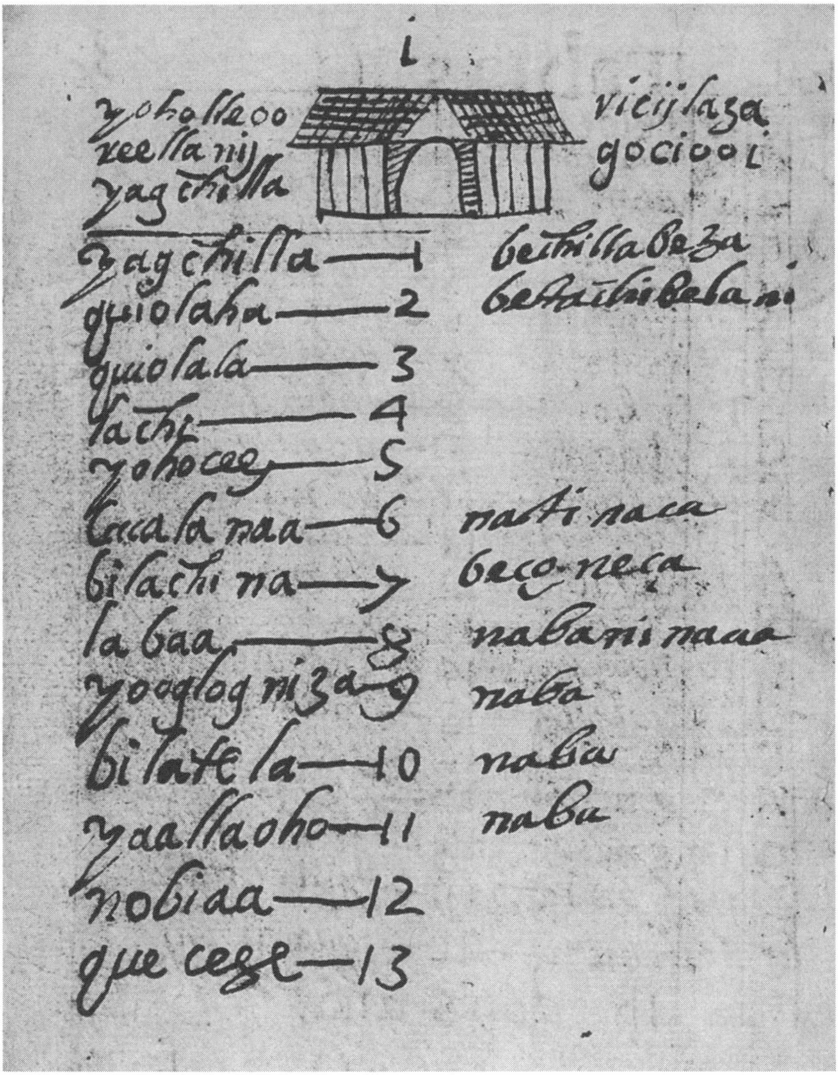

FIGURE 7.2 The First Trecena of the Zapotec 260-Day Count in Booklet 85a.
SOURCE: Gobierno de España. Ministerio de Cultura. Archivo General de Indias, México 882, 1405v

PAN-ZAPOTEC DEITIES AND
FOUNDATIONAL ANCESTORS

The dij dola propitiated a broad array of entities that fall into three
categories: Pan-Zapotec deities that were also worshipped in the Valley
of Oaxaca and in the Sola region; entities that share calendrical and
personal names with Northern Zapotec foundational ancestors; and
local entities worshipped in Lachirioag and Betaza. Table 7.1 proposes
various comparisons between the Pan-Zapotec deities named in Booklets 100 and 101 and the two most detailed colonial sources on Zapotec
deities: entries from Córdova's 1578 Spanish-Valley Zapotec dictionary
analyzed by Thomas Smith-Stark; and the "thirteen gods" Diego Luis
identified for Balsalobre in 1635 and 1654. Since the only known systematic ordering of thirteen deity names by a colonial Zapotec specialist
is Diego Luis's list, this order was followed in Table 7.1; even though
Diego Luis provided a different version of this list using Spanish terms
in 1635,[20] the table follows the Zapotec deity names he revealed in 1654.
Smith-Stark's influential proposal regarding a reconstructed order of
deity names has been noted along with the 1578 Córdova entries,[21] with
the number in Smith-Stark's list preceding the deity's name. Three other
sources also appear in this table: an analysis of iconographic elements in
preconquest Zapotec urns by Adam Sellen;[22] a Loxicha calendar investigated by Robert Weitlaner;[23] and a calendar from San Antonio Huitepec
analyzed by Ron Van Meer.[24] Both the Loxicha and the Huitepec calendars contain only nine names, and these two lists are only included
to highlight a contrast with Diego Luis's list. For broader comparative
purposes, a list of the Central Mexican Thirteen Lords of the Day is
also included.[25]

As depicted in Table 7.1, Northern Zapotec specialists worshipped at
least eight deities that were also venerated in the Valley of Oaxaca and
Sola. In Córdova's 1578 dictionary, these deities are called Piyè Tào / Piyè
Xòo, Coquì Xee / Coquì Cìlla, Copijcha, Cozòbi, Pezèelào, Huichàana,
Cocijo, and Cozàana. The most important category in this group is com-
posed by three separate names for creator deities, the first two of which
Diego Luis identifies as the first and eleventh deities in his list of thirteen
gods. The first one is Quitzino (also Chino, Ichinoo, Queechino, and
Piyè Tào / Piyè Xòo), a deity characterized by Diego Luis as "God Thirteen," and who, according to Smith-Stark, presided over all other deities.
The second is Cozàana (also Nosana or Coxana), a deity associated with
creation events and, according to Diego Luis, with deer and fish. Another
creator deity was Coqui Xee (also Ni Xee, or Ni Xee Tao Lopa), which
has no cognate in Diego Luis's list. A song in Booklet 100 identifies Ni

Xee Tao Lopa, "Great Beginning 8/11-Dew," as the father of foundational ancestor Lord 1-Cayman; Smith-Stark suggested that Coqui Xee is an epithet for the main creator deity, Cozàana.[26]

There also exist important correlations between six deities in the pan-Zapotec and the Postclassic Central Mexican pantheons. The Zapotec Piyè Tào / Quitzino and the Central Mexican deity Xiuhteuctli share two important commonalities: they both head a list of deities, and their names refer to a time count—the former to the 260-day count, the latter to the 365-day year. The remaining five deities also present clear parallels, both in their avocations and relative position with respect to Diego Luis's 1654 list, to five of the Central Mexican deities listed in two deity series: the Nine Lords of the Night and the Thirteen Lords of the Day. These deities, listed by their order as Lords of the Night in Table 7.1, are known by the Nahua names Centeotl, Mictlanteuctli, Chalchihuitl Icue, Tlahzolteotl, and Tlaloc.[27] These deities are correlated with the following pan-Zapotec deities: Cozòbi (also Loçucui, or Gozobi Tao), a maize deity that Córdova and Diego Luis portrayed as a god of harvests or maize; Pezèelào (also Huila, or Becelao Dao), a deity who presided over the Zapotec underworld; Huichàana Dao (also Nohuichana), Córdova's deity of procreation, and a goddess associated with birth-giving, fish, and rivers, according to Diego Luis; Lexee, a deity linked to sorcerers and thieves that, according to Smith-Stark, may be associated with Pixèe pecàla, Córdova's "demon of luxuriousness"; and Cocijo (also Loçio, or Gocio), associated with thunder and rainfall. My interpretation of the correlations between these six deities is in general agreement with the model proposed by Sellen and in partial agreement with that of Alcina Franch.[28]

A pan-Zapotec solar deity associated with hunters called Licuicha (also Niyoa, Coquieta, or Cobicha) may correlate with either the Lord of the Day Tonatiuh or the Lord of the Night Piltzinteuctli.[29] Finally, four other Central Mexican Lords of the Day—Quetzalcoatl, Tlahuizcalpanteuctli, Tezcatlipoca, and Tlalteuctli—and one more Lord of the Night—Tepeyollotl—may also share cosmological parallels with Zapotec deities, but this second set of correspondences is open to debate.

The songs in Booklets 100 and 101 include some sections devoted to the propitiation of Northern Zapotec foundational ancestors. Such practices have several points of contact with state Zapotec religious practices in the Late Formative (400 BCE–200 CE) and Classic periods (200–800 CE), which, according to Joyce Marcus's interpretation of archaeological and ethnohistorical data, featured the worship of deified ancestors.[30] The confessions compiled by Maldonado in 1704 and idolatry trials from at least eight Villa Alta Zapotec communities suggest that

TABLE 7.1 Zapotec and Central Mexican Sacred Beings in Preconquest and Colonial Sources

Córdova 1578b (Smith-Stark 1999)	Diego Luis, 1635 (AGN-Inq. 437-I, 3)	Diego Luis, 1654	Diego Luis name variants 1654	AGI-Mex 882, 1704 Booklet 100	AGI-Mex 882, 1704 Booklet 101	Loxicha calendar (Weitlaner 1961)	Huitepec calendar (Van Meer 2000)	Censer iconography (Sellen 2002)	9 Lords of the Night; 13 Lords of the Day (Boone 2007)
1. *Piyè tào, pìyè xòo* "god of all thirteen gods" (Córdova 1578b, 141r)	1. "god of all thirteen gods"	1. *Liraa quitzino* God Thirteen	*Liraa chino* AGN-Inq. 437-I 3:88r; *Lira quichino* AGN-Inq. 571:399r	*Quøechino* (Song 9)	*Betao ichinoo* (Song 6)	*Ndozin* Deity 13	*Natoriño*	Glyph U, Mask 5, (same as Cozaana)	1/1. Xiuhteuctli (Night/Day)
1. *Coqui xee, coqui cilla* Lord of creation/dawn *Ni xèe ni cillani*, the beginning of all things	12. "god who made all human beings" (?)			*Ni xee Tao Lopa* Great Beginning 8/11 Dew (Songs 3, 5)					9. Quetzalcoatl? (Day) 12. Tlahuizcalpanteuctli? (Day)
Pitào copijcha (Córdova 1578b, 383r)	2. "god of the hunt"	2. *Licuicha Niyoa* "god of the hunt"	*Liquicha Coquieta* Associated with hunting AGN-Inq. 571:399r	*Cobicha* (Song 1)	*Cobicha* (Song 9)	*Ndo'yet* deity of *novena* prayers	*Lguachoriñe*		4. Tonatiuh? (Day) 3. Piltzinteuctli? (Night)
6a. *Pitào quille pitào yage* deity of riches, merchants		3. *Coquee Laa* deity of riches	*Coquie Laa* cochineal intercessor AGN-Inq. 437-I-3:89v			*Beydo* deity of riches	*Oguilo*	Glyph X, Mask 6, Costume 3	?
7. *Pitào cozòbi*, deity of harvests	9. "god of maize and all foodstuffs"	4. *Locucui* deity of maize and harvests		*Gozobi tao* (Song 9) *Xonaxi Gozobi tao* (Song 12)		*Ndubdo* deity of maize	*Osucui*	Glyph L, Mask 2, Costume 1	4/7. Centeotl (Night/Day)
2. *Pitào pezèelao* Underworld deity, principal demon	5. "god of the dead who are in hell" 7. "Lucifer, god of hell"	5. *Leraa Huila* deity of Hell	*Coquie Cabila*, Underworld deity AGN-Inq. 437-I-3:95r	*Becelao dao* (Songs 6, 12)		*Kedo* King of evil	*Natobilia*	*Xicani* Glyph, Mask 2	5/6. Mictlanteuctli (Night/Day)
4. *Pitào huichàana*, deity of infants and fertility		6. *Nohuichana* deity of rivers, fish, and pregnant women		*Huichana dao*, (Song 3) *Huichana quiag lao* (Song 6)		*Ndan* deity of the ancestors	*Bichana*	Glyph P, Mask 9	6/3. Chalchihuitl Icue (Night/Day)

Córdova (Valley Zapotec)	Other colonial sources	Córdova glosses	AGN-Inquisition	Songs (source 1)	Songs (source 2)	Modern (Mse…)	Modern (Bexu…)	Glyph / Mask	Aztec equivalent
8. *Pitào xicàla* deity of dreams 8a. *Pìxèe pecàla* demon of luxuriousness	7. *Lexee* deity associated with sorcerers and thieves					*Mse* Malevolent deity	*Bexu*	Glyph F, Mask 7	7/5. Tlazolteotl (Night/Day)
	8. *Nonachi*, deity of illnesses					*Mbaz* Earth deity	*Yuache*		?
9. *Cocijo*, deity of rain and thunder	9. *Locio* deity of thunder			*Gaa Gocio* (9 Cociyos) (Song 10)	*Gocio* (Song 7)	*Mdi* deity of rain	*Yocio, Igosioó, osio*	Glyph M, Mask 1	9/8. Tlaloc (Night/Day)
	10. *Xonatzi Huila* Wife of Leera Huila and deity of illnesses and death	8. "goddess of hell, or the wife of said Lucifer"							?
1. *Pitào cozàana,* deity of animals/hunting *Cozàana tào,* Creator deity	11. *Cosana* Ancestors' deity, associated with water 13. "god of his ancestors" (?)		*Noçana guela* AGN-Inq. 573:290r *Nosana queya,* deity of deer AGN-Inq. 571:393r	*Coxana* (Songs 3, 6), *Betao coxana* (Song 9)				Glyph U, Mask 5, (same as Deity 13)	?
	12. *Leraa queche* deity of medicine								?
	13. *Lira cuee* deity of medicine								?
6. *Pitào piizi* deity of diviners 6b. *Pitào zii pitào yàa* deity of misery 6c. *Pitào tèe* deity of evil	4. "god of sorcerers"		*Leraa Huisi* deity of diviners AGN-Inq. 571-13:313r					Glyph Y Mask 4	10. Tezcatlipoca? (Day)
3. *Pitào xòo* deity of earthquakes									8. Tepeyollotl? (Night) 2. Tlalteuctli? (Day)
5. *Coqui lào* deity of fowls								Glyph X, Mask 6, Costume 3	?

SOURCES: AGN-Inq 437; AGI-Mex 882; Boone 2007; Córdova 1578b; Sellen 2002; Smith-Stark 1999; Van Meer 2000; Weitlaner 1961

local Zapotec religious practices were based on the memory of founding lineages. An ubiquitous category of effigies, ranging from carved or painted representations of individuals[31] to "hanks of hair" tied to pieces of cotton, was called *quiquiag yagtao* in Caxonos Zapotec, a term literally meaning "head(s) of the Great Tree" that was glossed in trial records as "heads of the ancestors or grandparents."[32] Communal celebrations took place at geographical locations with specific local names, usually in the outskirts of a village. Accordingly, one may ground the broad rubric of "Zapotec local ritual practices" in a particular terrain: that in which ancestors, foundational accounts, and sites for communal ceremonies converged within the social and spatial boundaries of a Zapotec queche—a sociopolitical unit with its own foundational narrative, ruling lineage(s), and territory.

Although our knowledge of founding ancestors of Northern Zapotec communities is still in flux, various Zapotec primordial titles and testaments provide information about the names, deeds, and lineage of some of them. I now turn to a brief discussion of three Zapotec foundational ancestors that appear both in Booklets 100 and 101 and in other Zapotec-language documents: Lord 1-Cayman, Great Eagle, and Great 4/11-Knot. This section provides only some illustrative examples of the ancestor worship practices, as depicted in these songs, which were targeted by idolatry eradicators.

A first example is Lord 1-Cayman. As noted by Michel Oudijk, several colonial Zapotec genealogical narratives list Lord 1-Cayman as a founding ancestor. In the Genealogy of San Lucas Quiaviní, a Valley Zapotec queche, the founder of Genealogy 2 is Coque Quiechilla, "Lord 1-Cayman," Quiechilla being the Valley equivalent of the Northern Zapotec Yagchila, 1-Cayman. This text also shows Lord 1-Cayman facing another ancestor, Lord 6-Death Great Eagle (Cogui Quielana Piçia Tao); the accompanying text refers to 1-Cayman with the Zapotec title *pichana*.[33] This document also states that Lord 1-Cayman was issued from a mythohistorical place of origin called *bille gaa billehe gache g[ue]la tini*, which Oudijk translates as "Cave Nine, Cave Seven, the Lake of Blood."[34] The primordial title of Tabaá also lists a Yaxila Veqini (1-Cayman Bird) as the ancestor of the Northern Zapotec queche of Xuquila,[35] and another Yagchila as Nelao's consort. Additionally, Frame 14 of the Lienzo de Tabaá lists a ruling couple called Lord 1-Cayman and Bixeag Lachi.

In Booklet 100, Lord 1-Cayman is mentioned in seven of the twelve stanzas in Song 5. This song probably refers to the very same founding ancestor who appears in the three sources mentioned above: the Genealogy of Quiaviní, the primordial title of Tabaá, and the Lienzo de

Tabaá. Moreover, Bixeag Lachi, whom the Lienzo de Tabaá identifies as Lord 1-Cayman's wife, makes an appearance in Stanza 8 of Song 5. In fact, Stanza 2 of Song 5 records the divine origin of Lord 1-Cayman as follows:[36]

biye   yagxo   lani   yagchila ni
On this [365-day] year 1-Earthquake, on this festivity of 1-Cayman

colag coque yagchila   xini   lopa   ni xee
Lord 1-Cayman was born, son of 8/11-Dew, the Beginning

Three criteria render this statement remarkable. First, the first line employs two elements when identifying a date: the 365-day year 1-Earthquake, and the 260-day date 1-Cayman. According to Javier Urcid, no known pre-Columbian Zapotec hieroglyphic text designates a date by referring to both year and day name, so this designation breaks with Classic-period Zapotec calendrical conventions.[37] Second, the epithet Nixee Tao Lopa, Great Beginning 8/11-Dew, mentioned several times in Songs 3 and 5 of Booklet 100, designates a creator deity (shown also in Table 7.1) as Lord 1-Cayman's father. Third, Lord 1-Cayman's birth date places him at the very beginning of Zapotec time: this date, Day 1-Cayman Year 1-Earthquake, is the first of 18,980 unique days contained within a cycle of fifty-two 365-day years.

The second example is Great Eagle. Several ancestors in colonial Zapotec sources have a version of Bicia Tao, "Great Eagle," as part of their name phrase. As noted above, the Genealogy of Quiaviní portrays a Lord 6-Death Great Eagle seated before Lord 1-Cayman; both lords are shown occupying high-backed chairs (*icpalli* in Nahuatl, *pecogo* in Zapotec) that highlight their status as legitimate lords from a founding lineage. This document also mentions a Coqui Picia Tao Quequeche, "Lord Great Eagle Quequeche." Furthermore, the Lienzo de Tabáa mentions two more ancestors who share this personal name: Coque Yeagela Besia Dao, "Lord Yeagela Great Eagle" in Frame 6, and Coque Yezina Bezia Dao, "Lord Yezina Great Eagle" in Frame 20. Additionally, the group of pictorial genealogies known as Lienzo de Guevea and Lienzo de Petapa depict an ancestor with a pictorial name glyph that is sometimes glossed in these texts as Biciya Tuo Rigula, "Old Great Eagle."[38] Unlike these texts, the songs of Villa Alta do not refer to individuals who combine the appellation of "Great Eagle" with other names; in any case, there are references to an individual called Great Eagle in Songs 5, 7, and 12 of Booklet 100, and once again in Song 5 of Booklet 101.

Bilatela Tao, or Great 4/11-Knot, provides a third instance of ancestor veneration. This was the personal name of a founding ancestor in Villa Alta, and one of the seven "brothers" that various Northern Zapotec sources identify as founding ancestors reputedly baptized by the Spanish in the 1520s. The primordial title of Tabáa calls Biladela Dao the "father of Tabáa"; Frame 26 of the Lienzo de Tabáa identifies Coque Biladela Dao as the son of Xo Dao, "Great 8-Earthquake." In addition, a will from Solaga dated in 1789 and transcribed by Oudijk lists Bilatela Dao as the third "brother" in a list of seven founders of Northern Zapotec communities, listed here from first to seventh: Bilapag Laguiag Xobego, Belaxila Yalaxila Yaxila, Bilatela Dao, don Juan de Velasco Diadela, Balachila, Tiolana, and Yaalao Lachixoza.[39] In the Villa Alta Songs, Bilatela Tao is mentioned in Songs 2 and 6 of Booklet 101. In Stanza 3, Song 6, a verse that mentions Xoo Dao is followed by a second verse that mentions Bilatela Tao and refers to the latter as *xini colaa*, "elder son." Hence, Song 6 refers to a Bilatela Tao who was the son of Great 8-Earthquake, a kinship statement that mirrors information conveyed in the Lienzo de Tabáa.

Furthermore, one of the best-documented examples of sacred objects tied to ancestral lineages appeared in Lachirioag's collective confession. On November 18, 1704, a group of notables that included, besides town officials, the caciques don Juan Martín and don Nicolás de Santiago, surrendered what was perhaps their most sacred possession: a round wooden box with a lid that contained "the root, or tree trunk, of their genealogy." This box was preserved in an important sacred site, a small cave known locally as *Yabe soa*, located on a cliff. Before performing a collective ceremony at this site, men and women bathed in separate groups for three days; then, after offering the blood of turkeys and burning juniper resin, or *yala vichi*, "the entire town said, 'If you are powerful, take away this illness that has befallen on us.'" Then, the celebrants ate the sacrificed turkeys, drank pulque, and ate uncooked maize tortillas. When Judge Aragón y Alcántara had the box opened, he saw "four flint lancets, four small stone idols of various shapes, and some shiny stones they call *guiag cachi* [precious stones]." A second box, which "belonged to the same sacrifice," yielded two bundles wrapped in *yaga guichi*, or "tree paper," paper made from tree bark, and was described as follows:

One had a small basket of sorts containing two ears of maize tied with a [yaga guichi] ribbon from which hung three shiny stones similar to the ones mentioned before. There was another small bundle wrapped in the same paper, and within, some chili peppers, a few seeds that seemed to be chia, and some beans and squash seeds, all of which was also wrapped in a thin piece of cloth along with some burnt coals. Once the second bundle was opened, it was ascertained that it contained, bundled in a black rag, several bunches of what seemed to be ocote leaves, held together by those same leaves; and two of the same stones already mentioned; and some feathers and a small seashell. Apparently, these bundles were stained with blood, which they said came from roosters.[40]

According to Lachirioag's officials, they used "similar instruments" to perform celebrations at another local sacred site called *Da Yego Tia Xono*, "River of Lineages Eight."[41] These bundles provided a link between the living and their ancestors, as the eldest member of "each generation or lineage" held custody of one such bundle, which was propitiated in times of collective need. The round box unveiled for the first time before Spanish eyes had a legendary provenance. It had been brought circa 1604 from the Caxonos town of Yatzachi, where it had previously resided for forty years, by don Cristóbal Martín Jaclaba (1-Rabbit). Don Cristóbal was the great-grandfather of the Lachirioag cacique don Juan Martín, a specialist who imposed calendrical names on local children and who also surrendered his own calendrical text, which he had obtained from a Solaga resident.

This description of Lachirioag's sacred bundle shares important structural parallels with Late Formative offering boxes. Marcus and Flannery analyzed several offering containers found under Structure 35, a temple built in the middle years of the Monte Albán II period (200 BCE–100 CE) in San José Mogote, the most important ceremonial center in the Valley of Oaxaca prior to the rise of Monte Albán.[42] Three of the boxes contained no artifacts. Two containers held important artifacts and were located under Structure 35's inner room. Along with jade beads and stone fragments, Feature 94 contained two jade statues, which probably represented sacrificed nobles. Feature 95 was a rectangular adobe box containing a ceramic effigy of a high-status person placed in a bowl and accompanied by a sacrificed quail; above, a figure with a Cocijo mask held a stick and a serpent's tongue, accompanied by four female effigies wearing Cocijo masks. Marcus and Flannery interpreted this offering as a burial scene depicting the transformation of a deceased lord into Cocijo. In spite of the vast iconographic differences between these offerings and the two bundles from Lachirioag, they share four points of convergence: both were enclosed in boxes placed in sacred sites; both featured a grouping of four important effigies as part of the offering complex; both contained stones or beads regarded as precious, either jade or "shiny stones"; and sacrificial blades were located near the boxes in both cases. Most importantly, both sets of offerings were tied to the worship of ancestral beings. In fact, the movement across the landscape of the Lachirioag offering, moved from Yatzachi by the head of a Zapotec lineage, resembles the well-documented transportation of "sacred bundles" by migrating Central Mexican peoples.[43]

THE TRANSITION FROM ZAPOTEC DIJ DOLA TO
DOMINICAN LIBANA

Both the dij dola in Booklets 100 and 101 and the libana in Booklets 102 and 103 resemble two other corpora of colonial Mesoamerican ritual songs: a corpus of ninety-one cuicatl transcribed in the second half of the sixteenth century by Nahua elites and now known as *Cantares Mexicanos*, and the *Cantares de Dzitbalché*, fifteen songs transcribed in late eighteenth-century Yucatec Maya orthography in Dzitbalché, Campeche.[44] Bierhorst and Karttunen and Lockhart argued that the Nahua *Cantares Mexicanos* feature a stanza structure that combines recurring combinations of verses in a predictable pattern.[45] In particular, Bierhorst described three stanza elements: a first section, which contains new information, and which he calls "verse"; a second, highly repetitive section, which he designates as "refrain"; and a third element, which he calls "litany." Since these three designations come from poetic traditions that greatly differ from those of Mesoamerican genres, I employ a modified form of Bierhorst's labels in my discussion of the Christian songs of Yalahui below: I use "theme" rather than "verse," keep the designation of "refrain," and refer to a stanza's "boundary markers" instead of "litanies."[46]

Two of the most significant conventions that these Zapotec and Nahuatl song genres share is the performative definition of boundaries between subunits through the utterance of syllables with ambiguous or unknown lexical content, and the pairing of song sections with percussion patterns. In both the Nahua and the Zapotec compositions, the end of each stanza is marked with a chain of syllables with no lexical content, such as *ayao, hiya, hoya*, which were an important component in the song's structure, even if their precise meaning is unknown.[47] Although the Zapotec libana employ phrases such as "Santa Maria, Hallelujah," these phrases perform exactly the same role those syllables have as boundary markers. In both the dij dola and the libana, these syllables or phrases function as divisions between stanzas, which are the basic performative unit in these genres.[48]

While the Nahua songs and the libana in Booklets 102 and 103 both feature an alphabetic transcription of percussion patterns that employs the syllables *ti, qui, co,* and *to*,[49] no such pattern appears in the dij dola in Booklets 100 and 101. Given the similarities between these percussion patterns, it is tempting to assume that the Dominicans who authored the libana used a transcription of the Nahua songs in *Cantares Mexicanos* as their model. However, the Nahua *Cantares*, the non-Christian dij dola, and the Christian libana all have in common two other crucial traits: the aforementioned lexical and nonlexical elements that mark stanza boundaries, and the alternation between new information and repetitive refrains. Therefore, these two genre conventions may have originated in one or more preconquest Nahua and Zapotec ritual genres that were the primary source for those three colonial alphabetic genres.

Pedro Vargas, Fernando Lópes, and Pedro Gonzalo, the authors and owners of the dij dola, embraced the preservation of Zapotec ancestral cults. In contrast, other natives in the region chose a more ambivalent path, which included one collaborative project with Dominicans. This project eventually yielded Booklets 102 and 103 from AGI México 882. Booklet 102 contains three brief songs: a six-stanza song celebrating the sacrifice of God's only child; a five-stanza song about the Virgin Mary; and a four-stanza song entitled "Elegant Speech about Saint Francis" (*libana queani* S[an] Fran[cis]co). Booklet 103 contains seventy-two stanzas, divided into twelve songs that address redemption, the passion of Christ, the mysteries of the Virgin, and celebrate Christ, the Virgin Mary, the Three Wise Men, God the Father, and Saint John the Baptist. A distinguishing dialectal feature of Booklets 102 and 103 is the usage of the voiceless alveolar affricate [ts] in words such as *guetze* (town) or *tzela* (a conjunction), which is a phoneme in colonial and contemporary dialects of Nexitzo and Bixanos Zapotec.[50]

Since Booklet 102 and 103 were therefore composed by speakers of Nexitzo or Bixanos Zapotec, their provenance may be established indirectly. In Maldonado's campaign records, there is only one instance in which the residents of a Nexitzo or Bixanos Zapotec town mentioned the surrender of "wooden drum songs": the confession of Yalahui, signed on November 24, 1704. This document stated that Juan Martín, son of Yalahui alcalde Miguel Martín, owned "a booklet with *teponaztli* songs"; both Miguel and another town official had consulted this booklet. These booklets were copies of earlier texts, for their irregular orthography—*Ahisaso guiristo* for Jesu Christo, *balacisco* for Francisco—indicates that Zapotec speakers copied these songs without Dominican supervision. The Yalahui officials also testified that no communal sacrifices took place in their town after the deaths of their local specialists in the early 1680s.[51] Nevertheless, Juan was accused of idolatry once again during the trial of his associate Juan Felipe in February 1706. While Miguel was being held in the royal jail due to his status as a suspected "teacher of idolatries," one of Yalahui's principales declared that Juan observed a delay before taking his wife into his new home shortly after getting married, for he awaited Juan Felipe's instructions regarding a propitious day for this activity.[52]

In spite of such suspicions against their owners, the Yalahui songs possess a sustained focus on the Virgin Mary. Authors of colonial doctrinal texts in Mesoamerican languages often emphasized Mary's role as mother of humankind's savior and exalted her compassion and humility before God the Father. Other than *Xonaxi*, the most frequent appellation of the Zapotec Mary is "mother of generous giving" (*xinaa quela huezaa lachi*), used to translate the canonical expression "Mother of Mercy." Furthermore, the use of Marian epithets was somewhat common in devotional literature in Mesoamerican languages. Yalahui's Song 1 refers to Mary as a "Royal Enclosure" (*lleeya yahui*),[53] which echoes the metaphorical designation of the beloved as an *hortus conclusus*, or enclosed orchard, in the Song of Songs (4:12). Winston-Allen has argued that, by the twelfth century, Marian texts in Latin embraced this evocative image as a designation for Mary's womb, unblemished by human conception.[54] The Song 1 stanza containing this metaphor states:

Booklet 102, Song 1, Stanza 3:

THEME:
godice   queag beo nizah naxij lleeya yahui   lijchij dios
She existed once, Azalea, Sweet Water, Royal Enclosure of the House of God

REFRAIN:
bezahlachijloo   quia lij benaachij   xilahni cuina bedao
You generously granted the true light to humankind: the servant of God Himself.

BOUNDARY MARKER:
ayahu ayau

Moreover, the Zapotec Marian epithets "Azalea,[55] Sweet Water" (*queag beo nizah naxij*) in this stanza's theme exemplify a rhetorical strategy that associated Christian entities with flowers and sweetness. In other songs in Booklets 102 and 103, both Mary and Jesus receive epithets that incorporate the term "flower." Besides "azalea," Mary is also called "sweet flower" (*gueag naxi*), and Christ is called a "good flower" (*gueag tzahui*) and "the dear flower born on Earth" (*gueag natzona golag guetze lao yoo*). In addition, the stative "it is sweet" (*naxij*) was used to describe Mary in other devotional Zapotec texts.[56] These Zapotec metaphors echo other designations of Mary as flower and garden in doctrinal texts in indigenous languages: for instance, an early seventeenth-century Nahuatl devotional text characterizes Mary as "God's sacred flowery enclosure, his sacred flowery land" (*in iteoxuchitepancaltzin Dios, in iteoxuchitlaltzin*),[57] and a seventeenth-century Quechua composition describes her as a flowery garden closed off by various types of Andean vines.[58]

In all likelihood, the Yalahui songs represent a later form of earlier doctrinal dramas penned by several Dominican missionaries in Valley Zapotec. One of the most celebrated authors of such dramas was Vicente de Villanueva, vicar of Teotitlán del Valle in the 1560s. According to Burgoa, Villanueva "rendered with great ease the mysteries of our Holy Faith in the poetic meter of the Indians' language, and he taught the Indians to stage performances about these mysteries using verses."[59] Furthermore, fray Alonso de la Anunciación composed and staged a Zapotec-language biblical drama in 1575 in Etla. One of Burgoa's teachers, fray Melchor de San Raymundo, composed a Zapotec play in verse about the martyrdom of St. Catherine.[60] Finally, fray Martín Giménez wrote doctrinal dramas in Zapotec and Spanish.[61]

Nonetheless, the Yalahui songs were part of a doctrinal strategy that employed a modified version of the Zapotec "idolatrous" dij dola genre to depict Christian teachings. As the Dominican Gaspar de los Reyes stated in the preface to his 1704 comparative grammar of Caxonos and Valley Zapotec,[62] no printed Christian texts in Caxonos or Nexitzo Zapotec were produced in the seventeenth century, with the exception of Pacheco de Silva's 1687 *Doctrina*.[63] In spite of this lack of known works, Reyes surmised, manuscript copies of doctrinal Zapotec texts must have been composed in the region, given that Villa Alta Dominicans were known to preach Zapotec sermons from the late sixteenth century onward. The Villa Alta libana are the only tangible proof that Reyes's assertion was not merely an expedient defense of Dominican evangelization during the most intensive eradication campaign ever carried out in the region. Indeed, these songs are the sole extant representatives of a bold evangelization experiment that emerged at an earlier moment in the evangelization dialogue, when doctrinal authors still believed that the replacement of Zapotec ancestors and sacred beings with Christian entities could be accomplished by giving Christianity a rhetorical foothold that mimicked ancestral Zapotec songs.

TWO VANTAGE POINTS ON THE CAXONOS REVOLT

The ancestral worship practices described above led civil, ecclesiastical, and mendicant authorities to investigate various idolatry allegations in Caxonos Zapotec queche during the period preceding the 1700 revolt. For instance, the alcalde mayor Velasco y Castilla investigated the activities of Mateo Luis of Yatzachi in 1668. This trial was initiated by two Dominicans who caught the defendant as he was about to offer a sacrifice to Betao Gocio, the Zapotec thunder deity, in order to catch fish. The friars sent him to Velasco y Castilla; before him, Luis reported an incantation, entered in Spanish in the trial records, in which he propitiated

Saint Andrew and Betao Gocio. Even though Luis showed remorse, he was sentenced to two hundred lashes. Similarly, in June 1684, the alcalde mayor Alonso Muñoz de Castilblanque and his associate Pedro Boza came upon some suspicious bundles in the possession of San Francisco resident Nicolás de Contreras. When Boza unwrapped them, he discovered several pieces of *yaguichi* paper, eight bloodied small bundles containing green and red bird feathers and small ocote branches, assorted feather bundles and a bird's head, two birds stuffed with herbs, and two human hair bundles that probably represented founding ancestors. Contreras fled town, along with twenty other men and their families, but six local residents were arrested. However, Castilblanque soon acknowledged that the case pertained to ecclesiastical jurisdiction, and he turned his records over to Bishop Sariñana.[64] Finally, two documents drafted to counter Maldonado's contention that idolatry had prospered due to Dominican leniency—a December 1704 letter from fray Joseph Castilla to his provincial and a July 1706 Dominican testimony—asserted that fifteen Dominicans uprooted idolatries in the late seventeenth century in the Caxonos Zapotec towns of Yatee, Yaa, San Francisco, Zoogocho, and Yatzachi.[65]

A more substantial uprising in the region preceded the Caxonos riot by a decade and a half. In November 1684, a large indigenous mob angered by excessive tributary obligations lay siege to the seat of royal justice in Choapa, trapping within the alcalde mayor of Villa Alta and several of his Spanish associates, but the rebels relented when armed succor arrived from Oaxaca City.[66] In any case, the 1700 uprising more closely resembled a confrontation that took place in the neighboring Caxonos towns of Zoogocho and Zoochila a decade earlier. On March 30, 1691, the Dominican José de Castilla, minister of Zoogocho, requested the support of alcalde mayor don Juan Manuel de Quiroz in order to carry out the arrests of several town officials. The next day, after celebrating mass in Zoogocho, Castilla closed the church's doors and then had the commissioner Francisco Calvo arrest six native officials, who were locked in the prison at neighboring Zoochila. Early in the morning of April 2, a native mob swarmed into Zoochila, liberated the officials, and threw Calvo in prison; Castilla and his supporters, including a Zoogocho principal, barricaded themselves in the local church. Fray Alonso de Vargas, vicar of San Francisco, convinced the rioters to free Calvo the following morning. Afterward, Castilla said mass and the native crowd kneeled, kissed his hands, and received his pardon.

Hence, in both Zoochila and San Francisco Caxonos, an uncertain point of equilibrium shortly after a riot was achieved through a Zapotec strategy that involved an organized show of strength and a public act of repentance.[67] Given how the threat of violence at Zoogocho was expediently dismantled, one may ask what led the natives of San Francisco to murder two fellow residents nine years later. Much in the way that don Diego dared reveal to an African slave closely guarded details about communal practices in Lachirioag four decades earlier, Jacinto de los Ángeles committed the transgression of alerting a handful of Spanish tradesmen about a communal celebration that was being held in the home of Joseph Flores, the head of the local confraternity of Saint Joseph. The Spaniards reported this news to the Dominicans, and don Juan Bautista joined their group later.

The documentary evidence about the Caxonos uprising underwent an important reorganization in the nineteenth century. In 1889, when the Oaxacan archbishop Eulogio Gillow investigated the 1700 riot in an eventually unsuccessful attempt to promote the beatification of don Juan and Jacinto before the Vatican,[68] the original trial records were dispersed. Gillow removed the 1700–1702 proceedings and other related documents from judicial archives and had them transcribed in a format resembling the original pagination; this set is still the most complete extant representation of the case. In any case, three separate Oaxaca archives now hold copies of original eighteenth-century documents that served as the basis for about 91 percent of the 1889 transcriptions.[69]

Archbishop Gillow's interpretation of the Caxonos trial records was not without equivocation. It should be noted here that there is no evidence that don Juan Bautista or Jacinto were native fiscales at the time when the celebration at Flores's house took place, although don Juan had indeed served as a fiscal some years earlier.[70] Both the original trial record, its surviving nineteenth-century copies, and a 1774 testimony drawn so that descendants of Jacinto continued to benefit from tribute exemption refer to both men solely as "Indians" or as *naturales*, "natives," and never as fiscales.[71] Hence, don Juan and Jacinto were discharging the dictates of their conscience rather than an official duty when they acted as informants. This is not a trivial matter, since the fact that these two men were not legitimate fiscales could have rendered their intervention even more intolerable in the eyes of Flores's supporters. Nonetheless, since this detail interfered with Gillow's emerging narrative about the martyrdom of don Juan and Jacinto in the 1880s, it appears that he unilaterally decided to identify them as fiscales, thus perpetuating an inaccuracy about the Caxonos revolt.[72]

The Caxonos records contain two distinct views about the ceremonies that precipitated the riot. Around 9:00 p.m. on September 14, 1700, Jacinto de los Ángeles told the ironsmith Diego de Mora, the carpenter Joseph de Valsalobre, and Valsalobre's apprentice Manuel Rodríguez, that the townspeople were engaged in "idolatries." Valsalobre notified the Dominican Gaspar de los Reyes, who was in his cell with don Juan Bautista—a small detail suggestive of social intimacy between these two men. This group, joined by Reyes's servant Diego Boorques, recruited the Dominican vicar Alonso de Vargas, the Spanish captain don Antonio Pinelo, and a few others, and raided Flores's house an hour or two later. The most spontaneous Spanish account of this celebration comes from the testimony of Mora, Valsalobre, Boorques, and Rodríguez, given before the alguacil Joseph Martín de la Sierra a day after the riot:

They arrived at the house they said belonged to Joseph Flores, where they saw many natives, both men and women, and young boys, with many torches and in a great silence. Having seen this, in a loud voice, [Vargas] said, "What is this shameful thing?" and Joseph de Valsalobre went into the house sword in hand, and all the Indians fled, except for town resident Sebastián Martín. In said house they found a doe that [the natives] had apparently been bleeding out, as it had not died yet, and on a table there were some images of saints placed face down, and on top of them some bowls filled with blood, and they also found some turkeys, plucked and headless, and much diabolic filth inside two woven palm containers and a cane box. Accompanied by the two [Dominicans], they made Martín carry the doe out, and they brought all of these things to the monastery.[73]

Valsalobre later amended his declaration to include more tantalizing details. On November 4, 1700, he emphasized blood as a motif in his testimony before the corregidor:

He saw three rooms full of male and female Indians, and he jumped into the main room, where Indians and youngsters of various ages were on their knees before a table. The most noticeable ones were don José de Seli, gobernador, and don Cristóbal de Robles and Juan Hernández, alcaldes of said town, for they wore pieces of cloth like small capes on their heads, and *huipiles* [native blouses] shaped like the white habits of the mendicants. On the table, [he] saw some *apastes*, or bowls, filled with blood and about three lit wax candles. . . . An Indian of said town called Sebastián Martín held something like a piece of hide with writing made of blood, which he showed to all of them, as if they were praying.[74]

A radically different description of this observance was recorded in sixteen testimonies in support of the Caxonos defendants, which Viceroy Sarmiento de Valladares and Oidor José de Osorio instructed Mier del Tojo to record in May 1701 in order to avoid a second riot. The declarations of the natives of Yatzachi, and of San Mateo, San Miguel and San Francisco Caxonos, several of which were local notables, displayed quite a different outlook on the celebration at Flores's home. While the scene that unfolded before the friars and their associates appeared to be a veritable catalog of idolatrous sacrifices—a demonic book, white robes, beheaded turkeys, a bleeding doe, and the sacrilegious use of saints' images—witnesses testifying on behalf of Flores and his associates offered an alternative view. Consider the deposition of Francisco Luis, who served as alcalde of San Francisco in 1699:

On the night of September 14 of last year, this witness and his five-year-old son, called Joseph, took one peso as a contribution to the confraternity of Saint Joseph to the house of Joseph Flores, who had invited his friends, *compadres* [people joined by ritual kinship links], and barrio neighbors to have dinner because he was finishing [his term] as [the head of] said confraternity. Around eight o'clock at night, as everyone was gathered there . . . the two parish ministers came into the house with some Spaniards who had swords . . . and with another official called Juan Bautista, and Jacinto de los Ángeles. They came into one of the houses of Joseph Flores, in which they had turkeys, *tamales, tortillas*, and a deer, and the blood they had extracted from it in order to make blood sausages. . . . Father fray Gaspar de los Reyes and Jacinto de los Ángeles came into the kitchen in which this witness and another man were, and the said Jacinto seized a piece of pork . . . and threw it to the dogs. This witness asked him, "Jacinto, what are you doing?" Then, the people in the other room ran away in fright, but this witness and the people who were with him went home.[75]

Like Valsalobre's evolving testimony, the declarations of some natives sympathetic to Flores also underwent transformations between earlier and later iterations on the record—for instance, witnesses initially denied having any knowledge about the two informants' fate. Therefore, it is not surprising to find that the testimony of Luis and other town officials, recorded eight months after the riot, echoed the denial of idolatrous intent that the Lachirioag defendants had attempted three decades earlier: the gathering in fact celebrated the end of Flores's term in the confraternity; the offerings were food for his guests; the doe had been bled to prepare sausages. Moreover, other witnesses asserted that the subsequent acts of violence against the monastery were inspired by public apprehension about armed Spanish presence and by the fact that a native had been shot and killed. One witness even reported that don Juan Bautista still owed the community some of the funds he received during his earlier tenure as fiscal.[76]

It would be a supremely ironic turn to find that Luis was in fact being candid about this observance. It is, after all, possible that this celebration was linked to Flores's service in a confraternity, and that the townspeople had preemptively confronted any idolatry suspicions that might stem from their unorthodox use of saints' images and deer blood. However, if the celebrants' motivation was oriented toward Zapotec cosmology, its significance remains unclear. Unlike many Northern Zapotec collective observances, this celebration was held indoors and not at a sacred site, rendering its motivation even more enigmatic. The meeting took place late at night on September 14, 1700, which was the transition between the piyè dates 12-Death (*benelana*) and 13-Deer (*yecechina*) in 3-Wind (*quiolahaa*), Year Forty-Two of the fifty-two Zapotec year count. These dates also fell at the beginning of a twenty-day period called Gaha in the Zapotec 365-day year (see Figure 5.3 in Chapter 5). One possibility is that the people of San Francisco were commemorating the end of the penultimate trecena in the 260-day count, which concluded on 13-Deer; another is that they were ending their observance of the arrival of Gaha, which had begun four days earlier, on September 10.

Alcalde mayor Mier del Tojo interpreted the events at Caxonos as a dangerous merging of rebellion and idolatry that had to be confronted with severity. In fact, he believed that the rebellion was linked to two indigenous caciques who had been successful in legal suits they brought against Spanish civil and ecclesiastic officials. In spite of such fears, however, there is no historical evidence linking these notables to the uprising. The first one was don Felipe de Santiago of Yatzona, who gained a sterling reputation in the 1680s as an effective legal representative of Zapotec communal interests against the economic interests of alcaldes mayores. Santiago, who eventually quarreled with his local ally don Joseph de Celis, was granted an order to be released from prison by the Audiencia at the worst possible moment—only a few days after the riot at Caxonos. Mier del Tojo, who did not trust Santiago due to his fame as an effective advocate for native communities, held him in prison until about 1702 while he was investigated for idolatry and involvement in the revolt.[77]

The second case provides another example of a juridically savvy cacique who attempted to turn the tide of civil and ecclesiastical justice in his favor, but was trumped due to the timing of the 1700 uprising. In November 1688, the local beneficiado Fernando de Villegas collected testimony about the suspicious activities of don Lorenzo Rosales y Arellano, cacique of the Chatino town of Santo Domingo Teoxomulco, and five of his associates: Pablo Hernández, Diego López, Diego Luis, Diego Salinas, and Juan Velasco. Allegedly, these men buried turkeys under house foundations and left offerings at sacred sites that included a cave called Quiela Liloo, "Water That Falls Suddenly." Rosales was also said to collect candles for such offerings, and to own a "book in which he saw the days, times, and hours that were good or bad," like the Chatino specialists who had given Diego Luis of Sola a calendar seven decades earlier. In 1699–1700, the Elotepec beneficiado Manuel de Espina Altamirano, as commissioned judge in the case, recorded testimony about how Rosales had severely punished several witnesses against him. Nonetheless, Rosales maintained that the motivation behind these proceedings was suspect. Following a legal strategy favored by other native caciques, Rosales journeyed to Mexico City and argued before the Audiencia that the case against him was provoked by a suit he filed against don Juan Martínez Morentín, Teozacualco's alcalde mayor, for having voided a land transaction between natives. Furthermore, he and his brother submitted that Espina Altamirano was moved by personal hatred. Rosales even turned himself in at Mexico City's ecclesiastical jail in July 1700, hoping to be freed after the charges against him were cleared. However, after the Caxonos revolt, Mier del Tojo employed Rosales's case as an argument for requesting the Audiencia's permission to act swiftly against the insurgents. Hence, Rosales remained incarcerated as of November 27, 1700, the last date in extant records, since the witnesses against him had not been ratified.[78]

Mier del Tojo proceeded against the Caxonos insurgents with the support of Oaxaca's corregidor, and the viceroy inspected the case, requesting reviews from his chief prosecutor, the Audiencia, and the oidor Osorio. Juan de Valdés, general advisor to the viceroy, wrote a concise summary of this case in January 1701. Making an argument previously used by alcaldes mayores to act against idolaters, Valdés invoked Laws 6 and 7, Book V, Title V of the *Recopilación de leyes de Indias*, which demanded that the viceroys support the ecclesiastic jurisdiction in idolatry cases, and concluded that the gravity of the crimes at Caxonos warranted civil intervention, even if they did not involve maleficio. Most importantly, Valdés cleared the field for handing death sentences by asserting that each of three offenses—sedition, rioting resulting in murder, and idolatry—warranted capital punishment.[79] Some of the rebels sentenced to death were local officials—the alcaldes don Cristóbal de Robles and José Luis, the regidor Pedro Pablo, and the cantor don José de Mendoza. The rest were those who decided to murder the informants at a meeting, a group including the avowed murderers Nicolás de Aquino and Francisco López, who also admitted to drinking some of their victims' blood. The garroting and quartering of the fifteen convicts was carried out two days after sentencing, and the heads and right hands of Aquino and López were placed on stakes in San Francisco's main square. Two defendants were paraded in an auto and received two hundred lashes, privation of office, and exile.

The trial's focus then shifted to defense attorney José de Ledesma's appeal against the suspended death sentence handed to the remaining seventeen defendants. It is difficult to reconcile Mier del Tojo's pitiless punishment with the disciplining of other indigenous rebels. After the 1660 Tehuantepec rebellion was quelled, only two natives were executed; even if the 1761 Yucatec Maya rebellion at Cisteil resulted in the death of several hundred native combatants, only nine of the rebels were put to death.[80] He also took the unusually cruel measure of placing each of the thirty-four defendants on a torture rack and applying a turn of the screw before recording their testimony ratification.[81] Perhaps this alcalde mayor enjoyed a broad degree of latitude regarding ecclesiastical claims on these idolaters since the bishopric's seat was vacant between 1700 and early 1702; indeed, the cathedral chapter held no recorded discussion of the Caxonos events.[82]

In a paradoxical turn, Mier del Tojo's career after the Caxonos trial, while highly accomplished, became entwined with sorcery suspicions. After completing this trial and his term as alcalde mayor in 1702, he became one of the most prosperous merchants in Oaxaca City. Shortly after his death in March 1730, some Oaxaca residents began spreading the rumor that he had lost his mind due to a sorcery act. In an attempt to profit from this tale, a business associate called Lucas Fortuna removed some of Mier del Tojo's property from his house after his death, claiming unpaid debts. His widow successfully sued Fortuna, recovered the removed possessions, and obtained a public retraction regarding her late husband's alleged bewitching in December 1731.[83]

MALDONADO'S EXTIRPATORY EXPERIMENTS

After his arrival in Oaxaca in July 1702, the newly elected bishop fray Ángel Maldonado decided to undertake painful reforms. Maldonado, a well-educated man, had a doctorate in theology from the University of Alcalá and had taught there for several years before becoming a *magister* in his order of Saint Benedict.[84] He soon realized that any measures toward reconciliation would have to address the pending appeal of the seventeen Caxonos defendants. In a move that mirrored a general pardon granted in August 1701 by the viceroy to all Caxonos residents not named as defendants, in December 1702 Maldonado issued a general absolution from idolatry convictions to all Villa Alta natives who confessed their transgressions and were not "teachers of idolatry." In spite of these reprieves, many of San Francisco's inhabitants left town due to harassment at the hands of loyalist gobernador don Gabriel de los Ángeles; in February 1703 the viceroy instructed Ángeles to halt this behavior.[85] Given the dispersal of the Caxonos trial records in the nineteenth century, the fate of the remaining seventeen defendants was in doubt since Gillow's time, given that the original autos did not include the outcome of Ledesma's appeal. However, several documents from a volume compiled by a notary public circa 1740 provide a coda to the case. According to these records, signed in 1703 by the viceroy, Bishop Maldonado, and Mier del Tojo's successor, Captain Diego de Rivera y Cotes, the Real Sala del Crimen in Mexico City nullified the suspended death sentence against fifteen of the seventeen remaining defendants, sentencing them instead to whipping and exile. Cotes, installed as alcalde mayor in early 1703, had these defendants transferred to a prison in Oaxaca. The bishop selected eleven of them and tried them as idolaters.[86]

In November 1702, Maldonado undertook an exhaustive visita of Villa Alta, during which he inspected seventeen beneficios, confirmed more than four thousand natives, heard idolatry trials, and sent several convicts to the new prison of idolaters he erected as a substitute for Sariñana's prison. As Maldonado later indicated in a 1708 Latin epistle to Clement XI, this first scrutiny only led him to suspect the natives concealed "even greater abominations."[87] In order to extract information about local rituals, the bishop appointed Joseph de Aragón y Alcántara, Sariñana's leading extirpator in the 1680s and then Ejutla's parish priest, as his visitador general, and took him along in his first visit.[88]

Furthermore, Maldonado set in motion an amnesty experiment that would leave an indelible mark in the social organization of ritual practices in the region. According to later testimony presented to the crown by Dominican Procurator General Antonio de Torres, the bishop selected one of the eleven defendants surrendered to him by the alcalde mayor, gave this native his pectoral to wear as an emblem, and ordered him to travel throughout Villa Alta announcing his absolution.[89] This messenger traveled from town to town in a festive manner, gathering native audiences to the sound of "drums, trumpets, and shawms."[90] Maldonado's offer, repeated in a proclamation by the alcalde mayor, was simple and non-negotiable: in exchange for denouncing their ritual specialists, turning in their clandestine ritual texts, and making a full confession about all their ritual practices, each community would benefit from a general absolution and an amnesty from further trials. Compliance with this directive generated heated debates. A Spanish carpenter who was in the Nexitzo Zapotec queche of San Miguel Tiltepec when the alcalde mayor's order arrived testified that several *guechea*, or malevolent ritual specialists, began arguing boisterously about who should be turned in before settling on a man called Nicolás Pacheco. In spite of Maldonado's absolution, Pacheco was eventually tried and jailed for sorcery in 1705 and released in 1708.[91]

These displays of authority, coupled with memories of the savage punishment of the Caxonos insurgents, may account for the overwhelming scale of the response to Maldonado's innovative overture. Between September 1704 and January 1705, the elected authorities of 104 indigenous communities in Villa Alta, representing a native population

of about sixty thousand,[92] journeyed to San Ildefonso, Villa Alta's cabecera, to register a petition for absolution, a confession regarding their
observances, or both. Thus, the officials of fifteen Bixanos Zapotec,
twenty-seven Caxonos Zapotec, twenty-six Nexitzo Zapotec, twenty-
nine Mixe, and seven Chinantec towns filed past either one of two experienced idolatry eradicators: Aragón y Alcántara, or commissioned judge
fray Diego de Cardona. A mestizo fluent in Caxonos Zapotec, Joseph de
Ramos,[93] translated their testimony into Spanish. After presenting brief
confessions in Spanish, town representatives were asked to name of their
"teachers of idolatries," identify named sites of ritual significance, describe their observances, and turn in any "instruments of idolatry" they
possessed, such as calendrical or ritual texts. The only exception to this
pattern was an eloquent and almost elegiac confession written in Caxonos Zapotec by Yalálag's cabildo. Maldonado's surrogates trusted the
confessants to make a full surrender of their ritual texts. For instance, in
the spring of 1706, don Juan Felipe, then fiscal of Yalahui, was accused
of having kept the "book of idolatries" he had brought to San Ildefonso
after the judge failed to ask him about it. This defendant argued, however, that the text in question was in fact a "Christian doctrine" and not
a calendrical booklet.[94]

According to these confessions and other accusations made in trials in
1702–6, during this period there were sixty-one Zapotec communities
in Villa Alta who had at least one resident specialist. About two-thirds
of these communities—thirty-nine queche—housed between one and
five specialists. As for the uppermost tier, fifteen queche had between
six and ten specialists, and only seven Zapotec queche—Betaza, San
Juan Xuquila, Lalopa, Tiltepec, Yagayo, Yalálag, and Yaxila—had more
than ten. The fact that Betaza yielded the largest number of alleged specialists in this sample, a total of thirty-two, resulted from an intensive
1703 idolatry investigation discussed below. Except for Yalálag, there
is no stable correlation between number of alleged specialists and 1703
population levels; for instance, while only four specialists were said to
live in Lachirioag, which had 1,242 tributaries at the time, twenty-four
allegedly resided in San Miguel Tiltepec, which had only 736 household
heads.[95]

Rather than carefully interrogating each defendant, as had been done
by many inquisitorial judges who had embraced a model epitomized by
the actions of Jacques Fournier against Cathar heretics in Montaillou
in the early fourteenth century,[96] Maldonado delegated his authority to
several representatives. Besides the indispensable Aragón y Alcántara,
they included Cardona, the San Ildefonso Dominican minister Joseph
de Contreras, and the priests Miguel Martínez de Salamanca, Domingo

Zenlí y Cerdán, and Juan Manuel de Urbina.[97] Alcalde mayor Cotes assisted the bishop, turning over the testimonies of about forty-five so-called "teachers of idolatry" imprisoned in the royal jail.[98] Instead of painstakingly recording allegations against defendants, Maldonado streamlined juridical practice by having only collective confessions and ritual texts entered into the record. This approach allowed Maldonado to build an impressive set of records regarding native idolatry across a vast geographical domain, which no legal proceeding of that age could have otherwise obtained. In some ways, such a practice rendered inconsequential fine-grained theological distinctions and allowed administrators to think, perhaps for the first time, of idolatry as a series of essentially interchangeable crimes of thought.

Maldonado's disillusionment with the state of doctrinal education in Villa Alta led him to clash with the interest of the Dominicans in preserving the status quo. Shortly after his 1704 Villa Alta visit, the bishop proposed to the crown the creation of six new curates. In an intermediate chapter celebrated in May 1705, the Dominicans agreed to this petition, but the order requested that these curates be filled with Dominicans. Maldonado agreed, and these regulars were given their appointment through the bishop, a novel form of intervention in matters that the Dominicans had long regarded as internal.

One crucial factor rendered this campaign a unique eradication exercise in colonial Spanish America: the surrender of 102 separate texts containing Zapotec calendars and four collections of ritual songs. Since these booklets were prime exhibits of the uneven results of Dominican evangelization in Villa Alta after almost 170 years, the bishop spared them from the flames and submitted them to the Council of the Indies to support his requests. Indeed, in August 1706, this prelate upped the ante by asking the crown to confirm the creation of eleven new curates—Zoochila, Tabaá, Yalálag, Betaza, Lachixila, Comaltepec, Latani, Santa María, Puxmetacan, Ayutla, and Atalacatepec.[99] Unsurprisingly, this new proposal was bitterly opposed by the Dominicans. In a report printed circa 1709, Dominican Procurator General Antonio de Torres contended that ecclesiastic and civil archives brimmed with idolatry proceedings because, since natives knew it was difficult to punish an entire town, "they attempt to include [all of the queche] in this crime, so that, having all become defendants, they may receive an absolution sooner in order to return with greater freedom to their idolatries, as it occurred during [Maldonado's] visit."[100] The bishop retorted that, during his first visit, he found the number of ministers to be inadequate, citing the example of the cabecera of San Ildefonso, which had only three ministers for six thousand inhabitants in twenty-two towns.[101] Torres countered that the rotation of Dominicans in one township was preferable to the appointment of a resident priest, because a variety of ministers was more conducive to uncovering idolatry. What both Torres and Maldonado agreed on was the deep roots of native devotions. Using a New Testament simile that equated God's word with seeds, the bishop complained in a letter to Clement XI: "Some of the seeds were poured on a stone, and from it issued a plant that lacked substance [*humorem*]. Others were poured among the thorns, and the thorns stifled their growth."[102]

This confrontation was interrupted in June 1712, when allies of the Dominicans convinced Philip V to remove Maldonado from Oaxaca by appointing him to Orihuela, a small but comfortable bishopric in Murcia, Spain. Since Maldonado had already reached an agreement with the Dominican provincial, he rejected this offer in December 1712, arguing that the newly minted consensus would solve the impasse over the curates.[103] The bishop's proposals went beyond ecclesiastical reforms. Both he and Cotes asked the crown to congregate all towns in Villa Alta into groups of four hundred married couples; they also recommended appointing Spanish-language teachers and allowing the alcalde mayor to name local representatives.[104] As Chance observed, native resistance to this measure was so great that some towns offered large bribes to the alcalde mayor if he desisted from carrying out congregaciones, and there is little evidence that they were carried through.[105] Indeed, two native nobles, don Pedro Velasco and don José de Mendoza, were briefly imprisoned by the viceroy when they complained about this project before the Audiencia.[106]

COMMUNAL RESISTANCE IN BETAZA

Toward the end of 1702, the bishop himself brought his absolution to the queche of San Melchor Betaza and Santo Tomás Lachitaa in Villa Alta. Betaza, a relatively large town, had an estimated population of 935 residents in 1703; its neighbor, Lachitaa, shared numerous kinship links with Betaza and had about 178 individuals. In spite of Maldonado's visit, Betaza and Lachitaa were not ready to renounce their devotions. According to Agustín Gonzalo Zárate, a former Betaza official and the specialist whose arrest would trigger a revolt, hardly a month had passed after this visit before the town engaged in another communal celebration. Sometime in the next year, through the mediation of specialists who were experienced interpreters of the visions produced by the hallucinogenic plant *cuana betao*, the queche asked its tutelary deities what would befall them. Two specialists—Simón de Santiago and Nicolás

Laws 6 and 7 in Book I, Title I of the Laws of the Indies allowed alcaldes mayores to try idolaters after consulting with the Audiencia,[130] Cotes should focus on the misappropriation of crown tribute and turn in the trial records to Maldonado upon request. Therefore, Cotes divided the defendants according to their participation in the financing of communal practices. Six of the specialists who did not participate in such efforts—Fabián de Vargas, Nicolás de Espina Aracena, Simón de Santiago, Pedro Cano, Nicolás de Celis, and Joseph de Celis—were released from jail, but their property was seized in order to cover fines and trial costs. The remaining defendants stayed in jail and also had their property seized. Although these trial records are incomplete, toward the end of this proceeding, Cotes received a Zapotec letter from the 1705 Betaza cabildo that promised to repay the amount of royal tribute formerly used to fund clandestine festivities. This sum was 168 pesos, or a six-real contribution from each married couple.[131]

Three of the six specialists freed by Cotes emerged from their imprisonment with an unscathed faith in their ancestors, if one believes a dramatic testimony conveyed by the Dominican provincial Joseph de Algaba. According to the Spaniard Tomás Gutiérrez Xijón, who was appointed as Spanish-language teacher and gobernador of Betaza after the beginning of the trial,

Nicolás Espina, Fabián Vargas, and Simón Santiago gathered most of the natives of [Betaza] after they left Villa Alta and returned, and said the town would find consolation because they were notifying them that their observances would remain. This was because the bishop was a native neither of Spain nor of the Indies, nor did he have his origin in this world: he was a descendant of their deities, who had sent him so he would favor, support, and sustain them. [These maestros] had seen it with their own eyes, because, after being incarcerated by the ministers, the bishop traveled to the sierra to deliver them from persecution.[132]

Nonetheless, both Xijón's status as newly appointed local representative of colonial power and this declaration's timing seem suspect. Xijón gave this testimony in Villa Alta on February 10, 1705, and reached Algaba quickly, since it appeared as a rebuke to Maldonado in a February 19 letter written by the Dominican in Oaxaca City. Either news about a renewed pact with the ancestors traveled fast, or Algaba chose to embellish his report. Furthermore, Xijón would not have been the only schoolteacher newly appointed after Maldonado's campaign to settle scores through idolatry accusations. In January 1706, Andrés Gabriel Gonzalo, a principal from Analco who taught Spanish in Yatee, accused don Gerónimo Manuel, Juan Mendes, and Nicolas de Espina of uttering ancient prayers in Zapotec. He even had one of don Gerónimo's suspicious phrases, which partially translates as "we believe in this our deity . . . ," entered into the record.[133] Not only did the relative succinctness and vagueness of this phrase inspire suspicion; moreover, the defendants were swiftly released after claiming that Andrés falsely accused them because a Yatee alcalde had scolded him for having an affair with a local woman, even though he had a wife in Analco.

A confrontation between Cotes and Gaspar de los Reyes, one of the two Dominicans who confronted the Caxonos rebels, suggests that the alcalde mayor sought to extract financial gain from alleged idolaters. In October 1705, Reyes was told by friar Nicolás Barzalobre, Betaza's parish priest, that several residents had been caught with "instruments of idolatry" four months earlier, as reported by the ever-vigilant Xijón. Reyes had a title as ecclesiastical judge with commission against idolaters issued by Maldonado in 1705, but this appointment did not include jurisdiction over Betaza, so he deposed the three alleged idolaters—local alcalde Mateo Martín and his sons Joseph and Francisco, denounced earlier as the source of macaw feathers employed in collective rituals—as inquisitorial commissioner of Yatee and San Juan Xuquila. Apparently, not only had Francisco conducted a suspect ceremony the day before Palm Sunday, but also a search of his house's roof yielded a bundle containing a stone idol, feathers, and some strands of white hair that were, quite literally, the aforementioned "heads of the ancestors."[134] Afterward, an indignant Reyes discovered that Cotes had released these defendants after receiving the handsome sum of 122 pesos. When Cotes learned about Reyes's inquiry, he asked that the friar be placed under house arrest; nevertheless, Reyes was determined to bring this irregularity to the Inquisition's attention, and he journeyed to Oaxaca and Mexico to plead his case. Maldonado—who, according to Reyes, formed an alliance with Cotes to counter Dominican influence in Oaxaca—accused Reyes of insubordination for leaving the province without his permission, and Cotes argued that Reyes was mentally unstable. The powerful Maldonado-Cotes alliance had the last word. Due to the resulting scandal, Reyes, who had gained renown as the author of a 1704 Caxonos and Valley Zapotec grammar, lost his post as commissioner. In June 1707 the Holy Office ruled that he could not be reinstated.[135]

Nonetheless, Maldonado's campaign would not silence the beating of the nicachi in Villa Alta. In September 1718, Mariana Martín of Lachitaa denounced some preparations for a communal ritual that included the drinking of a fermented beverage called *tepache*, the sacrifice of various roosters, and the performance of Zapotec songs. Alerted by Martín, a representative of the royal justice came to Lachitaa, only to discover that most of the town's adult residents had fled to the surrounding mountains, leaving behind two teponaztli drums, carved stones, feathers, and a fresh batch of tepache in the house of the proverbial poor widow, who denied having any knowledge about the feast. Mariana also described a communal ritual she had witnessed earlier:

It is true that in May [1718] there was another act of idolatry around seven in the morning. . . . She saw all the men from her town gather around. Then Gaspar Bautista and Fabian Luis, both from Betaza, began playing, one on the teponaztli and the other on a tortoise shell, and they were both singing in the language of the Valley in the ancient manner; the most she could understand was that they were saying *The stars are burning* . . . , and she could not hear better or see what they were doing due to the distance.[136]

It is with this evocative description that the performance of nicachi songs exits the extant documentary record. We can only speculate as to the reasons for the absence of further trials or accusations regarding the performance of this ritual genre: either many its practitioners died without passing on their knowledge, or, as is more likely, they continued this practice in greater secrecy and without risking detection from outsiders.

THE RISE AND FALL OF ZAPOTEC
COLLECTIVE RITUAL SPHERES

This chapter probed the documentary sources produced during Maldonado's eradication experiment in order to reconstruct and interpret four converging domains: local Northern Zapotec cosmologies; the social organization of devotions deeply anchored in such understandings of the universe; the eradication policies that targeted these practices; and native responses to these punitive projects. Below, I summarize the impact of the "invisible war" in southern Villa Alta queche with a final reflection on demography, local autonomy, factionalism, and prophecy.

The first phase in the third cycle of extirpation efforts in Central Mexico (1660s–1700s) was coterminous with a period of general demographic recovery in Villa Alta native communities. According to extant demographic data, Villa Alta experienced a substantial demographic recovery during the second half of the seventeenth century. Chance calculated by extrapolation a descent to 21.6 percent by 1622 of the 1548 total population levels, and a significant recovery by 1703.[137] By this year, the entire population of Villa Alta was up to 38 percent of the 1548 total, yielding a 175 percent increase between 1622 and 1703. The particular demographic success of Caxonos Zapotec communities placed them above their neighbors: while their number decreased to 37 percent of the 1548 population by 1568, their population grew by a factor of

1.5 between 1568 and 1622, and by a factor of 2.4 between 1622 and 1703. Nevertheless, one must pause before embracing the mechanistic explanation that increased population levels automatically resulted in the growth of the number of ritual specialists. Idolatry extirpation projects followed social and political dynamics independently from sustained demographic decay. An analysis centered on demographic dynamics cannot fully explain the fact that the rapport between social order and ritual practices differed from one community to another. Moreover, the responses of different queche to extirpation attempts were also variable.

In San Francisco Caxonos and Betaza, autonomy comprised several forms of political action, such as secession, land disputes against neighboring queche, the spontaneous organization of local confraternities, or the defense of communal lands, articulated in different ways within different native communities. The aftershocks of Maldonado's campaign were felt in various Villa Alta queche as various factions accused their enemies of idolatry with varying degrees of success between 1705 and 1706 in Roayaga,[138] Tiltepec,[139] and Yalahui.[140] The prospect of being sent to the perpetual prison was redoubtable to natives, as suggested by a 1707 accusation in Zapotec against a priest at Yagavila who casually threatened to send the local alcaldes to the *lichi guia perfeta* [sic] after a minor dispute.[141]

In San Francisco there was a relative consensus, led by practitioners such as Flores and opposed by a small faction headed by Bautista and Ángeles, that communal practices were to be performed in the relative privacy of domestic spaces. The solution advocated by Betaza officials was quite different, however, as it involved a dual arrangement for public Christian and local devotional practices that rested on financial contributions by household. The existence of a dual system in Betaza and Lachitaa was facilitated by their geographic isolation and by a relative laxity in Dominican evangelization policies. In these communities, a minimal definition of autonomy with respect to communal devotions included the refusal to involve any outsiders in a heated local discussion over the proper social and spatial realms in which local devotions were articulated. Hence, such an arrangement gave Betaza's religious field a different configuration from that of San Francisco Caxonos's, even if both towns were regarded as idolatrous by colonial authorities.

Although the sharp phrases that comment on the division between defenders and denouncers of Northern Zapotec devotions come down to us through Spanish translations, they remain vivid enough. Those who reneged traditional devotions threatened the pride vested in them and were described as servile beings who obtained their sustenance from licking the Spaniards' plates. The masculinity of those who refused to defend their ancestors was rhetorically put into question by denying them an iconic masculine garment, a pair of pants. Through a series of well-chosen epithets, a line was drawn between the feminized, those with loose tongues and those who sold their towns away, from those who proudly kept their representations of lineage heads and baptized their children with calendrical names. This local pride in the defense and veneration of lineage lines coexisted with other forms of honor and shame in colonial Spanish America, such as the honor that attached to legitimate birth and the shame that issued from sexual impropriety, public insulting words or gestures, and illegitimacy.[142]

During the second half of the seventeenth century, two policy changes began to have substantial effects in Villa Alta. On the one hand, two ruthlessly ambitious bishops, Sariñana and Maldonado, embraced a more severe set of legal measures and punitive efforts against alleged idolaters; on the other, the office of the alcalde mayor in Villa Alta expanded its reaches into idolatry extirpation measures and increased its economic and political impact among natives through a greater control of policies that appropriated goods and labor in native communities. In the most terrible of ways, local Zapotec deities had the last word. When Betaza's ritual specialists consulted their deities through the mediation of hallucinogens, they were told, according to Simón de Santiago, that they had fallen "into the hands of God the Father." Although we do not have a Zapotec transcription of his confession, the Spanish *en manos de*, "into the hands of" was probably a gloss of the ubiquitous term *lachinaa*, frequently used in several documentary contexts: testators used it to denote they were handing full control of their lands to their heirs,[143] or of their soul to Jesus Christ,[144] and town officials employed it to signify they were leaving an important decision in the hands of Spanish administrators.[145] This polysemic term was thus an apt summation of an epochal transition. Not only had a new cycle of civil and ecclesiastical administration arrived in Villa Alta, but the ancestral deities whose praises were sung in nicachi songs were about to leave their human charges in the care of God the Father.

CHAPTER 8

From Idolatry to *Maleficio*

Reform, Factionalism, and Institutional Conflicts in the Eighteenth Century

In the first two decades of the eighteenth century, anti-idolatry measures in Central Mexico underwent yet another substantial transition. In Oaxaca, Maldonado's extirpatory activities in Villa Alta in 1702–6 provided an unusual coda to an institutional crescendo that began shortly after the 1660 Tehuantepec rebellion. Accusations against Zapotec specialists tapered off after the 1710s, and Maldonado's coerced confiscation of ritual texts apparently drove literate specialists further into a social underground not documented in extant records. In the diocese of Mexico, a celebrated criollo intellectual transformed the institutional practices of the Provisorato de Indios y Chinos in the 1710s and 1720s. This chapter addresses these and other developments in policies against idolatry in the sees of Mexico and Oaxaca. First, focusing on Toluca, I inspect the transformation of procedural and punitive dynamics throughout the eighteenth century, evaluating how idolatry, superstition, hail casting, and maleficio were defined in the courtroom and exploring the medicalization of sorcery accusations. Then, I consider the relationship between local factionalism and idolatry accusations in Oaxaca, assess Maldonado's most enduring punitive legacy—the perpetual prison for idolaters—and inquire into one of the most substantial native sorcery trials in eighteenth-century Oaxaca: a case against several blood-sucking sorcerers in a Chinantec community in the 1750s. Finally, I address procedural conflict among competing jurisdictions, which involved a protracted dispute between the provisorato and the Inquisition as well as episodic confrontations between alcaldes mayores and the provisorato.

The providential preservation of indigenous idolatry, sorcery, and superstition proceedings conducted by the ecclesiastical judges of Toluca between the 1720s and the 1780s provides us with an unusually detailed perspective on ecclesiastical projects against native heterodoxy. Records at the Archivo Histórico del Arzobispado de México (AHAM) and the Archivo del Cabildo Catedralicio de México (ACM) contain thirty-eight separate accusations, trial summaries, and legal proceedings in the diocese of Mexico against sixty-one individually identifiable natives accused of crimes against the faith between 1691 and 1780. The original number of proceedings against indigenous heterodoxy was not a massive corpus; in 1767, the entire ensemble of such records between 1722 and 1766 was contained in one hundred eighty folios, or about forty folios per decade.[1] These cases concern defendants investigated by nine ecclesiastical judges, eight of which resided at the *cabecera* of San Joseph de Toluca.[2] Given the paucity of similar records in other regions near the Basin of Mexico, this corpus provides an extraordinary opportunity for a longitudinal analysis of accusations regarding matters of faith in native communities. The following section discusses this corpus, which describes activities undertaken during the tenure of four Mexican archbishops: Aguiar y Seijas (1680–98), Lanciego Eguiluz (1714–28), Vizarrón y Eguiarreta (1730–47), and Rubio y Salinas (1748–65). Table 8.1 provides an overview of the claims investigated by ecclesiastical judges in the region.

The civil jurisdictions of Toluca, Metepec, Tenango del Valle, and Temazcaltepec, twenty leagues to the west and southwest of the Basin of Mexico, enclosed a patchwork of sociolinguistic entities and civil districts. In the fifteenth century, Axayacatl's military conquest of the region resulted in the redistribution of land to Mexica allies and local lords.[3] Prior to the establishment of a Mexica garrison at Calixtlahuacan, Otomi, Matlatzinca, and Mazahua speakers predominated in the region,[4] and these languages coexisted with Nahuatl throughout colonial times. By the mid-sixteenth century, Toluca was divided into a cabecera and six barrios, roughly corresponding to the subdivisions established after the Mexica invasion, and its indigenous cabildo provided an equal number of alcaldes, regidores, and alguaciles mayores that represented the three main local "nations" as they existed before congregaciones: eighteen Matlatzinca, eighteen Nahua, and ten Otomi towns.[5] From the sixteenth century onward, the Franciscans established five cabeceras de doctrina at Toluca, Calimaya, Zinacantepec, Jilotepec, and Metepec;[6] the Augustinians founded convents at Malinalco and Ocuilan; and the archbishop of Mexico administered thirteen predominantly indigenous parishes in the region.[7] By the late seventeenth century, Vetancourt counted more than six thousand native subjects, nine indigenous confraternities, and twenty-one towns served by priests residing elsewhere.[8]

TABLE 8.1 *Extant Provisorato Proceedings in the Toluca Valley, 1691–1780*

Jurisdiction	Subdivisions	Local languages	Dates	Defendants' number and gender	Types of accusation
Toluca	Cacalomacan	Nahuatl	1765	1 W	Sorcery
	Calpoltitlan	Nahuatl	1729; 1736	1 M; 1 M	Sorcery
	Chachalolla	Nahuatl?	1759	1 W	Sorcery
	S. Mateo	Matlatzinca	1780	1 W	Sorcery
	Sta. Ana	Nahuatl	1760	1 W	Superstitious healing
	S. Bernardino	Matlatzinca?	1764	1 W	Sorcery
	S. Buenaventura	Otomi	1736	1 M	Hail casting
	Sta. Clara	Matlatzinca	1760	1 W	Sorcery
	Calixtlahuaca	Matlatzinca	1764	2 M	Sorcery
	S. Lorenzo	Matlatzinca, Otomi	1737; 1745; 1756; 1774; 1776	1 M; 1 M; 2 W; 1 M; 2 M	Idolatry; hail casting; sorcery
	S. Pablo	Otomi	1764	1 W	Sorcery
	Tlachaloya	Otomi	1754	6 W & 4 M	Idolatry
	Toluca	Multilingual	1729; 1747	1 M; 1 M	Superstitious healing; sorcery
Metepec	Metepec	Multilingual	1722	1 M	Superstitious healing
	Sta. Ana	Nahuatl	1765	1 W	Superstitious healing
	S. Antonio	Otomi	1727	1 M	Hail casting
	S. Felipe	Nahuatl?	1736	1 W	Superstitious healing
	S. Mateo Atenco	Nahuatl	1728	1 M	Superstitious worship
	Totocuitlapilco	Nahuatl	1734	1 M	Idolatry
	Zinacantepec	Otomi, Nahuatl	1742	2 M	Superstitious healing
Tenango del Valle	Calimaya	Multilingual	1691; 1745	2 M; 1 W & 1 M	Idolatry; superstitious healing
	Tepexuxuca	Nahuatl?	1726–27	1 W	Sorcery
	Tenango del Valle	Matlatzinca, Nahuatl	1747	2 W & 1 M	Sorcery; superstitious healing
Temazcaltepec	S. Mateo Totoltepec	Nahuatl	1754; 1756; 1764	1 M	Superstitious healing
	S. Pedro Totoltepec	Nahuatl	1728; 1756–58; 1758	1 W & 1 M; 1 M; 1 W & 1 M	Superstitious healing; sorcery

SOURCES: AHAM; García Castro 1999; Gerhard 1972

The Toluca corpus is a heterogeneous accretion of claims against indigenous practices falling into categories that were co-constructed by accusers, defendants, and ecclesiastical authorities. Our understanding of it is improved by employing four classifications that emerge out of the records: maleficio—the causing of illness through an implicit or explicit pact with the devil—superstition, idolatry, and hail casting. Two trends deserve particular note: the relative scarcity of idolatry accusations and the prevalence of maleficio claims. Surprisingly, in the eighteenth century Toluca did not see the rise of local ministers devoted to ferreting out traditional beliefs. Neither did the three sitting archbishops of Mexico between 1711 and 1765 share Bishop Maldonado's zeal for identifying and isolating heterodoxy among their parishioners. Therefore, the Toluca corpus lacks both a centralized ecclesiastical interpretation of native beliefs and ritual texts produced by native specialists. Plants, foodstuffs, and implements are sometimes called by their Nahuatl names, but only three ritual specialists were identified using Nahuatl terms,[9] and detailed lines of questioning regarding indigenous categories were rarely pursued by prosecutors.

THE PROVISORATO DE INDIOS UNDER CASTORENA Y URZÚA

Juan Ignacio de Castorena y Urzúa's reputation in Mexican historiography rests on both his work as the compiler of *Fama y obras pósthumas del fénix de México*, a 1700 edition of the poetry of Sor Juana Inés de la Cruz,[10] and his pioneering labor as editor of the 1722 *Gaceta de México*, the first periodical published in New Spain. His contemporaries knew him as a kinetic author, jurist, preacher, and public figure. After obtaining the degree of *licenciado* and doctor of laws in the early 1690s, he served as a temporary lecturer in law at the Royal University. Following in the steps of Juan Ruiz de Alarcón and other ambitious criollos, Castorena y Urzúa secured an advanced degree at a peninsular university, obtaining a doctorate in theology at Ávila in 1698. During a stay in Spain in 1697–1700, he gained a reputation as a stylish preacher and was appointed theologian and examiner by Madrid's nuncio.[11] In 1700, he returned to New Spain with a respectable *media ración*, a low-tier appointment in Mexico's cathedral chapter.[12] By March 1703, he was named rector of the Royal University and, as such, delivered a highly praised oration at the official welcome for the viceroy duke of Albuquerque.[13] His output as author of printed sermons and other literary works was outstanding for a man who also held several high ecclesiastical posts and compares favorably to the literary production of his fellow extirpators Sariñana and Maldonado.[14] Nonetheless, his exuberant tropes may not have impressed all audiences, as suggested by a set of sarcastic marginalia left by an anonymous reader in a copy of his 1696 *Abraham académico*, an oration written for the Royal University's celebration of the Immaculate Conception.[15]

Even if, as William B. Taylor remarks, a career in idolatry eradication proved an advantage for those vying for an appointment at a cathedral chapter,[16] Castorena y Urzúa traveled this path in reverse. When he was named deputy provisor de indios by the cathedral chapter upon the death of Archbishop Juan Ortega y Montañés, he had no experience as extirpator and his main merits were academic and literary. Still, this appointment was confirmed by the incoming archbishop, José Pérez de Lanciego Eguiluz y Mirafuentes.[17] Besides an early extant case in which an indigenous defendant was turned over to him by the Holy Office—the 1713 trial of midwife María la Colorada for love magic—his first significant action as provisor was the orchestration of a potentially controversial indigenous auto de fe.[18] Although no native had been paraded in an auto through the streets of Mexico City since don Carlos of Tetzcoco's execution in 1539, Castorena y Urzúa orchestrated a punitive pageant for five indigenous practitioners before the church of San José de los Naturales on August 5, 1714. He explained the reason for this innovation in punitive practices in an August 1714 letter to the Holy Office:

Even if by custom my predecessors punished each [idolater] in his own parish, forwarding the attestation of the sentence and the absolution to his parish priest, experience shows me that greater displays are required due to the slowness of the Indians, so they may receive our Holy Faith with greater reverence upon seeing our deep regard for it. In order to explain [our faith] to them, it was necessary to organize an auto with great solemnity; therefore, I decided to execute [the auto] in the manner of this Holy Tribunal.[19]

Far from objecting to this procedure, the Mexican inquisitors commended the provisor for his zeal. In order to address any legal contingency, he also notified the Council of Indies about this unusual auto, adding the evocative but unoriginal argument that, due to their rustic nature, native spectators would absorb the moral of the auto "through their eyes, rather than through their ears; through the representations they witness, rather than through the persuasions they hear."[20]

Two years later, the provisor once again showed his interest in exemplary punishment by ordering an auto in San Bartolomé Osolotepec in the jurisdiction of Tenango del Valle on February 23, 1716.[21] This proceeding, presided over by Nicolás Lópes Xardón, San Bartolomé's beneficiado, ecclesiastical judge, and Holy Office commissioner, was depicted in an extremely unusual painting shown in Figure 8.1.[22] Little is known about this event or the painting's commissioning. However, a legend on this work identifies the attending authorities, with ecclesiastic ones to the right and civil ones to the left of the ecclesiastical judge, who has his seat raised above the alguacil mayor; on his right, one sees a notary from the archbishopric, three attending priests, and three friars. Before the convicts stood the officiating priest, near an altar bearing the six tall candles they would hold during Mass; on their right sat the alcalde mayor of Toluca and two associates on a platform, while below it sat the corregidor and six indigenous officials holding their staffs of office. On the right behind the penitents stood a preacher on a pulpit, who perhaps translated the proceedings into Nahuatl, Otomi, or Matlatzinca, all spoken in the region. Various vivid details complete the scene: a clutch of women attired in bright colors stare in horror at the convicts, while two travelers and a peddler stand on the left fringe, and a boy plays with a dog on the right. Through a symbolically appropriate choice, the anonymous painter emphasized the political hierarchy displayed in this auto while denying us even a glance at the faces of the four males and two female penitents on its center stage, who keep their backs turned to us and stand straight in their tall corozas and perhaps borrowed European clothing.

In January 1723, Castorena y Urzúa approached the Holy Office seeking guidance regarding another unusual auto. Following a consultation with the Audiencia of Mexico in February 1722, Viceroy Marqués de Valero resolved to surrender to the provisor several cult objects confiscated in the Nayar region, in the diocese of Guadalajara, after a successful military campaign against Cora communities, which had until then preserved a relative measure of political and religious autonomy. Since the Jesuit missionaries in the Cora expedition had already burned the corpses of two ancestors that had been the focus of worship, the provisor now planned to destroy three cult objects of great significance: the remains of a deified ancestor called the Great Nayar, a stone figure called Tonati representing the sun, and a receptacle that reputedly held the blood of sacrificed children. The inquisitors did not oppose the auto, and these objects were paraded and demolished on August 31, 1723.[23] No spectator of this auto could doubt that one of its meanings was the dramatization of the destruction of an idolatrous polity now incorporated into the evangelical fold. These disciplinary displays were not merely didactic repudiations of native idolatry; they also signaled a new period in extirpation attempts in Mexico during which the provisor de indios claimed an increasingly centralized role as supervisor of extirpation efforts.[24] However, no such pageant would again take place in the streets of Mexico City in the following three decades, until Provisor Francisco

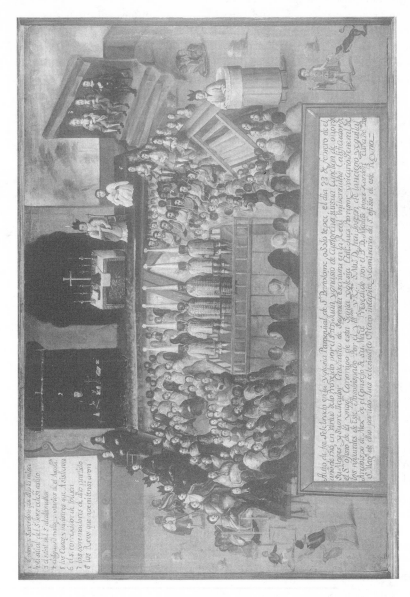

FIGURE 8.1 Depiction of an Auto Ordered by Provisor Castorena y Urzúa in 1716.

SOURCE: Museo Nacional de Arte, CONACULTA, INBA, Mexico

Ximénez Caso asked to borrow the ornaments used by inquisitorial authorities to discipline fourteen native idolaters on February 25, 1753.[25]

Such punitive fervor certainly did not hinder Castorena y Urzúa's career, for, when he stepped down as provisor after the death of Archbishop Lanciego Eguiluz, a handsome reward was already in the works. On July 6, 1729, a bull drafted by Pope Benedict XIII named Castorena y Urzúa Bishop of Yucatán, a post he occupied until his death in 1733.[26]

PROCEDURAL AND PUNITIVE POLICIES IN
TOLUCA'S PROVISORATO

Mexico's Provisorato de Indios y Chinos followed a standard set of legal procedures regarding indigenous crimes of faith, which is particularly noticeable from the administration of Castorena y Urzúa onward.[27] William B. Taylor suggested that eighteenth-century beneficiados enjoyed by virtue of their appointment the right to lead inquiries regarding accusations of idolatry, superstition, or sorcery against their native parishioners, and he cites a set of instructions on how to conduct native idolatry proceedings that circulated in the diocese of Tlaxcala circa 1746 as evidence of these faculties.[28] Nonetheless, there is evidence that this state of affairs was preceded by a change in the faculties against idolatry accorded to ecclesiastical judges. In the seventeenth century, ecclesiastical judges cited specific licenses against native idolaters granted them by their bishop or archbishop, or commissions from the provisor de indios.[29] These licenses were often quoted in the proceedings and in relaciones de méritos sent to the Council of the Indies. Nevertheless, the Toluca provisorato cases and other eighteenth-century proceedings show that this tendency to cite licenses or commissions came to an end, at least for proceedings heard in one's own parish. Hence, in the eighteenth century, ecclesiastical judges initiated native idolatry and sorcery proceedings involving their parishioners without specific licenses or commissions, but they were required to request further instructions from the provisorato.[30]

Most cases began with a written or oral accusation directed to an ecclesiastical judge or the provisor. In some cases, witnesses came forward in response to provisorato edicts, which mirrored Holy Office procedure in that they asked believers to volunteer information.[31] The judge could have these complaints transcribed by an escribano and exercised his discretion as to whether testimony would be sent to the provisorato.[32] This denunciation became a *cabeza de proceso,* the formal start to a proceeding, and then the judge compiled a *sumaria información* by recording the testimony of witnesses. Indigenous witnesses were usually deposed in their native tongue through a court interpreter or an ecclesiastic officer proficient in their language; frequently, the witnesses' native language was not specified. At least one witness was required to initiate a proceeding, but more than one was needed to secure a conviction,[33] and many cases featured at least three witnesses. Arrests could occur before or after the sumaria was reviewed by the judge. Defendants were usually sent to the district's royal jail, although women and older men were frequently placed in the custody, or *depósito*, of a local resident. Ecclesiastical courts relied on indigenous fiscales for locating witnesses or defendants. After the sumaria was collected, the provisor reviewed it and then returned it to the ecclesiastical judge so that he could *recibir la causa a prueba*, or collect the defendant's testimony and enter any other defense motions into the record. There was a time limit of at least one month, but extensions were granted. During this stage, the defendant secured a defense attorney and testified, and the testimony of all sumaria witnesses was ratified. Then, the trial reached its *estado de sentencia* and was sent to the provisor for final review and ruling. The civil justice performed the actual arrests, corporal punishments, or public auctions of the defendant's labor, for such actions could not be carried out by the clergy. In theory, trial records were archived by the provisorato, and parochial archives kept copies.

Unlike the diocese of Oaxaca, that of Mexico had a specialized functionary who oversaw all ecclesiastic proceedings against natives. As shown in Chapter 2, since the 1550s this official had been called provisor y vicario general de naturales, or de indios, and his duties included reviewing every diocesan trial involving natives, and handing down a final sentence. Cases seen by this official included indigenous bigamy, cohabitation, sexual improprieties, failure to comply with financial obligations to the church, and the triad on which this chapter focuses: sorcery, idolatry, and superstition. These faculties mirrored those of the provisor y vicario general, who dealt with nonindigenous subjects. Both provisores were often appointed by incoming archbishops, and the cathedral chapter also made appointments *en sede vacante*, or the interim between archbishops.

By the early eighteenth century, the provisor de indios began reviewing cases against *chinos*, or subjects of Asian origin living in the diocese of Mexico, and hence the office was renamed Provisorato *de Indios y Chinos*. One of the first such provisores was Castorena y Urzúa, who assumed this title before 1718.[34] The inclusion of both natives and chinos in the same jurisdiction followed institutional precedent in Mexico. From the late sixteenth century and until the early 1750s, the archdiocese allowed the Dominicans to administer a parish for *indios extravagantes*, or native migrants, in the heart of Mexico City. Although this parish originally served Mixtec and Zapotec speakers residing in this city, it eventually welcomed Asian migrants. Furthermore, since the Inquisition had previously punished the heterodox practices of chinos, this expansion in diocesan jurisdiction probably occurred after a consultation with the Holy Office.[35] In any case, the Inquisition retained its jurisdiction over natives in the Philippines, the region of origin for many chinos in Mexico.[36]

The Provisorato de Indios had relatively cordial relations with the Mexican Inquisition, at least in the first half of the eighteenth century. Hence, in various instances episcopal authorities learned about the involvement of nonnatives in heterodoxy and submitted court records to the Holy Office.[37] While inquisitors routinely rejected pursuing denunciations against natives,[38] they did record the testimony of almost any witness denouncing native improprieties, even if this step rarely led to prosecution.[39] Inquisitors occasionally assisted the civil and ordinary jurisdictions, always refraining from trying natives.[40]

Nevertheless, the provisorato's use of titles, insignia, and procedures that mirrored those of the Holy Office eventually led Mexican inquisitors onto a direct collision course with Archbishop Antonio de Lorenzana (1766–71) and his provisor de indios y chinos between 1766 and 1769. Greenleaf analyzed this dispute as prime evidence of jurisdictional conflict; my analysis extends his discussion into the nineteenth century.[41] This quarrel began in 1766, when the inquisitors learned that local ecclesiastical judge Mariano Yturria called himself a member of the Santo Oficio de la Inquisición ordinaria de los Indios y Chinos, the Holy Office of the Ordinary Inquisition of Indians and Chinese. A secret inquiry resulted in troubling revelations: not only had the provisorato de indios embraced the title of Inquisición Ordinaria de Indios y Chinos since the 1750s, but the provisorato also copied inquisitorial procedure in its autos, and inquisitorial insignia were on display in the provisorato's office and on official correspondence.[42] When Provisor de Indios Barrientos used the offending title in a 1769 edict, Inquisitor Julián de Amestoy approached Archbishop Lorenzana. Lorenzana retorted that since "time immemorial" the diocese's provisor had assumed the title of "Inquisitor of Indians," and later sent proof that the Vicar General of Madrid and Alcalá called himself inquisidor ordinario. In 1774, another edict referred to the provisorato as the Tribunal de la fe de Indios y Chinos,[43] and in 1775, two officials mistook Mexico's inquisitorial tribunal with this provisorato, boldly interrupting a meeting to deliver an indigenous prisoner.[44] Nonetheless, the Supreme Council of the Inquisition did not intervene, and the provisorato used those appellations until the early nineteenth century. In 1796, another edict made reference to a "Provisor and Inquisitor of the Indians";[45] in 1800, upon the death of Archbishop

Alonso Núñez de Haro y Peralta, the cathedral chapter appointed one of
its own, Manuel de Sandoval, as provisor, vicario general, and inquisidor
ordinario de indios y chinos.[46] In 1803 Juan de Cienfuegos again called
himself inquisidor de indios y chinos.[47]

The Mexican provisorato's disciplinary policies may be gauged
through seven proceedings that record a final sentence between the
1720s and 1730s. Three sentences consisted of a relatively moderate
penalty of twenty-five lashes,[48] which reflected the punitive calculus of
Provisor Miguel de Aldave: Francisco Diego, who promoted the superstitious cult of Guadalupe;[49] the superstitious healer Petrona María;[50] and
the healer Pascual de los Reyes.[51] A provisorato sentence from the late
1720s suggests that one hundred lashes and two years of labor or imprisonment amounted to a fair punishment for "diabolical" divination.[52]
This sentence, handed down in Zempoala, a town several leagues to the
northeast of Mexico City, focused on the actions of three defendants—
Antonio Rodríguez, his wife Isabel Francisca, and Antonia Melchora—
who ingested "a certain herb" in order to find a lost bolt of cloth and
were thus guilty of an implicit pact with the devil. In contrast, their three
associates were sentenced only to "public shame."

Sometimes, provisores exercised leniency. When Bartolomé Martín was
convicted of an "implicit pact" for conjuring hail, the provisorato's fiscal asked for two hundred lashes and four years of labor; however, Castorena y Urzúa reduced the sentence to one hundred lashes.[53] Furthermore,
some sentences depicted a detailed plan of spiritual reform. In 1736, Nicolás Martín, another convicted hail caster, was not sentenced to bodily punishment on account of his advanced age, but was instructed to attend mass
on Sundays and holy days for three months. Seizing an opportunity to turn
the old man into a walking example against native error, Provisor Pedro
Ramírez del Castillo instructed Nicolás to choose a permanent residence
so that "those he scandalized with his deceit would learn a lesson through
his punishment and reform."[54] In the same year, Ramírez del Castillo prescribed a similar course of action for Francisca Quiteria, a superstitious
healing convict from San Felipe Tlamimilolpan. Instead of receiving corporal punishment, she would be publicly absolved of her crime during a mass
in her locality and was ordered to hear masses for two months.

HAIL CASTING

The pan-Mesoamerican set of beliefs regarding the control of rain,
storms, and hail through prayer presented extirpators with an acute
ontological problem comparable to sorcery: Did these specialists exer-

cise control over nature, and if so, what was the source of such power? Jacinto de la Serna's mid-seventeenth-century *Manual* and three proceedings against "hail conjurers" provide evidence of ecclesiastical responses to this issue. In Nahua societies the term *teciuhtlazqui*, "hail caster, or hail fender," designated this specialty, and this is the term listed in Molina's dictionary, along with *teciuhtlazani*, "someone who drives hail away."[55] Sahagún noted the existence of a specialist called *nahualli teciuhqui teciuhtlazqui*, literally "nahual, seer, hail caster," who knew when it would rain and reminded the community to perform sacrifices for the lord of Tlalocan.[56] As noted by Roberto Martínez González,[57] the formulas employed by colonial teciuhtlazqueh differ from those found in Sahagún and may have followed a pattern of individualization.

De la Serna used various anecdotes to depict hail conjuring as an activity whose ontology was beyond doubt. In his *Manual*, he discussed several "hail conjurers" from San Mateo Xalatlaco and Tenango in the Toluca Valley punished circa 1611. He noted that there were up to ten hail casters in each of these towns, and that a public collection was taken to pay them. As proof of their power, he recounted that, as seven "eminent conjurers" prepared to drive away hail approaching from the east at Xalatlaco, one of them drove this mass so far that it devastated many fields to the west. Furthermore, de la Serna noted that these conjurers had a "pact with the Demon," but different techniques: some used prayers from the Roman Manual and then blew air at the clouds; others repeated incomprehensible words as they threatened the clouds with a live serpent curled around a staff; others yet ordered the lords of thunder and rain to go away as they blew air at the sky; finally, others invoked God, Mary, and Saint James to drive away the storm and finished their plea with an invocation of the Trinity.[58]

The trial against Gaspar de los Reyes of San Lorenzo provides evidence that hail casting continued to be seen as integral to the elective sphere into the 1740s. In July 1745, the fifty-year-old Gaspar was brought to Toluca's public jail under suspicion of being a hail conjurer. Gaspar admitted taking one peso from several men, but denied being a hail conjurer, and referred to this specialization as *texsipec*, a misspelled term used as an equivalent to the canonical teciuhtlazqui. While three witnesses attested to Gaspar's piety, two men indicated that his avocation was common knowledge in San Lorenzo. One of them testified that several local residents paid Gaspar to conjure hail for the previous four years; the defendant noted he was afraid of incurring in the wrath of the local priest and reluctantly agreed to cast hail after renegotiating his payment.[59]

The 1727 proceeding against Bartolomé Martín showcased two important continuities between his procedure and that of hail casters investigated by Ruiz de Alarcón and de la Serna a century earlier: a belief in divine initiation, and the use of the Trinity as an ally against stormy weather. Bartolomé, a ranch hand at Hacienda San Antonio, an Otomi-speaking area near Metepec, employed the following theological justification:

Although he cast spells against hail, that was a favor given to him by the Three Persons, Father, Son and the Holy Ghost, for one day there was a rainstorm as he looked after some oxen, and a bolt of lighting had fallen on him, wounding him from haunch to foot on his left side and leaving a burnt area. When he came to his senses, three angels appeared before him. They gave him strength and told him they were envoys from the Holy Trinity, and that they were bringing him the grace of casting spells against hail; then, they went back to Heaven.[60]

Bartolomé's initiation at the hands of a Christian entity bore an uncanny resemblance to the visions reported by Domingo Hernández, Mariana, and Juan de la Cruz to de la Serna and Ruiz de Alarcón a century earlier. While these seventeenth-century extirpators assumed those visions were self-serving fabrications, Castorena y Urzúa embraced a bureaucratic solution. He obtained a formal opinion from Joseph Flores Moreno, a professor of theology at the University of Mexico and the main ecclesiastical prosecutor in the diocese. Flores Moreno stated that, since Bartolomé did not know the basic doctrinal tenets or led an "exemplary" life, his claim of personal contact with God's angels was spurious. In his view, Bartolomé's false visions rendered him formally guilty of superstition, but his ontologically indubitable effectiveness issued from "an implicit pact with the devil."[61] A decade later, the investigation of another conjurer resulted in a more expedient proceeding. In 1736, after reviewing a trial against Nicolás Martín of San Buenaventura Toluca, Provisor Ramírez del Castillo merely called him a "superstitious fraud." Unlike his predecessor, this provisor did not need a review to conclude that only exemplary punishment would convince Nicolás's neighbors to reject his claims.[62]

IDOLATRY AND CLANDESTINE EFFIGIES

The Toluca provisorato corpus depicts a relative lack of concern with idolatry. Between 1691 and 1780, extant records refer to only three major idolatry investigations: the 1691 accusations against Domingo de San Juan and Juan Miguel of Calimaya, the 1737 arrest of Baltasar Francisco of San Lorenzo Toluca, and a 1754 inquiry at Hacienda Guadalupe Tlachaloya.

The información against Domingo illustrates the worship of a Nahua deity in a novel context. In May 1691, the Franciscan Juan de Gama informed Provisor de los Naturales José de Torres y Vergara about anonymous accusations against Domingo de San Juan, an indigenous cook at the Franciscan monastery of San Pedro y San Pablo Calimaya.[63] Domingo was said to bathe every Holy Saturday before visiting two lakes on a neighboring mountain range, where he offered wax candles and incense. Gama also indicated that, fourteen years earlier on a Good Friday, he and a Spaniard had surprised Domingo and his associate Juan Miguel as they imbibed a drink prepared with the *panquitzi* plant. This drink, which allowed them to "divine about things occult," was part of a celebration that included animal sacrifices honoring "the god of flowers."[64] This reference illuminates Domingo's likely cosmological motivations: the worship of Nahua deity Xochipilli, or "Flower Prince," as part of the celebration of Jesus's death and rebirth. Xochipilli's high profile as an agricultural deity associated with maize deity Centeotl and as a major character in the birth of the sun in the Codex Borgia may account for the persistence of its cult in eighteenth-century Toluca.[65] Having received Gama's accusation, the provisor commissioned ecclesiastical judge Juan Díaz del Castillo to collect testimonies about Domingo. All witnesses remarked on the contrast between Domingo's visibility as the monastery's cook and his status as an idolatry suspect. Three local witnesses corroborated Gama's suspicions about Domingo's activities on Holy Saturday and his use of an herb to summon "diabolic visions."[66] In fact, there was an earlier local example of the merging of ancient and Christian devotions during Holy Week. According to de la Serna, circa 1610 a "teacher of idolatries" from Teotenango traveled to the Sierra Nevada of Toluca to retrieve a stone effigy, which was concealed under several rosaries and then placed in the eucharist's custody by an unsuspecting priest before a Holy Thursday procession.[67]

A narrative regarding ancient devotions recurred in the accusations against Baltasar Francisco. In August 1737, the Franciscan Martín Calderón penned a note addressed to Toluca's ecclesiastical judge, Nicolás de Villegas, stating that Baltasar perpetrated a "superstitious fraud" by proclaiming that local residents should not enter a cave in the hill of Tolochi without first removing their rosaries and "invoking the demons." The passing reference to Tolochi provided another link to ancient beliefs: this hill located north of the colonial city of Toluca had been inhabited since Postclassic times by Matlatzinca settlers, and it was the likely location of a temple dedicated to their tutelary deity, Tolotzin.[68] Calderón also noted that locals visited a water source in the Tolochi cave to ask for an occupation that would give them sustenance, leaving behind incense and flower offerings.[69] Judge Villegas had Baltasar detained at a local *obraje*, or local workshop, but then transferred him to Toluca's Hospital of San Juan de Dios due to his poor health. Villegas eventually received authorization from the provisor to collect testimony, but Baltasar died shortly afterward.[70]

The most detailed account of a clandestine ritual celebration in the region appears in a 1754 *información* against ten workers from Guadalupe Tlachaloya, a hacienda north of Toluca near the Otomi-speaking area encompassing San Nicolás Tlachaloya. Late at night on September 28, 1754, Andrés de la Cruz, son of the owner of neighboring Hacienda Buenavista, and four of its associates entered an oratory collectively owned by Juan de la Cruz, Isidro López, and Antonio Francisco, three indigenous laborers. Inside, they found these men and their wives, a fourth couple, a widow, and a young woman. Much like the Spaniards who interrupted the ceremony at Caxonos half a century earlier, after a single glance Andrés and his companions decided this was an idolatrous celebration, given the presence of displays of elusive meaning. A few days later, these vigilantes brought six of the celebrants before Juan del Villar, Toluca's ecclesiastical judge.

The owners of Buenavista and Guadalupe Tlachaloya, who outranked all other witnesses, stepped forward to articulate a collective remembrance of two uncanny displays. On one side, a tallow candle burned before an altar with Christian saints. On the other, a wax candle burned before a multitudinous array of clay figurines. According to an inventory, these "dolls" included four male and female figures on horseback, a trumpet player, a friar, three angels, a guitar player, a woman grinding maize, a figurine with articulated limbs, several figures with darkened faces, two rabbits, a deer, three toads, two serpents, a scorpion, a pig, an eagle, a little horse, three fish figurines, a dove-shaped whistle, reproductions of kitchen implements, and a wooden doll with articulated limbs. Many offerings were placed in between these figurines, including some plants identified as *pipiltzitzintli*, "little nobleman,"[71] flowers, rolled tobacco cigarettes, flint, "glass of Moteuczoma" (obsidian glass), bread, maize ears, tortillas, tamales shaped into figurines, bananas, apples, and sugarcane. Suspended on the wall above the offerings was an arch made with cotton pieces attached to red-dyed wool threads, or *chomite*, which the judge interpreted as a rainbow. The celebrants also sang a prayer to the Holy Sacrament accompanied by guitar and harp.[72] Some of the celebrants justified themselves by saying that a female healer had told them to perform this ceremony for a sick child. Hence, this elective ceremony was probably a healing ritual under the patronage of archangels. The celebration took place on the eve of the feast of Archangels Michael, Gabriel, and Raphael, and the inventory noted the presence of three angel figurines.[73]

Indeed, the mere possession of anthropomorphic or zoomorphic figurines was seen as an indicator of idolatrous beliefs by both witnesses and judges. Nonindigenous subjects accused of consulting native specialists occasionally mentioned the use of effigies in Mexico City,[74] Aguascalientes,[75] and Zacatecas.[76] Furthermore, in December 1759, Domingo Gonsáles, the Otomi-speaking fiscal of San Pablo Autopan, testified that Santiago de la Cruz fashioned a maize dough figurine according to the instructions of Ana María, a healer and suspected sorcerer; Santiago was said to have placed this figurine and a small pot in the home of one of Ana María's alleged victims.[77] The April 1765 proceedings against alleged sorcerer Andrés Martín from San Pedro Totoltepec resulted in the discovery of several clay figurines hidden behind a piece of cloth in the oratory of a house. Andrés's landlady retrieved the effigies, which included three "in the shape of Moors," an African man, two candy sellers, a priest, a guitar player, two rabbits, and a bull.[78] The recurrence of guitar players and priests or friar effigies in both the Guadalupe Tlachaloya and Totoltepec inventories suggest shared but deeply opaque local motivations behind their use in clandestine ritual activities.[79]

NARRATING MALEFICIO IN THE COURTROOM

In his influential analysis of sorcery prosecution in seventeenth-century France, Robert Mandrou posited a rapid transition from fear to skepticism at civil courts over the course of a single decade. No such transition took place in eighteenth-century Toluca, for its ecclesiastical judges, echoing the beliefs of Spanish inquisitors in the sixteenth and seventeenth centuries, had already assumed a conservative and often skeptical position.[80] In their view, a sorcery conviction called for proof of an implicit or explicit pact with the devil and of illness or death caused by nonnatural means. This view set a high threshold for the construction of sorcery narratives in the courtroom. According to E. E. Evans-Pritchard's classical characterization of Zande sorcery in north-central Africa, suspicions of sorcery were used as a default explanation for almost any undesirable outcome in social and individual well-being and constituted a "natural philosophy."[81] Even though the fragmentary evidence from Toluca is not dense enough to reconstruct local sorcery ideologies, these accounts allow us to explore the logic of credible sorcery claims.

As witnesses filed before an often skeptical judge, they sought to present a depiction of sorcery that fit in a particular narrative arc. How did witnesses frame it? The first step was to present a formal written or oral complaint. However, the testimony of witnesses with family ties to the plaintiff was deemed insufficient. In 1722, Diego Martín of Metepec presented his brother, wife, and mother as the only witnesses regarding a sorcery accusation against Miguel de Santiago, but the proceedings were cut short when no more witnesses were found.[82] Several proceedings began with a complaint regarding illnesses suddenly contracted after conflictive interactions with suspected *hechiceros*, or sorcerers. Other narratives emphasized a point when cures by a specialist worsened an ailment. Two separate proceedings from Calpoltitlan illustrate both trends. In 1736, Felipe de San Juan regaled the court with a narrative of conflicts between his wife Martina Agustina and his neighbor Francisco Xavier: the latter grew angry with her when she refused to lend him broad beans, stole the sap of Martina's agaves, and threatened to take away everything she owned. These conflicts led Martina and Felipe to accuse Francisco of sorcery, a claim that gained urgency when Martina died a month later. Francisco denied having caused her death, even as he admitted to disagreements with this couple.[83] About a decade earlier, in 1729, the parents of Pedro Baltasar of Calpoltitlan denounced Nicolás Cocinero for causing the illness of his son, even if they themselves had called on Nicolás to perform a cure on their son's swollen leg.[84]

Some reputed sorcerers appeared in court to accuse their neighbors of damaging their reputation, which afforded them the opportunity to construct a preemptive narrative. In 1760, Sebastiana María of Santa Clara Toluca presented a writ stating she had been called a nahual by her brother, with whom she had quarreled, and a *puta hechicera*, "whore and sorcerer," by two other women, Bartola and Juachina. The judge called forth Bartola, who declared that Sebastiana once confided in her she was a sorcerer, but since this event happened "secretly and before no one," it carried little weight. Bartola also testified that her own sister, who suffered from leg pains that would not diminish even after a rubbing treatment from a Toluca physician, was told by another woman called Lucía that Sebastiana had bewitched her. Lucía had apparently seen Sebastiana climb to her roof and "roll about" on it after having an argument with her, and this vignette was presented as the root of public suspicions about Sebastiana.[85]

In other cases, alleged sorcerers pursued counterclaims vigorously. In 1756, Juana Clara of San Lorenzo Toluca presented a writ against three women who persisted in calling her a sorcerer, even though one of the accusers had been briefly jailed for such contentions. Juana demanded that these accusers be punished should they fail to justify their claims.[86] In 1761, Juana Clara was once again accused of sorcery by María Encarnación. Both women pursued a quarrel that first sprang between

María's husband and Juana's nephew; María reported that one of her breasts swelled to "monstrous" proportions and that she later expelled bristles from her mouth. Juana retorted in writing that she had already been detained and released for lack of evidence and asked that María furnish evidence backing her argument.[87] Moreover, a failed sorcery accusation could result in legal action against the accusers. In 1764, when Domingo Pascual of San Francisco Calixtlahuaca accused Bartolomé Santiago of causing a stomach illness leading to his son's death, Bartolomé's father Antonio Raphael, a cacique, submitted a writ asking that Domingo furnish proof of his allegations. Domingo hauled into court two agave leaves that, he declared, specified the date of his son's demise as predicted by Bartolomé, but the judge ruled that the meaning of this inscription "could not be ascertained." When Domingo could not find any witnesses, he desisted from his claim and was sentenced to pay legal costs and admonished not to make unfounded accusations again.[88]

Given these challenges, compelling sorcery narratives revolved around the feats of malevolent sorcerers, who often were said to boast about having control over a victim's health. Witnesses presented recollections of sorcerers' threats in court, believing they furnished unimpeachable proof of their malevolence. Evidence ranged from putative predictions—such as the above prophecy on maguey leaves—to highly evocative threats. For example, Francisco Xavier of Calpoltitlan told Felipe de San Juan when the latter suddenly fell ill, "if you begin to cry now, you will cry much more soon";[89] Baltasar Francisco of Toluca threatened to make a young woman dry up "like a *totopostle*," or toasted tortilla chip;[90] María Rosa of San Lorenzo told Pedro Tadeo, "Go on now, for you will have occasion to remember me";[91] and María Magdalena of Tenango del Valle, who told Petrona María that a spell someone else cast on her would not be cleared until Petrona was made to die and resurrect, also stated, "You will heal when God and I will it."[92]

In some instances, aggrieved parties took pains to leave evidence of sorcerers' threats before dying. In 1764, various witnesses from the Otomí town of San Pablo Hueyxoapan filed past Judge George Martínez to accuse Agustina María of sorcery.[93] Tomás Nicolás said Agustina caused the death of his first wife by making her drink pulque; when Tomás threatened to denounce Agustina to the authorities for bewitching his second wife, she regained her health after Agustina agreed to a cure. The most damaging evidence came from Rita Cristina, widow of don Joseph Valeriano, former gobernador of San Pablo: after attesting to a dispute Agustina had with her husband regarding tribute, she displayed a note allegedly written by don Joseph. This note, dated February 1761, stated in faltering Spanish that don Joseph attributed his illness to

Agustina, who had told him, "May the devils carry you away!" Felipe Tomás added his voice to this chorus by asserting that during a quarrel with Agustina she told him that "just as she had taken the life of his uncle [don Joseph], she would do the same with him."[94]

FROM MALEFICIO TO SUPERSTITION

The most Protean category in the Toluca corpus is superstition, a realm encompassing suspect healing practices, divination, offerings made in caves and mountain sites, and the unorthodox cult of Christian entities. The boundary between maleficio and superstitious healing seemed especially porous, as some healers' clients claimed they felt the effects of malevolence after a cure. For instance, in 1765, Desiderio Joseph Gutiérrez of Cacalomacan, who contracted a stomach illness shortly after a dispute with a woman called Manuela, resorted to five indigenous healers to regain his health. Gutiérrez's testimony provides an unusual sample of these healers' heterodox methodology: Juan Gabriel of Toluca prayed to the Holy Trinity, burned copal, and rubbed estafiate on clients' bodies; in addition to all that, Antonio de Cortés of Cacalomacan healed "in the name of the Virgin"; Manuela of Santa Ana Toluca diagnosed the illness as maleficio and used estafiate and other herbs; an anonymous curer from Ostotitlan, besides using Cortés's methods, also employed the smoke of coyote and "tiger" hides; finally, Hipólito Moreno of Ostotitlan burned coyote, wolf, and "tiger" hides, prescribed snake and vegetal powders, and cured "in the name of the Trinity."[95]

Although superstition was regarded as a lesser crime than sorcery, ecclesiastical judges took pains to distinguish "formal superstition" from mere deceit. In 1729, Provisor Aldave ruled that Pascual de los Reyes of Cuauhtla Amilpas was not "formally superstitious, but simply a liar" for pretending to extract bones and glass from his paying clients' bodies.[96] One of the most peculiar such cases was that of Francisco Diego of San Mateo Atenco. In 1728, Francisco told his neighbors that, besides having a vision of God the Father, an image of the Virgin of Guadalupe had also spoken to him and promised to give him five pesos so he would build her a dwelling, as well as one hundred pesos to buy fruit for the poor every week; she also granted him a staff so he would become gobernador. After proclaiming these revelations, many local residents flocked to Francisco's house, where they drank water from a container that held a flower, which he used to wipe the sweat off the brow of the Virgin's image. Throughout his trial, Francisco claimed he had not lied about these apparitions, but in his sentence Aldave noted with disdain that his account was implausible and that Francisco "did not even know the Christian doctrine" and thus was a "superstitious liar."[97]

The proceedings against two Nahua villagers from San Pedro Totoltepec between 1756 and 1765 illustrate several witnesses' pragmatic appraisal of the boundary between superstition and maleficio. These records also illustrate how collective perceptions of indigenous specialists operated independently from ecclesiastical dicta: while one of these men was regarded as an effective healer by Spaniards and natives, the other underwent a transformation from Christianized subject to malevolent healer. This narrative begins in 1756, when Jacinto Tapia, who had been disciplined once before for superstitious healing, was blamed for casting a spell on Marcela María, Jacinto Nicolás's wife. The source of the accusation was Andrés Martín, then imprisoned in Toluca's royal jail due to an accusation Tapia leveled against him. Jacinto Nicolás exposed this entanglement in a writ to the court in which he noted that, after Tapia failed to cure his wife of a growth on her neck, he visited Andrés in jail, who revealed that Tapia had bewitched Marcela.[98] Judge Villar imprisoned Jacinto Nicolás and summoned both Tapia and Andrés; Tapia portrayed himself as a Christian healer who healed with crosses and an indigo balm, and Andrés swore he cured with Christian prayers, estafiate,[99] animal fat, and palm oil. Jacinto Nicolás eventually changed his story and asserted that Marcela did not suffer from maleficio, but from an illness "given by God."[100]

Several years later, Andrés Martín was once more the target of an inquiry, now as a malevolent sorcerer. In March 1765, fray Juan Antonio Montes of Totoltepec reported that the death of a young man called Francisco Joseph caused a commotion, since it was public knowledge that Andrés Martín had forecast his death, even as Francisco pleaded with Andrés to let him live. Shortly after Francisco's death was made public, Andrés fled town, leading several witnesses to share their suspicions about him. Juan Ramos recounted how Francisco, his own nephew, told him that Andrés cast a spell on him and then prophesied he would die "in fright, as he yawned and hiccupped," which turned out to be an accurate description of Francisco's end.[101] Most strikingly, Petra Manuela, a mestiza who urged the dying youth to pray, said that Francisco bitterly retorted there was no use in praying, for the mighty Andrés had "even taken away the [Christian] doctrine" from him.[102]

In contrast with Andrés's trajectory, Jacinto Tapia's encounters with ecclesiastical justice did not dull his public renown as an effective healer. In 1764, as Tapia languished in Toluca's jail for continuing to engage in "superstitious" healing, a most unusual petition reached Provisor and Vicar General Manuel Barrientos y Cervantes in Mexico City. Its putative author was Joseph de Samaniego, a blind and ill Spaniard who took the extraordinary step of requesting a license from the provisor so he could benefit from Tapia's herbal remedies; this cure would take place before ecclesiastical authorities. Understandably, the archbishopric's prosecutor responded that allowing Tapia to minister to clients from his jail cell was "intolerable," and he instructed Judge Martínez in Toluca to investigate the circumstances under which Tapia might have tended to customers. Martínez summoned Samaniego, who explained that this petition was drafted by a go-between named Joseph Domingo de Rosas. As decreed by the provisor, Martínez admonished the jail keeper that no one should seek healing remedies from Tapia, under pain of excommunication.[103]

MEDICAL EXAMINATIONS
AND THE BOURBON REFORMS

By the middle years of the eighteenth century, ecclesiastical and civil authorities in Mexico and Oaxaca had begun a novel educational project: an attempt to install schools in native communities in order to promote the use of Spanish as a language of doctrinal instruction. As noted by William B. Taylor, even if an abundant number of royal cédulas issued in 1691, 1693, 1694, 1700, 1718, and 1720, mandated the establishment of Spanish-language schools in native towns, it was not until May 1720 that a major ecclesiastical figure, Archbishop Lanciego Eguiluz of Mexico, heeded royal orders and a 1716 viceregal decree by establishing these schools.[104] By January 1755, Archbishop Manuel José Rubio y Salinas and Provisor de Indios Ximénez Caro boasted about having established about 237 Spanish-language schools in 181 native communities in the diocese of Mexico since this archbishop was appointed to his see in 1747.[105] However, in the long term, in spite of the insistence on the substitution of native languages with Spanish by some of the bishops who participated in the 1771 Fourth Mexican Church Council, and in spite of repeated calls in cédulas from 1766, 1770, 1778, and 1782 for the establishment of Spanish-language schools in large numbers, the breadth and impact of Spanish-language education projects on native communities were circumscribed and modest.[106]

Another midcentury transition in ecclesiastical attitudes toward superstition and sorcery was signaled by a July 1754 edict from Archbishop Rubio y Salinas decreeing that any alleged native victim of sorcery would be examined by a physician before calling forth witnesses. The timing of this order was probably not fortuitous: it was issued shortly after the crown decreed the secularization of all indigenous parishes in the Americas in 1753, a measure directed toward increasing the efficiency of parish administration. According to the archbishop, his 1754 edict was motivated by the fact that his prosecutor had been forced to ask for the release of alleged sorcerers in all but one of several recent cases. Even when suspects were acquitted, the archbishop observed, their enemies damaged their social standing, since their property was confiscated and used for trial costs. Hence, Rubio y Salinas issued new directives:

After the accusation is presented, or after somebody comes in to complain about an Indian, the first step shall be to issue an auto so that the complainant may be examined by a physician (if one were available), a surgeon, or a barber, whose declarations will be recorded in detail. [The physicians] shall be asked not only about their opinion about the malady, but also about its symptoms. . . . If no one were available to perform this examination, the ecclesiastical judges shall examine the sick person's relatives and helpers, inquiring not only about the malady, but also about its beginnings, medicines previously administered, and anything observed during its progress. [The judges] should always provide a separate report about what they observe.[107]

While Rubio y Salinas's order formally established a medical review of alleged sorcery victims, this measure had been employed earlier in the century. When the priest Nicolás de Villegas accused Sebastiana Francisca of Tepexuxuca of bewitching his mother in 1726, he noted that Captain Antonio de Melo, experienced "in the art of surgery," examined the bones and herbs his mother expelled "through natural means" and noted her various afflictions. After this examination, Melo concluded that Villegas's mother did suffer from maleficio.[108]

Two cases depict the application of Rubio y Salinas's edict to specific accusations. In 1765, when María Joaquina of Santa Ana accused her neighbor Josefa of causing a stomach illness after forcing her to drink pulque, Judge Martínez had her examined by Bernardo López de Salazar, a surgery instructor licensed by the Protomedicato. López de Salazar promptly diagnosed María with aggravated colonic irritation; this ailment had first resulted in *cardialgia*, or heartburn, and later she contracted *ictericia flava*, or jaundice; therefore, this was a natural illness.[109] Another examination ordered by Judge Martínez in 1767 yielded much different results. After examining Juana María of San Pedro Totoltepec, Miguel Joseph de Garzias y Villanueva, a physician licensed by the Protomedicato, concluded she was the victim of maleficio. Garzias y Villanueva's diagnosis relied on the deployment of a specialized vocabulary: he noted that, given her "pituitary constitution, . . . and proper nutrition," it could not be explained why Juana suffered from "hemoptoic" episodes, vomited "atrabilious" matter not mixed with ingested food, suffered from pain near her esophagus, and had little thirst or hunger. This physician's claim of *maleficio* was founded in his belief that no natural causes, either internal or *procatárticas*,[110] could have caused Juana's illness.[111]

During the early Bourbon period, inquiries against native idolatry and superstition were not the exclusive province of the provisorato. For instance, in 1783, José Grediaga, the alcalde mayor's lieutenant at Tenango del Valle, investigated sorcery accusations against Félix Francisco and his wife María Sebastiana and concluded that the local escribano submitted them in bad faith, for they were motivated by the fact that the accused opposed a yearly collection for a communal litigation fund favored by the escribano.[112]

Furthermore, in the 1760s, civil justices intervened in two cases involving local cults and suspicions of idolatry. These cases, addressed only briefly below, illustrate the emergence of so-called "messianic" cults that were orchestrated by charismatic indigenous leaders seeking to carve out a space for heterodox Christian practices in local collective spheres. The first one concerned a heterodox cult in Yautepec in the early 1760s previously analyzed by Serge Gruzinski,[113] which was led by the Nahua specialist Antonio Pérez and featured the involvement of the mestiza Luisa Carrillo and a large number of natives.[114] The viceroy secured a royal order mandating a full inquiry into the case;[115] given Luisa's ethnic status, she was tried by the Holy Office and punished for idolatry in a May 1768 auto de fe along with other convicts.[116] In 1769, in the diocese of Puebla, Pedro de Leoz, alcalde mayor of Tulancingo, helped suppress the activities of a group of more than two hundred native celebrants drawn from seven localities who worshipped at a hilltop near San Mateo Tututepec. Their avowed leader was a man known as Diego or Juan Diego, said to regard himself as "another Messiah," and his retinue included a woman called María Isabel, allegedly worshipped as "Our Lady of Guadalupe." This regional cult had a decidedly hybrid bent, for cult effigies seized by authorities after a successful attack on the hilltop included images of Guadalupe and Saint Matthew borrowed from San Mateo's church, along with an image of a monkey's head, reputedly the "god of the maize and chile fields."[117]

FACTIONALISM AND IDOLATRY ALLEGATIONS
IN OAXACA

Several records provide a useful vantage point on a recurrent phenomenon in Oaxaca during the late seventeenth and early eighteenth centuries: the disclosure of idolatry and sorcery accusations against indigenous officials in the context of local factionalism. Ever since Bishop Zumárraga removed from office a native judge from Tlatelolco for idolatry in 1539,[118] ecclesiastical and civil authorities frequently followed a simple policy: any native official convicted of idolatry or superstition was removed from his post and usually forbidden from ever again assuming elective office.

Idolatry accusations were, more often than not, part of a complex socioreligious field in which political actors constantly shifted alliances and legal strategies. Two important cases exemplifying these shifts in the aftermath of the Caxonos rebellion were discussed in Chapter 7: the accusations against don Lorenzo Rosales of Teoxomulco, and don Felipe de Santiago of Yatzona.[119] Sometimes, the initiative was seized by local political leaders; thus, in 1733 don Pedro de Chávez y Guzmán, cacique and fiscal of Tlaxiaco, denounced several residents for idolatry and sorcery, and the Audiencia issued two orders to the alcalde mayor of Teposcolula requesting an inquiry.[120] The dismissal of local officers sometimes resulted in the need to organize new elections, as occurred in 1741 in Huajuapan.[121] Removal orders were, nonetheless, subject to appellation and review; hence, in 1697, after the alcalde mayor of Chichicapa and Cimatlán tried Gobernador Nicolás Pacheco for idolatry, the Audiencia first requested a copy of the trial records,[122] and then ruled that Pacheco be reinstated, for he had been acquitted.[123]

It was thus inevitable that idolatry inquiries would be used by political factions seeking to remove their opponents from office. An illustrative example from Villa Alta is the proceeding initiated by Sebastián de Santiago y Nicolás Gómez of Lalopa in 1714, who complained to an ecclesiastical official that Francisco de la Cruz, a specialist denounced during Maldonado's 1704 campaign, served as fiscal and had been chosen as gobernador in spite of an idolatry conviction that, they argued, barred him and his sons from holding elective office.[124] Another example comes from the district of Nexapa: in July 1727, a group of former town officials denounced Joseph and Sebastián de la Cruz, alcaldes of Santa Lucía Mecaltepec, for threatening to punish any town resident who confessed with the town's vicar after a small clay figurine was uncovered. However, the entire town council countered this charge by requesting that proof of their guilt be presented before the alcalde mayor. This accusation, which did not lead to a full inquest, probably originated in a rift dividing the vicar and its allies from town officials and a local family who was under investigation by the vicar for various offenses.[125] In fact, sorcery suspicions could haunt town officials for years. In 1727, Santiago de la Cruz was discharged from his post as gobernador of Ixtlahuaca because sixteen years earlier he had asked local residents to build a niche for an idol he sought to protect.[126] Some decades later, in 1767, Nicolás de la Cruz, escribano of Santo Domingo Tepuxtepeque, and several of his associates were accused by a neighbor of kneeling before a young local woman and worshipping her "like the Virgin"; their ceremonies included singing and the sacrifice of a young dog and several turkeys.[127]

One of the most important cases involving an idolatry accusation against a native cabildo in Oaxaca took place in Yalálag and resulted in a legal confrontation between them and the archbishop of Mexico and viceroy of New Spain. These indigenous officials, in fact, sought to exploit a gap in the colonial juridical system in order to fight removal from office. In July 1735, as a result of an indictment of many Yalálag residents for alleged cannibalism and child sacrifice handed down by Oaxaca bishop Francisco de Santiago y Calderón, the entire cabildo—gobernador Francisco Hernández, alcaldes Pedro de Aguilar and Fernando Martín, and regidores Francisco de la Cruz, Gerónimo de Espina, Diego Hernández, and Juan Mateo—was removed from office by the alcalde mayor.[128] The proceeding also alleged the culpability of maestros Antonio de la Cruz and Joseph Martín, sacrificers Santiago de Selis and Joseph de Yllescas, and recorded the involvement of twenty-two other residents, for a total of thirty-three defendants. Since no trial records are extant, no detailed narrative regarding these accusations survives.

However, the demoted officials concocted a clever legal strategy to regain their posts. Since the Laws of Indies expressly forbade interventions by civil or ecclesiastical authorities in elections within pueblos de indios, the deposed cabildo sent a complaint to the Audiencia stating that their alcalde mayor had stripped them of their offices without justification; no word was said about the pending idolatry accusations. Consequently, they obtained a royal decree ordering Eusebio Ferra y Carmona, the Audiencia's prosecutor, to reinstate Hernández, Aguilar, and Martín in their posts, and Ferra y Carmona carried out this order before November 1735. When Juan Antonio de Vizarrón y Eguiarreta, who served as both viceroy and archbishop of Mexico at the time, learned about these events, he annulled the decree obtained by these cabildo members and had them stripped from their offices again and arrested in January 1736. In a subsequent investigation, Ferra y Carmona was imprisoned and interrogated, but a curious development took place: the original decree sent by the Audiencia to reinstate the cabildo of Yalálag had disappeared and could not be found. The fact that this decree was never found suggests that either these officials destroyed it on purpose, or that the decree's execution was somehow facilitated by Ferra y Carmona. These Yalálag officials, along with twenty-one other defendants, paid a steep price: at the end of their trial, Bishop Santiago y Calderón sentenced them to perpetual incarceration at the idolaters' prison in Oaxaca.[129]

SORCERY AND POLITICAL CONFLICTS
IN THE CHINANTLA

On December 7, 1752, a Chinantec man called Francisco Ambrosio stood in the main square of Oxitlan, grasping a crucifix and bleeding from a horrendous gash. Francisco had just attempted to commit suicide by driving a knife into his neck, and Pedro Xixón Moreno, the local beneficiado, ordered the bells rung so that the entire town could gather to hear his deathbed confession about blood-sucking sorcery and human sacrifices allegedly perpetrated by one of two warring factions at Oxitlan. Francisco now openly declared that he and the mulatto Baltasar de Rivera, a member of the opposing faction, were responsible for the conflict's escalation. Nonetheless, Xixón would not extract a complete confession. Even though Francisco repeatedly asked for an escribano, the local officials fled the square in fear and left Xixón alone with the dying man. Hours later, as Francisco rested in his house, the town's official's congregated around his bed—to silence him rather than to hear him, in Xixón's telling. As Francisco steeled himself to speak, Juan Antonio Alcedo, *teniente de* (deputy) alcalde mayor, stepped forward and asked him with apparent solicitude, "Do you recognize me Francisco, my son? Do you realize that I am the teniente?" These words stopped Francisco short, and from then on he would not answer Xixón's questions.[130]

This revealing case was shaped by, and provides unusually detailed information about, three separate conflicts: the confrontation between two opposing factions at Oxitlan; a jurisdictional dispute between ecclesiastical and civil justice; and, more poignantly, the struggle to preserve a collective secret. The proceedings involved most of the inhabitants of San Lucas Oxitlan, a Chinantec-speaking community in the province of Teotila, a rugged transitional zone between the Zapotec sierra and the coastal plains of Veracruz. At the time, barely a generation had passed after a landmark event in regional evangelization efforts: in 1730, at the behest of Bishop Maldonado, the ecclesiastical judge of Yoloz, Nicolás de la Barreda, published the first doctrinal text in Chinantec,[131] a language whose tonal system had posed serious difficulties for missionaries.

As John Chance remarked, cooperative schemes in native Villa Alta communities yielded to "conflict and factionalism" by the eighteenth century,[132] exemplified by legal challenges against local elections presented by the losing faction or by protracted litigation that split villages into factions that periodically aligned with or denounced the two most influential representatives of colonial authority: the alcalde mayor and parish priests. Oxitlan was no exception to this trend, and the complex dispute that threatened the town's social stability in 1750–59 had its roots in a conflict over elections. The documentation reflects two dueling narratives, one authored by several ecclesiastical judges and the provisor and vicario general in Oaxaca City and another authored by don Andrés de Otañes and his brother, don Santiago, both alcaldes mayores of Teotila.

Don Andrés sought to keep the political power of the local clergy in check. In addition, don Andrés modeled himself after other alcaldes mayores who sought to maximize their returns from repartimientos de efectos by establishing alliances with indigenous cabildo officials.[133] According to the disgruntled ecclesiastical judge Joaquín de Echevarría y Haro, don Andrés was "an eternal buyer of his post" and a *caudillo*, a term he used in its contemporary sense. Don Andrés expanded his influence by confronting various ministers who opposed his designs. For instance, he demanded the accounting books of the district's confraternities under pain of fifty lashes, which he then modified before returning them. This fabrication allowed don Andrés to justify a petition to abolish these confraternities.[134]

The ecclesiastical narrative began with a surprisingly public revelation of secret malevolent devotions. In August 1750, Oxitlan's indigenous cabildo, headed by gobernador Juan Pascual, interrogated three local residents suspected of sorcery: a seventy-year-old woman called Petrona Lucía, and two younger men called Pedro Nicolás and Francisco Marcos. A keen observer of colonial power, Juan Pascual combined juridical torture with an auto: the three suspects were exhibited before their neighbors at a sacred site near a large silk-cotton tree outside town known as El Pochote;[135] when Petrona demurred, she was whipped several times. Among the people she denounced was Juan Luis, the reputed sorcerers' leader, and don Diego Bernardino, an influential former gobernador. The cabildo notified Manuel Riveros, Xalapa's ecclesiastical judge, and imprisoned several suspects.[136]

By December 1750, these prisoners, who had been released by order of the alcalde mayor, were accused of haunting residents by turning into animals. Judge Riveros promptly initiated proceedings against them by recording the testimony of Petrona, Pedro, and Francisco, who provided a frightful narrative of blood-sucking sorcery, child sacrifice, and shape-shifting. The witnesses also revealed that two of the sorcerers traveled to Mexico City to bribe don Santiago Otañes, who succeeded his brother as alcalde mayor by 1751, and later gave him loads of fish and cacao. In 1751 Riveros ordered the imprisonment and seizure of property of three witnesses and eleven suspects, also requesting the royal justice's assistance to carry them out.[137]

In his response to this request, don Santiago presented a counternarrative claiming that Riveros violated civil jurisdiction by attempting to intervene in a dispute between Oxitlan's cabildo and the alcaldía mayor.

According to don Santiago, his brother had deposed the 1750 cabildo led by Pascual due to "innovations and rebellion," and these officials were now behind the sorcery accusations against former allies of the alcalde mayor. To prove this claim, don Santiago submitted a letter from Riveros to don Bernardino in which he called him and his supporters "rogues" and demanded that he return to "legitimate gobernador" Juan Pascual a substantial amount of wax and cotton. This casual confession about an alcalde mayor's intervention in a native election speaks volumes about the political might of the Otañes brothers, for such actions often drew legal challenges from native officials, as seen in an unsuccessful suit brought by Latani and Yaveo in 1695,[138] and the aforementioned 1735 conflict at Yalálag. In the end, don Santiago stressed, Riveros's actions aggravated a rift, for Juan Pascual's cabildo sought ecclesiastical sanctuary in Oxitlan's church to avoid prosecution by the alcalde mayor. In fact, they remained in the church for the next several years, unable to leave without facing arrest.[139]

Don Santiago's response precipitated a legal dispute between him and Oaxaca's diocesan authorities. Provisor Lizardi appointed ecclesiastical judge Joaquín Lazarte to continue the proceedings, and the latter found that all witnesses stood by their earlier statements, so he once again asked don Santiago to assist him in enforcing an arrest and seizure order. Don Santiago astutely conditioned his compliance on having the right to inspect the trial records, for he knew that such a move provided access to privileged information. In response, Lazarte threatened him with excommunication. The bishopric's fiscal, Joseph Martínez, accused the alcalde mayor of *fautoría*, or enabling the defendants to commit their crimes.

In any case, this dispute had already been submitted to the Audiencia of Mexico for resolution. In October 1752, Provisor Alejandro Miranda, Lizardi's successor, commissioned ecclesiastical judge Francisco Rendón to continue the proceedings. The provisor's order cited a June 1752 Audiencia decision that was nothing short of Solomonic. The Audiencia decreed that sorcery crimes not involving heresy were *de mixto foro*— they fell under both ecclesiastical and civil jurisdiction—and in those instances, ecclesiastics should be assisted by and share their records with civil justices. Whenever sorcery involved heresy, as had occurred in this case, this was a "crime of faith," and ecclesiastics could carry out arrests with or without the assistance of civil judges.[140] Although don Santiago begrudgingly arrested the Oxitlan defendants, he continued to harass several witnesses in the case.[141]

Petrona Lucía, the prosecution's leading witness and an avowed sorcerer, presented a fantastically detailed account about a "government" of sorcerers in Oxitlan. Her confession was a catalog of horrors that resembled in its insistence on supernatural feats the 1738 sorcery confession by María Felipa de Alcaraz, a Spanish woman in Oaxaca City.[142] However, while Alcaraz resorted to a heavily European imaginary when she recounted how indigenous sorcerers led her through the air to the devil, Petrona tapped into a far more hybrid imaginary as she described shape-shifting sorcerers. Leonora María appeared as a queen on a carriage and as a blue snake; Felipe Pedro became a pig or a male goat; Rosa María took the shape of a dog or a serpent; and Francisco Ambrosio morphed into a goat. Petrona emphasized the activities of a family of sorcerers: Miguel Felipe, one of Rosa María's sons, sacrificed four of his sons and brought an illness into town from Córdoba, and her other son Marcos Felipe turned into a friar and said mass at El Pochote before a host prepared with fresh and dried blood. Moreover, former gobernador don Diego Bernardino followed Petrona and turned into a male goat and a horned ocelot to frighten her into silence. The two other witnesses used less fantastic descriptions, stating, for instance, that Juan Luis and Marcos Felipe did not turn into ecclesiastics, but simply donned clerical robes.

Blood sacrifice was the leitmotif running through these confessions: sorcerers offered human blood at El Pochote, extracted blood from women and young children donated for that purpose by their parents, and ate women and children. Except for a bloodied host, which seemingly indexes Jewish blood libel narratives,[143] all of the activities reported during these proceedings resemble Mesoamerican beliefs regarding shape-shifting and blood-sucking sorcery.[144] An important accusation involved the offering of blood and human bodies at the beginning of a construction project. Petrona and her fellow witnesses contended that Diego Mendes ate his own grandson and another child after the beams for a communal building were brought into town. The mulatto Baltasar de Rivera provided a more contextual narrative, based on legal records handed to his grandfather after he served as Oxitlan's gobernador. By consulting this private archive, Rivera learned that the gobernador Antonio Diego, grandfather of suspected sorcerer don Bernardino, had been sentenced to seven years' exile decades before. Don Antonio was turned in by the two alcaldes, who noticed that fresh blood had been splattered where the beams of a new roof joined the frame of Oxitlan's church. A trickle of blood from the church to the very door of don Antonio's house led them to uncover a jar full of blood, as well as blood-drenched tortillas under his bed.[145]

The Oxitlan jurisdictional battle resulted in a renewed concern from the Audiencia and the viceroy regarding the protection of ecclesiastical jurisdiction in Oaxaca. The Audiencia and Viceroy Marqués de las Amarillas supported efforts by the bishop of Oaxaca to receive civil assistance; thus, in 1757 a viceregal order directed the alcalde mayor of Guamelula to provide such assistance when asked.[146] In September 1782, the royal fiscal Ramón de Posada obtained the assistance of Villa Alta's alcalde mayor in an idolatry investigation led by the minister of Puxmetacan.[147] The viceroy further favored ecclesiastical jurisdiction through a December 1782 order instructing all alcaldes mayores of Oaxaca to assist ecclesiastical judges in punishing native idolaters without inspecting trial records or charging a fee;[148] they were also ordered to write back acknowledging receipt of this directive.[149] Nevertheless, Fiscal Posada regarded this latter order as damaging to both civil jurisdiction and indigenous interests, since it would allow priests, who were often motivated by "either outmoded zeal or cupidity," to punish their native charges without showing their commissions.[150]

PUNITIVE POLICIES IN EIGHTEENTH-CENTURY OAXACA

Maldonado's idolaters' jail continued to serve its mandate as permanent carceral space for native idolaters until the 1760s. Maldonado's successor, Bishop Francisco de Santiago y Calderón (1729–36) continued to hear idolatry trials. He also granted specific commissions against idolatry; for instance, in March 1730, he gave such a commission to Joseph de Noriega y Espina, vicario foráneo of Teozacualco.[151] In 1732, according to one of his letters to the crown, he was actively punishing idolaters and incarcerating maestros at the prison of idolaters, including notables such as don Antonio, cacique of Yalahui,[152] and he also confirmed about 120,000 parishioners in his first visita.[153] Santiago y Calderón adopted the establishment of Spanish-language schools as the cornerstone of his attempts to improve indigenous knowledge of the Christian doctrine and eradicate native ritual practices; by November 1734, he could boast to the crown that he had completed two visits of his diocese and had established "almost five hundred" Spanish-language schools in native communities. In this letter, he also mentioned having imprisoned "about seventy teachers of idolatry, given away by the Indians themselves" in the prisión perpetua.[154]

By the mid-eighteenth century, Maldonado's prisión perpetua may have begun to be used as the default ecclesiastic prison in Oaxaca City. This state of affairs is suggested by a 1758 letter from Bishop Buenaventura Blanco y Helguero (1753–64), in which he mentions his intention to build a second ecclesiastic prison, since he had been forced to incarcerate ecclesiastical subjects in the prisión perpetua, "mixed in with the native idolaters," for lack of space.[155] Figure 8.2 shows a late eighteenth-century drawing from Oaxaca's archiepiscopal archives that may have

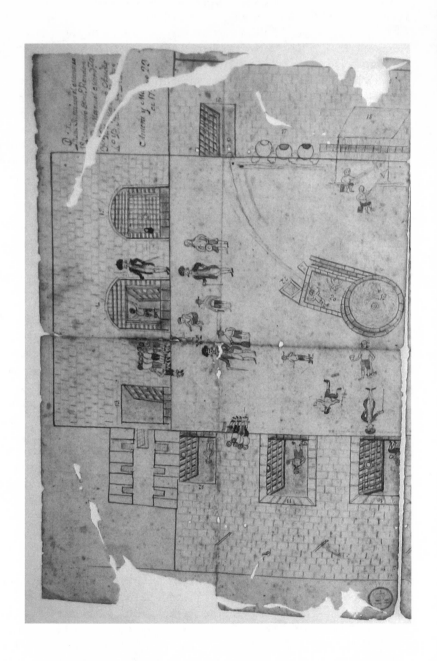

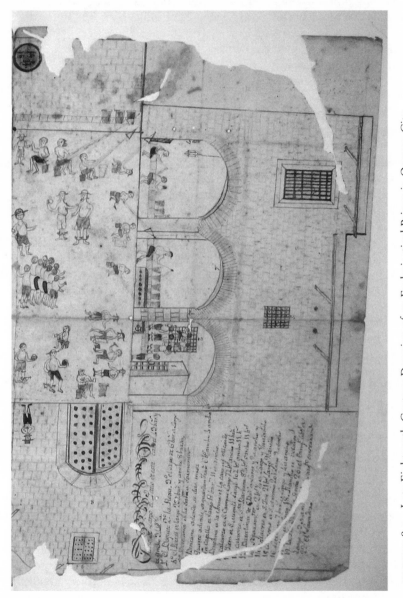

FIGURE 8.2 Late Eighteenth-Century Drawing of an Ecclesiastical Prison in Oaxaca City.

SOURCE: Archivo Histórico del Arzobispado de Oaxaca, uncatalogued

been made in the 1750s by order of Bishop Blanco to depict the prison's current state.[156]

This depiction shows a building designed not only to isolate and control but also to provide a carceral space where indigenous idolaters could bathe, rest, and engage in various crafts to earn their keep under the vigilance of their jailers. At the center of an enclosed courtyard 43 varas (36.1 meters) long and 34.75 varas (29.2 meters) wide, there is a round cistern with a tank and a washing station; near the cistern, the night watchman occupies a simple shelter. In fact, as attested by a 1762 petition drafted by the owner of a nearby orchard, a channel provided access to water outside the prison's walls.[157] More than fifty prisoners, apparently naked from the waist up, are scattered throughout this open space under the vigilant eye of seven figures in full European dress. Most of these convicts wear leg irons, many of them on both limbs, while a privileged few have one leg free and the other encased in iron. The only prisoners unimpeded by irons are those hard at work: seven of them weave on looms strapped to their waists, and a few others work on small objects. The wall on the illustration's bottom has a three-arch arcade with a reinforced door, a grille, and stocks. Above the arcade, a single large window was used by the priests who came to say Mass before the idolaters. Several doors lead from the courtyard to various rooms; clockwise from the bottom of the drawing, one finds the chapel, three cells named after Saints Campur, Michael, and Barbara, six holding cells and a door leading to several narrow cells (about 1.9 by 1 meters), and two cells named after Saints Joseph and Anthony. Physical punishment is not openly displayed in this sketch, with three exceptions. A prisoner with leg irons and arms held high stands at the entrance to the holding cells, apparently awaiting a whipping; by the stocks, an official holds up a lash. More ominously, above the arcade a barred window is identified as belonging to the *sala de tormentos*, "torture chamber."

A last glimpse at the fate of Maldonado's prison comes from a July 1765 letter from the cathedral chapter to the crown's prosecutor. In this document, the chapter, acting in lieu of the bishop due to a vacant episcopal seat, describes the "perpetual ecclesiastical prison" as being located "in an outlying district about eight or nine blocks from the Episcopal Palace, a building so ancient and badly constructed since its beginnings, that it is scarcely anything more than a great enclosure with shoddy walls and even worse roofing, being an uncomfortable dwelling even for the miserable Indians for whom it was conceived."[158] A series of autos drafted the same year by several Oaxaca clergy described the project of building a new ecclesiastical jail, with support from the bishop.[159]

Additionally, Bishop Blanco manifested his concern with idolatry by requesting that the crown approve more severe punishments. In 1755, Blanco complained that natives judged the seriousness of their crimes by the severity of their penalties and hoped that royal decrees reflected greater "strength and rigor" against them. In a second letter from 1758, Blanco also noted that the usual punishments, service in their home parishes and "a few lashes," did not keep them from idolatry. Blanco ended his missive with a request for the consideration of two bold innovations: either the expansion of legal faculties for bishops on indigenous matters, or the return of natives to inquisitorial jurisdiction. Not surprisingly, a 1763 royal response directed Blanco to continue with established legal practices and maintain his vigilant stance over idolatry as his proposal was considered.[160] The bishop's zeal was called into question, however, by a letter from a subdelegate of the Santa Cruzada bull who had several disagreements with Blanco. The Council of Indies recorded the subdelegate's accusation that Juan de Urueta, Blanco's provisor, charged indigenous idolatry defendants legal costs as exorbitant as 470 pesos per case.[161]

The last grand extirpatory gesture in late eighteenth-century Oaxaca took place in Mixe territory in 1781. As Bishop Joseph Gregorio de Ortigosa (1775–93) set out to complete a visita in Tehuantepec, the minister of Acatlan, a Mixe town in Nejapa, handed him a long list of idolaters in his parish. The number of suspects so shocked the bishop that he convened a meeting of theologians, who, perhaps bearing in mind Maldonado's 1704 campaign, decided to issue an edict forgiving all those who had avowed their transgressions and extending the pardon to anyone who made a new confession. Save for the five dependencies of Acatlan, no other pueblo de indios came forward. The bishop found that a majority of the parish's residents was implicated, and some of them even surrendered ritual texts. In spite of receiving a collective absolution, their pastor continued to find their behavior suspicious and later revealed that they "had invented another sacrifice" related to Ash Wednesday, the holiday on which the absolution had been given.[162]

Finally, in July 1785, Ortigosa's provisor sentenced idolatry and superstition defendant Antonio Pedro of Cotzocon, parish of Puxmetacan, to ten years' imprisonment in Puerto Rico.[163] In 1791, Reymundo Manuel de los Santos, a literate and politically savvy Mixe legal representative from Cotzocon, was imprisoned for idolatry and heresy in Oaxaca City's "ecclesiastical court's jail" during trial, since the prisión perpetua had ceased to exist.[164] This conviction was spearheaded by parish priest Antonio Pío Tinoco, who wanted to block de los Santos's appointment as local schoolteacher, complaining that he had become Cotzocon's "voice and caudillo." In 1794, de los Santos's sentence, which was as harsh as that handed out against Antonio, was modified on appeal to a fifty-league exile from Oaxaca City.[165]

MODERN EXTIRPATIONS AND
FADING BOURBON IDOLATRIES

Received historical narratives about social and political changes in the Bourbon years focus on a transition to greater institutional expediency, skepticism, and rationality.[166] While these observations may ring true in broader domains, this chapter shows that, in terms of ecclesiastical policies against native idolatry, sorcery, and superstition, a decisive transitional point occurred early rather than late in the eighteenth century, and that earlier policies continued to coexist with more streamlined procedures. In Mexico, a set of trials from Toluca allow us to follow Castorena y Urzúa's drive to reform the Provisorato de Indios y Chinos in the 1710s and 1720s by reinstating autos against idolaters in Mexico City, following a highly systematic legal procedure, and calling forth theological experts to assess specialists' claims. Subsequent provisores seemingly lacked Castorena y Urzúa's reformist spirit. However, an important modification, the requirement to have sorcery victims examined by a physician, was imposed by Archbishop Rubio y Salinas in the 1750s.

In Oaxaca, Maldonado's 1702–5 campaign in Villa Alta represented an expedient experiment, a modern extirpation *avant la lettre*, that did not result, paradoxically, in an institutionally codified approach to idolatry inquests. Hence, Bishop Ortigosa's 1781 amnesty offer, the only known attempt to replicate Maldonado's approach, did not result in multitudinous confessions. Sariñana's and Maldonado's most important legacy was the perpetual prison for idolaters, a punitive experiment that hovered between colonial and modern dynamics; the prison punished and isolated "teachers of idolatry" indefinitely as if they were contagious cases, but no institutional logic guaranteed its political and economic survival, and the project was abandoned by the 1760s. Oaxacan bishops remained committed to uprooting idolatry, nevertheless. For instance, as late as 1785, Provisor and Vicario General Antonio Ibáñez y Corvera noted that his court's archives held many idolatry trials, "conducted in succession almost year after year with no interruption."[167]

The evidence reviewed above also demonstrates that eighteenth-century indigenous sorcery accusations in Toluca and the Chinantla region were a far cry from the collective outcries that accompanied the witch hunts at Logroño or Loudun.[168] Even in the few examples when several witnesses corroborated sorcery accusations, their testimonies followed an accretive logic in which suspicions that gathered over several years established a sorcerer's public reputation. The construction of sorcery narratives was thus not a culminating event, but a reflection of more diffuse social processes. Thus, sorcery accusations were a public indictment of an individual's malevolence made by interested parties who shared a degree of intimacy with the accused.

If we agree with Charles Tilly that credit and blaming are "doubly social" in that they invoke one set of social relations through accusation, while the act of apportioning blame redefines such relations,[169] then it might be said that sorcery accusations both reflected preexisting personal rifts and reframed social relations. The awareness of this process led accusers to present richly detailed scenarios and the accused to object, sometimes preemptively, to a damaging accusation. Even if ecclesiastical and indigenous notions about sorcery easily converged in court narratives, indigenous denunciation dynamics often followed an autonomous logic. The best example of this disjunction is the dramatic Oxitlan case. When a political rift materialized between Juan Pascual and his associates—who claimed to have been legitimately elected as cabildo officials, and don Diego Bernardino's allies—who were supported by the alcalde mayor, the former faction accused the latter of sorcery and blood witchcraft. Although this denunciation was politically expedient, it did not materialize out of nothing; rather, it compressed many suspicions that the accusers regarded as plausible from their local cosmological perspective.

In both Mexico and Oaxaca, reports of idolatrous practices were relatively rare in the late eighteenth century. Hence, the two instances of local cults at Yautepec and the Sierra de Tototepec y Tenango, regarded as idolatrous by ecclesiastics and as messianic by contemporary scholars, were highly unusual occurrences.[170] In any case, provisores, ecclesiastical judges, and ministers continued to diligently record claims of native heterodoxy into the early nineteenth century. Some of these accusations manage to turn the tables on the Spanish; for instance, in 1775, a Yalálag native reported before an inquisitorial commissary that a Spaniard sold various powders that conferred good luck and the love of women in Oaxaca City's main square.[171] The 1796 trial of several natives from San Luis de la Paz led by Andrés Martínez deserves particular attention, even if it occurred in the western fringes of the Sierra Gorda and was overseen by diocesan authorities in Michoacán. A lengthy investigation unearthed complex allegations regarding the use of peyote and other hallucinogenic plants in connection with Christian observances.[172]

In the diocese of Mexico, the last extant colonial-period accusations regarding native heterodoxy concerned the cult of a skeletal effigy called "the Just Judge" in Amoles circa 1793,[173] the nocturnal devotions of a silver-plated "cross of justice" near Querétaro in 1817,[174] and the 1819 ecclesiastical proceedings against a native accused of performing superstitious divination in Calimaya.[175] The last known colonial superstition denouncement in Oaxaca concerns the trial of six officeholders from San Miguel Mixtepec suspected of performing rituals in a nearby cave. They were set free on bail in December 1815 and, like the 1735 Yalálag cabildo, they requested reinstatement in office for the three weeks that remained in their terms.[176]

In the end, the Bourbon ecclesiastical imagination persevered in its assessment of many native practices as inherently suspect. A February 1769 edict from Provisor and Inquisidor de los Indios Barrientos, which cited a 1765 cédula calling for vigilance against idolatry, contained a long list of suspect activities: collective dances to the beat of preconquest instruments (*nescuitiles*); live representations of the Nativity, Christ's Passion, or the Three Kings; *volador* dances; dances devoted to Saint James (*santiaguitos*); healing or divination involving pipiltzintzintli plants, peyote, hummingbirds, flowers, or "other herbs or animals"; offerings of dolls, candles left in caves, mountains, or rivers; hail conjuring; maleficio; the collective bathing of men and women; service by grooms in the home of their future in-laws; premarital celebrations that established whether the bride was pregnant; and dancing and excessive drinking during nine-day wakes. Most remarkably, the edict named various genres of illicit devotional texts that circulated "among Indians and Chinese," including illustrated divinatory texts, calendars citing "all the *naguales* of stars, elements, birds, fish, and other animals," Christian texts with names such as "Our Lord's Testament," and prayer books devoted to Saint James, Saint Bartholomew, and Saints Cosmas and Damian.[177]

Furthermore, Audiencia judge Antonio de Rivadeneira y Barrientos outlined sixty indigenous superstitions in the report he wrote as royal representative to the Mexican Fourth Provincial Council of 1771. Rivadeneira, who also opposed calls by ecclesiastics to discontinue the use of indigenous languages to teach the Christian doctrine,[178] seemed to possess extensive knowledge about suspicious observances. Besides hail casting and the use of pipiltzintzintli, peyote, and other plants, Rivadeneira sketched a variety of beliefs regarding animals and natural forces, suspect acts performed during life-cycle events and Christian celebrations, and everyday activities such as cooking, eating, buying and selling, or felling trees.[179] Thus, by the close of the colonial era, the extirpators' Lascasian net, cast over a seemingly boundless ocean of indigenous performances and behaviors, continued to trap an inexhaustible supply of suspect indigenous practices, even as sustained institutional interest in them waned.

CHAPTER 9

A Colonial Archipelago of Faith

Every year, beginning with the feast of Mary's Assumption on August 15 and continuing for about ten days, many people residing in or near the Northern Zapotec town of Betaza in Oaxaca walk up steep hillsides and through the thick brush atop Lom San Antonio, Saint Anthony's Hill. Eventually, they reach a small shelter under a large rock. There, they sacrifice turkeys and leave bread, alcohol, cigarettes, cacao beans, and other offerings for Xhan Li Yelyiu, the True Lord of the World, a local divine being whose sanctuary is that very shelter. Comparable celebrations unfold in many other local sacred sites on the outskirts of other Northern Zapotec communities. For instance, in San Andrés Yaa, a public fair held near an open-air chapel to celebrate the Invention of the Holy Cross on May 3 easily blends with a different set of observances that take place around a small pond located about one hundred meters away from the chapel. At this site, known as Head of the Town of San Andrés, individuals and families build dozens of crude reproductions of houses they hope the sacred beings who reside there will grant them, complete with multiple levels, garages, and cars in their driveways. Both sites are occasionally visited by individuals who hire ritual specialists to ask for well-being or to make specific demands, but many of them believe their petitions will be more effective when made on certain Christian holidays.[1]

Any outsider surveying such scenes may believe that there exists an unbroken devotional thread between the communal celebrations investigated by Bishop Maldonado in the early eighteenth century and these twenty-first century observances, or conclude that Christianity has lost a massive gambit, given the prominence accorded to local devotions at the end of five centuries of evangelization. After all, similar examples of devotions rooted in ancestral beliefs exist in many other Central Mexican communities.[2] Both conclusions would be misleading, however. While there exist multiple structural points of contact between some of the practices described in eighteenth-century records—for instance, the worship of Yabe, an entity mentioned in colonial ritual songs, continues at a sacred hilltop near Lachirioag—much has changed. Not only has the 260-day Central Mexican divinatory count faded completely from view, except in a handful of native communities,[3] but some specialists have substituted it with Christian calendars. Even if indigenous specialists in some communities continue to petition local and regional deities, these entities' names, attributions, and powers have shifted significantly. The beat of the nicachi or the teponaztli no longer summons native celebrants to sing and dance for Zapotec or Nahua sacred entities, although those instruments may still be used in other contexts. In other words, local collective and elective spheres have undergone multiple historical transformations since colonial times, and the projection of long-term continuities from the present into the past and vice versa would result, as Chance and Taylor argued regarding Mesoamerican cargo systems, in the re-creation of a dubious ethnographic past.[4]

I now turn to a discussion of five concluding reflections that summarize evidence presented in the previous chapters. After reviewing my approach to the sources and arguing that the multiplicity of local devotions did not constitute a unified religious field, I examine an important contrast between Mexico and Oaxaca in terms of native responses to idolatry suppression. Then, I contend that these native devotions should be understood as forms of epistemological dissent, which occasionally led to violent acts of resistance against colonial Christianity. After noting a major transition in forms of punishment from Zumárraga's disciplinary humanism to Sariñana's and Maldonado's isolation of idolaters, I close with a final assessment of the role that the written circulation of knowledge played in the reconfiguration of indigenous devotions.

First, it bears restating that this work has focused on indigenous collective and elective devotional practices through vantage points afforded by institutional projects that targeted these observances. By definition, many of the sources employed here emphasize the exceptional and the marginal. Such an emphasis leads to a highly bracketed analysis of the vast universe of colonial indigenous ritual practices that does not include, by design, the multiple manifestations of native devotional fervor regarded with minimal suspicion by ecclesiastics, such as local and regional Marian cults,[5] certain hybrid forms of religious art,[6] or some native confraternities.[7] Although idolatry eradicators targeted collective and elective spheres in indigenous communities, some native practitioners operated in urban markets whose clients were mostly Spaniards and castas,[8] but these domains recede from view when one focuses on idolatry extirpation records. Rather than deploying categories such as hybridity and syncretism, terms whose mere use never constitutes a full analysis, this project has emphasized a richly detailed, microsociological, "thick" ethnohistorical narrative and sociocultural and linguistic description of Nahua and Zapotec devotions. My goal in embracing such complexity was to illuminate the intricate interplay of individual and collective interest in public, private, and clandestine spaces. This project has also interpreted native forms of social consciousness about devotion through the deployment and investigation of narratives co-constructed by witnesses and judges, since the combination of narrative evidence and suspicious objects that indexed "idolatries" and "superstitions" was the pervasive coin of this juridical realm.

Such multiple narratives about indigenous devotions should prevent us from analyzing them as a unified phenomenon. The ritual practices prosecuted by civil and church authorities articulated local cosmological beliefs in myriad ways: while Northern Zapotec specialists kept the 365-day count current by linking it to the feast of Saint Matthias, Nahua specialists personified or called forth a wide variety of preconquest deities and Christian saints, each tied to a particular epithet and pragmatic end. In Toluca, specialists prescribed healing rituals that called for ceramic effigies made in Metepec, and nowhere else; in Oxitlan, Chinantec malevolent specialists were feared for their interest in human blood and their shape-shifting prowess.

Although these practices share important structural connections and affinities in various domains—such as divinatory time counts, the veneration of sacred sites, and the importance of animal and human blood sacrifice—each of these communities embraced Mesoamerican understandings of the cosmos and its order in different ways and articulated those beliefs selectively and in conjunction with Christian observances in so diverse a manner that their efforts defy meaningful classification. The very presence of diverging theories about the cosmos alongside Christian practices in a local religious field means that one cannot reduce the complexity of, say, local devotions in Betaza, Sola de Vega, or Atenango del Río, to a species of "peasant Christianity," even though some of those observances may superficially resemble the cult of the saints in pre-Reformation Spain.[9] In other words, to do justice to the conceptual, pragmatic, and sociocultural diversity of Central Mexican devotion, we must take as our guiding metaphor neither the hybridization nor the crystallization of indigenous and Christian beliefs, nor even the permanence of a static Mesoamerican substrate, but a sobering vision of a colonial archipelago of faith composed by hundreds of local cosmologies that incorporated insights and theories drawn from Mesoamerican and European beliefs following autonomous and historically contingent criteria.

Second, such complexity does not preclude certain general conclusions about indigenous responses. Charts 9.1 and 9.2 render visible an important phenomenon in accusation trends: a marked contrast in allegations by gender in the dioceses of Mexico and Oaxaca between the 1520s and the late eighteenth century. In Mexico, as shown in Chart 9.1, there are two important patterns: a sharp decrease in accusations against male noblemen and officeholders by the end of the sixteenth century, and a series of fluctuating increases in accusations against commoner female specialists that begins in the early seventeenth century. In Chapter 2 I argued that the decline of "natural lords" by the 1560s and the impact of doctrinal education resulted in the disassociation of traditional ritual practices with public office, and this change is reflected by the first trend. By contrast, the increase in accusations against females demonstrates that there was an increase in the visibility of female specialists in the elective sphere from the early seventeenth century onward. This pattern may have been motivated by two separate phenomena. First, as shown in Chapter 3, the data regarding deity-personification practices compiled by Ruiz de Alarcón suggests that a growing number of Nahua females entered the elective sphere in the early seventeenth century. This regional trend cannot be regarded as a general one. Nonetheless, the fact that by the early eighteenth century accusations against female specialists equaled those leveled against their male counterparts suggests that by that period there was some gender parity among specialists operating in the elective sphere. Moreover, this increase in accusations against females may also have been informed by a growing gender bias against female practitioners after the Counter-Reformation. As noted in Chapter 3, both Ruiz de Alarcón and de la Serna believed that women were particularly susceptible to being misled by the Devil, and this belief may have colored the perception of these and other enemies of idolatry.

It is instructive to briefly contrast these data with changes in witchcraft accusation patterns by gender in early modern Europe. A sample of witchcraft denunciations for the period 1300–1500 proves there was a sharp increase of more than 20 percent in accusations against women from the 1420s onward.[10] While the European data show a decisive increase with time, my data for the diocese of Mexico has important fluctuations: even though females are the majority of the accused between the 1610s and the 1630s, the 1710s and the 1720s, the 1750s and the 1760s, and the 1780s, they slide into the minority in all other periods. Hence, while the early modern European prosecutions suggest a more systemic bias regarding female specialists, this prejudice was not the sole factor driving gender bias in Central Mexico.

As shown in Charts 9.1 and 9.2, prosecution trends in Oaxaca were substantially different from those of Mexico. In a sharp contrast with the more egalitarian participation of female specialists in the elective sphere in Mexico, Zapotec, Mixe, Mixtec, Chinantec, and Cuicatec female practitioners were a small minority among the accused. Women account for about 2 percent or less in almost any given decade, including Villa Alta in 1700–1710, which is depicted on a broken y-axis in Chart 9.2 due to the high number of male practitioners (429). I interpret this trend as evidence that Oaxacan extirpators held a bias not regarding gender, but in terms of the social spaces where unorthodox practices tended to occur. By and large, civil and ecclesiastic authorities prosecuted idolatrous and superstitious acts that took place in the collective sphere. Due to various sociocultural and political factors that call for further analysis, colonial Zapotec women did not frequently participate in the exchange of clandestine ritual texts or assume a leading role in the organization of collective practices. Hence, the emphasis extirpators placed on collective devotions radically skewed the record in favor of allegations about male practitioners. This bias resulted in a relative lack of interest in investigating practices in the elective sphere, so these data provide by necessity limited information about specialists of either gender who worked primarily for households and families in Oaxaca.

The contrast outlined above highlights one crucial distinction between Nahua and Zapotec responses to evangelization and idolatry suppression policies. On the one hand, there was a marked decline in the participation of native officials in collective ritual practices from 1571 onward, and public Christian devotions became dominant in the collective sphere of many Nahua localities by the early seventeenth century. On the other hand, several Zapotec communities continued to favor the reproduction of collective ritual practices as a local, often disputed political project, even in the face of large-scale extirpation attempts. Hence, evangelization and extirpation attempts in Oaxaca tended to focus on the repression of collective ritual practices, which inspired some communities to defend a measure of local political autonomy. In Mexico, this trend ran in the opposite direction: local accusations made by indigenous plaintiffs against specialists in the elective sphere were commonplace and had to be carefully managed by ecclesiastical judges by the eighteenth century, as shown in Chapter 8, as they became entangled with individual disputes and enmities.

Third, this longitudinal analysis of indigenous responses to evangelization and idolatry eradication projects forces us to reconsider their status as forms of resistance. It could be argued that the myriad ways in which some indigenous believers eroded the dominance of orthodox

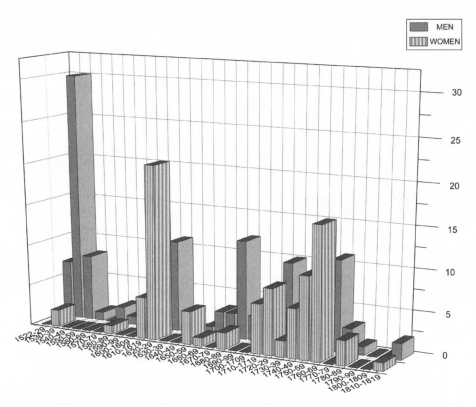

CHART 9.1   Extant Accusations Against Indigenous Specialists in Mexico by Gender.

SOURCES: ACM; AGI; AGN; AGOP; AHAM; AHAO; ALC; AHJO; BMNA; NL

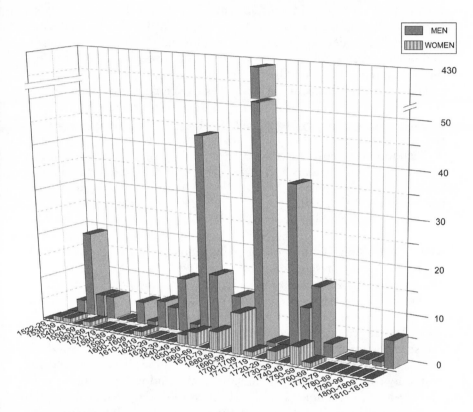

CHART 9.2   Extant Accusations Against Indigenous Specialists in Oaxaca by Gender. 1700–1709 data not to scale (429 accusations against males; 9 against females).

SOURCES: ACM; AGI; AGN; AGOP; AHAM; AHAO; ALC; AHJO; BMNA; NL

Christianity amounted to what James Scott famously termed "everyday forms of resistance."[11] Nevertheless, this explanation rehearses a dichotomy that may have existed only in the mind of extirpators: devoted Christian ministers waging an invisible war against their apparently meek but surreptitiously recalcitrant parishioners. No such simple binary existed, as demonstrated by the activities of indigenous political actors examined in Chapters 6 and 7 who opposed both collective and elective unorthodox devotions, and by the complex contredanse of allegations about healing and sorcery examined in Chapter 8. Thus, recasting this vast universe of acts of dissent against Christian norms as somehow equal or uniform forms of quotidian resistance does not take into account the diversity of indigenous forms of consciousness that inspired such acts; as suggested by Steven Stern, peasant and native consciousness formation and deployment is problematic, and never easily predictable.[12]

Therefore, I propose that the broadest rubric one may use to conceptualize the determined decentering of orthodox Christianity by native believers is that of epistemological dissent. By minimizing the importance of local devotional acts, one runs the risk of occupying the same conceptual zone claimed by secular extirpators in seventeenth-century Central Mexico, who attributed "idolatrous" and "superstitious" acts not to the decisions of fully conscious individuals, but to the workings of a demonic agency present behind every native devotion. If we choose to conceptualize indigenous subjects as social actors who performed elective and collective practices in a conscious manner, then it follows we should take very seriously the ontological claims that anchored their beliefs.

In Oaxaca, calendar specialists believed in a three-tiered temporal and spatial continuum through which twenty groups of thirteen days rotated endlessly. In the Cohuixca-Tlalhuica region, Nahua specialists held sway over illness, the agricultural cycle, and individual destinies by embodying preconquest deities through the performance of highly marked speech acts. In Toluca, specialists healed by staging carefully arrayed cosmological tableaus involving offerings and ceramic effigies and drove hail away by invoking Christian and non-Christian entities. Each of these observances, and many others briefly outlined in the preceding chapters, epitomized local theories of knowledge about time, the cosmos, and the social order. Each of these devotional orientations instantiated a de facto act of epistemological dissent with Christian ontological claims, as diverse strategies that confronted and adopted Christian beliefs at the same time.

Furthermore, I examined more direct, violent forms of resistance in Chapters 6 and 7. In terms of collective observances, various indigenous town councils—such as those of Betaza, Lachirioag, Yalálag, and

Oxitlan in Oaxaca—promoted internal strife as they cast their lot with that of their ancestors and traditional practices, embracing a cosmological and political vision that by necessity excluded other ways of organizing and performing collective devotions in public spaces. This was a struggle over local autonomy, which in these communities became both an argument over what constituted the true structure of the world, and a sociopolitical project that sought to implant such a theory as the dominant one in local public spaces.

Fourth, these confrontations were not merely symbolic, for they left behind a long wake of political conflicts, property seizures, social scandals, intractable enmities, intense but short-lived rebellions, and hundreds of indigenous bodies incarcerated, maimed, disciplined, or destroyed. Ever since Bishop Zumárraga's extirpation campaign of the late 1530s, the canonical procedure for the disciplining of indigenous specialists in Central Mexico had been public exemplary punishment. Echoing Foucault's influential treatment of public punishment during the "classical age," one could interpret autos featuring native convicts as a matrix of dominance that was, simultaneously, the imprinting of state power on its subjects' bodies,[13] a "political ritual,"[14] an "exercise of 'terror'" that also counted as a "triumph of the law,"[15] and an act of violence that incriminated its audience as guarantors and coparticipants.[16]

Nonetheless, the public punishments meted out against idolaters in Central Mexico were species of Christian discipline and indoctrination that cannot be fully accounted by this Foucaldian model. Ecclesiastic authorities viewed such displays of might primarily as the continuation of evangelization efforts by other means. From their vantage point, bodily punishment was only the most visible form of a broader disciplinary complex, and it served three distinct goals. First, it reminded native audiences that idolatry, sorcery, and superstition were serious transgressions that should be as feared as the punishment they attracted, a point best exemplified by the 1560 mock burning of several Zapotec idolaters in Teiticpac, which reenacted hellish fire for a nearly neophyte audience. Second, physical disciplining was but the beginning of a path toward reform for transgressors, which also included measures such as service in churches and hospitals, temporary exile from their places of residence, and payment of legal costs and damages to aggrieved parties. Third, Oaxaca's "perpetual prison" instantiated an important division between two forms of punishment: one directed toward "contagious" idolaters permanently isolated from the colonial social body; and another one toward those regarded as redeemable.

Additionally, the disciplinary calculus of bishops and alcaldes mayores was far from uniform. Although the relative scarcity of complete trial records do not allow for a full quantitative consideration of sentences, it can be stated that physical punishments for indigenous crimes against the faith varied widely between Mexico and Oaxaca. Excluding suicides and penitents who died in prison, the extant record of physical punishment reflects six executions,[17] one convict sentenced to two hundred lashes,[18] fifteen to one hundred lashes,[19] two to fifty lashes,[20] three to twenty-five lashes,[21] and one to four lashes in the diocese of Mexico.[22] As for Oaxaca, there exist records of seventeen executions counting the 1702 Caxonos trial,[23] one convict reputedly condemned to five hundred lashes,[24] and six convicts who received two hundred lashes.[25] Even though these data are by no means exhaustive, they do suggest that idolaters paid a higher, more systematic punitive cost in Oaxaca, while authorities in Mexico were inclined to prescribe a broad range of degrees of physical penitence, with the horrifying figure of one hundred lashes as a common penitence for crimes against Christianity.

A radical turn in the characterization of idolatry, ushered in by the late seventeenth century, was rendered possible by the symbolic inclusion of native subjects into the Spanish monarchy's political body. A lucid example of this recasting appears in Jacinto de la Serna's mid-seventeenth-century *Manual* when he contends that, even if God's judgment against idolaters resulted in epidemics among indigenous people, Spaniards should succor them, because

[Indigenous people] are a nation so useful to the political life of this Monarchy of Spain, that [the monarchy's] conservation depends on it because everyone lives enchained to the labor of these Indians, and they are necessary for all because at this present time, there is no thing that can work without them, neither mines, nor the fields, nor the factories, nor the buildings because they are the blood of the mystical body of the Monarchy.[26]

Here, de la Serna acknowledged the importance of native subjects in a pregnant metaphor. Indians were to the monarchy as blood was to the body, both a source of sustenance and an inert component to be managed. In doing so, this author cited an early modern characterization, discussed in detail in a classic work by Ernst Kantorowicz,[27] of the two bodies of a Christian king: one mortal and corruptible, and another imagined as a political body whose visible head was any legitimate occupant of the throne. De la Serna presented this arrangement as "mystical" because it resolved a crucial contradiction of colonial rule: in spite of separate legal spheres, natives and Spaniards were metaphorically reunited in a naturalized assemblage.

As asserted by Foucault, a criminal's body was placed at the "opposite pole" of the monarchy's body, thus becoming a symbolic antithesis of the king.[28] Indigenous idolaters, however, were conceptualized as the opposite of virtuous native Christians and as impure and dangerous elements within the Spanish monarchy's social body. In the late seventeenth century, Bishop Sariñana began treating idolatry defendants like infectious cases, and this move facilitated the emergence of an innovative punitive institution in Oaxaca City: a perpetual prison, echoed on a smaller scale by Villavicencio in his parish at Tlacotepec. Eternal spiritual warfare had acquired an equally permanent form of punishment. In a legal culture where imprisonment was a side effect rather than a penalty in and of itself, this institution threatened idolaters with a fate worse than forced labor, exile, or perhaps even execution. By building their prisons, Bishops Sariñana and Maldonado acquired the capacity to administer a form of social death on a large scale to recidivist idolaters, who became quarantined from their social networks.

Furthermore, Maldonado embraced a novel approach: the bureaucratized extirpation campaign, which delegated authority and focused on the systematic harvesting of volunteered confessions at a regional and demographic scale never attained before or ever since in New Spain. In the diocese of Mexico, Castorena y Urzúa began standardizing legal procedure at the Provisorato de Indios y Chinos, brought theological experts to confront hail casters, and reintroduced indigenous autos in Mexico City. Perhaps not coincidentally, these three zealous extirpators were also known for their public eloquence: various printed publications preserved their most popular sermons, and Castorena y Urzúa edited both Sor Juana's poetry and the *Gaceta de México* before turning his attention to idolaters. Both punitive programs brought praise from idolatry eradicators not only in their respective dioceses but also in Guatemala and Zacatecas: in 1704, the alcalde mayor of Zapotitlan and Suchitepequez raised the possibility of sending nine especially pernicious specialists to Oaxaca's perpetual prison;[29] in 1723, the legendary Franciscan missionary fray Antonio Márgil de Jesús, writing from the Colegio de Guadalupe in Zacatecas, noted the urgent need for a perpetual prison for idolaters in Guatemala City and suggested that Castorena y Urzúa incarcerate six idolatrous "popes" from Querétaro, so they would reveal the identities of other specialists in the region.[30]

Paradoxically, this eternal war against impurity in the body of the monarchy did not result in institutional continuity. In a discussion of inquisitorial practices in colonial Peru, Irene Silverblatt turns to Hannah Arendt to propose a relationship between the Spanish Inquisition and "the subterranean stream" of a Western history of state control of racial categories through bureaucratic and punitive practices. From this perspective, the Inquisition appears to be a surprisingly modern institution.[31] In New Spain, Oaxaca's perpetual prison, Maldonado's bureaucratized extirpations, and the use of medical experts to adjudicate sorcery claims all seem to replicate *avant la lettre* the modern practices of perpetual incarceration, impersonal record-keeping in carceral systems, and the use of scientific testimony in court. These projects were, like so many other colonial legal and political proposals, subject to the vagaries of colonial enforcement. The most enduring of these projects was Oaxaca's prison for idolaters, for it survived the demise of Sariñana and Maldonado and provided continuity in punitive policies for five decades until its decline in the 1760s. Nevertheless, Maldonado's eradication experiment was a unique gambit that no other enemy of idolatry managed to replicate. Furthermore, there is no evidence regarding the systematic incorporation of medical expert testimony to sorcery proceedings, which made only occasional appearances in proceedings held between the 1760s and the 1780s in Toluca. These profound disjunctions in continuity and enforcement should prevent us from describing colonial extirpation in Central Mexico as an increasingly rationalized and systematic project.

Finally, I argued in Chapter 5 that an unexpected consequence of the alphabetization of idolaters was the emergence of several textual genres that preserved knowledge about local cosmological theories, the Postclassic calendar, and various propitiation techniques. We can tentatively date the beginning of this appropriation of European literacy practices on a large territorial scale—from the southwestern Oaxaca coast to central Oaxaca and the Cohuixca-Tlalhuica region near the Basin of Mexico—to the early seventeenth century, even if its origins are still poorly understood. The analysis of texts by indigenous practitioners and the recontextualization of detailed linguistic data compiled by knowledgeable missionaries and secular clergymen provide an epistemic perspective on native devotions that goes far beyond that furnished by legal records, which feature far thicker layers of mediation from juridical, ecclesiastic, and civil discourses. The emergence and reproduction of clandestine native ritual and devotional genres during this period, and their eighteenth-century sequels, is a phenomenon demanding a multidisciplinary approach that maintains a firm footing in the institutional history of colonial extirpation. Hence, Chapters 3 through 7 posited an analysis of these native genres through multiple case studies, the discourse analysis of native sources, the placement of such sources in their intellectual and social context, and the comparative analysis of the oral and written transmission of ritual knowledge.

In Central Mexico, a small but significant number of literate idolaters appropriated European forms of alphabetic literacy to reproduce and represent as authoritative various ritual and calendrical genres. This move cannot be fully understood if we take orality, alphabetic writing, and literacy to be monolithic systems that imprint the same unified logic on the societies in which they exist. Three lines of evidence discussed in Chapters 3, 4, 5, 7, and 8 indicate that the various epistemological, intellectual, and discursive assumptions inhabiting European writing systems were not inexorably mapped onto the idolaters' booklets. First, ritual specialists came into the possession of alphabetic literacy in an idiosyncratic way that accentuated individual and local stances. Having acquired literacy in preparation for service in local civil or church hierarchies, some specialists used Spanish letters to reflect local phonemic norms; others used the Arabic numerical system in unexpected ways, or appropriated the haphazard use of punctuation in early modern imprints. Second, clandestine ritual texts did not displace oral genres or end the oral transmission of ritual knowledge. As noted in Chapter 5, in northern Oaxaca, the region of origin of the largest extant corpus of clandestine native ritual literature in colonial Spanish America, specialists circulated written and oral versions of the 260-day count and its structure without contradiction. Ritual-text users and owners both in this region and in south-central Oaxaca appropriated texts in a variety of ways, putting into question the existence of a categorical distinction between literate and illiterate. Third, the rapports among literacy practices, specialist networks, communities of readers, and pragmatic aims varied widely from one locality to another. In Sola, a small network of literate specialists circulated calendrical texts using at least two Zapotec variants. In Villa Alta, broader networks operating across larger distances and a wider variety of Zapotec variants facilitated the exchange of calendars and fostered the transcription of entire ritual performances and cosmological narratives. In and near the Toluca Valley, some indigenous authors transposed Spanish almanacs, while others reinterpreted Christian teachings.

The uneven survival of trial records, the linguistic difficulties that accompany the translation of native clandestine genres, and the multiple lacunae in the sources about colonial indigenous devotions have all contributed to blotting out the concreteness of Nahua and Zapotec ritual specialists as historical subjects. My work has been motivated by the premise that, in spite of these difficulties, the first task before us concerns returning the "invisible war" between colonial judges and native practitioners to the realm of the discernible. By outlining periods, discussing the changes in extirpation policies, and establishing a chronology of extirpation campaigns in Mexico and Oaxaca, this project proposed a historical narrative about the activities of these extirpators.

Yet this is the barest of beginnings. Through the mere fact of their survival in the Cohuixca-Tlalhuica region and in Villa Alta, several sources hint at the existence of a clandestine intellectual sphere whose conditions of production—literate native church officials, an interested audience, access to both native ritual knowledge and European devotional texts—existed in other communities in Central Mexico. This book endeavored to open an avenue of research devoted to historical actors that barely missed total obliteration: the emerging "local ethnological history"[32] of native authors of devotional texts that circulated clandestinely in the interstitial spaces of the monarchy's social body. Future students seeking to walk along this path face three considerable challenges: to rescue these native authors from relative oblivion through the recovery, interpretation, and translation of their works; to assess the collective consciousness of their work as an intellectual enterprise; and to place these resolute writers within the staggeringly diverse context of the colonial devotional archipelago they inhabited.

Glossary

A: Arawak
M: Mixtec
N: Nahuatl
S: Spanish
Z: Zapotec

alcalde   S. local magistrate and cabildo member

alcalde mayor   S. chief magistrate; deputy alcaldes mayores were tenientes de alcalde mayor

alguacil   S. town constable

altepetl   N. Nahua polity

alternancia   S. policy of filling posts by alternating between those born in Spain and criollos

Audiencia   S. high court

auto (de fe)   S. formal public punishment in the manner of the Inquisition

bachiller   S. title for the holder of a first university degree

beneficiado   S. clergy appointed to a beneficio, a curate endowed with an income

cabecera   S. head town

cabildo   S. city or town council

cacao   N. *cacahuatl*, chocolate

cacique   A. chief

calpolli   N. altepetl subdivision

cargo   S. position in a town council

casta   S. term for those of mixed Native, European, and/or African descent

cédula   S. royal decree

chalchihuitl   N. precious green stone

cochineal   a red dye from an insect that feeds on the nopal cactus *cofradía*   S. confraternity.

colaní   Z: calendar specialist

compadre   S. godfather, ritual kinship relationship

congregaciones   S: the merging and consolidation of indigenous population centers

copal(li)   N. incense

corregidor   S. royal official who served as governor of a district

criollo   S. a person born in the Indies of Spain-born parents

cuacu   M. image

cuana betao   Z. *Turbina corymbosa*; see ololiuhqui

doctrina   S. administrative unit established by missionaries, roughly equivalent to a parish

encomendero   S. possessor of an encomienda

encomienda   S. grant of a group of natives for labor and to pay tribute

escribano   S. notary

fanega   S. dry measure equal to about 1.6 bushels

fiscal (indígena)   S. native charged with supervising Christian practices in a locality; a nonindigenous fiscal was a court prosecutor

guechea   Z. a malevolent ritual specialist

huehuetl   N. large drum

huija tao   Z. "Great Seer," high Zapotec priest

intendencia   S. political division introduced in 1786, when 116 civil jurisdictions were grouped into nine intendencias

juez de comisión   S. commissioned judge

laní   Z. a single day in the Zapotec 260-day count

licenciado   S. title for the holder of an advanced university degree

legua   S. league; a linear measure equal to 4.19 km

macehualli   N. commoner; *macehualtin*, pl.

maestro de idolatría   S. "teacher of idolatry," a ritual specialist who instructed others

memorial   S. formal document addressed to the king or his representatives

mestizo   S. a person of mixed indigenous and Spanish origin

ñuu   M. Mixtec polity

obraje   S. a workshop or mill requiring physically demanding labor

oidor   S. judge of the high court

ololiuhqui   N. *Turbina corymbosa*

Omnímoda   S. "Exponi Nobis," 1522 papal bull granting temporary episcopal powers to regulars

ordinario   S. sitting bishop or archbishop in a see

peso   S. monetary unit equal to 28.7 grams, eight reales

peso de oro S. valued at 450 maravedís, equal to one castellano

piciyetl N. lime-cured tobacco used in rituals

pigana, bigana, vigana Z. young assistant to Zapotec ritual specialist

pilli N. noble

pipiltzintzintli N. possibly *Salvia divinorum*

piyè, biyè Z. time or time count; designates both the 260-day count, and a cycle of thirteen *yza*

pitào Z. deity, powerful being

principal S. prominent person in a town

provincial S. chief administrator of a mendicant province, chosen by election

provisor S. chief prosecutor in a diocesan tribunal; a *provisor de indios* investigated charges against natives in the diocese

pulque N. alcoholic beverage made from agave

pueblo de indios S. indigenous community legally recognized as such

queche, gueche, yeche, yetze Z. Zapotec polity

quetzalli N. beautiful green feather

quichi, guichi Z. native paper or written text

ración S. full appointment at the cathedral council; a lesser appointment was a *media ración*

real S. monetary unit equal to one-eighth of a peso

real patronato S. faculty granted by the Vatican to the kings of Spain allowing them to collect church and appoint candidates for ecclesiastical posts in the Indies

regidor S. town councilman

relación S. account, chronicle

repartimiento de efectos (or *de mercancías*) S. the forced sale of goods to natives at an artificially high price

residencia S. conduct of affairs of an official after his term of office

sujeto S. subject town

temazcalli N. sweat bath

tenexietl N. type of tobacco with a wide ritual usage

teocalli N. temple

teotl N. deity, borrowed into Spanish as *teule*

teponaztli N. small, hollow, wooden drum with two musical tones

tequitlahto N. labor draft official

tetlachihuianih N. malevolent specialists

teyollocuanih N. "Human Heart Eaters," malevolent specialists

títulos primordiales S. "primordial titles," or indigenous foundational narratives, sometimes backdated to early colonial times

tlacateccatl N. military title for captive takers

tlacochcalcatl　N. military title for captive takers

tlamacazqui　N. priest

tlahtoani　N. ruler, speaker, king

topil　N. minor town official

tzitzimimeh　N. skeletal supernatural entities associated
with creation events and the end of eras in Nahua cosmology

vara　S. linear unit of measure equal to 0.84 meters, about 33 inches

vecino　S. resident, head of household

vicario foráneo　S. adjunct vicar

vicario y juez eclesiástico　S. vicar and ecclesiastic judge

visitador　S. royal inspector

volador　S. native dancer who descends from a tall pole attached by a rope

xihuitl　N. a 365-day divided into eighteen 20-day periods and a 5-day period
　　when *nemi ontemi*, "one lives in vain"

yza　Z. a 365-day year structurally similar to the *xihuitl*

SOURCES: AHJO; Córdova 1578a, 1578b; Covarrubias [1611] 1994; Molina [1571] 1992; Sahagún 1950–1982.

Abbreviations

ACM	Archivo del Cabildo Catedralicio de México	
	-L	Legajos
	-Litig	Litigios
AGEO	Archivo General del Estado de Oaxaca (Mexico)	
	-AM	Alcaldes Mayores
	-Obisp	Obispado de Oaxaca
AGI	Archivo General de Indias (Spain)	
	-Cont	Contratación
	-Escr	Escribanía
	-Indif	Indiferente General
	-Inq	Inquisición
	-Just	Justicia
	-Merc	Libro de Mercedes
	-Mex	Audiencia de México
	-MP	Mapas y Planos
	-Patr	Patronato
AGN	Archivo General de la Nación (Mexico)	
	-AM	Alcaldes Mayores
	-BN	Bienes Nacionales
	-Carc	Cárceles y Presidios
	-Civ	Civil
	-Cler	Clero Regular y Secular
	-Crim	Criminal
	-GPar	General de Parte
	-Ind	Indios
	-Inq	Inquisición
	-Jud	Judicial

-Matr	Matrimonios
-RC	Reales Cédulas
-Tier	Tierras
-UE	Unidad Eclesiástica

AGOP   Archivio Generale dell'Ordine dei Predicatori (Italy)
    -SH   Provincia S. Hyppoliti

AGPEO   Archivo General del Poder Ejecutivo del Estado de Oaxaca (Mexico)

AGSA   Archivio Generale dell'Ordine di Sant'Agostino (Italy)

AHAM   Archivo Histórico del Arzobispado de México (Mexico)

Cajas   (indicated by number)
    -Var   Varios

AHAO   Archivo Histórico del Arzobispado de Oaxaca (Mexico)
    -Dioc   Diocesano / Gobierno
    -LCab   Libros de Cabildo
    -Mart   Mártires de Caxonos

AHJO   Archivo Histórico del Poder Judicial de Oaxaca (Mexico)
    -TEP   Archivo Judicial de Teposcolula
    -Civ   Civil
    -Crim   Criminal
    -VA   Archivo Judicial de Villa Alta
    -Civ   Civil
    -Crim   Criminal
    -YAU   Archivo Judicial de Yautepec

AHN   Archivo Histórico Nacional (Spain)
    -DocInd   Documentos de Indias
    -Inq   Inquisición

ALC   Archivo del Lic. Luis Castañeda (Mexico)

AMO   Archivo Parroquial de La Merced, Oaxaca (Mexico)

ANO   Archivo de Notarías del Estado de Oaxaca (Mexico)
    -Álvarez   José Álvarez Aragón
    -Benaias   Diego Benaias

APF   Archivio di Propaganda Fide (Italy)
    -SOCG   Scritti Originale Riferite alla Congregazione Generale

ARAO   Archivo de la Reforma Agraria del Estado de Oaxaca (Mexico)

ASV	Archivio Segreto Vaticano (Vatican)
-AC	Ad Cardenali
-Arm	Armadii
-AV	Ad Vescovi
-BulPr	Bullae Praedicatorum
-ReLat	Registri Laterani
-SecBr	Secretariae Brevi
-SS	Secretaria di Stato
BBO	Biblioteca Francisco de Burgoa, Oaxaca (Mexico)
-DomGob	Dominicos Gobierno
BCN	Biblioteca Centrale Nazionale (Italy)
-Gesu	Fondo Gesuitico
BMNA	Biblioteca del Museo Nacional de Antropología (Mexico)
-ColAnt	Colección Antigua
BNE	Biblioteca Nacional de España (Spain)
BNF	Bibliothèque Nationale de France
-Mex	Fonds Mexicain
BNM	Biblioteca Nacional de México
-Imp	Impresos
BRAH	Biblioteca de la Real Academia de Historia (Spain)
-MemNE	Memorias de la Nueva España
BRP	Biblioteca del Real Palacio, Madrid (Spain)
JCB	John Carter Brown Library (USA)
-CodInd	Codex Indianorum
-CodSp	Codex Spaniorum
MNAM	Museo Nacional de Arte (Mexico)
NL	Newberry Library (USA)
-Ayer	Edward Ayer Collection
RBE	Real Biblioteca de El Escorial (Spain)
TL	Tozzer Library, Harvard University (USA)
TRO	Tropenmuseum, Amsterdam (Netherlands)

Notes

Chapter 1

1. An *encomienda* was a royal grant to conquerors and their descendants of a group of natives; the encomendero collected tribute and was expected to foster native evangelization. Most encomiendas reverted to the crown by the late sixteenth century. At least another Villa Alta encomienda besides Lachirioag lasted into the eighteenth century (Gerhard 1972, 372).

2. The most commonly used monetary units in New Spain were the peso and the real. One peso equaled eight reales; one real divided into halves, quarters, and eighths. The daily wages for a nonindentured agricultural laborer ranged between two and three reales.

3. AHJO-VA Crim 23, 42v–44r.

4. Ibid., 71r; my emphasis.

5. See Tavárez 2002, for a full version of this argument.

6. Gruzinski 1989; Pardo 2004.

7. Cervantes 1994; Gruzinski 2002; MacCormack 1991.

8. Balsalobre [1656] 1892, 234.

9. In this work I employ standardized spellings for Classical Nahuatl and Spanish terms. Recurring Zapotec terms reflect the Valley Zapotec orthography used in Córdova 1578b. Nahua and Spanish personal and place names are spelled as they appear in documents, but I modernized the spelling if several variants exist. I have added orthographic accents to proper names, following usage in Mexican historical journals. All translations from the Nahuatl, Zapotec, Spanish, Italian, Latin, and French are my own, unless otherwise noted.

10. Clendinnen 1987; García Icazbalceta 1947; Greenleaf 1962, 1965, 1969, 1985, 1991; Gruzinski 1985, 1988, 1993; Jiménez Moreno and Mateos 1940; Klor de Alva 1981, 1982, 1991; Lafaye 1976; Lea 1906; Medina 1905; Moreno de los Arcos 1991; Padden 1970; Ricard 1966; Scholes and Adams 1938, 1952; Scholes and Roys 1938; Terraciano 2001; Sepúlveda y Herrera 1999.

11. Alcina Franch 1993, 1998; Berlin 1988; Coe and Whittaker 1982; Gruzinski 1988; Lara Cisneros 2002; Ruiz de Alarcón 1984; Sáenz de Santa María 1969.

12. There exist eight Mixtec historical records and four Maya calendrical texts produced before the conquest (Boone 2007).

13. Isthmus Zapotec local history is represented in the various versions of the *lienzos*, pictorial documents painted on cloth, of Guevea, Petapa, and Huilotepec; Valley Zapotec history is depicted through the genealogies of Macuilxochitl, Quialoo, and San Lucas Quiaviní; Sierra Zapotec history is represented in the lienzos of Tabaá and Tiltepec (Oudijk 2000).

14. Postclassic refers to the period between AD 750–800 and contact time (1519). The Late Postclassic covers the time between the early fourteenth century and 1519.

15. De la Serna 1892; Edmonson 1988; Quiñones Keber 1995.

16. Córdova 1578b, 400v.

17. Córdova 1578a, 202–4.

18. Caso 1965, 932.

19. Kaufman 2000; Justeson and Tavárez 2007.

20. See Sahagún 1981, book 2, for a description of the xihuitl. Regarding the debate about preconquest leap year corrections in Mesoamerica, see Prem 2008, 89–99; Tena 1987, 61–75.

21. Tavárez and Justeson 2008; Urcid 2001.

22. Córdova 1578b, 332v; *yeche, yetze,* or *quetze* in other Zapotec variants.

23. Berdan et al. 1996; Lockhart 1992; and Schroeder 1991 analyze altepetl structure.

24. See, for instance, López Austin 1973a.

25. Bourdieu 1971.

26. Farriss 1984, 294–97.

27. Departing from Robin Horton's (1971, 1975) microcosm-macrocosm conversion model for sub-Saharan Africa, Farriss proposed that both Christian and Mesoamerican ritual practices were organized into three social categories: universal, parochial, and private. However, as Stanley Tambiah (1990, 131) lucidly suggests, in Horton's model the macrocosmic level may be understood as a veiled form of monotheism. My model addresses this criticism by proposing that the universal sphere is intrinsically linked to "parochial" and private levels.

28. Asad 1986.

29. Durkheim [1912] 2001, 257.

30. Kirchhoff, Odena Güemes, and Reyes García 1989.

31. Sugiyama 2004.

32. See López Austin and López Luján 2009 for an exhaustive interpretation of the structure and iconography of the Templo Mayor in Tenochtitlan. For other Mesoamerican ceremonial centers, see Joyce 2004; Marcus and Flannery 1996; Sugiyama 2004.

33. Marcus and Flannery 1996; Sahagún 1950–1982, 1990.

34. Sahagún 1950–1982.

35. In their analysis of blood witchcraft in Tlaxcala, Nutini and Roberts (1993, 14) embrace an ontological distinction between witchcraft and sorcery "regardless of whether it is made on the ground by the actors themselves."

36. López Austin 1967a.

37. Murray 1962; Ginzburg 1992; Henningsen 1980; Kieckhefer 1976.

38. Evans-Pritchard 1965; Tambiah 1981.

39. Kelly and Kaplan 1990.

40. Sahlins 1985.

41. Turner 1977.

42. Halbertal and Margalit 1992.

43. Aquinas 1948, 476–77: *Summa Theologiae*, Quaestio XCIV, Articulus 1.

44. Aquinas 1948, 481–82: *Summa Theologiae*, Quaestio XCIV, Articulus 4. For a précis of the link between idolatry and blasphemy in Aquinas, see Villa-Flores 2006, 23.

45. Bernand and Gruzinski 1992, 209–10.

46. This term is analyzed as *tla-teo-toqui-liz-tli*; Lockhart (2001, 239) notes that *toca* means considering something to be something else, "usually without sufficient grounds."

47. This solution appears in Feria 1567 and in various Northern Zapotec texts. Córdova (1578b, 227v) lists *quela pezèlào*, an abstract noun based on the name of the Lord of the Underworld; *quela huezàa*, "the giving," and *quela huezète*, "adoration." Feria's formula prevailed.

48. See Isaiah 40:18–20, 44, 9–20; Jeremiah 10:1–5; and Habakkuk 2:18–19 (Halbertal and Margalit 1992, 19). Aquinas's *Summa* (1948, 481) cites Proverbs 21, noting that images of wood and stone were made in antiquity out of affection for departed rulers.

49. Ginzburg 1985; for a critique, see Rosaldo 1986.

50. Bernand and Gruzinski 1992.

51. Balsalobre [1656] 1892, 251–60; and Sánchez de Aguilar 1892, 31–74.

52. Villavicencio 1692.

53. See *Jacobellis v. Ohio*, 378 U.S. 184 (1964), a decision written by Justice Potter Stewart.

54. Certeau 1982, 1988; Christian 1981b; Ginzburg 1980, 1985.

55. Duviols 1971, 2003; Griffiths 1995; Griffiths and Cervantes 1999; MacCormack 1991; Millones 1979; Mills 1997; Salomon 1987; Wachtel 1992.

56. Chuchiak 2000; Viqueira 1997a.

57. Alberro 1988; Berlin 1988; Greenleaf 1985; Sánchez de Aguilar 1892, 17–122.

58. For an overview of the legal adjudication of indigenous and casta status, see Cope 1988. Tavárez 2009a analyzes three seventeenth-century cases in which inquisitors adjudicated the status of defendants claiming indigenous identities.

59. For some examples of clergy appointed as jueces de comisión contra idolatrías in Mexico, see AGN-Inq UE 182, no. 4 (1584); AGN-Inq 303 (1624); AGN-Inq 776, no. 25 (1724). For Oaxaca, see AGN-Inq 249, no. 23 (ca. 1600); AGN-Inq 573-I (1656); AGI-Indif 216, no. 140 (1703); AGI-Indif 217, no. 33 (1704). These titles and faculties are based on juridical practice in Mexico and Oaxaca; Chuchiak 2000 provides a discussion of somewhat diverging arrangements in Yucatán's Provisorato de Indios.

60. For Oaxaca, see AGI-Indif 3000, no. 217 (ca. 1616); AGI-Mex 355 (1620); AGN-Inq 573 (1656). For Mexico, see AGI-Mex 337 (1610).

61. For Oaxaca, see AGN-Inq 249, no. 23 (1596); AGI-Mex 878 (1703).

62. For Mexico, see AGN-Inq 674, no. 26 (1688); AHAM 18, no. 36 (1691);

ACM-Litig 7–17.1, 1363–64 (1729); for Oaxaca, see AGN-BN 1076, no. 10 (1674); AGI-Indif 300, no. 229 (1702); AGN-Inq 734 (1705); AGN-Inq 898, no. 55 (1746); AGN-Inq 960, no. 17 (1750, 1752).

63. Civil native idolatry and sorcery trials in Mexico begin by 1530 with the trial of the Phurépecha Caltzontzi (Scholes and Adams 1952) and continue at least until 1737 (AGN-Inq 862, no. 36). In Oaxaca, they begin in the 1530s (AGI-Just 191, no. 2) and continue until 1800 (AHJO-TEP Crim 1285).

64. Scholes and Adams 1952, 45–68.

65. In September 1539, former native priest Tlilanci underwent water torture in Izúcar. Since he did not confess and the evidence against him was weak, he was absolved (González Obregón 1912, 189–90).

66. González Obregón 1912, 138–39; see Chapter 2 below.

67. AGN-Inq 42, no. 20; see Chapter 2 below.

68. AGI-Mex 358, no. 7; Burgoa [1674] 1989, vol. 2, 88–92; see Chapter 2 below.

69. AGI-Mex 358, no. 3 bis; see Chapter 2 below.

70. ALC 1270-3, 58–110; AHAO-Mart S-4, 550–603; see Chapter 8 below.

71. Spicer 1967.

72. Taylor 1996, 48.

73. Ginzburg 1979, 186.

74. The following data are not included in my quantitative analysis: seven natives punished by Ponce de León in 1610 (AGI-Mex 337); twenty-six Juquila specialists disciplined by Sariñana in 1690 (AGI-Mex 357); and seventy maestros jailed by Santiago y Calderón in 1734 (AGI-Mex 877).

75. AGN-Inq 1282, no. 11.

76. AGN-Crim 308, no. 1.

77. Lara Cisneros 2002, 148.

78. Gerhard 1972, 17–18.

79. Smith 1992, 114.

Chapter 2

1. In the Late Postclassic, a ruler's calendrical name was rarely used in public monuments (Emily Umberger, personal communication, 1996). However, don Carlos's calendrical name was used in trial records and in a 1564 letter by Juan de San Antonio of Tetzcoco (Chimalpahin 1997, vol. 2, 225, 227).

2. AGN-Inq 1305, no. 13, 37r; see Chapter 9 below.

3. González Obregón 1910, 29, 83.

4. García Icazbalceta 1947; Greenleaf 1962, 1969, 1985; Ricard 1966; Gruzinski 1993.

5. Klor de Alva 1991.

6. Aguirre Beltrán 1963; Alberro 1988; Baudot 1990, 1995; Greenleaf 1962, 1969, 1985; Gruzinski 1988, 1993, 2002; Kubler 1948; Klor de Alva 1982, 1991, 1999; Moreno de los Arcos 1991; Ricard 1966.

7. Aquinas 1948, 481–82: *Summa Theologiae*, Quaestio XCIV, Articulus 4.

8. Burkhart 1989, 175.

9. In his first extant letter, Gante identified himself as Peter van der Moer of Ayghem, near Ghent (Gante in Spanish). This 1529 text, which contains one of the earliest evangelization accounts from New Spain, was published in Zierikzeee 1534.

10. This group of Franciscans included Motolinia, Valencia, and Ciudad Real (Ricard 1966, 21–23).

11. Baudot 1990; Schwaller 1987.

12. Diego Valadés (1579, 222), Gante's student and personal secretary, recorded this refusal.

13. Letter from Gante to the Franciscans of Flanders, 1529 (Torre Villar 1973, 74). For a discussion of this school, see Burkhart 1996; Kobayashi 1974.

14. *Ca ye ixquich i*[n] *ma moteneoa y*[n] *toteoh yn totlatucauh y*[n] *Iesu Christo,* or "This is all. May our deity, our Lord Jesus Christ be praised" (Zierikzee 1534, 127r).

15. There are forty-two extant pictorial catechisms from Mexico; similar works also existed in Peru. Some have glosses in Nahuatl, Otomi, Mazahua, or Spanish. Normann 1985 provides a systematic stylistic categorization. Individual catechisms have been analyzed among others by Dean 1989; Galarza 1980. Along with Elizabeth Boone and Louise Burkhart, I am currently involved in a collaborative analysis of BNF-Mex 399, an unusual pictorial catechism from San Sebastián Atzacualco with annotations from several readers.

16. There exist surviving Nahuatl texts only from Escalona, Gante, and Olmos (A. León-Portilla 1988; Zulaica y Gárate [1939] 1991).

17. Gante 1547, [1553] 1981.

18. Dominican Order 1550.

19. Cruz and Badiano 1940.

20. See Reyes García 2002.

21. RBE d-IV-7; JCB-CodInd 23. Torquemada ([1615] 1969, 436) states that Rodríguez translated the proverbs of Solomon, and the "four books of the *Contemptus mundi,* although the last twenty chapters were missing from the third book; those were recently translated by Father fray Juan Bautista [Viseo] while he was the Guardian of Tetzcoco."

22. Burgoa [1674] 1989, vol. 2, 126.

23. Burgoa [1674] 1989, vol. 1, 267.

24. See, for instance, J. Anunciación 1575, 1577; Bautista Viseo 1599, 1600a, 1600b, 1606; Molina [1546] 1675, [1569] 1984, [1571] 1992; Sahagún [1583] 1993.

25. Lockhart 1992, 1994.

26. Terraciano 2001, 92.

27. Greenleaf 1985, 20–21. However, Lea (1906, vol. 3, 196) held that, in the absence of licensed American ecclesiastical authorities, the Audiencia designated Inquisition officials directly. Thus, when Córdoba died in 1525, the Audiencia would have named Martín de Valencia commissary of the Holy Office.

28. See García Icazbalceta 1881, 112, who quotes book 3, chaps. 4–6 of Mendieta's *Historia.*

29. Medina 1905, I, 114. Moreno de los Arcos (1991, 34), following an

interpretation that dates back to Agustín Dávila Padilla, proposes that Valencia obtained inquisitorial faculties by an application of the Omnímoda.

30. Medina 1905, I, 115, 120.

31. AGN-Inq 40, no. 4. Juan Fernández del Castillo was accused of obtaining a dog-shaped effigy from a native. There also exists a 1528 accusation against an indigenous woman who served Fernando Morzillo's wife (AGN-Inq 1, no. 27, 138r). Nineteenth-century indices list a proceeding (AGN-Inq 1, no. 1) for cohabitation against a native called Marcos, but this document is no longer extant.

32. See Phelan 1970, for a discussion of Fiore's influence on Franciscan millenarist thought.

33. Zierikzee 1534, 126r–27r, 123v–24r, 122r–23r.

34. For a sobering view on multitudinous baptisms, see Cline 1993.

35. Mendieta 1997, vol. 2, 283–84 (book 5, chap. 9).

36. Greenleaf (1962, xx) notes that García Icazbalceta claimed that Valencia presided over the execution of natives.

37. Motolinia [1858] 1990, 34.

38. Mendieta 1997, vol. 1, 385–93 (book 3, chaps. 24–26). A shorter account probably derived from Mendieta appears in Muñoz Camargo 1998, 237–39.

39. BNAH, Colección Antigua 273 (II), 739, *Anales antiguos de México y sus contornos*, José F. Ramírez. The *Anales de Diego García* (ibid., 983) state that Valencia had these Tlaxcalteca lords hanged (Sepúlveda y Herrera 1999, 37).

40. Muñoz Camargo 1981, 216v, 262v.

41. Mendieta 1997, vol. 1, 394–97 (book 3, chap. 27). This event is retold in Muñoz Camargo 1998, 239–41; however, unlike Mendieta, Muñoz Camargo asserts this act went unpunished.

42. BNAH, Colección Antigua 273 (II), 914, *Anales antiguos de México y sus contornos*, José F. Ramírez (Sepúlveda y Herrera 1999, 39).

43. BNF-Mex 303.

44. Elliott 2006, 120–21.

45. López 1576, 73v–64r.

46. Scholes and Adams 1952.

47. AGI-Just 191, no. 2, cited throughout this paragraph. This is the earliest extant idolatry case from Oaxaca.

48. Native elites were occasionally punished with *aperreamientos* in early postconquest times. An indigenous artist portrayed the aperreamiento of seven Coyohuacan lords by Cortés (BNF-Mex 374) in a vivid drawing modeled after a European illustration (Gruzinski, personal communication, 1998).

49. None of these witnesses had a Christian name; they were designated instead by their Zapotec calendrical names. The Spanish notary's transcription of these names is not precise enough to yield an unambiguous interpretation. Yagaeche is 1-Lizard or 1-Jaguar, Bineche is 12-Lizard or 12-Jaguar, Guezalao is 13-Monkey, 13-Crow, or 13-Face, and Nalao is 4-Crow, 4- or 8-Monkey, or 11-Face.

50. Paul III named López de Zárate as first bishop of Oaxaca on July 11, 1535 (ASV-ReLat 1615, 238v–40r).

51. Martínez Sola 1998.

52. Cummins 2003.

53. In his 1529 letter, Gante states that certain priests "did not have wives, and in their stead they had boys, whom they abused" (Zierikzee 1534, 125v).

54. Greenleaf 1962, 41.

55. Kubler 1948, vol. 1, 10.

56. Greenleaf 1962, 35.

57. Zumárraga's title, giving him full powers as inquisitorial judge, appears in García Icazbalceta 1881, 78–79.

58. AGN-Inq 40, no. 2.

59. AGN-Inq 40, no. 8; González Obregón 1910, 205–15.

60. AGN-Inq 30, no. 7A. This vicar used inquisitorial faculties without specifying their source, but may have acted under Omnímoda provisions.

61. González Obregón 1912, 85–89. Aguilar punished Suchicalcatl, Tezcacoatl, and Collin, and he seized cult effigies at a cave near the Augustinian monastery.

62. NL Ayer Ms 1277.

63. AGN-Inq 37, no. 1, vs. Francisco for bigamy; AGN-Inq 34, no. 6, vs. Tomás and María for cohabitation.

64. Gibson 1964; Greenleaf 1962, 1969, 1991; Grunberg 1998; Gruzinski 1988, 1993, 2001; Klor de Alva 1981, 1982, 1991; Moreno de los Arcos 1991; Padden 1970; Ricard 1966.

65. The careers of Olmos and other early missionary authors are discussed in Baudot 1995.

66. The first edition of *Reprobación* appeared circa 1530 and a second edition printed in 1541 (Christian 1981a, chap. 4; Ciruelo 1977).

67. Olmos [1553] 1990, 42: *yuhqui yn tlatoani mochichiuhticatca, yn iuh mochichiuayah tlatoque ye uecauh yn iquac mahceuaya.*

68. Cervantes 1994.

69. Molina ([1571] 1992, 63r–v) defines *nahualli* as "witch" and *nahuallotl* as "necromancy." In any case, there is a broad semantic field covered by verbal compounds employing the nominal root *nahual-*, which include deceit (*nitenahuallia*), stalking (*nahuallachia*), and mistrust (*nitenahualhuica*).

70. González Obregón 1912, 179.

71. Ibid., 180–82.

72. Tetepanquetzal and Cuauhtemoc were hanged in Honduras in 1525, after a swift trial in which Cortés accused them of plotting against him (Chimalpahin 1997, vol. 1, 169).

73. These nine defendants were Antonio Tlacatec[c]atl or Tlacateuctli, an Otomi priest exiled from Tlanocopan in 1536 (González Obregón 1912, 15); Martín Tlacochcalcatl, Francisco Huycinabal, and Pedro Tlacatec[c]atl of Atzcapotzalco, punished in Atzcapotzalco and in the public markets of Mexico in 1538 (ibid., 107); Marcos Hernández Atlabcatl, judge and principal of Tlatelolco, punished in the Tlatelolco market, barred from holding office, and exiled for two years in 1539 (ibid., 110); Cristóbal, cacique of Ocuituco, whipped in the streets of Mexico along with his wife Catalina and sentenced to three years' hard labor at the mines in 1539 (ibid., 172–74); Don Juan, cacique

of Matlactlan, punished with four lashes and sentenced to sit among children at a doctrinal school (AGN-Inq 40, no. 8); and don Carlos Chichimecateuctli, of Tetzcoco.

74. Foucault 1977, 34.

75. Ibid.; see also 23–30.

76. Chimalpahin 1997, vol. 2, 40, *auh ynic tlatiloc tlateotoquiliztli ytech tlan.* For a discussion of Chimalpahin's works, see Schroeder 1991; and Schroeder, Cruz, Roa-de-la-Carrera, and Tavárez 2010.

77. BNF-Mex 217, 6v.

78. For preconquest lords and rulers "the title of office acted almost like a second appellation" (Lockhart 1992, 118).

79. According to Sahagún (1950–1982, book 1, 55), the taker of four captives in battle was called "the tlacateccatl, the tlacochcalcatl, the *quauhtlahto*." These title holders belonged to a war council called Tequioacacalli or Quauhcalli (ibid., book 8, 43). Chimalpahin asserted that Itzcoatl was the first to bestow the titles of tlacateccatl and tlacochcalcatl (Schroeder 1991, 173).

80. Carrasco 1984, 60.

81. Lockhart 1992, 485. According to Rémi Siméon (1984, 559), Vetancourt and Clavijero (1945) defined tlacateccatl as one of three titles for three "judges" in preconquest tribunals, the remaining ones being *cuauhnochtli* and *tlailotlac.*

82. González Obregón 1912, 5–7.

83. Ibid., 56, 57, 63.

84. Gruzinski 2001, 30–60. For an analysis of the Israelite conception of idols, see Halbertal and Margalit 1992.

85. AGN-Inq 212, no. 7, 39v.

86. In November 1538, three principales, Martín the Tlacochcalcatl, Pedro the Tlacateuctli, and Francisco Huycinabal from Atzcapotzalco were brought before Zumárraga, along with cult effigies of Huitzilopochtli, Tlalocateotl, Cihuacoatl, "Tlamacinga," and "Cialeuque" found in their houses. These men confessed to having ordered some of their associates to observe a hundred-day seclusion period away from women to honor Tezcatlipoca, and one of Pedro's associates said he ordered him to adopt the Matlatzinca calendrical name "Evatuto" (González Obregón 1912, 100–104), perhaps a corruption of *In thaati*, "Wind" (Caso 1945, 108).

87. AGN-Inq 37, no. 3.

88. Chimalpahin 1997, vol. 1, 169.

89. If Tlacochcalcatl Nanahuatzin was indeed appointed native ruler of Mexico, he would have held this title circa 1524–25. Chimalpahin (1997, vol. 2, 38–39) wrote that, after Cuauhtemoc's execution in 1525, Cortés appointed two noblemen as rulers: first, don Juan Velásquez Tlacotzin, who died before taking office, and then don Andrés de Tapia Motelchiutzin.

90. González Obregón 1912, 117.

91. Schroeder (1991, 210) notes that some rulers and calpolli heads bore the title of tlailotlac, perhaps originally an ethnic designation linked to Tlailotlacan, one of Tetzcoco's six subdivisions (Offner 1983, 111). Lockhart (1992, 39, 485) notes that the main official of Coyoacán held the title of Mixcoatlailotlac.

92. González Obregón 1912, 122. Francisco gave their names as Tocoal, Culua, Totepeu, Ciguateque Paueca, Chachicinayotecatl, Culua Tlapisque [Colhua Tlapixqui], and Achicatl [Achacatl].

93. González Obregón 1912, 177–78. Besides Huitzilopochtli and Quetzalcoatl, the only other major deity in this list is "Heart of the Community" (*Altepetl Iyollo*). The "wind figure" may refer to Ehecatl; Macuiltonale figures in an incantation recorded a century later (Ruiz de Alarcón 1984, 230); Macuyl Masiciual granted success in war after her image was wrapped in the flayed skin of a male victim.

94. González Obregón 1912, 21–27.

95. Torquemada [1615] 1969, 84.

96. González Obregón 1912, 60, 67.

97. Gruzinski 1988, 37–38.

98. Ibid., 25, 26.

99. Ibid., 60, 64.

100. Sahagún 1950–1982, book 10, 192: *Ic quitoque in vevetque, in aqujn oonmjc oteut, qujtoaia, ca on-teut, q, n, ca oonmjc. auh injc motlapololtique, in aço ic tlacamachozque in tlatoque catca, mochintin moteotocaque, in jquac mjcque. Cequjntin qujnmjxiptlatique tonatiuh, cequjintin metztli.*

101. See, for instance, Kirchhoff, Odena Güemes, and Reyes García 1989.

102. López Austin 1973a.

103. Molina [1571] 1992, 45v, 95v; he also lists the terms *nicnixiptlayotia*, "I make something in my own image," and *niteixiptlati*, "I assist in someone's place, or I represent someone in a play." The nominal root *-ixiptla* is an inalienable possession and as such has no absolutive ending: it is either "someone's substitute" (*te-ixiptla*), or "X's substitute" (*i-ixiptla*). Clendinnen (1990, 122) mistakenly uses *-ixiptla* as if it could be detached from its referent and mistranslates it as "god-representation."

104. Sahagún 1950–1982, book 10, 143: *yn uel quimoteotia tla[l]ticpac.*

105. Sahagún 1950–1982, book 2, 61, 62, 64, 143, 148, 150.

106. Ibid., 122.

107. Ibid., 66; see also Durán 1967.

108. Hvidtfeldt 1958, 82–89, 95.

109. Sahagún 1950–1982, book 2, 66: *ypampa ca nel ye ytlaçoteouh ypan quimati.*

110. González Obregón 1912, 56.

111. Weber 1968, I, 114.

112. González Obregón 1912, 60.

113. Sahagún 1986, quoted in Nicholson 1971, 410.

114. The thesis that political intrigue played a role in this trial is not novel; García Icazbalceta (1947) considered this possibility, as well as Ricard (1966, 273), who refused to pass judgment on it.

115. González Obregón 1910, 2–7, 39–48, 48–54. Francisco's, Cristóbal's, and don Alonso's accounts converged on all substantial points, and they ratified their testimony on September 24 (73–75).

116. González Obregón 1910, 6.

117. AGN-Inq 30, no. 7A.

118. González Obregón 1910, 3, 41.

119. Ibid., 59, 43. This speech figure was recorded in Spanish at trial.

120. Ibid., 42, 45, 46.

121. AGN-Civ 1271, no. 5, 173r.

122. Chimalpahin 1997, vol. 2, 40–41: *çan tlatilloc yn tlacatl Don carlos ahuachpitzactzin tlatohuani tetzcuco yn tlahtocat chiuhcnauhxihuitl* [. . .] *fiscal catca yn ihquac yn ypan inyn don fr. Juan de çumarraga obispo achto Mexico.*

123. Both Ricard (1966) and Greenleaf (1962), following Chimalpahin, believed that don Carlos became ruler of Tetzcoco in 1531. Nonetheless, Gibson (1964, 170, 511) noted, as I do below in greater detail, that several statements made at the trial showed that don Carlos was still a pretender to the rulership in the summer of 1539 (AGN-Inq 2, no. 10, 253r, 259v, and 263v).

124. González Obregón 1910, 67.

125. Don Carlos is called "principal and vecino" at the beginning of the trial (González Obregón 1910, 1). Elsewhere, he is designated as "principal" (ibid., 14), "vecino" (ibid., 48), and "Indian" (ibid., 69, 79). The only exception to this pattern occurs in Cristóbal's deposition, who referred to don Carlos as cacique once in passing (ibid., 5). During his interrogation, don Carlos never called himself a cacique (ibid., 55).

126. Chimalpahin 1997, vol. 2, 200–203. This account was penned by don Pablo Ahuachpain, don Francisco de Andrada, don Lorenzo, or a fourth anonymous principal. For a discussion of succession procedures in Tenochtitlan and Tetzcoco in the early colonial period, see Gibson 1964, 168–73.

127. Ibid., 194–99. Although don Carlos's age is not overtly stated at trial, during his interrogation he states that he was married in the church around 1535 and that he was baptized fifteen years earlier (González Obregón 1910, 56); he also had a natural son aged ten or eleven in 1539 (ibid., 37).

128. González Obregón 1910, 33–35. Carrasco (1984) observed that the remarriage of Nahua widowed noblewomen with their former husbands' brothers prevented the splitting of patrimonial lands.

129. Ibid., 32–33.

130. Ibid., 56; Chimalpahin 1997, vol. 2, 224–27.

131. Don (2010) speculated that don Carlos took office either in late February or early March (198), or in April or May 1539 (172), and surmised that all mentions to him as tlahtoani were redacted after his death (188). Nonetheless, as noted above, don Pedro's own widow dated his demise to late April 1539 at the earliest, no extant sixteenth-century evidence confirms don Carlos's appointment as tlahtoani, and Chimalpahin, the main Nahua annalist who identified don Carlos as a ruler, did so some sixty years after the Tetzcoca's execution.

132. Carrasco 1984, 46.

133. González Obregón 1912, 89, 97.

134. AGN-Inq 30, no. 7A.

135. González Obregón 1912, 202.

136. AGN-Inq 212, no. 7, 30r–35r.

137. González Obregón 1910, 66–79.

138. Ibid., 84; Ricard 1966, 196.

139. Greenleaf 1962, 74; Greenleaf 1985, 123; Lea 1906, vol. 3, 210.

140. AGN-Inq 212, no. 7, 51r–52r (regarding don Pedro), and 71r (regarding don Antón).

141. Ibid., 57r, 61r (don Pedro), 77v, 78r (don Antón).

142. García Icazabalceta, cited in Klor de Alva 1991, 13.

143. Ibid., 63r and 64r (don Pedro), 80r (don Antón). In don Pedro's case, Rodrigo de Albornoz, the crown's accountant and a leading encomendero, posted one thousand pesos de oro as guarantee.

144. ASV-Arm XLI 39, 253r.

145. Zumárraga's testament is transcribed in García Icazbalceta 1881, 176–81.

146. Greenleaf 1969, 75.

147. A fragmentary proceeding circa 1546 against the caciques of Tamazulapa (AGN-Inq 37, no. 11 bis) is extant, but Tello de Sandoval did not intervene directly in it.

148. See Terraciano 2001, 279–83; and Sepúlveda y Herrera 1999.

149. AGN-Inq 37, no. 7.

150. Terraciano 2001, 262.

151. Sepúlveda y Herrera 1999, 80.

152. AGN-Inq 37, no. 10.

153. Ibid., no. 11.

154. Ibid., no. 10.

155. Ibid., no. 6; see also Terraciano 2001, 263, 273.

156. AGN-Inq 37, no. 11 bis. A transcription of this trial appears in Boletín del AGN, 1934.

157. Gerhard 1972, 160.

158. AGN-Inq 42, no. 20. The outcome of this proceeding is unknown.

159. Teotlalco was a corregimiento without a permanent doctrinal establishment; see Gerhard 1972, 310.

160. AGN-Inq 37, no. 12.

161. This was the Cohuixca polity of Tzompanco, a Triple Alliance tributary that became a mining center shortly after 1521 (Gerhard 1972, 316).

162. AGN-Inq 40, no. 9.

163. See Lorenzana 1769b; Huerga Teruelo 1991; Greenleaf (1969) gives a date of 1554 without citing a source.

164. Greenleaf 1985, 28.

165. Traslosheros 2002, 493–94; the cohabitation proceedings come from AGN-Matr. c. 128. Traslosheros observed that a provisor de indios was also mentioned in a 1561 cédula and a 1567 letter by Montúfar.

166. Greenleaf (1965, 141) believed that provisores de indios began investigating native heterodoxy only after 1571.

167. Ibid., 495–96.

168. This order is discussed in García Icazbalceta 1881, 9, who quotes AGI-Merc, vol. 3, 89r.

169. Reyes García 2002, 157–61; *q[uin]paquilli yn innequatequiliz* means, "he washed away their baptism." According to Reyes García, these annals,

which focus on events occurring between 1564 and 1569, were written by a group of Nahua authors that included a feather-work specialist, the escribanos Francisco Quauhtli and Domingo Leonardo, the writer Cristóbal Quauhtli, and an anonymous escribano. I thank García Garagarza (2010) for discussing his illuminating analysis of Teton's case with me. See Burkhart 1989, 42, 83, for a contextual discussion of the tzitzimimeh.

170. See Scholes and Adams 1938; Chuchiak 2005. Landa's native allies defended him in 1567 (AHN-DocInd 200), while his native enemies denounced him (AHN-DocInd 202). He successfully argued his actions were justified by the Omnímoda, and canonical experts decreed his use of force was not excessive.

171. Mörner 1970.

172. Gibson 1964.

173. For the Basin of Mexico, see Gibson 1964; for Toluca, see Menegus-Bornemann 1991; for Cuernavaca, see Haskett 1991.

174. Martínez Sola 1998, 300.

175. Except for Espinosa's exploits, recounted in *Palestra historial*, all these extirpators appear in *Geográfica descripción*.

176. Burgoa [1674] 1989, vol. 2, 339–59.

177. A recent interpretation of a 1554 *memorial* by don Juan Cortés in AGI-Escr 160b, no. 1 (Zeitlin 1994, 2003) suggests that Burgoa's account resulted from a merger of oral and written accounts. In this document, don Juan refers to his father and grandfather with the Nahuatl titles *Huizquiauitl* and *Yecaquiahuitl*, respectively. If these titles are read as *Itzquiyahuitl* (Flint Rain) and *ehecaquiyahuitl* (Wind Rain), it becomes clear that they are translations of the Zapotec titles *Cocijo* (qu)*eza* (Thunder Flint) and *Cocijo pij* (Thunder Wind). Based on the historical information provided by don Juan, Oudijk proposed that don Juan's grandfather was the original Cocijopij, conqueror of Tehuantepec, while don Juan's father was a certain Cocijoeza who died circa 1502 in Tehuantepec. Thus, the Cocijoeza known to Burgoa as a ruler in Zaachila would either be a historical character other than don Juan's father, or a conflation of several characters (Oudijk 2000, 34–40).

178. See Zeitlin 2005, chap. 2; and Zeitlin and Thomas 1992.

179. Zeitlin and Thomas 1992.

180. Burgoa [1674] 1989, vol. 2, 350; the text misspells the title as *Huipa too*. Burgoa glossed this term as "seer" and "watchtower," and Córdova (1578b, 299v) reported that *Huía tào* or *vuija táo* was a "pope or priest of the Devil; only he went in and offered sacrifices in his sanct[um] sanctorum, where the idols were."

181. A similar title, *Lachi Queche*, "Heart of the Town," appears in the Zapotec songs that will be discussed below in Chapter 7.

182. Burgoa [1674] 1989, vol. 2, 351. Furthermore, the jewels given as offerings were confiscated.

183. San Mateo Teiticpac, or Río Hondo, was in the jurisdiction of Cimatlán and Chichicapa. A corregimiento since 1534, Teiticpac was shaken by a native revolt in 1547 (AGI-Patr 181, ramo 11).

184. Burgoa [1674] 1989, vol. 2, 88–92.

185. AGI-Mex 358, no. 7.

186. Burgoa [1670] 1989, 96.

187. The Dominican mission was supported by a 1556 cédula; see Chance 1989.

188. BBO-DomGob 29.

189. AGI-Mex 358, no. 3 bis.

190. AGI-Mex 358.

191. In Guaxolotitlan, fray Matías de Puertocarrero and a fray Domingo imprisoned some natives with the support of the civil justice until they agreed to write the crown asking for more Dominicans (AGI-Mex 358, no. 10).

192. AGI-Mex 358.

193. Montúfar's difficulties continued until his death. In March 1568, he banished the cathedral's dean and imprisoned some seculars for plotting against him. Upon his death, the cathedral chapter asked the king in May 1572 that the new archbishop be a theologian competent in civil affairs, and not a mere friar (AGI-Mex 336 A).

194. Martínez Sola 1998, 302–13.

195. Cook and Borah (1979) may have overestimated preconquest and early colonial populations by taking at face value figures for newly converted Indians—six million in Central Mexico by 1540, according to Torquemada ([1615] 1969).

196. Sanders 1976, 1979.

197. Whitmore 1992.

198. See Coe and Whittaker 1982, 16.

199. In Central Mexico, multiregional epidemics occurred in 1520–21, 1545–48, 1576–80, 1595–97, and 1629–31, and regional epidemics took place in 1531, 1559–60, 1563–64, 1595, 1604–7, and 1633–34 (Gibson 1964; Cook and Lovell 1991).

200. Klor de Alva 1991.

201. Foucault 1977.

Chapter 3

1. Greenleaf 1985, 32; his source is Cuevas 1921–1928.

2. Medina 1905, vol. 1, 483, 488.

3. Lea 1906, vol. 1, 199.

4. Lea 1906; Greenleaf 1969.

5. A cédula issued on December 30, 1571, excluded Indians from the jurisdiction of the new inquisitorial tribunals in the Indies and stated that any native transgressions against the faith fell within the ordinario's purview. This order was reissued on February 23, 1575 (Lea 1922, 210–11).

6. A list of mandatory Christian holidays for natives appears in León 1611.

7. Borah 1983.

8. Greenleaf 1965; Villa-Flores 2008.

9. AGI-Mex 69, ramo 4, no. 47.

10. AGI-Mex 357; both letters are dated on January 2.

11. One exception is a 1605 accusation before the Holy Office against the Spaniard Sebastián de la Cruz from Izúcar, for keeping effigies of his Nahua wife's ancestors at home (AGN-Inq 281, no. 35).

12. Two periods in particular were characterized by multiregional epidemics and pandemics, 1576–80, and 1595–97; see Gibson 1964.

13. AGI-Mex 336 A.

14. AGI-Mex 69, ramo 4, no. 55.

15. AGI-Mex 336 A.

16. AGI-Mex 336 B.

17. For a detailed discussion of this period, see Poole 1987.

18. AGI-Mex 336 B.

19. See Klor de Alva et al. 1988; and M. León-Portilla 2002. For a discussion of the compilation of the Sahaguntine corpus, see Bustamante García 1990.

20. AGI-Mex 336 B.

21. AGI-Mex 336 A.

22. Torquemada [1615] 1969, 549 (book 20, chap. 46).

23. AGN-Inq, vol. 43, no. 6, 197r–230v). On the First Mexican Council, see Lorenzana 1769a, 143–44.

24. Nesvig 2009, 155–60. The policies of the Third Mexican Council regarding doctrinal texts in indigenous languages appear in Lorenzana 1769b, 14.

25. This paragraph summarizes several observations in Truman 2003; see also Schwartz 2008, 144–48. For a discussion of inquisitorial attempts to censor printed works in late sixteenth-century New Spain, see Nesvig 2009, 229–44.

26. Benassar 1979.

27. Kamen 1998, 133.

28. Bouza 2001.

29. See Bernand and Gruzinski 1992, for a discussion of links between seventeenth-century idolatry discourses and the Counter-Reformation. San Andrés Epazoyucan was located northeast of the Basin of Mexico and inhabited by Nahuatl and Otomi speakers. An Augustinian parish was established there toward 1540 (Gerhard 1972, 68–69).

30. AGN-BN 497, no. 30.

31. Ibid., 4r–v.

32. Teotlalco's gobernador had made offerings to Tlaloc in 1546. By 1569, this jurisdiction had lost some population due to migration, and parishes had been established in two of its largest settlements, Teotlalco and Cuitlatenamic (Gerhard 1972, 310–11).

33. AGN-Inq UE 182, no. 4. I thank Guadalupe Cruz Soto (1993) for sharing her research with me.

34. Although some of Sahagún's informants noted that ololiuhqui was also called *coatl xoxouhqui* (Quezada 1989, 47–48), there are separate references to temecatl in Sahagún's *Códice Matritense* and the works of Francisco Hernández (López Austin 1975, 66).

35. Ponce de León 1892. This manuscript is kept at the BMNA and was translated in Ruiz de Alarcón 1984. According to Clavijero, this work was acquired by Boturini (BCN-Gesu 1255/5, 12v).

36. De la Serna 1892, 287–88. The "Marquesado," a term encompassing some of Cortés's former holdings, refers here to northern Morelos and the Toluca Valley.

37. De la Serna 1892, 288. Teotenango was Tenango del Valle's original name.

38. The resumé of Gil de la Barrera, García Guerra's provisor and vicario general de indios, does not mention any involvement in extirpation efforts (AGN-Indif 3000).

39. As a 1608 request for a cathedral chapter post shows, Bocanegra was prefect of the Anunciata Congregation and rector of the Colegio de San Pedro y San Pablo in Mexico City; later, he served as vicar of Taxco (AGI-Mex 228, no. 23).

40. AGI-Mex 28, no. 7.

41. AGI-Mex 337. Chapters 6 and 7 of Joshua recount the divinely ordained execution of some members of the tribe of Judah for failing to hand over silver and gold spoils to be consecrated by priests.

42. Moreover, Ruiz de Alarcón (1984, 47) recounts a case in which some specialists designated as *teyollocuanih*, "Human Heart Eaters," and *tetlachihuiani* were accused of killing many residents of Coyuca with ashes they received from other *tlatlacatecoloh*, or malevolent specialists. The authorities consulted Dr. Juan Cano, a professor of law at the Royal University, who recommended the death penalty.

43. This practice, which Ruiz de Alarcón reported as well, recalls the Mexica practice of making amaranth seed figures representing drowning or accidental burial victims for ritual consumption during the feast of Tepeilhuitl (Sahagún 1950–1982, book 2, 132–33).

44. See Haskett 1991, 2005, for the Nahua appropriation of heraldic seals.

45. De la Serna 1892, 291–92: *Nican motenehua in nelli Cristiano in quipohuaz, in quicaquiz, in itlatlauhtiliz in totecuyo Christo yn itlazonantzin in Santa Maria yn itlatlauhtiloca; yehuantin in motenehua in quauhtli in ocelotl yn macehualtin imatlapal, in cuitlapilli, in huilatzitzin, yn motolinia, yn macehualtin in çacatla nemi.*

46. M. León-Portilla 1983, 53–54.

47. AGN-Indif 299.

48. Ibid.

49. Coe and Whittaker 1982, 13.

50. AGN-Indif 299; AGI-Mex 231, no. 11.

51. AGI-Mex 38, no. 34, Letters of Viceroy Duque de Albuquerque.

52. Atenango's first resident priest arrived circa 1600 (Gerhard 1972, 113), too early a date for Hernando's career.

53. AGN-Inq 304, no. 39, 266v–67r.

54. Ibid., 265v–66v; see also Greenleaf 1965, 146–47.

55. The Holy Office investigation against Ruiz de Alarcón for usurpation of faculties was not unique. In 1625, an allegation was recorded against fray Gerardo de Porras, prior of the Augustinian convent of Chiauhtla and Holy Office commissioner, for punishing a native ololiuhqui user in an auto (AGN-Inq 510, no. 133, 588r).

56. Warren (1973, 83) states that Ruiz de Alarcón was named ecclesiastical judge in 1617, but I have not found any documentary evidence in support of this claim.

57. ACM-Litig L-8, 275r–88r.

58. AGI-Mex 231, no. 11.

59. The appointments granted to extirpators Gonzalo Curiel (AGN-Indif 300, no. 217) and Torres Cortés in Oaxaca (AGN-Inq 573-I, 144v–51v), or even Sánchez de Aguilar in Yucatán (AGI-Mex 299), show that these documents explicitly mentioned a license to try natives for idolatry or superstition.

60. AGN-Inq 303, 78r. Ruiz de Alarcón's commission probably outlined powers against idolaters. In this 1624 letter, Ruiz de Alarcón implicitly noted his exercise of such powers by referring to two different notaries: a Gaspar Ruiz; and the bachiller Alonso Sánches Holgado, former vicar of Tepecuacuilco.

61. AGI-Mex 357.

62. This is the only known copy of this work, and it is catalogued as BMNA-ColAnt 160.

63. In the Late Postclassic, a broad ethnic and linguistic division existed to the southwest of the Basin of Mexico. Most communities in what is now northern Guerrero were part of Cohuixcatlalpan, while communities in southwestern and central Morelos were in Tlalhuicatlalpan (Sahagún 1950–1982, book 6). The Cohuixca-Tlalhuica distinction was used as a category in the *Relaciones Geográficas* of the 1580s. For an overview of ethnic differentiation in Nahua communities, see Berdan et al. 2008.

64. López Austin 1966, 1967a.

65. Evidence suggests that two Nahuatl variants are represented in Ruiz de Alarcón's text, the Tlalhuica and the Cohuixca dialects. Coe and Whittaker (1982, 319–21) noted three features that may correspond to distinguishing traits of the Tlalhuica and Cohuixca dialects: endings in /-ik/ rather than in /-ki/, *achtotipa*, "first," versus *achtopa* or *achtocopa*, and the occasional preservation of stem-final vowels.

66. See López Austin 1967b; Ruiz de Alarcón 1984; and Coe and Whittaker 1982.

67. AGN-BN 596, no. 45. I thank Jonathan Amith for sharing his notes about this document with me.

68. Xolotl was both the name of a deity and a personal name.

69. Ruiz de Alarcón 1984, 148.

70. Ibid., 28–29.

71. Garibay 1954; M. León-Portilla 1983; Karttunen and Lockhart 1980.

72. M. León-Portilla 1983, 47–62.

73. Garibay 1954, 59–106; Karttunen and Lockhart 1980, 11–15; M. León-Portilla 1983, 29–31.

74. See Sahagún 1950–1982, 1986, [1583] 1993.

75. Bautista Viseo 1600b; see Léon-Portilla and Silva Galeana 1990.

76. López Austin 1967b, 1975.

77. Jakobson 1987, 146–47; Tambiah 1981, 135–36.

78. See Hymes 1981; Tedlock 1987.

79. Garibay (1954, 19). Nahua *difrasismos* were composed of two terms that convey a third, absent notion, often metonymically.

80. Bricker 1974, 368–73.

81. Ruiz de Alarcón 1984, 231. Following Caso, Andrews and Hassig point out that 4-Reed was a calendrical name common to Notahtzin Nonantzin (Our Father, Our Mother), Tlahuizcalpanteuctli (Lord of the House of Dawn, an aspect of Quetzalcoatl), Citlalli Icue (Her Skirt Is A Star), Tonatiuh (Sun Disk), and Tonacateuctli (Lord of Our Flesh).

82. /na: . wi . a: . katl/ (4) /mi . li:n . ti . kah/ (4). I rely on Canger's (1986) characterization of syllabic clusters in Classical Nahuatl; see also Lastra 1986.

83. Kripke 1980.

84. Ruiz de Alarcón 1984, 88, 97.

85. Ibid., 129.

86. Austin 1975.

87. Ibid., 151.

88. See Ruiz de Alarcón 1984, 151; López Austin 1970, 16.

89. This pair figured as a primeval couple devoted to divination in Nahua creation accounts (Nicholson 1971, 401).

90. Ruiz de Alarcón 1984, 56.

91. This was a secondary rationalization on the part of specialists, who divided this name into its etymological components, *cipac*-(tli), "lizard," and *tonal*-(li), "sun, destiny."

92. According to Jonghe (1905), this passage in Thévet's *Cosmographie*, also known as *Histoyre de Mechique*, is a French-language version of Olmos's earlier work written circa 1543, which Mendieta cited in the foreword to book 2 of his *Historia*.

93. Thévet 1575, vol. 1, 998v: *pour ceste cause estoit ce Dieux aymé des autres, & l'appelloient* [Tlazohpilli], *c'est à dire Seigneur bien amé.* See also Nicholson 1971, 401.

94. Sahagún 1950–1982, book 2, 60–62; Hvidtfeldt 1957.

95. Nicholson 1971, 417.

96. Ruiz de Alarcón 1984, 222.

97. See Ruiz de Alarcón 1984; Nicholson 1971.

98. This narrative is markedly similar to the *Leyenda de los Soles* in the Codex Chimalpopoca (see Bierhorst 1992).

99. The epithet Nanahuatzin-Xiuhpiltzin was used by several specialists to address fire (Ruiz de Alarcón 1984, 97, 104).

100. See Ruiz de Alarcón 1984, 127, 129, 125.

101. Ruiz de Alarcón (1984, 208) suggests that female specialists could also perform this cure.

102. Nicholson 1971, 418–19.

103. Ibid., 398.

104. De la Serna 1892, 287.

105. Barlow [1949] 1992.

106. Acuña 1986, 115.

107. Coe and Whittaker 1982, 10.

108. Acuña 1986, 79.

109. Ibid., 31.

110. Gibson 1964; Mörner 1970.

111. Gerhard 1972, 111–14.

112. BMNA-ColAnt 336, no. 26.

113. Ruiz de Alarcón 1984, 148. Olmos ([1553] 1990, 47–49) observed earlier that more women than men became ritual specialists.

114. De la Serna 1892, 294.

115. See AGI-Mex 31, no. 11; AGI-Mex 76, ramo 15, no. 83; AGI-Mex 804 (1633–34); AGI-Indif 161, no. 296; AGI-Indif 194, no. 4; and AGI-Indif 2998, no. 409.

116. ACM-Litig L-8, "Relación que Don Juan de Velázquez hizo . . . ," 59r–60r. In Peru, the king selected one of three regulars nominated by their superiors.

117. Ibid., 71r–v.

118. Schwaller 1999, 3–7.

119. Alva [1634] 1999, 74–77, Sell's translation (1999).

120. Ibid., 86–87, Sell's translation (1999).

121. Ibid., 81, 85; Schwaller 1999, 11.

122. Alva [1634] 1999, 56.

123. AGI-Mex 337, Letters of Mañozca.

124. Ibid.

125. Boturini 1746, 21–22. Boturini's copy may be the one now owned by the Biblioteca Nacional de España (BNE Ms. 19634); see Sáenz de Santa María 1969.

126. JCB-CodSp 75.

127. Schroeder 2000, 49–55.

128. San Gregorio closed after the death of Rodríguez Puebla in 1848, and sometime after this date, these three manuscripts were moved to the Biblioteca del Museo Nacional and published for the first time in 1892.

129. Hoffmann (1995, 316) stresses that this plant is now widely known as *Turbina corymbosa*.

130. Hernández 1986, 110.

131. Fields 2008.

132. Monardes 1574, 47v.

133. Cárdenas [1591] 1965, 172.

134. Sahagún gave *coatl xoxouhqui*, or "Green Snake," as a name for ololiuhqui (Aguirre Beltrán 1963, 127). Hernández argued that *coaxihuitl* was an alternative designation for ololiuhqui, since, he noted, it resembled a serpent.

135. Hernández 1651, 8.

136. Sahagún 1950–1982, book 10.

137. Farfán 1579, 205r. A mixture of piciyetl leaves and wine was recommended as an emetic and for dislodging humors from head and stomach.

138. Ruiz de Alarcón 1984, 218.

139. Ibid., 199–200.

140. Ibid., 249–50.

141. Ibid., 67.

142. Ibid., 60, 67.

143. This method was also reported by Zapotec specialists; see AHJO-VA Civ 117, 39r.

144. AGN-Inq UE 182, no. 4; Cruz Soto 1993, 172–74.

145. AGN-Inq 510, n. 133, 588r.

146. AGN-Inq 303, 78r.

147. Ruiz de Alarcón 1984, 65.

148. Ibid., 60.

149. Aguirre Beltrán 1963, 131. His sources are, respectively, AGN-Inq 339, n. 33; AGN-Inq 435, n. 12; AGN-Inq 342, n. 15; AGN-Inq 363, n. 28.

150. The extant accusations against Nahua officeholders were of little substance. In 1621, a Mexico City resident accused Juana Isabel, perhaps a daughter of the cacique of Tlatelolco, of claiming to be able to turn herself into a dog, but the Inquisition did not pursue this case (AGN-Inq 486, no. 65). During a 1635 inquiry regarding the idolatrous use of a Postclassic ceremonial site near Malinalco, this town's gobernador was named as a potential suspect (Lisa Sousa, personal communication, 2010). In 1655, Pablo Jacinto, principal of San Juan Teotlalco, was accused of sorcery, but the civil justice found no supporting evidence and he regained his post in 1656 (AGN-Ind 20, no. 259 bis).

151. As noted below in Chapter 6, one of the few exceptions is Gregorio Juan's syncretic cult at Xicotepec and Ayohuizcuauhtla in the diocese of Puebla in 1659 (Gruzinski 1988).

152. Lewis 2003.

153. Alberro 1988; Quezada 1989, 1991.

154. De la Serna 1892, 302–3; Losa 1642, 112r–14r.

155. Sánchez de Ordiales insisted that his consultation was made without malice (AGN-Inq 348, no. 4).

156. Ruiz de Alarcón 1984, 184–85.

157. De la Serna 1892, 305–6. For a discussion of the personification of illnesses in the *Tratado*, see Raby 2006.

158. Ruiz de Alarcón 1984, 66–67.

159. Gruzinski 1992, 1993.

160. Silverblatt 1987, 181. For a discussion of economic incentives for female healers in colonial Guatemala, see Few 2002.

Chapter 4

1. There is no extant documentation regarding Oaxacan idolatry trials in 1560–95 other than the debates between the Audiencia and Bishop Albuquerque in 1562 and 1576 regarding Dominican extirpation efforts.

2. The province of Santiago was divided into two provinces at the 1592 Dominican general chapter. The Dominicans had Antonio de Cáceres, bishop of Astorga and confessor of Philip II, act as referee regarding this province's boundary conflicts. Although Cáceres decided that the diocesan boundaries of Mexico and Tlaxcala would determine those of Santiago, this province claimed the Mixtec doctrinas of northwestern Oaxaca. This claim was withdrawn at the

1596 Dominican chapter, and Cáceres's scheme was confirmed by a September 1599 decree from the Dominican superior and a November 1599 decree from Clement VIII (ASV-SecBr 289, 32r–35r).

3. Griffiths 1995; Mills 1997.

4. AGI-Mex 232, no. 25.

5. The relación de méritos was a genre employed by secular priests to present a summary of their education and ecclesiastical career to the real patronato when applying for ecclesiastical appointments. See Chuchiak 2002.

6. AGI-Mex 232, no. 25; AGI-Mex 355; AGN-Indif 3000.

7. AGN-Inq 249, no. 23, 190r, 196v.

8. Ibid., 192r.

9. Bohórquez was named Bishop of Venezuela on July 18, 1611 (ASV-AV 15, 80v–81r); on November 13, 1617, he was promoted to the bishopric of Oaxaca (ASV-AV 15, 157r), and received permission to be sworn in by either the cathedral dean of Venezuela or Oaxaca (ASV-SecBr 554, 328r–v).

10. Gay 1998, 342.

11. AGN-Inq 510, no. 133, cited in Greenleaf 1965, 146. AGN-Inq 303-I, 354, no. 8, 9; Alberro 1992, 137.

12. AGI-Mex 301.

13. AGN-Indif 3000, no. 229.

14. Ibid.

15. AGN-Indif 3000, no. 217.

16. Ibid.; AGI-Mex 357.

17. AGN-Inq 329, no. 13.

18. Although Leonel de Cervantes Carvajal was appointed as Bohórquez's successor on February 18, 1636 (ASV-AC 17, 112v), he died in Mexico City in 1637 before assuming his post. Benavides was elected bishop of Oaxaca on June 27, 1639 (ASV-AC 17, 187v–88r).

19. Burgoa [1674] 1989, vol. 2, 228–31.

20. Córdova 1987, 228v. This observance resembles a Nahua practice reported by Durán (1967, vol. 1, 157): to ward off pollution, straws were passed through one's tongue, each one a metonymical representation of a misdeed.

21. APF-SOCG 259, 253r–79r.

22. Gay 1998, 336.

23. See AGI-Mex 357; Gay 1998, 337–39.

24. This controversy is illustrated by a September 20, 1642, papal bull. At the request of the procurator general of the Dominican province of Santiago, Urban VIII confirmed the official policy on alternancia: in a four-chapter cycle, the first and fourth ones would elect Spanish and criollo candidates for provincial from the Puebla friary, while the second and third chapters would elect criollo and Spanish candidates from the Mexico City friary (ASV-BulPr VI 116). This concern with alternancia was shared by other regulars. At least since 1629, the Augustinians listed their members in Mexico by origin (AGSA Aa 47); a decade later, fray Pedro Nieto, a former Augustinian procurator general, complained to Propaganda Fide about the lack of qualified Spanish regulars in New Spain (APF-SOCG 259, 169r).

25. AGOP-SH XIII.12735, 1649.

26. ASV-BulPr VI 95, 1634.

27. AGOP-SH XIII.11250 1649, 2r–4r.

28. In Tilantongo, Sebastián Gómez was accused of giving his wife Magdalena Gaytán a remedy called *yucuño* in Mixtec, which provoked an abortion and also induced paralysis and deafness. AHJO-TEP Crim 89. For domestic violence in Mixtec households, see Terraciano 1998.

29. Sánchez was ordered to pay two pesos to the royal justice, two pesos for masses to be said for the sake of López's soul, and three pesos for legal costs (AHJO-TEP Crim 79).

30. AHJO-TEP Crim 4, no. 12, 1r–4v. For more information about Toyna Yoco, see Terraciano 2001, 262.

31. AHJO-TEP Crim 302.

32. AHJO-TEP Crim 492.

33. Ibid. Due to this trial's poor state of preservation, it cannot be determined whether Portocarrero punished the alcalde Palomares.

34. AHAO-LCab 1653–1656.

35. Balsalobre [1656] 1892, 232.

36. AGI-Mex 357.

37. Gerhard 1972, 51.

38. María de la Cruz of Ictlan was surprised placing cacao grains in the clothes of a dead man whose corpse was being prepared for burial (AGN-Inq 573-I).

39. Cuevas 1921–28, vol. 2, 112–14.

40. AHAO-LCab 1642.

41. AHAO-Dioc Caja 3; AGN-Inq 442, no. 2.

42. The Inquisición *ramo* at the AGN (AGN-Inq) contains trials against the subjects listed below by volume and folio numbers, which were heard by Balsalobre between November 1653 and January 1658: Diego Luis: 437-I-3 (66r–99v); Marcos Ruiz: 456 (563r–73r); Melchor López: 456 (574r–82v); Matías Luis: 456 (583r–89v); Lorenzo Martín: 456 (590r–98v); Melchor Xuárez: 456 (599r–611r); Martín de Orozco, Margarita Cortés, don Felipe Cortés, doña Ana de Ayala: 457-2 (40r–59r); Juan Luis: 438-II-14 (332v–36v) and 431 (296r–98v); Pedro and Agustín de Mendoza: 457-4 (65r–79v); Marcial Ramírez: 456 (557r–62r); Pascual García: 584-3 (26r–36v); Miguel Martín and Gracia Margarita 456–13 (542r–611r); sacrifices near San Dionisio Titicpaqui: 573 (261r–65r); thirty-two native clients of sixteen Sola maestros: 571 (361r–405r); Gaspar González Lalaa: 571–13 (305r–20r); Felipe Encomendero: 575 (565r–69v). Ecclesiastical judge Trujillo heard confessions from forty-four native clients of four Sola maestros: 573 (155r–73v, 212v–50v), and confessions from twenty-two native clients of eight Sola maestros: 573 (285r–316r). Escribano Aldrete drafted una información on Balsalobre's behalf: 457 (121r–42v), and inquisitor Medina Rico led an inquiry into Balsalobre's *Relación Auténtica*: 445-2 (412r–17v).

43. Gerhard 1972, 73.

44. Ibid.; AGN-Inq 437-I, no. 3.

45. AGN-Inq 437-I, no. 3; Berlin 1988.

46. AGN-Inq 438, no. 2, 456, 573.

47. Diego Luis offered contradictory testimony about when he became a specialist. In his February 4, 1654, statement, he said he had been a maestro for twenty-two years both before and after 1632; later, he asserted he had become a maestro "twenty-two years ago," which justifies a 1632 starting date (AGN-Inq 437-I-3).

48. The vicar confiscated this booklet, and it remained in Sola's church archive until 1654, when it was retrieved by Balsalobre during Diego Luis's interrogation. Diego Luis said he found this manuscript before 1632 and brought it to Luis López, who taught him "how to use it" (AGN-Inq 437-I, no. 3).

49. AGN-Inq 437-I-3, 74r.

50. Ibid.

51. *Colaní* is composed by the agentive prefix *co-* and the nominal root *lani,* "festivity," so it literally translates as "maker of feasts, celebrations." Córdova (1578b, 10r) translates *huechilla* as "diviner," and *colanij* as "someone who makes forecasts" (ibid., 13v).

52. Balsalobre [1656] 1892, 243.

53. AGN-Inq 573, 155r–73v, 212v–50v.

54. Ibid., 285r–316r.

55. AGN-Inq 571, 361r–405r.

56. AGN-Inq 575, 565r–69v.

57. For a lengthier analysis, see Berlin 1988.

58. AGN-Inq 571 no. 13, 573.

59. AGN-Inq 431, 438, no. 2.

60. AGN-Inq 571.

61. AGN-Inq 456, 437-I no. 3.

62. AGN-Inq 571, 573.

63. AGN-Inq 437-I, no. 3.

64. AGN-Inq 573.

65. AGN-Inq 571.

66. AGN-Inq 573.

67. AGN-Inq 456, no. 13.

68. AGN-Inq 437-I, no. 3.

69. Ibid.

70. AGN-Inq 457, 121r–42v.

71. Balsalobre [1656] 1892, 247–48.

72. AGN-Inq 445-II, 412v. This controversy is discussed in Greenleaf 1965, 144–45.

73. Alberro 1988, 35–40.

74. Paradoxically, we owe the preservation of Balsalobre's autos to two fortuitous shortcomings: Hevia y Valdés's violation of inquisitorial protocol, and the Holy Office's inefficiency regarding the return of these documents.

Chapter 5

1. Gerhard (1972, 371) notes that this former encomienda town was not mentioned in records after 1743; Chance (1989, 81) indicates that it was eventually renamed Roavela.

2. Caso (1965, 932) established 600 BCE as the antiquity of the earliest known epigraphic representation of this calendar through a Mixteca Alta radio-carbon date linked to ceramics that closely resemble Monte Albán I assemblages.

3. AGI-Mex 882, 914r.

4. Lockhart 1992, 383.

5. Ibid., 384.

6. For a sample of alphabetic genres in Maya languages, Mixtec, Nahuatl, and Zapotec, see Restall, Sousa, and Terraciano 2005.

7. Havelock 1982.

8. Harris 1989, 328.

9. Houston 1994, 37, 39.

10. Goody 1987.

11. Córdova 1578b, 182v. *Huezée quíchi* may be glossed as "Maker of tree-bark paper," and *huecàa yye* as "Maker of images." *Pèni huílla* means "singer," and *péni huelàba yye* is "reader or reciter of images" (ibid., 241v). In Córdova's work, the term *quijchi tija*—literally, "Tree-bark paper of lineages"—is given the qualifier *colàça*, "(of) ancient times," and it is rendered in Spanish as "Native book with figures" (ibid., 244v).

12. Some of the glosses in Córdova (ibid.) for the root -*yye* include: "Cipher. *Yye nagána nolòhuinice tòbi latícha*, [or] *yye*" (108v); "To be drawn. *Ti-yè-a* [or] *ti-yèe-a*. A drawing. *Na-yye*" (114r); "Any sort of writing. *Tícha, yye cáa quíchi, yye nacàa quíchi, tícha nacáa*" (182v); "A single letter. *Yye, lána, lána yye*" (142v); "To draw a figure . . . *Tozèea, tocàaya yye*" (196v); "To paint. *Tozèea, tocàaya yye*" (315v). For a less likely etymological interpretation of piyè as "wind flower," see Cruz 2007, 335–36.

13. From *nahualli*, shape-changing religious specialist. *Nahuallotl* was an abstract noun that referred to the capacity of being a *nahualli*, or the actions performed by one. This statement comes from book 8, folio 192v of the *Códice Matritense*, and it is discussed in López Austin 1973a, 175. A similar statement also occurs in the *Florentine Codex* (Sahagún 1950–1982, book 10, 191).

14. López Austin 1973a.

15. Torquemada ([1615] 1969) appropriated this description from a manu-script authored by Mendieta, which circulated among Franciscans in the late sixteenth century, but remained unpublished until 1870 (Baudot 1995).

16. Valadés 1579, 227.

17. Motolinia [1858] 1990, 2.

18. While Mignolo (1996) uses Motolinia's interpretation to argue that it epitomized the demonization of nonhistorical genres, Cañizares-Esguerra (2001) contends that the Spanish did not summarily reject the information recorded in Mesoamerican pictographic genres due to suspicions about their origin.

19. See Galarza 1980; Kellogg 1995; Romero Frizzi 1996, 2003; Romero Frizzi and Vázquez 2003.

20. Gruzinski 1993; Wood 2003.

21. Galarza 1980; Lockhart 1992; Oudijk 2000; Schroeder 1991; Whitecot-ton 1977, 1990.

22. Burkhart 1995.

23. Berlin 1988.
24. Alcina Franch 1993, 1998.
25. Hanks 1987, 2010.
26. Rappaport 1998.
27. See Chartier 1992, 1996.
28. Ruiz de Alarcón 1892, 157.
29. Ibid., 164.
30. BMNA-ColAnt 160, 42v.
31. Ruiz de Alarcón 1892, 217.
32. Lockhart 1992, 259.
33. López Austin (1966, 1967a, 1967b) claims this incantation was used by *temacpalihtotiqueh*, the thieving Aztec hypnotists (Sahagún 1950–1982, book 4).
34. Ruiz de Alarcón 1984, 78–80.
35. BMNA-ColAnt 160, 91v, as translated by Andrews and Hassig.
36. Ruiz de Alarcón 1984, 251.
37. This element refers to the piciyetl's association with the nine-tiered Nahua cosmos (López Austin 1973a, 1984; Tavárez 1999).
38. Some sections of this manuscript were published by the Maya Society (Anonymous 1935), based on a photostat made by Willam Gates (NL-Ayer MS 1675).
39. As in other 260-day counts, one would expect these twenty day signs to possess numerical coefficients from one to thirteen. In 1756, Mariano Veytia copied this correlation, now preserved as BNF-Mex 249, and erroneously identified as a Phurépecha calendar. Caso (1945, 95–96) correctly identified this count as a Matlatzinca calendar.

In his publication, Caso referred to versions of this count published by Veytia in his *Historia antigua de México* and by Ramírez in the *Anales del Museo Nacional* in 1905.
40. Li [1495] 1999.
41. Reprinted as E. Martínez [1606] 1948.
42. Leonard [1949] 1992, 160, 164, 201.
43. Códice Mendieta 1971, 255–58, cited in Mathes 1982, 33.
44. BNF-Mex 23–24.
45. See Mengin 1952.
46. López Austin 1973b.
47. BNF-Mex 381, 49.
48. Chimalpahin 1997, vol. 2, 128–29.
49. My translation departs slightly from the one in Chimalpahin 1997, vol. 2, 129, because I believe that Chimalpahin omits the morpheme *-tla-* in *Ipan quicuepa in ilhuica*[tla]*matinimeh*, yielding *Ipan quicuepa in ilhuicamatinimeh*. Molina (1992, 37v) translates *Ilhuicatlamatini* as "astrologer."
50. Li 1510, b verso to b ii recto, my emphases: **Siguen se los planetas** Del *primer cielo : y del septimo* **planeta que es la luna que tiene enel su assiento** *El primero cielo es donde tiene su assiento la luna: que es el inferior planeta y seteno: el qual esta constituydo en*[e]*l mas baxo circulo dela espera: y en espacio d*[e] *ocho años consuma su circulo. y es señor del seteno & ultimo clima.*

51. BNF-Mex 381, 49–50, my emphases: *Domi*[n]*go. Sigue se llos planetas. primero gramatica ca tlatohuani lunes el segoto mercielo* **planetas ques la llona que tiene en el su** *asie*[n]*to tetzacatl martes. el tercero ytel marius. tercero planetas cabalero miercoles. el segoto ciello ytel melgorio que es planetas ticitl yetz.*

52. TRO Ms. 3523–2. This manuscript features several hands, and a note toward the end identifies one of its owners in 1748. I am currently working on a comparison of this work with BNF-Mex 381.

53. BNF-Mex 381, 48–49: *Primero Planeta. Nica*[n] *pohuallo yn izqui si*[g] *nos, yn iquac aries tleticpacticate yn iquac leon tlanepa*[n]*tlaticate yn iquac sagitarius t*[l]*etl yntzi*[n]*tlaticate yn izqui* [i]*llhuitl tlahuica, yn iquac taurus tlalticpacticate yn iquac Virgon tlallinepa*[n]*tlaticate yn iquac capricornios tlalliynci*[n]*tlaticate yn iquac Seminis yehecatl ti*[c]*pacticate yn iquac libra yehecatl nepa*[n]*tlaticate yn iquac aquarius yehecatl tzintlaticate yn iquac ca*[n] *cer atl ticpacticate yn iquac Secorbius atl nepa*[n]*tlaticate yn iquac pilcis atl tzintlaticate.*

An alternative translation for "and [this is] what his work is, what happens here on Earth when he is born," is: "and what[ever] his work is, it will be done here on Earth."

54. BNF-Mex 381, 50: *Y*[n] *nica*[n] *micuiliuhtica yn izqui tlama*[n]*tli y*[n] *planetas y*[n] *tlacatiliztli, yn queni*[n] [ç]*an leportorion ypa*[n] *tlacatli nican motenehuan yn iquac Domigo tlahuizcalpa*[n] *motocayotia la primera olas*[un?] *yoa*[n] *onca tlacati yn tlatoque y*[n] *macenhualli tlacatiz yoa*[n] *ytla ytequiuh mochihuan nica*[n] *t*[laltic]*p*[a]*c yn iquac tlacati ypiltzintli nima*[n] *notzaloz yn quimatia ylepordorion [sic] quitemelahuiliz yn queni*[n] *leon yn ipa*[n] *tlacatin quihualcuitaci yn inacayo huel mahuiztic chalchihuitl teoxihuitl quetzaliztli yn ixtelolo temamauhti yn inacayo ce*[n]*ca chichiltic. Auh ynic nemi y*[n] *t*[laltic] *p*[a]*c ce*[n]*ca ymacaxoni ce*[n]*ca yxteyo yn iquac mococohua huel apaloz yn iquac macoz yn tlaquali amo quicahuaz ça*[n] *tequi*[tl] *tlaquatoz ytla*[h] *ypa*[n] *pehuaz. yn itoca leon niman iciuhca miquiz ahuel patiz yn tlacatilizpa*[n]*.*

With regards to my translation of *amo quicahuaz ça*[n] *tequi*[tl] *tlaquatoz,* see Molina [1571] 1992, 14v: "*çan tequitl oacico.* He barely arrived, and then left." Regarding my rendering of *ytla*[h] *ypa*[n] *pehuaz,* see Molina [1571] 1992, 41v: "*Ipam pepeua.* A madman who was periods of lucidity."

55. López Austin 1973b, 290: *yn imixpan nepechteco yuan cencayollo tlapallihui yollochicahuaque.*

56. E. Martínez [1606] 1948, 23.

57. Jauss 1982, 19, 23.

58. AGI-Mex 301, and Mexico 357.

59. AGN-Indif 3000, no. 217.

60. AGN-Inq 437-I-3.

61. AGN-Inq 456, 592v–93r.

62. Balsalobre [1656] 1892, 241.

63. Berlin 1988.

64. AGN-Inq 456, 577r–v.

65. Ibid., 558r–v.

66. Ibid., 547r.

67. Ibid., 544v.

68. Ibid., 545r.

69. AGN-Inq 457, 67r.

70. AGN-Inq 456, 577r.

71. Ibid., 558r.

72. These ethnic designations follow the usage proposed in Castellanos 2003; also see Rendón 1995.

73. See Restall and Kellogg 1998; Rojas Rabiela, Rea López, and Medina Lima 1999.

74. The quantitative data about Zapotec texts in this paragraph come from Oudijk 2006.

75. Alcina Franch (1993) numbered the Villa Alta calendrical booklets as Calendars 1–99, and this numeration is used at AGI; nevertheless, some of these booklets contain two different calendars, or split the same calendar into two booklets. Since there are in fact 103 separate copies of the calendar bound into 99 booklets, Alcina Franch's system identifies separate booklets, but not separate calendars.

76. Booklets 47, 63, 66, and 85 contain multiple calendars, and Booklet 87 contains a section of the calendar completed by one of the fragments bound in Booklet 85.

77. Zilbermann 1966; Alcina Franch 1993, 1998.

78. First, the original eighteenth-century page numbers present discontinuities that can only be explained by two separate attempts at pagination. Second, some booklets labeled with the name of their owner are not currently located adjacent to the corresponding community's confession. Third, booklets by Caxonos Zapotec speakers do not have a systematic distribution in the corpus, even though most Caxonos Zapotec confessions appear before 654v in AGI-Mex 882.

79. Córdova 1578a, 204–12.

80. While the colonial Zapotec piyè shares this structure with other Mesoamerican calendars, it also possesses two distinctive features. First, unlike all other counts, where numbers precede day signs, Zapotec day names are followed by a written number (Yagchila 1, Quiolaha 2, etc.). Second, each of the 260 Zapotec day names contain two elements: the first one is a prefix; and the second is one of twenty nominal roots. For instance, the day name 1-Cayman is composed by *yag-* and *-chila*.

81. Córdova 1578a, 202.

82. See Justeson and Tavárez 2007, for a discussion of this system.

83. Gates 1931.

84. The correlation between the piyè and the Gregorian calendar allows for 1671 or 1690 as possible dates of production; given the timing of Maldonado's campaign, the most likely date is the latter.

85. AGI-Mex 882, 1369r; Tavárez and Justeson 2008.

86. Booklet 87 bears on its front cover the inscription *Juan Mathias es M*[aest]*ro*, "Juan Mathias is a teacher [of idolatries]." There is only one Juan Mathías identified as a maestro (AGI-Mex 882, 914r) in the confessions.

87. Córdova (1578b, 150r) glosses "For the sun to be eclipsed" as *t-ati, ti-tágo*, and *ti-gáchi*.

88. Córdova (1578b, 161r), "For something to catch fire. *Tiàaqui, coyàqui*" (161r); and "To be consumed by fire, see burn. *Tiàaquia táaquia, teyáaquia*" (336v).

89. Two lunar eclipses were visible in Mesoamerica in 1693. Moreover, eclipses take place at the new moon and full moon nearest the nodes of the eclipse cycle. The nodes occur at intervals just short of two piyè cycles (520 days). Thus, two eclipses occurring at these intervals, as it is the case for those of August 23, 1691, and January 21, 1693, would be assigned near adjacent dates in the Zapotec count.

90. Caso (1928, 1965) contended that the yza, or 365-day count, is attested in the hieroglyphic inscriptions of Monte Albán in the year-bearer system.

91. Alcina Franch 1993, 138–39. The towns were Cacalotepec, San Juan Xuquila, Tanetze, Tiltepeque, Yaee, Yatao, Yatoni, and Xosa. Of those towns reporting specific Christian holidays in February, Yaee was the only town to have embraced the feast of the Purification (February 2) rather than Saint Matthias's day (AGI-Mex 882, 1310r).

92. AGI-Mex 882, 1456r. The Catholic Church later moved this holiday to May 14.

93. AGI-Mex 882, 1542r, 1543r. Both towns also performed these observances on their patron saint's day.

94. AGI-Mex 882, 1512v.

95. Ibid., 1144r.

96. Justeson and Tavárez 2007, 25–27, 56.

97. Booklets 8, 17, 19, 24, 25, 31, 323, 43, 44, 45, 49, 50, 52, 58, 59, 64, 74, 85–1, 88, and 97.

98. Booklets 22, 24, 31, and 32; Booklets 31 and 32 contain the same text with diverging spellings.

99. Booklets 43, 49, 58, 59, 74, 88, and 97.

100. Córdova 1578b, 244v. An annotation in Booklet 81 designates its contents as *Libro quichi tia queani xotao*, "Book, paper of the lineages of our grandfathers" (AGI-Mex 882, 1368r).

101. AGI-Mex 882, 1365r.

102. Ibid., 1319v.

103. Ibid., 483v.

104. Chance 1989, 22.

105. AGI-Mex 882, 1347r.

106. Ibid., 511v–12v.

107. Ibid., 694r–95v, 1458r,

108. Ibid., 998r, 1000r.

109. Ibid., 914v.

110. Ibid., 1542r.

111. AGI-Mex 882, 615r–16v. Although Lachixila may have had Chinantec residents (Chance 1989, 25, 35), many of its inhabitants spoke Bixanos Zapotec in the early 1700s. Three maestros from this town declared their ritual sites were

called "in our language" Guia Yabechi, Guiag Gozana, and Guia Goxio, all of them Zapotec names.

112. The demographic data cited here comes from Chance 1989, 48–52.

113. AGI-Mex 882, 182r–84v, 299v, 430r.

114. Gerhard 1972, 96.

115. Ibid., 50, 72.

116. Due to the relative abundance of Nahua mundane texts, researchers have privileged their study in historical and philological surveys. See Karttunen and Lockhart 1976; Lockhart 1992.

117. Farriss 1984, 341.

118. Rafael 1988, 44–54, 121.

119. Derrida's theory of logocentrism and about the radical difference between orality and the written sign rests on an ambitious survey of the properties of writing that goes from Plato's *Phaedrus* to Rousseau's *Essai sur l'Origine des Langues* (Derrida 1967). However, one of Derrida's crucial assumptions—the absence of linguistic signs prior to the emergence of writing—is based on a Greco-Latin conception of writing that excludes, in both historical and epistemic terms, the Mesoamerican writing systems. Mignolo 1996 provides a critique of the application of Derrida's notion of logocentrism to Mesoamerican texts.

120. Chartier 1992, 4–5.

121. Watt 1991; Chartier 1996.

122. Certeau 1984, 175–76.

123. See, for instance, Goody 1987.

124. Chartier 1996, 138–39.

Chapter 6

1. Mills 1997, 15.

2. Nutini and Bell 1980; Nutini 1988.

3. Mills 1997, 14–15.

4. Aguirre Beltrán 1963; Alberro 1992; Griffiths and Cervantes 1999; and Gruzinski 1993, 2002.

5. Peña Montenegro [1668] 1995, vol. 1, 458–83; Mills 1997, 102.

6. Lorenzana 1769b.

7. Gruzinski 1988.

8. AGI-Mex 78, ramo 1, no. 13, image 335.

9. Ibid., image 349.

10. Gruzinski 1988.

11. AGN-Cler 191, 433v.

12. AGN-Inq 605, no. 10, 443r.

13. AGN-Ind 24, no. 121 bis.

14. AGN-GenPar 13, no. 178, 205v.

15. AGN-BN 596, no. 11.

16. AGI-Mex 69, ramo 4, no. 47.

17. AGN-RC Duplicadas 30, no. 1365. There is no indication of outcome.

18. López Austin 1970; Burkhart 1989.

19. AGN-BN 596, no. 112.

20. Sahagún 1950–1982, book 4, 41, 101.

21. Lorenzana 1769b.

22. AGN-Inq 674, no. 15.

23. AGN-BN 596, no. 29.

24. AGN-Inq 531, no. 10; AGN-Inq 706, no. 27.

25. AGI-Mex 338.

26. AGN-Indif 215, no. 45.

27. Balsalobre [1656] 1892, 234. The Latin quotes come from Ephesians 6:11–18, and I provide here a translation from the King James Version of the Scriptures.

28. Gosner 1998, 59; see also, Aramoni Calderón 1992.

29. See Zeitlin 2005; Spores 1998. Zeitlin (2005, 170) notes that, while Diego Fajardo, one of Avellán's predecessors, was also murdered a decade before, Fajardo's death was not directly tied to a native revolt. For repartimiento policies in Oaxaca, see Baskes 2000.

30. Díaz-Polanco et al. 1996.

31. See Katz 1990; for a comparative view, see Stern 1987.

32. Zeitlin 2005, 171–84. I thank Judith Zeitlin for generously sharing her transcription and analysis of the 1662 letter (AGI-Mex 600, 675r–83v).

33. ASV-SS Vescovi e Prelati 62, 124r–27r, May 3, 1676.

34. ASV-SS Vescovi e Prelati 62, 135r–36r.

35. AGI-Mex 357.

36. In fact, del Puerto himself was reputed to be of Zapotec origin. Del Puerto, born in Minas de Chichicapa, left for Mexico City after having been denied ordination by the bishop of Oaxaca. In Mexico, he had a brilliant ecclesiastical career, becoming a member of the cathedral chapter and provisor and vicar general of the archbishopric. He returned to Oaxaca in triumph after his appointment as bishop (BRAH-MemNE vol. 32, 130v).

37. AGOP-SH XIII.12760.

38. AGI-Mex 881.

39. Excerpts from a few of these trials were published in Fuente 1947–1948, and in Ríos Morales 1994, and they are briefly discussed in Zaballa 2005.

40. AHJO-TEP 502. Melchor de Morales and his niece Catalina de Mendoza were surprised by two neighbors as they burned copal in a censer in the backyard of Mendoza's house; the neighbors reported this was an act of sorcery against the alcalde Domingo de Ayala, whom both defendants despised (AHJO-TEP 502).

41. See AHJO-VA Crim 19, 20, 22, and 23.

42. Ibid., 19.

43. Ibid., 20.

44. Ibid., 22.

45. Ibid., 23.

46. Chance 1989; Fuente 1947–1948.

47. AHJO-VA Crim 25. This trial is discussed in Chapter 7.

48. AGI-Mex 357; AGOP-SH XIII.12760.

49. Alberro 1988; Greenleaf 1969; Lea 1906.

50. They are, respectively, AHJO-VA Crim 19, and AHJO-VA Crim 22.

51. A Spanish translation of Vargas's prayer reads: "Whoever You are, You who are here, take this [turkey] blood, and make my land plot give a good yield" (AHJO-VA 19, 8v).

52. AHJO-VA Crim 19, 2r.

53. Villegas y Sandoval probably took into account the fact that Luis de Vargas's father had been convicted of practicing ritual sacrifices by don Gerónimo de Bañuelos, alcalde mayor of Villa Alta in 1640–42. Vargas senior fled town and was never punished (AHJO-VA 19, 4r).

54. AHJO-VA Crim 19, 8v–11v; AHJO-VA Crim 20, 1r–20r.

55. Some court officials formed a closely knit group who remained in their posts for decades, providing a procedural continuity valued by the alcaldes mayores. At the close of the seventeenth century, this group included Nicolás de Vargas as interpreter, Ramón de Vargas as a formal witness, and Diego and Joseph Martínez de la Sierra as alguaciles mayores.

56. For a discussion of trials of indigenous defendants claiming they were deceived by the devil, see Sousa 2002.

57. AHJO-VA Crim 22, 18v, 23v.

58. AHJO-VA Crim 23, 14r.

59. Ibid., 37v–38r.

60. The appellations *tie*, "deer," *tio*, "lion," *beag*, "squirrel," and *bayo*, "wild boar" are not standard Zapotec calendrical names.

61. AHJO-VA Crim 23, 38v.

62. Ibid., 43r–v.

63. This was not the sole difficulty regarding Cabrera's credibility. In his final declaration, he contradicted don Diego Martín's earlier depositions. While don Diego claimed to have accompanied Cabrera as he spied on the nocturnal meetings, Cabrera declared he had spied on the natives by himself.

64. AHJO-VA Crim 23, 71r.

65. Fernández de Santa Cruz showed his interest in idolatry extirpation in a 1684 letter to the crown (AGN-Cler 191, 432r–34v) in which he commented on suspicions of idolatry in Tlapa and advocated the appointment of ministers with linguistic abilities in isolated communities.

66. Gerhard 1972, 309.

67. AGN-BN 1076, no. 10.

68. AGN-Inq 674, no. 26.

69. AGN-Inq 669, no. 10, 488v–89r.

70. Michael Swanton, personal communication, 2008.

71. AGN-Inq 674, no. 26.

72. For a lengthier discussion of Nicolasa's case, see Tavárez 2009a. For an overview of the adjudication of sangre and status in New Spain, see Martínez 2008.

73. Villavicencio 1692, 125–35.

74. Villavicencio described practices from the environs of the Basin of Mexico

and the Puebla region. For instance, he depicted the worship of river water in a town near Atrisco, a Franciscan parish west of Puebla. Circa 1677, the Franciscan minister of Atrisco surprised several natives as they pulled a cart themselves, instead of using oxen; on this cart rode a container with water from the Jocopa River, along with copal-burning censers. This friar tried the celebrants and sentenced them to several years of forced labor (Villavicencio 1692, 51).

75. Sariñana 1666, 1r–133r. For an account of this commemoration, see Cañeque 2004, 131–32.

76. Sariñana [1668] 1968.

77. Sariñana 1666, illustration between folios 56 and 57.

78. Sariñana 1681, 4r–5v. For an overview of the 1680 Pueblo rebellion, see Knaut 1997.

79. Ibid., 12v.

80. Alberro 1988.

81. Gareis 1999, 234.

82. AGN-Indif 215, no. 45.

83. Ibid., no. 44.

84. AGN-Indif 214, no. 33.

85. Ibid., no. 34.

86. Ibid., no. 35.

87. AGI-Mex 357, 1693.

88. AGI-Mex 358, 878. Again, he refused to extract legal costs from these defendants.

89. AGI-Mex 357.

90. Ibid. Grado directed his philanthropy to other projects. Circa 1693, he offered three haciendas and a field in Ejutla to the Jesuits so they established a seminar to educate twelve priests who would preach in Zapotec and Mixtec towns. Nevertheless, this proposal, inspired by the Jesuit Colegio de San Gregorio in Mexico City, was rejected by the Jesuits (Gay 1998, 372).

91. Paradoxically, this Chatino community would eventually become a popular pilgrimage site for the most revered contemporary Marian devotion in Oaxaca, the Virgin of Juquila.

92. AGI-Mex 357. The probable location of the prison may be inferred from a 1706 transfer identifying Grado's landholdings in Oaxaca City as "a few one-story houses located on the street that descends from the Royal Hospital of San Cosme and San Damián to the so-called *barrio de China* in this city, which adjoin the main residential house of [Grado]" (ANO-Álvarez, June 25, 1706). Hence, the prison was located a few blocks to the southwest of the cathedral, in the location of the former Barrio de China.

93. Gay 1998, 385.

94. Hidalgo was also chaplain of the cathedral choir; later, he served as ecclesiastical prosecutor under both Sariñana and Maldonado (AGN-Indif 215, no. 45).

95. AHAO-LCab, 1697.

96. A dry measure equal to about 1.6 bushels.

97. ANO-Benaias, August 9, 1703. The bequeathed land was a rectangle measuring 116 by 67 varas (one vara equaled 0.84 meters). Manuel Esparza

(1996; personal communication, 1999) believes that the orchard where the prison was built was near the southwest corner of the Alameda de Juárez. Indeed, the street now called Benito Juárez was known as Calle de la Perpetua well into the nineteenth century.

Chapter 7

1. This description combines witness accounts from three sources: a September 19, 1700, letter to the Dominican provincial from Vargas and Reyes (AMO Caxonos trial records, 54r); the testimony of four Spaniards before an alguacil on September 16, 1700 (ibid., 94r–99v); and the testimony of Joseph de la Trinidad, Captain Pinelo's mulatto slave, before the corregidor of Oaxaca on October 26, 1700 (ibid., 182v–84r).

2. AGI-Cont 5456, no. 3, ramo 15; AGEO-AM 12, no. 9. Mier del Tojo was originally appointed in 1695.

3. ALC 1270, 161v–69v; AHAO-Mart S-4, 615–31; Gillow [1889] 1990, 174–81.

4. Bourdieu 1971.

5. See Alcina Franch 1993, for a tabulation of Zapotec ritual practices in Villa Alta, using the categories devised by idolatry extirpators.

6. These songs, which have no Spanish gloss, have never been translated. Details of this discussion are drawn from my ongoing translation project, which, besides colonial Northern Zapotec texts, is informed by linguistic information in Agüero 1666; Butler 1997; Córdova 1578a, 1578b; Cueva n.d.; Feria 1567; Kaufman 2004; Levanto 1776; Martín 1696; A. Martínez [1633] 1872; Munro and López 1999; Pacheco de Silva [1687] 1752; Reyes [1704] 1891; Smith-Stark, Bogard, and López Cruz 1993; and Smith-Stark 1999, 2003, 2008.

7. Córdova (1578b, 69v) translates *tij, ticha tij,* and *tij tólani* as "song." The root *tòla* is included in the verb *tòllaya,* which meant both "I beat on drums" (ibid., 44r), and "I sing" (ibid., 70v). There may be a semantic link between this term and a different item with similar spelling, *tòla,* which in pre-Columbian times designated pieces of straw that were used to draw blood from one's tongue as a sacrifice before a pigana, or Zapotec specialist. Tòla was recruited by the Dominicans as the translation for the term "sin" in Valley Zapotec (ibid., 228v).

8. Córdova 1578b, 316v, 324v. Paradoxically, by the nineteenth century, this term came to designate Zapotec religious speeches regarded as suspect by the Catholic Church, particularly in the Isthmus. I thank Manuel Ríos Morales and Víctor de la Cruz for this insight.

9. One of these songs, devoted to God the Father, contains the variant "song and elegant speech" (*di libana*) as a genre designation (AGI-Mex 882, Booklet 103).

10. AGI-Mex 882, 296v–97r.

11. Bierhorst 1985, 72–74.

12. Burgoa [1674] 1989, vol. 1, 371.

13. Lópes described the text as "a book made of half a paper sheet, old and

dirty, in which he said were contained the days for giving Gentile names" (AGI-Mex 882, 183v).

14. AHJO-VA Crim 79.

15. AHJO-VA Crim 117, 16r–18r.

16. See Taube 2004; and Boone 2007, 114–17.

17. The day list of Booklet 11 was written by a speaker of Caxonos Zapotec, while some auguries were written by a speaker of Nexitzo or Bixanos Zapotec.

18. In Caxonos Zapotec, *laci* refers to "turns" taken by time units, such as months. In Valley Zapotec, *lleto*, a possible *ledo* cognate, appears in the phrase *quelani yania lleto, yania tito colaça loo xilayoo bezeloo*, "you shall complete the full destruction of idolatry" (Feria 1567, 23v). Some Northern Zapotec texts use *lledo*, perhaps /yedo/, in the stock phrase *diacalachi xana dieo Dios lledo llela nabani quea*, "our lord God wishes to end my life" (AHJO-VA Civ 369, 3r, Tabaá, 1750).

19. Miller (1998) also regarded the Zapotec cosmos as containing three separate houses associated with the twenty trecenas, but I have arrived at somewhat different translations than those he proposed for Calendar 85. Cruz (2007, 364) argued that this rotating scheme reflects the four cardinal directions. Such an interpretation rests on reading references to the House of Earth as an alternation between West and East, even though there is no support for this hypothesis in the Villa Alta calendrical corpus.

20. AGN-Inq 437-I, 3, 75v.

21. Smith-Stark 1999.

22. Sellen 2002, 213–32.

23. Weitlaner et al. 1958.

24. Van Meer 2000.

25. For two other proposals regarding Zapotec deities, see Alcina Franch 1993, table 16; and Cruz 2007, 409–10.

26. All three variants of this epithet contain the element *xee*, which may be glossed as "beginning," based on two of Córdova's (1578b, 140v, 141r) glosses: "Infinite god with no beginning, they called him, without knowing who he was" (*Coqui xèe, coqui cílla, xèe tao*).

27. Boone 2007, 44–49.

28. Alcina Franch 1993, table 16; Sellen 2002, 231. I agree with Alcina Franch in terms of the correlations he proposed regarding Mictlanteuctli, Centeotl, and Tlaloc.

29. Both the Sola (*licuicha*) and the Caxonos Zapotec (*cobicha*) name for this solar deity are cognates of *ko-kwitza*, the proto-Zapotecan term for "sun" or "day" (Kaufman 2004).

30. See Flannery and Marcus 1983; Marcus and Flannery 1996.

31. See the declarations of Joseph Hernández from San Pablo Caxonos, AGI-Mex 882, 301v; and Pedro Gonzalo from Yaa, AGI-Mex 882, 305v.

32. See, for example, AHJO Crim 49. Yagtao or "Great Tree" may be a metaphor referring to ancestral origins and genealogies.

33. Oudijk 2000, 141–52; see also Oudijk, 2003.

34. Oudijk 2008.

35. This community, near Tanetze, should not be confused with the Chatino-speaking Santa Catarina Juquila discussed above in Chapter 6, or the Mixe-speaking Xuquila in the alcaldía mayor of Nexapa (Chance 1989, 83).

36. AGI-Mex 882, 190v.

37. Urcid, personal communication, 2005.

38. Whitecotton 1990; Oudijk and Jansen 1999.

39. Oudijk 2003.

40. AGI-Mex 882, 156v–57r.

41. A similar name still designates a site in the outskirts of Lachirioag.

42. Marcus and Flannery 1994, 415–18.

43. See, for instance, Boone 1994; and Kirchhoff Odena Güemes, and Reyes García 1989.

44. Barrera Vázquez 1965; Nájera Coronado 2007.

45. Bierhorst 1985, 42; Karttunen and Lockhart 1980, 15–65.

46. A full version of this argument appears in Tavárez 2009b.

47. For a discussion of epistemological issues raised by the existence of these syllables, see Tomlinson 2007.

48. Occasionally, the stanza end is marked not by sung syllables, but by a well-formed sentence, such as "Sing, you brothers" in Song 67 from *Cantares Mexicanos*, or *Santa Maria alleluya* in Song 3, Villa Alta Booklet 102.

49. The presence of percussion patterns in the Christian libana and their suspicious absence in the non-Christian dij dola suggest that these patterns were not transcribed by traditional Zapotec specialists.

50. In Caxonos Zapotec, the variant in which Booklets 100 and 101 were written, this phoneme is realized as a voiceless alveopalatal affricate in the same words, yielding the orthographic variants *gueche* and *chela*. These two variants define an isogloss dividing central Villa Alta into Nexitzo and Bixanos variants to the northwest and northeast, and the Caxonos variant to the south.

51. AGI-Mex 882, 430r.

52. AHJO-VA Crim 133, 1v, 21v, 37r.

53. Córdova (1578b) glosses *léea* as "orchard" (222v), "patio" (305v); in several Villa Alta testaments, *leya* and *lea* are glossed as "patio" or "enclosure." *Yahui* is a Nexitzo Zapotec cognate of the Valley Zapotec term *quéhui* or *quihui*, "palace, royal house" (341v), "regal" (80v, 98r, 212r), or even "something old or ancient" (27v–28r). See Tavárez 2006a, for a detailed discussion of these songs.

54. Winston-Allen 1997, quoted in Burkhart 2001, 15. Córdova (1578b, 157v) lists two Valley Zapotec terms for the expression "to become pregnant": one used only for Mary (*tàca lào xínia*), and four commonplace variants (*tiyóo xíni lània, ticáa xínia, ticá tàoya, ticcàa lào xínia*).

55. The term *gueag beo* is reflected in the contemporary Caxonos Zapotec *yej pi'o*, "azalea" (Long 1999, 299).

56. For instance, in its Salve Regina, Feria (1567, 56v) called the Virgin "Oh life, sweetness" (*quela nabanniè, quela naxiè*), and Pacheco de Silva ([1687] 1752, 35r) used *naxij* in such expressions as "the sweet, pure womb of the Lady of us all, the Virgin Mary" (*lehe naxij naiaari quie Xonaaxi quie reheo Rabaani Maria*).

57. Bautista Viseo 1606, transcribed and translated in Burkhart 2001, 16.

58. See Durston 2007, for Marian metaphors in doctrinal Quechua.

59. Burgoa [1674] 1989, vol. 2, 126.

60. Ibid., vol. 1, 267.

61. Peñafiel 1981, xxix.

62. Reyes [1704] 1891.

63. According to de la Fuente [1949] 1979, a nineteenth-century reprint of this *Doctrina* was still consulted with reverence in Yalálag in the 1930s.

64. AHJO-VA Crim 25; AHJO-VA Crim 49.

65. AGI-Mex 881; AGI-Mex 882.

66. AGPEO 6, no. 9.

67. AHAO-Mart S-1, 1–3.

68. A nineteenth-century cycle of paintings at the church of San Juan de Dios in Oaxaca City depicts an idealized narrative about the "Martyrs of Caxonos"; see McIntyre 1997. Furthermore, Traffano (2001) discusses church policies toward Oaxaca natives in the nineteenth century; Wright-Rios (2009) analyzes Gillow's pastoral administration.

69. The records Gillow had transcribed in 1889 comprise about 633 non-duplicated pages and are kept at the AHAO as Mártires de Caxonos S-1, S-2, and S-3 (1–530 and 642–83); S-4 (numbered 530–641); and S-15; some of these pages are duplicates. Gillow's transcription bears various paginations, and I cite the most recent one. I compared this set with three different sets of documents: a section of the original Caxonos records now kept at La Merced (AMO Caxonos trial records 5r–189v), which are interspersed with an idolatry case against don Lorenzo Rosales; another set of originals at the AHAO, ff. 203r–74r, and four sets of photocopies of the original records in the collection of don Luis Castañeda (ALC 1270-1, 1–56; ALC 1270-2, 5–18; ALC 1270-3, 57–147; ALC 1270-4, 148–62). This comparison suggests that the 1889 transcriptions are accurate. Only about fifty-four pages from these transcriptions cannot be matched with originals or photocopies of originals. A section of the original proceedings, now housed along with some relevant records from 1775 in a judicial archive (AHJO-VA Crim 6, no. 18) was published as Ballesteros César 2004.

70. AHAO-Mart, 269r, original records.

71. AMO Caxonos trial records; AHAO Mártires de Caxonos S-1, S-2, S-3, S-4, and 203r–74r; ALC 1270-1, 1270-2, 1270-3, 1270-4; Ballesteros César 2004, 31–35.

72. Gillow [1889] 1990, 103. Yannakakis 2008, 66–68, following Gillow, identifies these two informants as fiscales.

73. AMO Caxonos trial records, 95r–v. This testimony was confirmed by Pinelo and five other witnesses. An earlier analysis of this statement appeared in Tavárez 2006b.

74. AHAO-Mart S-3, pp. 375–76.

75. AHAO-Mart, 265v–66v, original autos.

76. Ibid., 269r, original autos; also, see ALC 1270-1; and AHAO-Mart S-2.

77. See AGN-Civ 343, no. 3, particularly 244r–59r. An insightful analysis of the activities of Santiago and Celis appears in Yannakakis 2008, 39–58.

78. AMO Caxonos trial records, 18r–25r; 30r–33v; 70r–79v. As noted by Rosales's attorney Fernando de Gálvez, his client's case was mistakenly sewn together with proceedings about the Caxonos uprising.

79. AHAO-Mart S-2, 419–22.

80. Spores 1998, 41; Patch 1998, 79.

81. AHAO-Mart S-4, 550–603.

82. AHAO-LCab 1700–1701.

83. Mier del Tojo's standing is reflected by a 1699 suit contending he was the legitimate executor of the prominent merchant don Francisco de Dávila y Medina, and challenging claims made by the alcalde mayor of Miahuatlán (AGEO-AM 19, no. 10).

84. Gay 1998, 387.

85. AGN-Tier 2958, no. 204.

86. ALC Box 19, Archives of escribano Páez de la Cadena, 93r–98v.

87. AGI-Mex 880.

88. AGI-Mex 877.

89. This detail was provided in a report to the crown written circa 1710 by Antonio de Torres, procurator general of the Dominicans in Oaxaca (AGI-Mex 880). Although Maldonado wrote a point-by-point rebuttal, he remained suspiciously silent on the subject of this peculiar emissary.

90. AGI-Mex 882, 114r.

91. AHJO-VA Crim 129, 21v.

92. AGI-Mex 880.

93. Ramos, from the barrio of Analco in San Ildefonso, became the official interpreter for the civil court at Villa Alta sometime after 1673, when his predecessor, the equally powerful Nicolás de Vargas, was assassinated by a cuckolded husband. Ramos was the sole heir to the landholdings of his father, the wealthy mestizo Nicolás de Chaves (AHJO-VA Civ 141). His cultural roots in Analco are evidenced by the fact that his translations reflected the phonology of Caxonos Zapotec, the variant heard near the head town of San Ildefonso, rather than that of Nexitzo or Bixanos. For instance, he rendered Yetzelálag as "Guechelala."

94. AHJO-VA Crim 133, 1v–3v, 12r–13r. This trial is incomplete.

95. Chance 1989, 48–63.

96. Le Roy Ladurie 1975.

97. AGI-Mex 879; AGI-Mex 882.

98. AGI-Mex 882, 296r–391v.

99. AGI-Mex 880; AGI-Mex 881.

100. AGI-Mex 880.

101. Maldonado ca. 1720.

102. AGI-Mex 880.

103. Ibid.

104. AGI-Mex 882.

105. Chance 1989, 167.

106. ALC Box 19, Archives of escribano Páez de la Cadena, 99r–100v.

107. Santiago also reported eating insects resembling dung beetles in the early rainy season in order to find lost objects (AHJO-VA Crim 117, 39r).

108. AHJO-VA Crim 117, 33r. For Yagtao, see note 32 above.

109. AHJO-VA Crim 117, 39v–40r.

110. Ibid., 37v.

111. Reko 1945, 44, 61.

112. Hoffmann (1995, 316) states that the brown seeds of a plant obtained in Oaxaca and identified by him as *Turbina corymbosa* are known as *badoh*, a term cognate with (cuana) betao. While Córdova's 1578 *Vocabulario* does not refer to any cuana betao cognate, it designates a type of vision-inducing mushrooms as *pèya çòo* (*Vea çoo* in Villa Alta), *nocuàna penèeche*, and *coopà tào*, and describes *Nocuàna còhui* as a vision-inducing fruit with small protuberances.

113. AHJO-VA 117, 39r.

114. Chance 1989, 48–63.

115. This abridged liturgical year featured Epiphany (which also celebrated Betaza's patron saint), Christ's purification at the Temple, Easter, the feast of the Holy Spirit, Corpus Christi, Our Lady of the Rosary, All Saints, and Christmas. Before 1704, visiting priests performed these celebrations in a site between Betaza and Lachitaa (AHJO-VA Crim 117, 28v, 27v).

116. Ibid., 60r.

117. Ibid., 24r–v.

118. For Cancuc, see Gosner 1992, 1998; Viqueira 1997b.

119. AHJO-VA Crim 117, 60r.

120. Yalálag held an important place due to its location on the road between Oaxaca and Villa Alta's capital, as well as its relatively large population—about 1,577 residents in 1703 (Chance 1989, 48).

121. AHJO-VA Crim 117, 9r.

122. While there were no conflicts between Yalálag and Betaza during this period, Betaza and Lachitaa had land conflicts with their northern neighbor, San Andres Yaa; see AHJO-VA Crim 207.

123. AHJO-VA Crim 117, 17v.

124. Ibid., 28v.

125. Ibid., 47v, 49v: Gaspar Bautista, Fabian Luis, Joseph Luis, and Juan Gerónimo.

126. Central Mexican indigenous confraternities routinely constituted themselves as money-lending enterprises. For instance, during the 1760s in the Nahua community of Tlapa in central Guerrero, the "money of the saint" provided income for confraternity expenses. Local residents borrowed amounts from this fund at usurious rates, which ranged between 25 and 100 percent; both principal and interest were repaid by the year's end (Dehouve 1988).

127. AHJO-VA Crim 117, 17r–v.

128. Ibid., 28v.

129. Ibid., 51r–v.

130. Ibid., 62v; see also Sánchez Bella 1992; Sarmiento Donate 1988.

131. This yields a 1705 estimate of 224 families in Betaza, only slightly higher than Chance's (1989) figure of 203 families.

132. AGI-Mex 882, 105v.

133. AHJO-VA 8, exp. 20, 2v. The alleged prayer begins with the generic formula *varegli lachi neto betao . . . que neto.*

134. AHJO-VA Crim 8, exp. 11, 1r–13r.

135. AGN-Inq 734, 418r–40r; AGN-RC duplicadas, vol. 42, no. 352. Greenleaf (1965, 147–48) does not mention Reyes's revelations regarding Cotes's behavior.

136. AHJO-VA Crim 184, 2v–3r.

137. Chance 1989.

138. AHJO-VA Crim 8, exp. 19.

139. AHJO-VA Crim 129, 21v.

140. AHJO-VA Crim 133.

141. AHJO-VA Civ 98, 1r.

142. See Twinam (1999) for a comprehensive perspective on honor and status in colonial Latin America.

143. AHJO-VA Civ 44, 17r; AHJO-VA Civ 93, 1r.

144. AHJO-VA Civ 144, 5v.

145. AHJO-VA Civ 93, 6r; AHJO-VA Civ 96, 10r.

Chapter 8

1. AHAM 13, no. 165, 1r.

2. The trials discussed below were heard by the following ecclesiastical judges in the periods indicated between parentheses: Juan Díaz del Castillo (1691) under Provisor Torres y Vergara; Juan Varón de Lara (1722–29) under Provisores Castorena y Urzúa and Aldave; Nicolás de Villegas (1734–37), Diego de Orosco (1742), Gerónimo Carranza (a judge at Calimaya, 1745), and Juan del Villar (1747–56), all under Provisor Ramírez del Castillo; George Martínez (1758–67) and Mathías Joseph de Eguiluz (1761) under Provisores Ximénez Caso and/or Manuel de Barrientos y Lomelí; and Alejo Antonio Betancourt (1774-1780) under Provisor Miguel Primo de Rivera. All of them resided at Toluca, except for Carranza. Original trial records were kept at the provisorato in Mexico City, and a copy was sent back to Toluca (AHAM 17, no. 233).

3. García Castro 1999, 75.

4. Gerhard 1972, 330; Galinier 1990, cited in Lara Cisneros 2002, 55.

5. García Castro 1999, 196, 199.

6. Jarquín Ortega 1990, 74.

7. García Castro 1999, 148, 153.

8. See Vetancourt [1698] 1982, part 4, 61–62.

9. The healer María la Juachina of Calimaya was identified as a healer who cast off *ehecameh*, or dangerous "winds" (AHAM 1767a); Pedro Nicolás of San Francisco Zinacantepec was called a ticitl by his clients (AHAM 26, no. 414); and Gaspar de los Reyes was identified as a hail caster in Nahuatl (AHAM 1748–49).

10. Alatorre and Tenorio (1998) argue that Castorena y Urzúa may even be the author of the 1691 "Letter by Serafina de Cristo," an important letter in Sor Juana's correspondence.

11. AGN-Indif 215, no. 45.

12. AGI-Contr 5460, no. 1, ramo 17. See Taylor 1996, 121–22, for a discussion of cathedral chapter offices.

13. AGN-Indif 214.

14. Besides the *Fama* and the *Gaceta*, his works as author or editor include *Abraham Académico en el Racional Iucio de los Doctores . . .* (1696); *La planta de la concepción, descalza de cvlpa . . .* (1700); *Cíngulos del Espíritu . . .* (1703); *Fructo de bendicion de la rosa de Castilla y la flor de lyz francesa . . .* (1709); *Raçones de la lealtad, cláusulas de la finesa en Elogio de las Hazañas . . .* (1711?); *Parabién de las letras a las armas . . .* (published in *Festivo triduo*, 1712); *El predicador convertido en los principios de su predicación . . .* (1719); *Ocupación angélica dolorosa . . .* (1720; *Novena angélica dolorosa . . .* (1720; reprinted in 1763); *El congregante prevenido . . .* (1724, 1725); *El complemento de los designios del Hijo de Dios . . .* (1725); *Las Indias entendidas por estar religiosamente sacramentadas . . .* (1725); *El minero mas feliz . . .* (1728); *Escuela Mystica de María Santíssima . . .* (1731); and *Noticias verídicas y formidables de las gravíssimas penas que padecen los condenados en el infierno . . .* (1731).

15. BNM-Imp RSM 1697 M4COF. As Castorena y Urzúa launches into an enthusiastic panegyric of Mary, he glosses a Latin phrase by jurist Giacomo Menochio as "Feathers in the Sun. Rays in the Birds." His unimpressed reader quips, "Feathers to the wind, voices in the air, all that is missing is a guitar."

16. Taylor 1996, 120.

17. AGN-Indif 215, no. 45.

18. AGN-Inq 753.

19. AGN-Inq 1305, no. 13, 37r.

20. AGI-Mex 278.

21. Gerhard 1972, 273.

22. This painting is now at the Museo Nacional de Arte (CONACULTA, INBA) in Mexico City.

23. AGN-Inq 803, no. 52. For a discussion of Cora religiosity, see Warner 2002.

24. This tendency coincides with the reorganization of criminal courts in Mexico City in the first quarter of the eighteenth century (Haslip-Viera 1999).

25. AGN-Inq 803, no. 52. The inquisitors judiciously refused to lend out their paraphernalia.

26. AGI-MP, Bulas y Breves 377, ramo 4, no. 3a.

27. An example of a case in which this description of procedure was followed to the letter is that of Sebastiana Francisca of Tepexuxuca in 1726 (see note 30).

28. Taylor 1996, 158, 604.

29. For a Toluca example, see AHAM 18, no. 36, 1r (1691).

30. Occasionally, parish priests overstepped these boundaries. In 1726, after Sebastiana Francisca of Tepexuxuca was turned over to the provisorato by the priest Nicolás de Villegas on suspicion of having cast a spell on his mother, she complained that Villegas had her in shackles at an associate's home for two months. She had also been suspended from a roof beam for several hours. The provisor did not reprehend Villegas, however (AHAM 15, no. 206, 9r–v).

31. For a 1744 proclamation, see AGN-Inq 1168, no. 16.

32. If an escribano was not present, the ecclesiastic judge could have testimony written down before two witnesses of his choice; see AHAM 1764b, "Autos de fe . . . contra Agustina Maria," 4v.

33. See Provisor Aldave's ruling in AHAM 16, no. 221, 1v.

34. AHAM 10, no. 142, 1r.

35. See, for instance, the 1652 inquisitorial trial for divination and sorcery of Antón Chino from Cochin, a slave living in Coyoacán (AGN-Inq 456, 55r–98r). For an overview of indios extravagantes, see O'Hara 2010, 40–43, 93–95.

36. See, for example, two autos by the inquisitorial commissary of Manila, one regarding the crafting of idols for the king of Siam in the home of don Benito Carrasco in 1719 (AGN-Inq 780, no. 4, 344r–54r), and another about an idol found with the belongings of don Fernando Bustamante y Rueda, a former governor of the Philippines, in 1720 (AGN-Inq 784, no. 20, ff. 1r–4v (1759);

37. See, for instance, AGN-Inq 776, no. 25 (1724); AGN-Inq 943, no. 10, 363r–66v (1756).

38. See AGN-Inq 753, 639r–53r (1713); AGN-Inq 1046, 204r–13v (1721); AGN-Inq 901, no. 36, 328r–37v (1744); AGN-Inq 1001, no. 4, 344r–54r (1759); AGN-Inq 1042, no. 4 (1764); AGN-Inq 966, no. 21 (1759); AGN-Inq 1331, no. 4, 107r–19v (1790).

39. There exist many examples; for instance, the extant set of accusations for the period 1705–20 includes AGN-Inq 729, no. 19 (1705); AGN-Inq 1122, no. 8 (1713); AGN-Inq 878, no. 13 (1713); AGN-Inq 878, no. 40 (1713); AGN-Inq 878, no. 46 (1716); AGN-Inq 552-I, no. 2 (1716); AGN-Inq 757, 289r (1716); AGN-Inq 1051, 138r, 140r (1718); AGN-Inq 817-II, no. 19 (1727).

40. For example, in 1737 Chilpancingo's inquisitorial commissary participated in an inquiry against nonnative idolaters (AGN-Inq 862, no. 36, 256r–78r). Unusually (Greenleaf 1965, 164), in 1785–87 the Holy Office initiated a trial against five natives from Hunucmá, Campeche, for idolatry (AGN-Inq 1256, no. 1, 1r–91v).

41. Greenleaf 1965, 159–63.

42. AGN-Inq 1037, no. 6, 248r–97r.

43. AGN-Inq 1168, no. 16, 232r–37r.

44. AGN-Inq 1037, no. 6, 290r–97r.

45. Quezada 1989, 109–10.

46. ACM L o, C 2, E 1, 1r–v.

47. AHAM 147, no. 6, 1r.

48. For a measure of contrast see AGN-Ind 24, no. 121, which records one hundred lashes and ten years' exile for don Francisco de Alvarado, cacique of Tlapa, for idolatry.

49. AHAM 16, no. 223.

50. Ibid., no. 221.

51. AHAM 17, no. 233.

52. ACM-Litig 7–17.1, 1363–4, 2 ff. This sentence is neither signed nor dated, but Joseph Joaquín Flores Moreno served as the provisorato's fiscal in this proceeding and in the 1729 trial of Pascual de los Reyes.

53. AHAM 15, no. 215, 1v–2r; Bartolomé was entitled to wages after the court recouped all of his proceeding's costs.

54. AHAM 23, no. 347b, 1r–2r.

55. Molina [1571] 1992, 92v.

56. Garibay 1946, 2, 135–254, 167–74.

57. Martínez González 2006, 36.

58. De la Serna 1892, 289–90.

59. AHAM 1748–49, 1r–3r.

60. AHAM 15, no. 215, 1r–v. He also invoked the Christ of Chalma, Our Lady of Guadalupe of Los Remedios, and San Antonio.

61. Ibid., 1v.

62. AHAM 23, no. 347b, 1r–2r.

63. This was Torres y Vergara's first post, granted him by Archbishop Eguiar y Seijas in the late 1680s; he would eventually serve the diocese as judge of testaments in 1692–1727 (Aguirre Salvador 2001, 83).

64. AHAM 18, no. 36, 3v.

65. Nicholson 1971, 417; Boone 2007, 197–99.

66. AHAM 18, no. 36, 1v–2v. They agreed this herb was called *paquinchi* or *panquischi*, noting, in an enigmatic aside, that its Spanish name was *bangui*.

67. De la Serna 1892, 293.

68. Romero 1956.

69. AHAM 52, no. 8, 1r.

70. Ibid., 3r.

71. This plant may be *Salvia divinorum*.

72. AHAM 73, exp. 20, 1r–v, 5v.

73. Ibid., 2v.

74. AGN-Inq 1122, no. 8, 147r–48r (1713).

75. AGN-Inq 821, 580r–v (1728).

76. AGN-Inq 1455, no. 5, 31r–32r (1812).

77. AHAM 1764a.

78. AHAM 92, no. 14, 4v.

79. Two more cases provide further evidence of the ritual use of clay effigies. In 1734, Diego Lele of San Miguel Totocuitlapilco was accused of going to the water spring at Apitzalco to place an offering that included *tzoalli* or amaranth dough (see Sahagún 1950–1982, book 2, 71, 145–46, 175–76), and clay effigies (AHAM 20, no. 311). In 1742, Diego Nicolás of Zinacantepec was told by Pedro Nicolás to take some "dolls from Metepec" to a nearby mountain so that Diego's illness "would stick to them" (AHAM 26, no. 414, 1r–2v).

80. Mandrou 1980; Kamen 1998.

81. Evans-Pritchard 1937, 63–65.

82. AHAM 13, no. 165.

83. AHAM-Var no. 347–1, 9 ff.

84. AHAM 17, no. 231.

85. AHAM 1760, "Contra Sebastiana María."

86. AHAM 1756, "Juana Clara viuda de Juan Leonardo."

87. AHAM 1756, "Contra Maria Rosa y Juana Clara por maléficas," 1761.

88. AHAM 1764b, "Contra Domingo Pascual y Antonio Rafael . . . por hechiceros."

89. AHAM Varios, no. 347–1, 1v.

90. AHAM 52, no. 8, 1r.

91. AHAM, 1756, "Contra Maria Rosa y Juana Clara por maléficas," 1761, 4v.

92. AHAM 63, nò. 34.

93. Vetancourt [1698] 1982, vol. 4, 62.

94. AHAM C 1764b, "Contra Agustina María . . . por hechicera."

95. AHAM 1765, "Desiderio Joseph Gutierrez denuncia."

96. AHAM 17, no. 233.

97. AHAM 16, no. 223, 1v–2v.

98. AHAM 1756, "Andres Martin y Jacinto Tapia . . . por curanderos," 1r–v.

99. From the Nahuatl *iztauhyatl; Artemisia ludoviciana* ssp. *mexicana*, a plant used for gastrointestinal diseases. Iztauhyatl is mentioned in the Codex Badianus (26r, 35r, 37r, 37v, 50r, 55v) and by Sahagún (1950–1982, book 10, 165, 140; book 11, 149, 165). See also Heinrich 2002, 107–17.

100. AHAM 1756, "Contra Andres Martin y Jacinto Tapia," 4r–v.

101. AHAM 92, no. 14, 6r–v.

102. Ibid., 4r.

103. AHAM 1764a, "Diligencias sobre la cura que Joseph Antonio de Samaniego."

104. Taylor 1996, 334, 706.

105. AGI-Mex 1937, Rubio y Salinas to the king, April 30, 1755, 12v.

106. Taylor 1996, 340–42; see also Heath 1972.

107. AHAM 1754, "Edicto del Arzobispo Rubio y Salinas sobre causas de maleficios contra indios." For parish secularization, see Taylor 1996, 83–86.

108. AHAM 15, no. 206, 3v.

109. AHAM 17, no. 233, "María Joachina casada con Marcelo Francisco."

110. Spanish physicians defined *causas procatárticas* as those located outside the patient's body; see Fragoso and Díaz 1627, 83.

111. AHAM 97, no. 26, 1r–v.

112. AGN-Crim 208, 135r–46r. I thank William B. Taylor for generously sharing this important reference with me.

113. Gruzinski 1988, 105–72.

114. AGN-Inq 1073, no. 2, 13r–119v and 225r–53r; AGN-Inq 1032, no. 3, 30r–36v; AGN-Inq 1000, no. 21, 291r–99v; AGI-Mex 1696.

115. AGN-BN 992, no. 557, 1r–4r; AGN-RC Originales 82, no. 72; AGN-RC Originales 86, no. 140, 298r–307r.

116. AGN-Inq 1094, 117v.

117. AGN-Crim 308, no. 1, 11r–14v; Taylor 1979, 124; Gruzinski 1988, 209.

118. AGN-Inq 42, no. 17.

119. Moreover, Calvo (2009) provides a microhistorical account of conflicts in Yatzona.

120. AGN-Ind 53, no. 180, 197r–98v.

121. AGN-Ind 55, exp. 21, 8r–v

122. AGN-Ind 33, no. 139, 92r–93v.

123. Ibid., no. 170, 117r–18r.

124. This accusation is misfiled with a different case in AHJO-VA Civ 61. I thank Yanna Yannakakis for sharing her notes on this case with me.

125. AHJO-YAU 1739, 1r–3v.

126. AGN-Ind 51, no. 134, 144r–v.

127. AGEO-Obisp 2, no. 5, 1r–3r.

128. AHJO-VA Crim 225.

129. AHJO-VA Crim 227.

130. AGN-Inq 960, no. 17, 283v–84v.

131. This work, *Doctrina christiana en lengua chinanteca*, was modeled after Ripalda's catechism and primarily reflected the Chinantec spoken near San Pedro Yoloz, Barreda's parish.

132. Chance 1989, 134–35.

133. Ibid., 146–47; Carmagnani 1988.

134. AGN-Inq 966, no. 21, 1v–2v.

135. "Pochote" is the Hispanicized form of the Nahuatl *pochotl*, "silk-cotton tree."

136. AGN-Inq 960, no. 17, 265r–66r, 286r.

137. Ibid., 271r–72r.

138. In this case, the Audiencia supported the alcalde mayor's intervention due to a revolt in Choapa. See Yannakakis 2008, 41–43.

139. Ibid., 272v–73v, 275r–v.

140. Ibid., 276r–82r.

141. AGN-Inq 966, no. 21, 2v–3v.

142. AGN-Inq 876, no. 41, 225r–77v. See Gruzinski 1978.

143. Dundes 1992.

144. Nutini and Roberts 1993.

145. AGN-Inq 960, no. 17, 286v–87r.

146. AGN-GenPar 41, no. 144, 85r.

147. AGN-AM 8, 34r–v; AGN-AM 4, 236r–v.

148. AGN-AM 5, 21r–22r. This order was issued to the alcaldes mayores of Zimatlán, Teococuilco, Teotitlán del Camino, Tehuacán de las Granadas, Oaxaca, Villa Alta, Xicayán (de Nieto), Nejapa, Tehuantepec, Teutila, Cuatro Villas, Jalapa, Miahuatlán, Juxtlahuaca, Nochixtlán, and Teposcolula.

149. Responses were sent back from Teotila (AGN-AM 4, 236r–v; AGN-AM 8, 189r–90r), Antequera, Nejapa, Nochixtlán (AGN-AM 8, 271r–v, 32r–v, 43r–v), and Zimatlán (AGN-AM 9, 132r–v).

150. AGI-Mex 2582, Testimony of Fiscal Posada, 5r–6r.

151. AGN-Indif 145, no. 64.

152. AHJO-VA Crim 125.

153. AGI-Mex 877.

154. Ibid.

155. AGI-Mex 2585, Letter from Bishop Blanco (March 20, 1758).

156. This drawing is archived at the AHAO; its date (*Ma< . . . > 175< . . . >*) and some of the legends are illegible due to rips in the document, but the style and hand suggest it was made in the late eighteenth century. A legend lists five

prison officials: Santiago el Mantero, Antonio Rendón, Manuel Mendoza, someone with the last name Arras, and a fifth person.

157. AHAO-Dioc 1762.

158. AGI-Mex 357.

159. AGN-Carc, no. 3, 1r–158v.

160. AGI-Mex 2585, Letters from Bishop Blanco (March 3, 1755; March 20, 1758; April 25, 1763); Response from the Royal fiscal to Bishop Blanco (December 21, 1763).

161. Ibid., Testimony from the Subdelegado de Cruzada in Oaxaca, not dated.

162. AGI-Mex 2587, Visita of Bishop Ortigosa, November 20, 1784, 11v–13v. For Mixe cosmology, see Lipp 1998; for Mixe territoriality and social organization, see Barros 2007.

163. AGN-Inq 256, no. 10, 146r–47v.

164. AGN-BN 149, no. 25, 1r–6r.

165. AGN-Jud 8, no. 12, 201r–47r.

166. For a recent discussion of this issue, see Silverblatt 2004; Schwartz 2008.

167. AGN-Inq 1256, no. 10, 146r–47r.

168. Henningsen 1980; Certeau 2000.

169. Tilly 2008, 3.

170. Gruzinski 1988, 1993; and Taylor 1979.

171. AGN-Inq 1128, no. 6, 208r–14r; the accuser later recanted this claim.

172. Lara Cisneros 2002, 148–60.

173. AGN-Inq 1049, no. 24, 286r–87v.

174. AGN-Inq 1465, 85r–87r.

175. AGN-BN 663, no. 30, 1r–19v.

176. AGEO 16, no. 30, 1r–1v.

177. This broadsheet is inserted in AGN-Inq 1037, no. 6, and cited in Greenleaf 1965. For its impact on Nahuatl theater, see Burkhart 2010.

178. BRP 1462; JCB-CodInd 52.

179. JCB-CodSp 52, 251r–65v; this source is discussed in detail in Taylor 1996, 72–73.

Chapter 9

1. These descriptions are based on interviews and fieldwork conducted in the spring of 2008 with Fidel Cacho González, municipal president of Upper Betaza; don Bartolo Cosme Jiménez, a town elder at San Andrés Yaa; and Aurelia Cano, a ritual specialist from Lachirioag.

2. See, for example, Lupo 1995; Monaghan 1999; Sandstrom 1992.

3. Lipp 1998 Stresser-Péan 2009; Weitlaner et al. 1958; Weitlaner and De Cicco 1961. Some sections of a Northern Zapotec calendar that was copied in the nineteenth century appear in Zanhe Xbab Sa 2006.

4. Chance 1996; Chance and Taylor 1985.

5. Brading 2001; Poole 1995; Nutini 1988.

6. See, for instance, Cummins 1995; Gruzinski 2002.

7. Dehouve 1988; Gruzinski 1985, 1990; Lavrín 1988; Schroeder 2000; Taylor 1994, 1996.

8. See Lewis 2003.

9. The most influential analysis of such peasant Christianities appears in Christian 1981a, 1981b.

10. Smith 1992, 119–20.

11. Scott 1985.

12. Stern 1987, 15.

13. Foucault 1977, 1–5.

14. Ibid., 47.

15. Ibid., 49.

16. Ibid., 58.

17. BNAH, Colección Antigua 273 (II); AGN-Inq 2-II, no. 2.

18. AHAM 15, no. 215.

19. AGN-Inq 38, no. 7; Boletín del AGN 1941, 213; AGN-Inq 37, no. 2; AGN-Inq 30, no. 9; AGN-Inq 212, no. 7; ACM-Litig 7–17.1, 1363–4.

20. AGN-Inq 212, no. 7; AGN-Inq 510–II, no. 112.

21. AHAM 16, no. 223; AHAM 16, no. 221; AHAM 17, no. 233.

22. AGN-Inq 40, no. 8.

23. AGI-Just 191, no. 2; AHAO-Mart S-1 to S-4.

24. AGN-Inq 510, no. 133; Greenleaf 1965, 146.

25. AHJO-VA Crim 19, 22, 25; AHAO-Mart S-1 to S-4.

26. De la Serna 1892, 287.

27. See Kantorowicz 1957.

28. Foucault 1977, 28–29.

29. Sáenz de Santa María 1981, 495.

30. Lamadrid 1951, 354–55.

31. Silverblatt 2004, 25–27, 220–22.

32. Friedrich 1977, 130; Friedrich 1986.

Bibliography

Acosta, José. [1590] 1962. *Historia natural y moral de las Indias*. Mexico: Fondo de Cultura Económica.

Acuña, René. 1986. *Relaciones geográficas del siglo XVI: Mexico*. Vol. II. Mexico: Universidad Nacional Autónoma de México.

Agüero, Cristóbal de. 1666. *Misceláneo Espiritual en el idioma Zapoteco*. Mexico: Francisco Rodríguez Lupercio.

Aguirre Beltrán, Gonzalo. 1963. *Medicina y magia: El proceso de aculturación en el México colonial*. Mexico: Instituto Nacional Indigenista.

Aguirre Salvador, Rodolfo. 2001. "Los catedráticos juristas de México." In *Universidad y sociedad en Hispanoamérica: grupos de poder, siglos XVIII y XIX*, ed. Margarita Menegus Bornemann, 63–114. Mexico: Universidad Nacional Autonoma de México, Centro de Estudios sobre la Universidad.

Alatorre, Antonio, and Martha Lilia Tenorio. 1998. *Serafina y Sor Juana: Con tres apéndices*. Mexico: Colegio de México.

Alberro, Solange. 1988. *Inquisición y sociedad en Mexico, 1571–1700*. Mexico: Fondo de Cultura Económica.

———. 1992. *Del gachupín al criollo*. Mexico: Colegio de México.

Alcina Franch, José. 1993. *Calendario y religión entre los zapotecos*. Mexico: Universidad Nacional Autónoma de México.

———. 1998. "Mapas y calendarios zapotecos; siglos XVI y XVII." In *Historia del Arte en Oaxaca*, vol. 2, 173–91. Oaxaca, Mexico: Consejo Nacional para la Cultura y las Artes, Gobierno de Oaxaca.

Alva, Bartolomé de. [1634] 1999. *A Guide to Confession Large and Small in the Mexican Language, 1634*. Trans. and ed. Barry Sell, John F. Schwaller, and Lu Ann Homza. Norman: University of Oklahoma Press.

Andrews, J. Richard. 1975. *Introduction to Classical Nahuatl*. Austin: University of Texas Press.

Anonymous. 1935. *Ayer MS Planetary Calendar en Lengua Nahuatl del año 1639*. Publication 17. Baltimore, MD: The Maya Society.

Anunciación, Domingo. 1565. *Doctrina Christiana breve y compendiosa*. Mexico: Pedro Ocharte.

Anunciación, Juan. 1575. *Doctrina Christiana muy cumplida*. Mexico: Pedro Balli.

————. 1577. *Sermonario en lengua mexicana.* Mexico: Antonio Ricardo.

Aquinas, Thomas. 1948. *Summa Theologiae.* Rome: Marietti.

Aramoni Calderón, Dolores. 1992. *Los refugios de lo sagrado. Religiosidad, conflicto y resistencia entre los zoques de Chiapas.* Mexico: Consejo Nacional para la Cultura y las Artes.

Asad, Talal. 1986. "Medieval Heresy: An Anthropological View." *Social History* 11 (3): 345–62.

Austin, John Langshaw. 1975. *How to Do Things with Words.* Cambridge, MA: Harvard University Press.

Ballesteros César, Claudia. 2004. *Los documentos de San Francisco Caxonos.* Oaxaca, Mexico: Archivo Histórico Judicial de Oaxaca, Proveedora Escolar, IAGO.

Balsalobre, Gonzalo. [1656] 1892. "Relación auténtica de las idolatrías, supersticiones, vanas observancias de los indios del obispado de Oaxaca." *Anales del Museo Nacional de México* (1ª Época) 6: 229–60.

Barlow, Robert. [1949] 1992. *La extensión del imperio de los Culhua-Mexica.* Mexico: Instituto Nacional de Antropología e Historia, Universidad de las Américas.

Barreda, Nicolás de la. 1730. *Doctrina Christiana en Lengua Chinanteca, añadida la Explicacion de los Principales Mysterios de la Fee.* Mexico: Herederos de la Viuda de Francisco Rodríguez Lupercio.

Barrera Vázquez, Alfredo. 1965. *El libro de los Cantares de Dzitbalché.* Mexico: Instituto Nacional de Antropología e Historia.

Barros, Alonso. 2007. "Cien años de guerras mixes: territorialidades prehispánicas, expansión burocrática y zapotequización en el Istmo de Tehuantepec durante el siglo XVI." *Historia Mexicana* 57 (2): 325–403.

Baskes, Jeremy. 2000. *Indians, Merchants, and Markets: A Reinterpretation of the Repartimiento and Spanish-Indian Economic Relations in Colonial Oaxaca, 1750-1821.* Stanford: Stanford University Press

Baudot, Georges. 1990. *La pugna franciscana por México.* Mexico: Consejo Nacional para la Cultura y las Artes.

————. 1995. *Utopia and History in Mexico: The First Chroniclers of Mexican Civilization, 1520–1569.* Niwot: University Press of Colorado.

Bautista Viseo, Fray Juan. 1599. *Confesionario en lengua mexicana y castellana.* Tlatilulco: Melchior Ocharte.

————. 1600a. *Advertencias para los confessores de los naturales.* Tlatilulco: Melchior Ocharte.

————. 1600b. *Huehuehtlahtolli.* Tlatelolco: Melchior Ocharte.

————. 1606. *Sermonario en Lengua mexicana.* Mexico: Casa de Diego Lopez Daualos.

Benassar, Bartolomé. 1979. *L'Inquisition espagnole, XVe–XIXe siècle.* Paris: Hachette.

Berdan, Frances F., Elizabeth Boone, et al. 1996. *Aztec Imperial Strategies.* Washington, DC: Dumbarton Oaks Research Library and Collection.

Berdan, Frances F., John K. Chance, Alan R. Sandstrom, Barbara L. Stark, James M. Taggart, and Emily Umberger. 2008. *Ethnic identity in Nahua*

Mesoamerica: The View from Archaeology, Art History, Ethnohistory, and Contemporary Ethnography. Salt Lake City: University of Utah Press.

Berlin Neubart, Heinrich. 1988. *Idolatría y supersticion entre los indios de Oaxaca.* Mexico: Ediciones Toledo.

Bernand, Carmen, and Serge Gruzinski. 1992. *De la idolatría: Una arqueología de las ciencias religiosas.* Mexico: Fondo de Cultura Económica.

Bierhorst, John. 1985. *Cantares Mexicanos: Songs of the Aztecs.* Stanford: Stanford University Press.

———. 1992. *Codex Chimalpopoca.* Tucson: University of Arizona Press.

Boletín del AGN. 1934. "Fragmento de un proceso de indios antropófagos." Vol. 5 (2): 169–73.

———. 1941. "Proceso contra Ana de Xochimilco." Vol. 12: 211–13.

Boone, Elizabeth. 2007. *Cycles of Time and Meaning in the Mexican Books of Fate.* Austin: University of Texas Press.

Boone, Elizabeth, and Walter Mignolo, eds. 1994. *Writing Without Words: Ancient Literacies in Mesoamerica and the Andes.* Durham, NC: Duke University Press.

Borah, Woodrow. 1951. *New Spain's Century of Depression.* Ibero Americana 35. Berkeley: University of California Press.

———. 1983. *Justice by Insurance: The General Indian Court of Colonial Mexico and the Legal Aides of the Half-Real.* Berkeley: University of California Press.

Boturini, Lorenzo. 1746. *Idea de una nueva historia general de la América septentrional.* Madrid: Juan de Zúñiga.

Bourdieu, Pierre. 1971. "Genèse et structure du champ religieux." *Revue Française de Sociologie* 12: 295–334.

Bouza, Fernando. 2001. *Corre manuscrito: Una historia cultural del Siglo de Oro.* Madrid: Marcial Pons Historia.

Brading, David A. 2001. *Mexican Phoenix: Our Lady of Guadalupe, Image and Tradition Across Five Centuries.* Cambridge: Cambridge University Press.

Bricker, Victoria Reifler. 1974. "The Ethnographic Context of Some Traditional Mayan Speech Genres." In *Explorations in the Ethnography of Speaking,* ed. Richard Bauman and Joel Sherzer, 368–88. New York: Cambridge University Press.

Burgoa, Fray Francisco de. [1670] 1989. *Palestra historial.* Mexico: Editorial Porrúa.

———. [1674] 1989. *Geográfica descripción.* 2 vols. Mexico: Editorial Porrúa.

Burkhart, Louise. 1989. *The Slippery Earth: Nahua-Christian Moral Dialogue in Sixteenth-Century Mexico.* Tucson: University of Arizona Press.

———. 1995. "The Voyage of Saint Amaro: A Spanish legend in Nahuatl Literature." *Colonial Latin American Review* 4: 29–57.

———. 1996. *Holy Wednesday: A Nahua Drama from Early Colonial Mexico.* Philadelphia: University of Pennsylvania Press.

———. 2001. *Before Guadalupe: The Virgin Mary in Early Colonial Nahuatl Literature.* Albany: Institute for Mesoamerican Studies, SUNY-Albany.

———. 2010. "Pageantry, Passion, and Punishment. Eighteenth-Century Nahuatl

Community Theater." In *Nahuatl Theater, Volume 4. Nahua Christianity in Performance*, eds. Barry Sell and Louise Burkhart, 3–50. Norman: University of Oklahoma Press.

Bustamante García, Jesús. 1990. *Fray Bernardino de Sahagún: Una revisión crítica de los manuscritos y de su proceso de composición*. Mexico: UNAM.

Butler, Ines. 1997. *Vocabulario zapoteco de Yatzachi el Bajo*. Mexico: Instituto Lingüístico de Verano.

Calvo, Thomas. 2009. *Vivre dans la Sierra zapotèque du Mexique, 1674–1707*. Paris: L'Harmattan.

Canger, Una. 1986. "Los dialectos del náhuatl de Guerrero." In *Primer coloquio de arqueología y etnohistoria del estado de Guerrero*, Instituto Nacional de Antropología e Historia, 281–94. Mexico: Instituto Nacional de Antropología e Historia.

Cañeque, Alejandro. 2004. *The King's Living Image: The Culture and Politics of Viceregal Power in Colonial Mexico*. New York: Routledge.

Cañizares-Esguerra, Jorge. 2001. *How to Write the History of the New World: Histories, Epistemologies, and Identities in the Eighteenth-Century Atlantic World*. Stanford: Stanford University Press.

Cárdenas, Juan de. [1591] 1965. *Problemas y secretos maravillosos de las Indias*. Mexico: Bibliófilos Mexicanos.

Carmagnani, Marcelo. 1988. *El regreso de los dioses: El proceso de reconstitución de la identidad étnica en Oaxaca, siglos XVII y XVIII*. Mexico: Fondo de Cultura Económica.

Carrasco, Pedro. 1984. "Royal Marriages in Ancient Mexico." In *Explorations in Ethnohistory*, ed. H. R. Harvey and Hanns J. Prem, 41–81. Albuquerque: University of New Mexico Press.

Cartas de Indias. 1877. Madrid: Imprenta de Manuel G. Hernández.

Caso, Alfonso. 1928. *Las Estelas Zapotecas*. Monografías del Museo Nacional de Arqueología, Historia, y Etnografía. Mexico: Talleres Gráficos de la Nación.

———. 1939. "La Correlación de los Años Azteca y Cristiano." *Revista Mexicana de Estudios Antropológicos* 3: 11–45.

———. 1945. "El Calendario Matlatzinca." *Revista Mexicana de Estudios Antropológicos* 8: 95–109.

———. 1965. "Zapotec Writing and Calendar." *In Handbook of Middle American Indians*, vol. 3, ed. Robert Wachope and Gordon R. Willey, 931–47. Austin: University of Texas Press.

Castellanos, Javier. 2003. *Diccionario Zapoteco-Español, Español-Zapoteco. Variante Xhon*. Oaxaca, Mexico: Ediciones Conocimiento Indígena.

Certeau, Michel de. 1982. *La fable mystique. XVIe – XVIIe siècle*. Paris: Gallimard.

———. 1984. *The Practice of Everyday Life*. Berkeley: University of California Press.

———. 1988. *The Writing of History*. New York: Columbia University Press.

———. 2000. *The Possession at Loudun*. Chicago: University of Chicago Press.

Cervantes, Fernando. 1994. *The Devil in the New World*. New Haven, CT: Yale University Press.

Chance, John K. 1989. *The Conquest of the Sierra*. Norman: University of Oklahoma Press.

———. 1992. "Colonial Ethnohistory of Oaxaca." In *Supplement to the Handbook of Middle American Indians: Ethnohistory*, ed. Victoria Bricker, 165–89. Austin: University of Texas Press.

———. 1996. "Mesoamerica's Ethnographic Past." *Ethnohistory* 43 (3): 379–403.

Chance, John, and William B. Taylor. 1985. "Cofradías and Cargos: An Historical Perspective on the Mesoamerican Civil-Religious Hierarchy." *American Ethnologist* 12: 1–26.

Chartier, Roger. 1992. *The Order of Books: Readers, Authors and Libraries in Europe Between the Fourteenth and Eighteenth Centuries*. Cambridge, MA: Polity Press.

———. 1996. *Culture écrite et société. L'ordre des livres (XIVe–XVIIIe siècle)*. Paris: Albin Michel.

Chimalpahin Quauhtlehuanitzin, Domingo Francisco de San Antón Muñón. 1997. *Codex Chimalpahin*. 2 vols. Trans. and ed. Arthur J. O. Anderson and Susan Schroeder. Norman: University of Oklahoma Press.

Christian Jr., William A. 1981a. *Apparitions in Late Medieval and Renaissance Spain*. Princeton, NJ: Princeton University Press.

———. 1981b. *Local Religion in Sixteenth-Century Spain*. Princeton, NJ: Princeton University Press.

Chuchiak, John F. 2000. "The Indian Inquisition and the Extirpation of Idolatry: The Process of Punishment in the Provisorato de Indios of the Diocese of Yucatán, 1563–1812." Doctoral dissertation, Tulane University.

———. 2002. "Toward a Regional Definition of Idolatry: Reexamining Idolatry Trials in the *Relaciones de Méritos* and Their Role in Defining the Concept of Idolatria en Colonial Yucatán, 1570–1780." *Journal of Early Modern History* 6 (2): 1–29.

———. 2005. "In Servitio Dei: Fray Diego de Landa, The Franciscan Order, and the Return of the Extirpation of Idolatry in the Colonial Diocese of Yucatán, 1573–1579." *The Americas* 61 (4): 611–46.

Ciruelo, Fray Pedro. 1977. *A Treatise Reproving All Superstitions and Forms of Witchcraft*. Trans. E. Maio and D. Pearson. Rutherford, NJ: Fairleigh Dickinson University Press.

Clavijero, Francisco Javier. 1945. *Historia Antigua de México*. 4 vols. Mexico: Editorial Porrúa.

Clendinnen, Inga. 1987. *Ambivalent Conquests: Maya and Spaniard in Yucatan, 1517–1570*. Cambridge: Cambridge University Press.

———. 1990. "Ways to the Sacred: Reconstructing Religion in Sixteenth-Century Mexico." *History and Anthropology* 5: 105–41.

Cline, Sarah L. 1993. "The Spiritual Conquest Reexamined: Baptism and Christian Marriage in Early Sixteenth-Century Mexico." *Hispanic American Historical Review* 73 (3): 453–80.

Coe, Michael, and Richard Whittaker. 1982. *Aztec Sorcerers in Seventeenth-Century Mexico*. Albany: Institute for Mesoamerican Studies, SUNY-Albany.

Cook, Noble David, and W. George Lovell, eds. 1991. *Secret Judgments of God: Old World Disease in Colonial Spanish America*. Norman: University of Oklahoma Press.

Cook, Sherburne F., and Woodrow W. Borah. 1979. *Essays in Population History: Mexico and California*. Vol. 3. Berkeley: University of California Press.

Cope, R. Douglas. 1994. *The Limits of Racial Domination: Plebeian Society in Colonial Mexico City, 1660–1720*. Madison: University of Wisconsin Press.

Córdova, Fray Juan de. 1578a. *Arte en lengua zapoteca*. Mexico: Pedro Balli.

———. 1578b. *Vocabulario en lengua zapoteca*. Mexico: Pedro Ocharte and Antonio Ricardo.

Covarrubias Orozco, Sebastián de. [1611] 1994. *Tesoro de la lengua castellana o española*. Madrid: Editorial Castalia.

Cruz, Martín de la, and Juan Badiano. 1940. *The Badianus Manuscript (Codex Barberini, Latin 241) Vatican Library: An Aztec Herbal of 1552*. Baltimore, MD: Johns Hopkins University Press.

Cruz, Víctor. 2007. *El pensamiento de los* binnigula'sa': *Cosmovisión, religión, y calendario, con especial referencia a los* binnizá. Mexico: Publicaciones de la Casa Chata.

Cruz Soto, Irma Guadalupe. 1993. *Magdalena Papalo y Joseph Chicon: Dos médicos nahuas del siglo XVI*. BA thesis, History Department. Mexico: Universidad Nacional Autónoma de México.

Cueva, Fray Pedro de la. N.d. *Parábolas y exemplos sacados de las costumbres del campo*. Manuscript, BNF. Photostat reproduction, TL.

Cuevas, Mariano. 1921–1928. *Historia de la iglesia en México*. 5 vols. Mexico: Ediciones Porrúa.

Cummins, Thomas. 1995. "Colonial Ekphrasis." In *Reframing the Renaissance: Visual Culture in Europe and Latin America, 1450–1650*, ed. Claire Farago, 152–76. New Haven, CT: Yale University Press.

———. 2003. "To Serve Man: Pre-Columbian Art, Western Discourses of Idolatry, and Cannibalism." *RES* 42: 109–30.

Dean, Caroline. 1989. "Praying with Pictures: A Reading of the Libro de Oraciones." *Journal of Latin American Lore* 15 (2): 211–73.

Dehouve, Danièle. 1988. "The 'Money of the Saint': Ceremonial organization and monetary capital in Tlapa, Guerrero, Mexico." In *Manipulating the Saints. Religious Brotherhoods and Social Integration in Post-Conquest Latin America*, ed. A. Meyers and D. E. Hopkins, 149–74. Hamburg, Germany: WAYASBAH.

Derrida, Jacques. 1967. *De la Grammatologie*. Paris: Les Éditions de Minuit.

Díaz-Polanco, Héctor, et al. 1996. *El Fuego de la inobediencia. Autonomía y rebelión india en el obispado de Oaxaca*. Mexico: Centro de Investigaciones y Estudios en Antropología Social.

Dominican Order. 1550. *Doctrina Christiana en le[n]gua española y mexicana*. Mexico: Juan Pablos.

Don, Patricia Lopes. 2010. *Bonfires of Culture: Franciscans, Indigenous Leaders, and the Inquisition in Early Mexico, 1524–1540*. Norman: University of Oklahoma Press.

Dundes, Alan. 1992. *The Blood Libel Legend: A Casebook in Anti-Semitic Folklore*. Madison: University of Wisconsin Press.

Durán, Fray Diego. 1967. *Historia de las Indias de Nueva España e islas de Tierra Firme*. Mexico: Editorial Porrúa.

Durkheim, Émile. [1912] 2001. *The Elementary Forms of Religious Life*. Oxford: Oxford University Press.

Durston, Alan. 2007. *Pastoral Quechua: The History of Christian Translation in Colonial Peru, 1550–1650*. Terre Haute, IL: University of Notre Dame Press.

Duviols, Pierre. 1971. *La lutte contre les religions autochtones dans le Pérou colonial; l'extirpation de l'idolâtrie entre 1532 et 1660*. Lima: Institut Français d'Études Andines.

———. 2003. *Proceso y visitas de idolatrías. Cajatambo, siglo XVII*. Lima: Pontificia Universidad Católica del Perú.

Edmonson, Munro. 1988. *The Book of the Year: Middle American Calendrical Systems*. Salt Lake City: University of Utah Press.

Elliott, John H. 2006. *Empires of the Atlantic World: Britain and Spain in America 1492–1830*. New Haven, CT: Yale University Press.

Esparza, Manuel. 1996. *Santo Domingo Grande: Hechura y reflejo de nuestra sociedad*. Oaxaca, Mexico: Carteles Editores.

Evans-Pritchard, Edward E. 1937. *Witchcraft, Oracles, and Magic Among the Azande*. Oxford: Clarendon Press.

———. 1965. *Theories of Primitive Religion*. Oxford: Clarendon Press.

Farfán, Agustín. 1579. *Tratado breve de Medicina, y de todas las Enfermedades, que cada passo se ofrecen*. Mexico: Antonio Ricardo.

Farriss, Nancy M. 1984. *Maya Society Under Colonial Rule*. Princeton, NJ: Princeton University Press.

Feria, Pedro de. 1567. *Doctrina christiana en lengua castellana y çapoteca*. Mexico: Pedro Ocharte.

Few, Martha. 2002. *Women Who Live Evil Lives: Gender, Religion, and the Politics of Power in Colonial Guatemala*. Austin: University of Texas Press.

Fields, Sherry. 2008. *Pestilence and Headcolds: Encountering Illness in Colonial Mexico*. New York: Columbia University Press.

Flannery, Kent, and Joyce Marcus, eds. 1983. *The Cloud People: Divergent Evolution of the Zapotec and Mixtec Civilizations*. New York: Academic Press.

Foucault, Michel. 1977. *Discipline and Punish: The Birth of the Prison*. London: Penguin Books.

Fragoso, Juan, and Francisco Díaz. 1627. *Cirugia vniuersal, aora nueuamenta añadida*. Madrid: Viuda de Alonso Martín.

Friedrich, Paul. 1977. *Agrarian Revolt in a Mexican Village*. Chicago: University of Chicago Press.

———. 1986. *The Princes of Naranja: An Essay in Anthrohistorical Method*. Austin: University of Texas Press.

Fuente, Julio de la. 1947–1948. "Documentos para la etnografía e historia zapotecas." *Anales del Instituto Nacional de Antropología e Historia*, vol. 3.

———. [1949] 1979. *Yalálag; una villa zapoteca serrana*. Mexico: Museo Nacional de Antropología e Historia, Instituto Nacional Indigenista.

Galarza, Joaquín. 1980. *Doctrina christiana: Méthode pour l'analyse d'un manuscrit pictographique mexicain du XVIIIe siècle avec application a la première prière: le Pater Noster*. Paris: Société d'Ethnographie.

Galinier, Jacques. 1990. *La mitad del mundo: Cuerpo y cosmos en los rituales otomíes*. Mexico: Universidad Nacional Autónoma de México, Instituto Nacional Indigenista.

Gante, Pedro de. 1547. *Doctrina Christiana en lengua mexicana*. Mexico: Juan Cronenberg.

———. [1553] 1981. *Doctrina Christiana en lengua mexicana*. Mexico: Editorial Jus.

García Castro, René. 1999. *Indios, territorio y poder en la provincia matlatzinca: la negociación del espacio político de los pueblos otomianos, siglos XV–XII*. Mexico: CIESAS, Instituto Nacional de Antropología e Historia, and El Colegio Mexiquense.

García Garagarza, León. 2010. "The Descent of the Tzitzimimeh: The Spanish Conquest and the Colonization of New Spain as the Fulfillment of Nahua Eschatology." Doctoral dissertation, University of California, Los Angeles.

García Icazbalceta, Joaquín. 1881. *Don Fray Juan de Zumárraga, primer obispo y arzobispo de México*. Mexico: Antigua Librería de Andrade y Morales.

———. 1947. *Don Fray Juan de Zumárraga, primer obispo y arzobispo de México*. 4 vols. Mexico: Editorial Porrúa.

Gareis, Iris. 1999. "Repression and Cultural Change: The 'Extirpation of Idolatry' in Colonial Peru." In *Spiritual Encounters: Interactions Between Christianity and Native Religions in Colonial America*, ed. N. Griffiths and F. Cervantes, 230–54. Lincoln: University of Nebraska Press.

Garibay K., Angel María. 1946. "Paralipómenos de Sahagún." *Tlalocan* 2–3: 167–74, 135–254.

———. 1954. *Historia de la literatura náhuatl*. Mexico: Editorial Porrúa.

Gates, William E. 1931. "A Lanquin Kekchi Calendar." *Maya Society Quarterly* 1 (1): 29-32.

Gay, José Antonio. 1998. *Historia de Oaxaca*. Mexico: Editorial Porrúa.

Gerhard, Peter. 1972. *A Guide to the Historical Geography of New Spain*. Norman: University of Oklahoma Press.

Gibson, Charles. 1964. *The Aztecs Under Spanish Rule*. Stanford: Stanford University Press.

Gillow, Eulogio. [1889] 1990. *Apuntes históricos sobre la idolatría e introducción del cristianismo en Oaxaca*. Mexico: Ediciones Toledo.

Ginzburg, Carlo. 1979. "Il nome e il come: Scambio ineguale e mercato storiografico." *Quaderni Storici* 40: 181–90.

———. 1980. *The Cheese and the Worms*. Baltimore, MD: Johns Hopkins University Press.

————. 1985. *The Night Battles: Witchcraft and Agrarian Cults in the Sixteenth and Seventeenth Centuries.* New York: Penguin Books.

————. 1992. *Ecstasies: Deciphering the Witches' Sabbath.* New York: Penguin Books.

González Obregón, Luis. 1910. *Proceso inquisitorial del cacique de Texcoco, Don Carlos Chichimeca tecutli.* Mexico: Guerrero Hermanos.

————. 1912. *Procesos de indios idólatras y hechiceros.* Mexico: Guerrero Hermanos.

Goody, Jack. 1987. *The Interface Between the Written and the Oral.* Cambridge: Cambridge University Press.

Gosner, Kevin. 1992. *Soldiers of the Virgin: The Moral Economy of a Colonial Maya Rebellion.* Tucson: University of Arizona Press.

————. 1998. "Religion and Rebellion in Colonial Chiapas." In *Native Resistance and the Pax Colonial in New Spain,* ed. Susan Schroeder, 47–66. Lincoln: University of Nebraska Press.

Greenleaf, Richard E. 1962. *Zumárraga and the Mexican Inquisition, 1536–1543.* Washington, DC: Academy of Franciscan History.

————. 1965. "The Inquisition and the Indians of New Spain: A Study in Jurisdictional Confusion." *The Americas* 22 (2): 138–66.

————. 1969. *The Mexican Inquisition of the Sixteenth Century.* Albuquerque: University of New Mexico Press.

————. 1978. "The Mexican Inquisition and the Indians: Sources for the Ethnohistorian." *The Americas* 34 (3): 315–44.

————. 1985. *Inquisicion y sociedad en el México colonial.* Madrid: J. Porrúa Turanzas.

————. 1991. "Historiography of the Mexican Inquisition: Evolution of Interpretations and Methodologies." In *Cultural Encounters,* ed. M. Perry and A. Cruz, 248–76. Berkeley: University of California Press.

Griffiths, Nicholas. 1995. *The Cross and the Serpent.* Norman: University of Oklahoma Press.

Griffiths, Nicolas, and Fernando Cervantes, eds. 1999. *Spiritual Encounters.* Lincoln: University of Nebraska Press.

Grunberg, Bernard. 1998. *L'Inquisition apostolique au Mexique: histoire d'une institution et de son impact dans une société coloniale (1521–1571).* Paris: L'Harmattan.

Gruzinski, Serge. 1978. "Indios reales y fantásticos en documentos de la Inquisición." *Boletín del AGN* 6: 18–39.

————. 1985. "La 'segunda aculturación': El estado ilustrado y la religiosidad indígena en Nueva España (1775–1800)." *Estudios de Historia Novohispana* 8: 175–201.

————. 1988. *Man-Gods in the Mexican Highlands.* Stanford: Stanford University Press.

————. 1989. "Individualization and Acculturation: Confession Among the Nahuas of Mexico from the Sixteenth to the Eighteenth Century." In *Sexuality and Marriage in Colonial Latin America,* ed. Asunción Lavrín, 96–117. Lincoln: University of Nebraska Press.

———. 1993. *The Conquest of Mexico*. Cambridge, MA: Polity Press.

———. 2001. *Images at War: Mexico from Columbus to Blade Runner (1492–2019)*. Durham, NC: Duke University Press.

———. 2002. *The Mestizo Mind: The Intellectual Dynamics of Colonization and Globalization*. New York: Routledge.

Halbertal, Moshe, and Avishai Margalit. 1992. *Idolatry*. Cambridge, MA: Harvard University Press.

Hanks, William F. 1987. "Discourse Genres in a Theory of Practice." *American Ethnologist* 14 (4): 668–92.

———. 2010. *Converting Words: Maya in the Age of the Cross*. Berkeley: University of California Press.

Harris, William V. 1989. *Ancient Literacy*. Cambridge, MA: Harvard University Press.

Haskett, Robert. 1991. *Indigenous Rulers: An Ethnohistory of Town Government in Colonial Cuernavaca*. Albuquerque: University of New Mexico Press.

———. 2005. *Visions of Paradise: Primordial Titles and Mesoamerican History in Cuernavaca*. Norman: University of Oklahoma Press.

Haslip-Viera, Gabriel. 1999. *Crime and Punishment in Late Colonial Mexico City, 1692–1810*. Albuquerque: University of New Mexico Press.

Havelock, Eric. 1982. *The Literate Revolution in Greece and its Cultural Consequences*. Princeton, NJ: Princeton University Press.

Heath, Shirley Brice. 1972. *Telling Tongues: Language Policy in Mexico, Colony to Nation*. New York: Teachers College Press.

Heinrich, Michael. 2002. "Ethnobotany, Phytochemistry and Biological/Pharmacological Activities of *Artemisia ludoviciana* ssp. *mexicana* (Estafiate)." In *Artemisia*, ed. Colin Wright, 107–17. Boca Raton, LA: CRC Press.

Henningsen, Gustav. 1980. *The Witches' Advocate: Basque Witchcraft and the Spanish Inquisition, 1609–1614*. Reno: University of Nevada Press.

Hernández, Francisco. 1651. *Nova plantarum, animalium et mineralium Mexicanorum*. Rome: n.p.

———. 1986. *Antigüedades de la Nueva España*. Madrid: Historia 16.

Hoffmann, Albert. 1995. "Medical Chemistry's Debt to Ethnobotany." In *Ethnobotany: Evolution of A Discipline*, ed. Richard Schultes and Siri von Reis, 311–19. Portland, OR: Dioscorides.

Horton, Robin. 1971. "African Conversion." *Africa* 41: 85–108.

———. 1975. "On the Rationality of Conversion." *Africa* 45: 219–35, 373–99.

Houston, Stephen. 1994. "Literacy Among the Pre-Columbian Maya: A Comparative Perspective." In *Writing Without Words: Ancient Literacies in Mesoamerica and the Andes*, ed. Elizabeth Boone and Walter Mignolo, 27–49. Durham, NC: Duke University Press.

Huerga Teruelo, Álvaro. 1991. "Proyecto de Santa Cruz la Real." *Actas del III Congreso Internacional Los Dominicos y el Nuevo Mundo*. Granada.

Hvidtfeldt, Arild. 1958. *Teotl and *ixiptlatli: Central Conceptions in Ancient Mexican Religion*. Copenhagen: Munksgaard.

Hymes, Dell. 1981. *"In Vain I Tried to Tell You": Essays in Native American Ethnopoetics*. Philadelphia: University of Pennsylvania Press.

Jakobson, Roman. 1987. *Language in Literature*. Cambridge, MA: Harvard University Press.

Jarquín Ortega, María Teresa. 1990. *Formación y desarrollo de un pueblo novohispano: Metepec en el Valle de Toluca*. Metepec: Colegio Mexiquense, H. Ayuntamiento de Metepec.

Jauss, Hans Robert. 1982. *Toward an Aesthetic of Reception*. Minneapolis: University of Minnesota Press.

Jiménez H., Víctor, and Rogelio González M. 1992. *El Ex-Obispado de Oaxaca: Un caso singular en la arquitectura colonial mexicana*. Mexico: CODEX Editores

Jiménez Moreno, Wigberto, and Salvador Mateos. 1940. *Códice Yanhuitlán*. Mexico: Museo Nacional, Instituto Nacional de Antropología e Historia.

Jonghe, Edouard de. 1905. *Histoyre du Mechique: Manuscrit français inédit du XVIe siècle*. Paris: Société des Americanistes.

Joyce, Arthur. 2004. "Sacred Space and Social Relations in the Valley of Oaxaca." In *Mesoamerican Archaeology*, ed. Julia Hendon and Rosemary Joyce, 192–216. New York: Wiley-Blackwell.

Justeson, John, and David Tavárez. 2007. "The Correlation of the Colonial Northern Zapotec Calendar with European Chronology." In *Cultural Astronomy in New World Cosmologies: Essays in Honor of Anthony Aveni*, ed. Clive Ruggles and Gary Urton, 19–96. Niwot: University of Colorado Press.

Kamen, Henry. 1998. *The Spanish Inquisition: A Historical Revision*. New Haven, CT: Yale University Press.

Kantorowicz, Ernst H. 1957. *The King's Two Bodies: A Study in Mediaeval Political Theology*. Princeton, NJ: Princeton University Press.

Karttunen, Frances. 1983. *An Analytical Dictionary of Nahuatl*. Austin: University of Texas Press.

Karttunen, Frances, and James Lockhart. 1976. *Nahuatl in the Middle Years: Language Contact Phenomena in Texts of the Colonial Period*. Berkeley: University of California Press.

———. 1980. "La estructura de la poesía náhuatl vista por sus variantes." *Estudios de Cultura Náhuatl* 14: 15–65.

———. 1987. *The Art of Nahuatl Speech: The Bancroft Dialogues*. Los Angeles: UCLA Latin American Center Publications, University of California.

Katz, Friedrich. 1990. "Las rebeliones rurales en el México precortesiano y colonial." In *Revuelta, rebelión y revolución*, ed. Friedrich Katz, 65–93. Mexico: Ediciones Era.

Kaufman, Terrence. 2000. The Day Names of the Meso-American Calendar. Unpublished manuscript, 105 pp.

———. 2004. Proto-Zapotec Reconstructions. Unpublished manuscript, 77 pp.

Kellogg, Susan. 1995. *Law and the Transformation of Aztec Culture, 1500–1700*. Norman: University of Oklahoma Press.

Kelly, John, and Martha Kaplan. 1990. "History, Structure and Ritual." *Annual Review of Anthropology* 119: 119–50.

Kieckhefer, Richard. 1976. *European Witch Trials: Their Foundations in*

Popular and Learned Culture, 1300–1500. Berkeley: University of California Press.

Kirchhoff, Paul, Lina Odena Güemes, and Luis Reyes García. 1989. *Historia tolteca-chichimeca.* Mexico: Centro de Investigaciones y Estudios en Antropología Social, Fondo de Cultura Económica.

Klor de Alva, J. Jorge. 1981. "Martín Ocelotl: Clandestine Cult Leader." In *Struggle and Survival in Colonial America,* ed. D. Sweet and G. Nash, 128–41. Berkeley: University of California Press.

———. 1982. "Spiritual Conflict and Accommodation in New Spain: Towards a Typology of Aztec Responses to Christianity." In *The Inca and Aztec States,* ed. George Collier et al., 345–66. New York: Academic Press.

———. 1991. "Colonizing Souls: The Failure of the Indian Inquisition and the Rise of Penitential Discipline." In *Cultural Encounters,* ed. M. Perry and A. Cruz, 3–22. Berkeley: University of California Press.

———. 1999. "'Telling Lives': Confessional Autobiography and the Reconstruction of the Nahua Self." In *Spiritual Encounters,* ed. Nicolas Griffiths and Fernando Cervantes, 136–62. Lincoln: University of Nebraska Press.

Klor de Alva, J. Jorge, H. B. Nicholson, and Eloise Quiñones Keber, eds. 1988. *The Work of Bernardino de Sahagún: Pioneer Ethnographer of Sixteenth-Century Aztec Mexico.* Albany and Austin: Institute for Mesoamerican Studies, SUNY-Albany, and University of Texas Press.

Knaut, Andrew L. 1997. *The Pueblo Revolt of 1680: Conquest and Resistance in Seventeenth-Century New Mexico.* Norman: University of Oklahoma Press.

Kobayashi, José María. 1974. *La educación como conquista: Empresa franciscana en México.* Mexico: Colegio de México.

Kripke, Saul. 1980. *Naming and Necessity.* Cambridge, MA: Harvard University Press.

Kubler, George. 1948. *Mexican Architecture of the Sixteenth Century.* 2 vols. New Haven, CT: Yale University Press.

Lafaye, Jacques. 1976. *Quetzalcoatl and Guadalupe: The Formation of Mexican National Consciousness, 1531–1813.* Chicago: University of Chicago Press.

Lamadrid, Lázaro. 1951. "The Letters of Margil in the Archivo de la Recolección in Guatemala." *The Americas* 7 (3): 325–55.

Lara Cisneros, Gerardo. 2002. *El cristianismo en el espejo indígena: Religiosidad en el occidente de la Sierra Gorda, siglo XVIII.* Mexico: Instituto Nacional de Antropología e Historia.

Lastra, Yolanda. 1986. *Las áreas dialectales del náhuatl moderno.* Mexico: Universidad Nacional Autónoma de México.

Lavrín, Asunción. 1988. "Diversity and Disparity: Rural and Urban Confraternities in Eighteenth-Century Mexico." In *Manipulating the Saints: Religious Brotherhoods and Social Integration in Post-Conquest Latin America,* ed. A. Meyers and D. E. Hopkins, 67–100. Hamburg, Germany: WAYASBAH.

Le Roy Ladurie, Emmanuel. 1975. *Montaillou, village occitan de 1294 à 1324.* Paris: Editions Gallimard.

Lea, Henry Charles. 1906. *A History of the Inquisition of Spain.* 4 vols. New York and London: The Macmillan Company.

———. 1922. *A History of the Inquisition of the Middle Ages.* New York: Macmillan.

León, Fray Martín de. 1611. *Camino del Cielo en Lengua Mexicana.* Mexico: Diego López Dávalos.

León-Portilla, Ascención H. de. 1988. *Tepuztlahcuilolli. Impresos en náhuatl.* 2 vols. Mexico: Universidad Nacional Autónoma de México.

León-Portilla, Miguel. 1983. "Cuicatl y Tlahtolli: Las formas de expresión en náhuatl." *Estudios de Cultura Náhuatl* 16: 13–108.

———. 2002. *Bernardino de Sahagun, First Anthropologist.* Norman: University of Oklahoma Press.

León-Portilla, Miguel, and Librado Silva Galeana. 1990. *Testimonios de la antigua palabra.* Madrid: Historia 16.

Leonard, Irving. [1949] 1992. *Books of the Brave: Being an Account of Books and of Men in the Spanish Conquest and Settlement of the Sixteenth-Century New World.* Berkeley: University of California Press.

Levanto, fray Leonardo. 1776. *Catecismo en lengua zapoteca.* Puebla, Mexico: Viuda de Miguel de Ortega.

Lewis, Laura A. 2003. *Hall of Mirrors: Power, Witchcraft, and Caste in Colonial Mexico.* Durham, NC: Duke University Press.

Li, Andrés de. [1495] 1999. *Reportorio de los tiempos.* Ed. Laura Delbrugge. London: Tamesis.

———. 1510. *Reportorio de los tiempos.* Seville, Spain: Jacob Cromberger.

Lipp, Frank. 1998. *The Mixe of Oaxaca: Religion, Ritual, and Healing.* Austin: University of Texas Press.

Lockhart, James. 1992. *The Nahuas After the Conquest.* Stanford: Stanford University Press.

———. 2001. *Nahuatl as Written: Lessons in Older Written Nahuatl, with Copious Examples and Texts* (Nahuatl Series, No. 6). Stanford: Stanford University Press.

Long, Rebecca. 1999. *Diccionario zapoteco de San Bartolomé Zoogocho, Oaxaca.* Mexico: Instituto Lingüístico de Verano.

López, Gregorio. 1576. *Las siete partidas del sabio rey Don Alonso el Nono.* Salamanca, Spain: Domingo de Portonarijs Ursino.

López Austin, Alfredo. 1966. "Los temacpalitotique: Brujos, profanadores, ladrones y violadores." *Estudios de Cultura Náhuatl* 6: 97–117.

———. 1967a. "Cuarenta clases de magos del mundo náhuatl." *Estudios de Cultura Náhuatl* 7: 87–117.

———. 1967b. "Términos del nahuallatolli." *Historia Mexicana* 17: 1–36.

———. 1970. "Conjuros médicos de los nahuas." *Revista de la Universidad de México* 24 (11): 1–16.

———. 1973a. *Hombre-dios: Religión y política en el mundo náhuatl.* Mexico: Universidad Nacional Autónoma de México.

———. 1973b. "Un repertorio de los tiempos en idioma náhuatl." *Anales de Antropología* 10: 285–96.

———. 1975. *Textos de medicina náhuatl*. Mexico: Universidad Nacional Autónoma de México.

López Austin, Alfredo, and Leonardo López Luján. 2009. *Monte Sagrado-Templo Mayor: El cerro y la pirámide en la tradición religiosa mesoamericana*. Mexico: Universidad Nacional Autónoma de México.

López de Hinojosos, Alonso. [1595] 1977. *Suma y recopilación de cirugía con un arte para sangrar muy útil y provechosa*. Mexico: Academia Nacional de Medicina.

Lorenzana, Francisco Antonio. 1769a. *Concilios Provinciales Primero y Segundo, celebrados en la . . . ciudad de México . . . en los años de 1555 y 1565*. Mexico: Imprenta del Superior Gobierno.

———. 1769b. *III Concilium Mexicanus . . .* Mexico: Imprenta del Superior Gobierno.

Losa, Francisco. 1642. *Vida que el siervo de Dios Gregorio Lopez hizo en algunos lugares de la Nueva España*. Madrid: Imprenta Real.

Lupo, Alessandro. 1995. *La tierra nos escucha*. Mexico: Consejo Nacional para la Cultura y las Artes, Instituto Nacional Indigenista.

MacCormack, Sabine. 1991. *Religion in the Andes: Vision and Imagination in Early Colonial Peru*. Princeton, NJ: Princeton University Press.

Maldonado, Ángel. ca. 1720. *Respuesta que da D. Fr. Angel Maldonado . . . a un informe, y manifiesto, que ha hecho Fr. Antonio de Torres . . .* Madrid.

Mandrou, Robert. 1980. *Magistrats et sorciers en France au XVIIe siècle: Une analyse de psychologie historique*. Paris: Seuil.

Marcus, Joyce, and Kent Flannery. 1994. "Ancient Zapotec Ritual and Religion: An Application of the Direct Historical Approach." In *The Ancient Mind: Elements of Cognitive Archaeology*, ed. Colin Renfrew and Ezra Zubrow, 55–74. Cambridge: Cambridge University Press.

———. 1996. *Zapotec Civilization*. London: Thames and Hudson.

Martín, Juan. 1696. Bvcabulario de la Lengua Castellena [*sic*] y Zapoteca Nexitza. Manuscript, Newberry Library.

Martínez, Alonso. [1633] 1872. *Manual breve y compendioso para empesar a aprender lengua çapoteca*, JCB-CodInd 70.

Martínez, Enrico. [1606] 1948. *Reportorio de los tiempos e historia natural de Nueva España*. Mexico: Secretaría de Educación Pública.

Martínez, María Elena. 2008. *Genealogical Fictions: Limpieza de Sangre, Religion, and Gender in Colonial Mexico*. Stanford: Stanford University Press.

Martínez González, Roberto. 2006. "Sobre la función social del buen nahualli." *Revista Española de Antropología Americana* 36 (2): 39–63.

Martínez Sola, María del Carmen. 1998. *El obispo fray Bernardo de Albuquerque. El marquesado del valle de Oaxaca en el siglo XVI*. Oaxaca, Mexico: Instituto Oaxaqueño de las Culturas.

Mathes, Miguel. 1982. *Santa Cruz de Tlatelolco: la primera biblioteca académica de las Américas*. Mexico: Archivo Histórico Diplomático Mexicano 12, cuarta época, Secretaría de Relaciones Exteriores.

McIntyre, Kellen K. 1997. *The Venerable Martyrs of Caxonos: An 1890 Painted*

History of Zapotec Rebellion in 1700. Doctoral dissertation, Art History Department, University of New Mexico.

Medina, José Toribio. 1905. *Historia del tribunal del Santo oficio de la inquisición en México*. Santiago, Chile: Imprenta Elzeviriana.

Meer, Ron van. 2000. "Análisis e interpretación de un libro calendárico zapoteco: El Manuscrito de San Antonio Huitepec." *Cuadernos del Sur* 15 (6): 37–74.

Mendieta, Gerónimo de. 1997. *Historia eclesiástica indiana*. 2 vols. Mexico: Consejo Nacional para la Cultura y las Artes.

Menegus-Bornemann, Margarita. 1991. *Del señorío a la república de indios. El caso de Toluca: 1500–1600*. Madrid: Ministerio de Agricultura, Pesca y Alimentación.

Mengin, Ernest. 1952. "Commentaire du Codex Mexicanus, nos. 23–24, BNP." *Journal de la Société des Americanistes* 41: 387–498.

Mignolo, Walter. 1996. *The Darker Side of the Renaissance*. Durham, NC: Duke University Press.

Miller, Arthur. 1991. "Transformations of Time and Space: Oaxaca, Mexico, circa 1500–1700." In *Images of Memory: On Remembering and Representation*, ed. Susanne Küchler and Walter Melion, 141–75. Washington, DC: Smithsonian Institution Press.

———. 1998. "Espacio, tiempo y poder entre los zapotecas de la sierra." *Acervos: Boletín de los Archivos y Bibliotecas de Oaxaca* 10 (3): 17–20.

Millones, Luis. 1979. "Religion and Power in the Andes: Idolatrous Curacas of the Central Sierra." *Ethnohistory* 26 (3): 143–263.

Mills, Kenneth. 1997. *Idolatry and its Enemies*. Princeton, NJ: Princeton University Press.

Molina, Fray Alonso de. [1546] 1675. *Doctrina christiana y cathecismo en lengua mexicana*. Mexico: Viuda de Bernardo Calderón.

———. [1569] 1984. *Confesionario mayor en la lengua mexicana y castellana*. Mexico: Universidad Nacional Autónoma de México.

———. [1571] 1992. *Vocabulario en lengua Castellana y Mexicana y Mexicana y Castellana*. Mexico: Editorial Porrúa.

Monaghan, John. 1999. *The Covenants with Earth and Rain: Exchange, Sacrifice, and Revelation in Mixtec Sociality*. Norman: University of Oklahoma Press.

Monardes, Nicolás. 1574. *Primera y segunda parte de la historia de las cosas que se traen de nuestras Indias Occidentales que sirven en medicina*. Seville, Spain: Alonso Escrivano.

Moreno de los Arcos, Roberto. 1991. "New Spain's Inquisition for Indians from the Sixteenth to the Nineteenth Century." In *Cultural Encounters*, ed. M. Perry and A. Cruz, 23–36. Berkeley: University of California Press.

Mörner, Magnus. 1970. *La corona española y los foráneos en los pueblos de indios de América*. Instituto de Estudios Ibero-Americanos, Serie A, Monografía 1. Stockholm, Sweden, and Castellón, Spain: Almqvist and Wiksell, Armengot.

Motolinia [Fray Toribio Benavente]. [1858] 1990. *Historia de los indios de la Nueva España*. Mexico: Editorial Porrúa.

Munro, Pamela, and Felipe H. López. 1999. *Di'cyonary X:tèe'n Dìi'zh Sah Sann Lu'uc. San Lucas Quiavini Zapotec Dictionary.* 2 vols. Los Angeles: UCLA Chicano Studies Research Center Publications.

Muñoz Camargo, Diego. 1981. *Descripción de la ciudad y provincia de Tlaxcala de las Indias y del Mar Océano para el buen gobierno y ennoblecimiento dellas.* Mexico: Universidad Nacional Autónoma de México.

———. 1998. *Historia de Tlaxcala: Ms. 210 de la Biblioteca Nacional de París.* Tlaxcala, Mexico: Gobierno del Estado de Tlaxcala, Centro de Investigaciones y Estudios Superiores en Antropología Social, Universidad Autónoma de Tlaxcala.

Murray, Margaret. 1962. *The Witch-Cult in Western Europe.* Oxford: Clarendon Press.

Nájera Coronado, Martha. 2007. *Los Cantares de Dzitbalché en la tradición religiosa mesoamericana.* Mexico: Universidad Nacional Autónoma de México.

Nesvig, Martin. 2009. *Ideology and Inquisition: The World of the Censors in Early Mexico.* New Haven, CT: Yale University Press.

Nicholson, Henry B. 1971. "Religion in Pre-Hispanic Central Mexico." *Handbook of Middle American Indians* 10: 395–446.

Normann, Anne Whited. 1985. *Testerian codices.* Doctoral dissertation, Anthropology Department, Tulane University.

Nutini, Hugo G. 1988. *Todos Santos in Rural Tlaxcala.* Princeton, NJ: Princeton University Press.

Nutini, Hugo G., and Betty Bell. 1980. *Ritual Kinship, Volume One: The Structure and Historical Development of the Compadrazgo System in Rural Tlaxcala.* Princeton, NJ: Princeton University Press.

Nutini, Hugo G., and John Roberts. 1993. *Bloodsucking Witchcraft.* Tucson: University of Arizona Press.

Offner, Jerome A. 1983. *Law and Politics in Aztec Texcoco.* Cambridge: Cambridge University Press.

O'Hara, Matthew D. 2010. *A Flock Divided: Race, Religion, and Politics in Mexico, 1749-1857.* Durham, NC: Duke University Press.

Olmos, Fray Andrés de. [1553] 1990. *Tratado de hechicerías y sortilegios.* Ed. Georges Baudot. Mexico: Universidad Nacional Autónoma de México.

Oudijk, Michel. 2000. *Historiography of the Bènizàa: The Postclassic and Early Colonial Periods (1000–1600 A.D.).* Leiden, Germany: CNWS Publications, vol. 84.

———. 2003. "Espacio y escritura: El Lienzo de Tabáa I." In *Escritura zapoteca: 2,500 años de historia*, ed. María de los Ángeles Romero Frizzi, 341–91. Mexico: CIESAS, Instituto Nacional de Antropología e Historia, Porrúa, CONACULTA.

———. 2006. "Los documentos zapotecos coloniales." Paper presented at the Francisco Belmar Conference on Otomanguean Languages. Oaxaca City, Mexico, April 21, 2006.

———. 2008. "The Postclassic Period in the Valley of Oaxaca: The Archaeological and Ethnohistorical Records." In *After Monte Alban: Transformation and Negotiation in Oaxaca, Mexico*, ed. Jeffrey P. Blomster, 95–118. Boulder: University Press of Colorado.

Oudijk, Michel, and Maarten Jansen. 1999. "Changing History in the Lienzos de Guevea and Santo Domingo Petapa." *Ethnohistory* 47 (2): 281–331.

Pacheco de Silva, Francisco. [1687] 1752. *Doctrina Christiana en lengua Zapoteca Nexitza*. Mexico: Imprenta de Francisco Xavier Sánchez.

Padden, Robert C. 1970. *The Hummingbird and the Hawk: Conquest and Sovereignty in the Valley of Mexico, 1503–1541*. New York: Harper & Row.

Pardo, Osvaldo. 2004. *The Origins of Mexican Catholicism: Nahua Rituals and Christian Sacraments in Sixteenth-Century Mexico*. Ann Arbor: University of Michigan Press.

Patch, Robert W. 1998. "Culture, Community and 'Rebellion' in the Yucatec Maya Uprising of 1761." In *Native Resistance and the Pax Colonial in New Spain*, ed. Susan Schroeder, 67–83. Lincoln: University of Nebraska Press.

Peña Montenegro, Alonso de la. [1668] 1995. *Itinerario para párrocos de indios*, vol. 1. Madrid: Consejo Superior de Investigaciones Científicas.

Peñafiel, Antonio, ed. 1981. *Gramática zapoteca de autor anónimo*. Oaxaca, Mexico: Ediciones Toledo.

Phelan, John Leddy. 1970. *The Milennial Kingdom of the Franciscans in the New World*. Berkeley: University of California Press.

Ponce de León, Pedro. 1892. *Breve relación de los dioses y ritos de la gentilidad*. Anales del Museo Nacional de México (Primera época) 6: 3–11.

Poole, Stafford. 1987. *Pedro Moya de Contreras: Catholic Reform and Royal Power in New Spain, 1571–1591*. Berkeley: University of California Press.

———. 1995. *Our Lady of Guadalupe: The Origins and Sources of a Mexican National Symbol, 1531–1797*. Tucson: University of Arizona Press.

Prem, Hanns J. 2008. *Manual de la antigua cronología mexicana*. Mexico: Centro de Investigaciones y Estudios en Antropología Social, Miguel Porrúa.

Quezada, Noemí. 1989. *Enfermedad y maleficio: El curandero en el México colonial*. Mexico: Universidad Nacional Autónoma de México.

———. 1991. "The Inquisition's Repression of Curanderos." In *Cultural Encounters*, ed. M. Perry and A. Cruz, 37–57. Berkeley: University of California Press.

Quiñones Keber, Eloise. 1995. *Codex Telleriano-Remensis: Ritual, Divination, and History in a Pictorial Aztec Manuscript*. Austin: University of Texas Press.

Raby, Dominique. 2006. "Mujer Blanca y Dolor Verde. Uso de los colores, del género y de los lazos de parentesco en el Tratado de Ruiz de Alarcón." *Estudios de Cultura Náhuatl* 37: 294–315.

Rafael, Vicente. 1988. *Contracting Colonialism: Translation and Conversion in Tagalog Society Under Early Spanish Rule*. Ithaca, NY: Cornell University Press.

Rappaport, Joanne. 1998. *The Politics of Memory: Native Historical Interpretation in the Colombian Andes*. Durham, NC: Duke University Press.

Reko, Blas. 1945. *Mitobotánica zapoteca*. Tacubaya, Mexico: n.p.

Rendón, Juan José. 1995. *Diversificación de las lenguas zapotecas*. Mexico: Centro de Investigaciones y Estudios en Antropología Social, IOC.

Restall, Matthew, and Susan Kellogg, eds. 1998. *Dead Giveaways: Indigenous*

Testaments of Colonial Mesoamerica and the Andes. Salt Lake City: University of Utah Press.

Restall, Matthew, Lisa Sousa, and Kevin Terraciano. 2005. *Mesoamerican Voices. Native Language Writings from Colonial Mexico, Yucatan, and Guatemala*. Cambridge: Cambridge University Press.

Reyes, Gaspar de los. [1704] 1891. *Arte de la Lengua Zapoteca Serrana*. Oaxaca, Mexico: Imprenta del Estado.

Reyes García, Luis. 2002. *Cómo te confundes? Acaso no somos conquistados?: Anales de Juan Bautista*. Mexico: Centro de Investigaciones y Estudios Superiores en Antropología Social, Biblioteca Lorenzo Boturini, Insigne y Nacional Basílica de Guadalupe.

Ricard, Robert. 1966. *The Spiritual Conquest of Mexico*. Berkeley: University of California Press.

Ríos Morales, Manuel. 1994. *Los zapotecos de la sierra norte de Oaxaca: Antología etnográfica*. Oaxaca, Mexico: Centro de Investigaciones y Estudios en Antropología Social-Oaxaca.

Rojas Rabiela, Teresa, E. Rea López, and C. Medina Lima. 1999. *Vida y bienes olvidados: Testamentos indígenas novohispanos*. 3 vols. Mexico: Centro de Investigaciones y Estudios en Antropología Social-CONACYT.

Romero, Javier. 1956. *El Dios Tolotzin*. Mexico: Fondo Mexicano del Libro.

Romero Frizzi, María de los Ángeles. 1996. *El sol y la cruz: Los pueblos indios de Oaxaca colonial*. Mexico: Centro de Investigaciones y Estudios en Antropología Social, Instituto Nacional Indigenista.

———. 2003. "Los zapotecos, la escritura, y la historia." In *Escritura zapoteca: 2500 años de historia*, ed. M. Romero Frizzi, 13–69. Mexico: Instituto Nacional de Antropología e Historia, Centro de Investigaciones y Estudios en Antropología Social.

Romero Frizzi, María de los Ángeles, and Juana Vázquez. 2003. "Memoria y escritura: La memoria de Xuquila." In *Escritura zapoteca: 2500 años de historia*, ed. M. Romero Frizzi, 393–448. Mexico: Instituto Nacional de Antropología e Historia, Centro de Investigaciones y Estudios en Antropología Social.

Rosaldo, Renato. 1986. "From the Door of His Tent: The Fieldworker and the Inquisitor." In *Writing Culture*, ed. James Clifford and George Marcus, 77–97. Berkeley: University of California Press.

Ruiz de Alarcón, Hernando. 1892. *Tratado de las supersticiones y costumbres gentílicas que oy viuen entre los indios naturales desta Nueva España*. Anales del Museo Nacional de México (Primera época) 6: 125–223.

———. 1984. *Treatise on the Heathen Institutions that Today Live Among the Indians Native to this New Spain (1629)*. Trans. and ed. J. Richard Andrews and Ross Hassig. Norman: University of Oklahoma Press.

Sáenz de Santa María, Carmelo. 1969. "Un formulario mágico mexicano: El 'Manual de ministros de indios' del doctor Jacinto de la Serna." *Revista de Indias* 29 (115–18): 531–79.

———. 1981. "Una revisión etnorreligiosa de la Guatemala de 1704, según fray Antonio Márgil de Jesús." *Revista de Indias* 41: 445–97.

Sahagún, Bernardino de. 1950–1982. *The Florentine Codex: General History of the Things of New Spain*. Books 1–12, 13 vols. Trans. and ed. Arthur J. O. Anderson and Charles E. Dibble. Salt Lake City: University of Utah Press.

———. 1986. *Coloquios y doctrina cristiana*. Trans. and ed. Miguel León-Portilla. Mexico: Universidad Nacional Autónoma de México.

———. 1990. *Breve compendio de los ritos idolátricos que los indios de esta Nueva España usaban en tiempo de su infidelidad*. Mexico: Lince Editores.

———. [1583] 1993. *Bernardino de Sahagún's* Psalmodia Christiana. Trans. and ed. Arthur J. O. Anderson. Salt Lake City: University of Utah Press.

Sahlins, Marshall. 1985. *Islands of History*. Chicago: University of Chicago Press.

Salomon, Frank. 1987. "Ancestor Cults and Resistance to the State in Arequipa, ca. 1748–1754." In *Resistance, Rebellion and Consciousness in the Andean Peasant World*, ed. Steven J. Stern, 148–65. Madison: University of Wisconsin Press.

Sánchez de Aguilar, Pedro. 1892. "Informe contra idolorum cultores." *Anales del Museo Nacional de México* (1ª Época) 6.

Sánchez Bella, Ismael, ed. 1992. *Recopilación de las Indias por Antonio de León Pinelo*. 3 vols. Mexico: Miguel Porrúa.

Sanders, William T. 1976. "The Population of the Central Mexican Symbiotic Region, the Basin of Mexico, and the Teotihuacán Valley in the Sixteenth Century." In *The Native Population of the Americas in 1492*, ed. W. Denevan, 85–150. Madison: University of Wisconsin Press.

———. 1979. *The Basin of Mexico: Ecological Processes in the Evolution of a Civilization*. New York: Academic Press.

Sandstrom, Alan. 1992. *Corn Is Our Blood: Culture and Ethnic Identity in a Contemporary Aztec Indian Village*. Norman: University of Oklahoma Press.

Sariñana, Isidro. 1666. *Llanto del occidente en el ocaso del más claro sol de las Españas* . . . Mexico: Bernardo Calderón.

———. [1668] 1968. "La catedral de México en 1668: Noticia breve de la solemne, deseada, última dedicación del Templo Metropolitano de México." Ed. Francisco de la Maza. *Anales del Instituto de Investigaciones Estéticas* 37, Supplement 2.

———. 1681. *Oración fúnebre* . . . *en las exequias de veinte y un religiosos de la regular observancia de seráphico P.S. Francisco* . . . Mexico: Viuda de Bernardo Calderón.

Sarmiento Donate, Alberto. 1988. *De las Leyes de Indias. Antología de la Recopilación de 1681*. Mexico: SEP.

Scholes, France, and Eleanore Adams. 1938. *Don Diego Quijada, Alcalde Mayor de Yucatán, 1561–1565*. Mexico: Editorial Porrúa.

———. 1952. *Proceso contra Tzinticha Tangaxoan, el Caltzontzin, formado por Nuño de Guzmán, año de 1530*. Mexico: Editorial Porrúa.

Scholes, France, and Ralph Roys. 1938. *Fray Diego de Landa and the Problem of Idolatry in Yucatán*. Washington, DC: Carnegie Institution.

Schroeder, Susan. 1991. *Chimalpahin and the Kingdoms of Chalco*. Tucson: University of Arizona Press.

———. 2000. "Jesuits, Nahuas, and the Good Death Society in Mexico City, 1710–1767." *Hispanic American Historical Review* 80 (I): 43–76.

Schroeder, Susan, Anne Cruz, Cristián Roa-de-la-Carrera, and David Tavárez. 2010. *Chimalpahin's Conquest: A Nahua Historian's Rewriting of Francisco López de Gómara's* La conquista de Mexico. Stanford: Stanford University Press.

Schwaller, John F. 1987. *The Church and Clergy in Sixteenth-Century Mexico.* Albuquerque: University of New Mexico Press.

———. 1999. "Don Bartolomé de Alva, Nahuatl Scholar of the Seventeenth Century." In *A Guide to Confession Large and Small in the Mexican Language, 1634,* trans. and ed. Barry Sell, John F. Schwaller, and Lu Ann Hozma, 3–15. Norman: University of Oklahoma Press.

Schwartz, Stuart B. 2008. *All Can Be Saved: Religious Tolerance and Salvation in the Iberian Atlantic World.* New Haven, CT: Yale University Press.

Scott, James C. 1985. *Weapons of the Weak: Everyday Forms of Peasant Resistance.* New Haven, CT: Yale University Press.

Sell, Barry. 1999. "The Classical Age of Nahuatl Publications and Don Bartolomé de Alva's Confessionario of 1634." In *A Guide to Confession Large and Small in the Mexican Language, 1634,* trans. and ed. Barry Sell, John F. Schwaller, and Lu Ann Hozma, 18–32. Norman: University of Oklahoma Press.

Sellen, Adam. 2002. *Las vasijas efigie zapotecas: Los ancestros personificadores de divinidades.* Doctoral dissertation in Mesoamerican Studies, Universidad Nacional Autónoma de México.

Sepúlveda y Herrera, María Teresa. 1999. *Proceso por idolatría al cacique, gobernadores y sacerdotes de Yanhuitlán, 1544–1546.* Mexico: Instituto Nacional de Antropología e Historia.

Serna, Jacinto de la. 1892. *Manual de Ministros de Indios para el conocimiento de sus idolatrías y extirpación de ellas.* Anales del Museo Nacional de México (Primera época) 6: 261–475.

Silverblatt, Irene. 1987. *Moon, Sun, and Witches: Gender Ideologies and Class in Inca and Colonial Peru.* Princeton, NJ: Princeton University Press.

———. 2004. *Modern Inquisitions: Peru and the Colonial Origins of the Civilized World.* Durham, NC: Duke University Press.

Siméon, Rémi. 1984. *Diccionario de la lengua náhuatl o mexicana.* Josefina Oliva de Coll, trad. Mexico: Siglo XXI Editores.

Smith, Philip. 1992. "A Quantitative Evaluation of Demographic, Gender and Social Transformation Theories of the Rise of European Witch Hunting, 1300–1500." *Historical Social Research* 17 (4) 64: 99–127.

Smith-Stark, Thomas. 1999. "Dioses, sacerdotes, y sacrificio—una mirada a la religion zapoteca a través del Vocabulario en lengua Çapoteca (1578) de Juan de Cordova." In *La religión de los Binnigula'sa',* ed. Víctor de la Cruz and Marcus Winter, 89–195. Oaxaca, Mexico: Instituto Estatal de Educación Pública de Oaxaca, Instituto Oaxaqueño de las Culturas.

———. 2003. "La ortografía del zapoteco en el Vocabulario de fray Juan de Córdova." In *Escritura zapoteca: 2,500 años de historia,* ed. María de los Ángeles Romero Frizzi, 393–448. Mexico: CIESAS, Instituto Nacional de Antropología e Historia, Porrúa, CONACULTA.

————. 2008. "La flexión de tiempo, aspecto y modo en el verbo del zapoteco colonial del valle de Oaxaca." In *Memorias del Coloquio Francisco Belmar*, ed. Áurea López Cruz and Michael Swanton, 377–419. Oaxaca, Mexico: Biblioteca Francisco de Burgoa.

Smith-Stark, Thomas C., Sergio Bogard, and Ausencia López Cruz. 1993. *Electronic Archive of the Vocabvlario en lengva çapoteca* by Juan de Córdova. Word Perfect 8, 7.7 MB.

Sousa, Lisa. 2002. "The Devil and Deviance in Native Criminal Narratives from Early Mexico." *The Americas* 59 (2): 161–79.

Spicer, Edward H. 1967. *Cycles of Conquest: The Impact of Spain, Mexico, and the United States on Indians of the Southwest, 1533–1960.* Tucson: University of Arizona Press.

Spores, Ronald. 1998. "Differential Responses to Colonial Control among the Mixtecs and Zapotecs of Oaxaca." In *Native Resistance and the Pax Colonial in New Spain*, ed. Susan Schroeder, 30–46. Lincoln: University of Nebraska Press.

Stern, Steve J. 1987. "New Approaches to the Study of Peasant Rebellion and Consciousness: Implications of the Andean Experience." In *Resistance, Rebellion and Consciousness in the Andean Peasant World*, ed. Steven Stern, 3–25. Madison: University of Wisconsin Press.

Stresser-Péan, Guy. 2009. *The Sun God and the Savior: The Christianization of the Nahua and Totonac in the Sierra Norte de Puebla, Mexico.* Boulder: University of Colorado Press.

Sugiyama, Saburo. 2004. "Governance and Polity at Classic Teotihuacan." In *Mesoamerican Archaeology*, ed. Julia Hendon and Rosemary Joyce, 97–123. New York: Wiley-Blackwell.

Tambiah, Stanley J. 1981. *A Performative Approach to Ritual.* London: British Academy.

————. 1990. *Magic, Science, Religion, and the Scope of Rationality.* Cambridge: Cambridge University Press.

Taube, Karl. 2004. "Aztec Religion: Creation, Sacrifice, and Renewal." In *The Aztec Empire*, ed. Felipe Solís, 169–77. New York: The Solomon Guggenheim Museum.

Tavárez, David. 1999. "La idolatría letrada: Un análisis comparativo de textos clandestinos rituales y devocionales en comunidades nahuas y zapotecas, 1613–1654." *Historia Mexicana* 49 (2): 197–252.

————. 2000. "Naming the Trinity: From Ideologies of Translation to Dialectics of Reception in Colonial Nahua Texts, 1547–1771." *Colonial Latin American Review* 9 (1): 21–47.

————. 2002. "Idolatry as an Ontological Question: Native Consciousness and Juridical Proof in Colonial Mexico." *Journal of Early Modern History* 6 (2): 114–39.

————. 2006a. "The Passion According to the Wooden Drum: The Christian Appropriation of a Zapotec Ritual Genre in New Spain." *The Americas* 62 (3): 413–44.

————. 2006b. "Autonomy, Honor, and the Ancestors: Confrontations over

Local Devotions in Colonial Oaxaca." In *Local Religion in Colonial Mexico*, ed. Martin Nesvig, 119–44. Albuquerque: University of New Mexico Press.

———. 2009a. "Legally Indian: Inquisitorial Readings of Indigenous Identities in New Spain." In *Imperial Subjects: Race and Identity in Colonial Latin America*, ed. Andrew B. Fisher and Matthew O'Hara, 81–100. Durham, NC: Duke University Press.

———. 2009b. "Los cantos zapotecos de Villa Alta: Dos géneros rituales indígenas y sus correspondencias con los Cantares Mexicanos." *Estudios de Cultura Náhuatl* 39: 87–126.

Tavárez, David, and John Justeson. 2008. "Eclipse Records in a Corpus of Colonial Zapotec 260-day Calendars." *Ancient Mesoamerica* 19: 1 (2008): 67–81.

Taylor, William B. 1979. *Drinking, Homicide and Rebellion in Colonial Mexican Villages*. Stanford: Stanford University Press.

———. 1994. "Santiago's Horse: Christianity and Colonial Indian Resistance in the Heartland of New Spain." In *Violence, Resistance, and Survival in the Americas: Native Americans and the Legacy of Conquest*, ed. William B. Taylor and Franklin Pease, 153–89. Washington, DC: Smithsonian Institution Press.

———. 1996. *Magistrates of the Sacred*. Stanford: Stanford University Press.

Tedlock, Dennis. 1987. "Hearing a Voice in an Ancient Text: Quiché Maya Poetics in Performance." In *Native American Discourse: Poetics and Rhetoric*, ed. Joel Sherzer and Anthony Woodbury, 140–75. Cambridge: Cambridge University Press.

Tena, Rafael. 1987. *El calendario mexica y la cronografía*. Mexico: Instituto Nacional de Antropología e Historia.

Terraciano, Kevin. 1998. "Crime and Culture in Colonial Mexico: The Case of the Mixtec Murder Note." *Ethnohistory* 45 (4): 709–45.

———. 2001. *The Mixtecs of Colonial Oaxaca*. Stanford: Stanford University Press.

Thévet, André. 1575. *La cosmographie vniuerselle d'André Theuet*. Paris: Pierre L'Huillier.

Tilly, Charles. 2008. *Credit and Blame*. Princeton, NJ: Princeton University Press.

Tomlinson, Gary. 2007. *The Singing of the New World: Indigenous Voice in the Era of European Contact*. Cambridge: Cambridge University Press.

Torquemada, Fray Juan de. [1615] 1969. *Monarquía indiana*. 3 vols. Mexico: Editorial Porrúa.

Torre Villar, Ernesto de la. 1973. *Fray Pedro de Gante*. Mexico: Seminario de Cultura Mexicana, Universidad Nacional Autónoma de México.

Traffano, Daniela. 2001. *Indios, curas y nación: La sociedad indígena frente a un proceso de secularización: Oaxaca, siglo XIX*. Turin, Italy: OTTO.

Traslosheros, Jorge. 2002. "El tribunal eclesiástico y los indios en el Arzobispado de México, hasta 1630." *Historia Mexicana* 51 (3): 485–516.

Truman, R. W. 2003. "Censorship in Spain: 1558–1631." Paper delivered at the History of Censorship Conference, Princeton University, September 26–27, 2003.

Turner, Victor Witter. 1977. *The Ritual Process: Structure and Anti-Structure.* Ithaca, NY: Cornell University Press.

Twinam, Ann. 1999. *Public Lives, Private Secrets: Gender, Honor, Sexuality, and Illegitimacy in Colonial Spanish America.* Stanford: Stanford University Press.

Urcid, Javier. 2001. *Zapotec Hieroglyphic Writing.* Studies in Pre-Columbian Art & Archaeology, Number 34. Washington, DC: Dumbarton Oaks Research Library and Collection.

Valadés, Diego. 1579. *Rhetorica Christiana.* Perugia, Italy: Petrumiacobum Petrutium.

Van Meer, Ron. 2000. "Análisis e interpretación de un libro calendárico zapoteco: El Manuscrito de San Antonio Huitepec". *Cuadernos del Sur* 15 (6): 37-74.

Vetancourt, Agustín de. [1698] 1982. *Teatro mexicano.* Mexico: Editorial Porrúa.

Villa-Flores, Javier. 2006. *Dangerous Speech: A Social History of Blasphemy in Colonial Mexico.* Tucson: University of Arizona Press.

———. 2008. "Wandering Swindlers: Imposture, Style, and the Inquisition's Pedagogy of Fear in Colonial Mexico." *Colonial Latin American Review* 17 (2): 251-72.

Villavicencio, Luis Diego Jaimes Ricardo. 1692. *Luz y método para extirpar idolatrías.* Puebla, Mexico: Diego Fernández de León.

Viqueira, Juan Pedro. 1997a. "Una fuente olvidada: El Juzgado Ordinario Diocesano." In *Las fuentes eclesiásticas para la historia social de México,* ed. Brian Connaughton and Andrés Lira, 81–99. Mexico: UAM-Iztapalapa and Instituto Mora.

———. 1997b. *Indios rebeldes e idólatras: Dos ensayos históricos sobre la rebelión india de Cancuc, Chiapas, acaecida en el año de 1712.* Mexico: Centro de Investigaciones y Estudios en Antropología Social.

Wachtel, Nathan. 1992. *La vision des vaincus: Les indiens du Pérou devant la conquête espagnole.* Paris: Gallimard.

Warner, Rick. 2002. "'Ambivalent Conversions' in Nayarit: Shifting Views of Idolatry." *Journal of Early Modern History* 6 (2): 168–84.

Warren, J. Benedict. 1973. "An Introductory Survey of Secular Writings in the European Tradition on Colonial Middle America, 1503–1818." In *Handbook of Middle American Indians* 13: 42–137. Austin: University of Texas Press.

Watt, Tessa. 1991. *Cheap Print and Popular Piety, 1550–1640.* Cambridge: Cambridge University Press.

Weber, Max. 1968. *Economy and Society.* New York: Bedminster Press.

Weitlaner, Roberto, and Gabriel De Cicco. 1961. "La jerarquía de los dioses zapotecos del sur." *Proceedings of the Thirty-Fourth International Congress of Americanists,* 695–710, Vienna.

Weitlaner, Roberto, et al. 1958. "Calendario de los zapotecos del sur." *Proceedings of the Thirty-Second International Congress of Americanists,* 296–99. Munksgaard.

Whitecotton, Joseph. 1977. *The Zapotecs: Princes, Priests and Peasants.* Norman: University of Oklahoma Press.

————. 1990. _Zapotec Elite Ethnohistory. Pictorial Genealogies from Eastern Oaxaca._ Nashville, TN: Vanderbilt University Publications in Anthropology, no. 39.

Whitmore, Thomas. 1992. _Disease and Death in Early Colonial Mexico: Simulating Amerindian Depopulation._ Dellplain Latin American Studies, no. 28. Boulder, CO: Westview Press.

Winston-Allen, Anne. 1997. _Stories of the Rose: The Making of the Rosary in the Middle Ages._ University Park: Pennsylvania State University Press.

Wood, Stephanie. 2003. _Trascending Conquest: Nahua Views of Spanish Colonial Mexico._ Norman: University of Oklahoma Press.

Wright-Rios, Edward. 2009. _Revolutions in Mexican Catholicism: Reform and Revelation in Oaxaca, 1887–1934._ Durham, NC: Duke University Press.

Yannakakis, Yanna. 2008. _The Art of Being In-Between: Native Intermediaries, Indian Identity, and Local Rule in Colonial Oaxaca._ Durham, NC: Duke University Press.

Zaballa, Ana de. 2005. "Jurisdicción de los tribunales eclesiásticos novohispanos sobre la heterodoxia indígena. Una aproximación a su estudio." In _Nuevas perspectivas sobre el castigo de la heterodoxia en la Nueva España. Siglos XVI–XVIII,_ ed. Ana de Zaballa, 57–78. Bilbao, Spain: Servicio Editorial Universidad País Vasco.

Zanhe Xbab Sa, A.C. 2006. _Lha Bene: El nombre propio en zapoteco._ Oaxaca, Mexico: Ediciones Conocimiento Indígena.

Zeitlin, Judith. 1994. "La pintura, la escritura, y el discurso colonial sobre la historia: una perspectiva desde el Istmo de Tehuantepec." Paper presented at the Second Annual Colloquium on Zapotec Studies. Oaxaca, Mexico.

————. 2003. "Recordando a los reyes: El lienzo de Guevea y el discurso histórico de la época colonial." In _Escritura zapoteca: 2,500 años de historia,_ ed. María de los Ángeles Romero Frizzi, 265–304. Mexico: CIESAS, Instituto Nacional de Antropología e Historia, Porrúa, CONACULTA.

————. 2005. _Cultural Politics in Colonial Tehuantepec: Community and State Among the Isthmus Zapotec, 1500–1750._ Stanford: Stanford University Press.

Zeitlin, Judith, and Lillian Thomas. 1992. "Spanish Justice and the Indian Cacique: Disjunctive Political Systems in Sixteenth-Century Tehuantepec." _Ethnohistory_ 39: 285–315.

Zierikzee, Amandus van. 1534. _Chronica compendiosissima ab exordio mundi._ Antwerp, Netherlands: Simon Cocus.

Zilbermann, Cristina. 1966. "Idolatrías de Oaxaca en el siglo XVIII." _Actas del XXXVI Congreso Internacional de Americanistas_ 2: 111–23. Seville.

Zulaica y Gárate, Román. [1939] 1991. _Los franciscanos y la imprenta en México en el siglo XVI._ Mexico: Universidad Nacional Autónoma de México.

Index

The letters f and t after a page number indicate figures and tables, respectively. Endnote references are indicated by n (or nn, for multiple notes), followed by note number. *Passim* denotes a cluster of references within a given page range.

de Espina Aracena—ingested cuana betao before the entire town, who awaited a response assembled outside the *Yoo Yagtao*, or "House of the Ancestral Origins," a location that provided them with the darkness and quiet their visions required. Santiago revealed that, after pleading with Bezelao, Lord of the Underworld, to keep him from dying from drinking cuana betao mixture, he was able to converse with some "little people" he called the Guitzana Tao Lords, and also with an entity called Golana and a woman called Vixea Guxio, all of whom answered questions posed by the queche.[107] To this list, the specialist Zárate added three more names. One was Copa Yeche, "Keeper of the Community"; another was Huichana, the aforementioned pan-Zapotec goddess of procreation; the third was an enigmatic entity known as Naa Bene Yactina Goxio.[108]

Santiago, the eldest of the two, would later testify that the deities of Betaza had revealed "that they had fallen into the hands of God the Father, that the Christian doctrine would come into town, and that the Spaniards would come in and take away their parents and grandparents—meaning their idols. The first would be Lord 1-Cayman, and in fact, he was brought out and burned in the town square of [Villa Alta] later."[109] Santiago's elegiac tone was echoed by Aracena, who confessed that the queche deities had told them that "the law of their ancestors would be lost; the Spaniards will come and take away the things we have from our ancestors."[110]

Santiago's visions were generated through a common practice in many northern Oaxacan communities. The Villa Alta confessions feature many reported instances of the divinatory use of a plant usually called cuana betao, "deity plant" or, less frequently, *cuana xonaxi*, "Lady Plant." Cuana betao is probably *Turbina corymbosa*, a plant with seeds with hallucinogenic properties called ololiuhqui in Nahuatl. This identification is based on the work of Blas Reko,[111] who reported in the 1930s that *Turbina corymbosa* was called *badoo* in Valley Zapotec and *cuan bdoa* in Northern Zapotec, both cognates of cuana betao.[112] As in the Nahua context, Zapotec specialists grounded up large amounts of this plant's seeds and drank them with water.[113] The officials of twenty-nine Zapotec and Mixe towns confessed to having cuana betao users. The total number of cuana betao drinkers was 136 out of 390 individually identifiable practitioners in the 1702–6 records, and 97 percent of these specialists were male. Only 21 percent of them were specifically identified as maestros, a fact suggesting that this ritual pursuit might have been open to various ranks of specialists. Moreover, the confessions reveal great diversity in the distribution of cuana betao drinkers, which depended not on population density, but on sociocultural variables. For example, Betaza, which had about 203 tributaries in 1703, had only five cuana betao users, a low ratio in comparison to the fifteen drinkers at Lachixila, which had 377 household heads in the same year.[114] Twenty-one towns had between one and four cuana betao users, and only six communities had seven or more: Lachixila, Reagui, Yalahui, Yaveo, Yaxoni, and Yelagui.

Prior to 1704, Betaza celebrated only seven Christian yearly holidays under the supervision of a visiting priest.[115] Due to concerns about the bishop's visit, communal celebrations were carried out only three times in 1703, as opposed to eight to ten times in the previous year. Later that year, visiting priest fray Francisco de Orozco came to ask the people of Betaza to surrender their ritual implements, but they denied having any.[116] After this visit, Betaza's officials called a communal meeting and discussed whether they would surrender their specialists and texts. According to Zárate, the entire town asserted that, rather than turn in their ritual implements, "they would first surrender and give up their own blood."[117] Following a pattern of intercommunity communication also pursued during the Cancuc rebellion,[118] Betaza's town council sent letters to neighboring queche pleading for their support. According to Juan Martín de Cabueñas, Betaza's gobernador, the cabildo asked the neighboring communities of Yaa, Yatee, and Lachirioag not to break ranks with Betaza and not to turn in their idols or fruit stocks, which were used for the illegal production of alcohol.[119]

Betaza and Lachitaa's communal resolve was tested by several incidents on December 17, 1703, at a fair at Yalálag.[120] Among the crowds of outsiders in the town square, the Spaniard Bernardo García recognized Agustín Gonzalo Zárate, a Betaza specialist whose detention had been requested by Bishop Maldonado. Another visitor from Betaza was don Pedro de Paz, a former alcalde and gobernador who approached one of the regidores of Yalálag and scolded him by asking if he and his neighbors were women, for "it would be better if they wore their women's petticoats, or else why should they have turned in their idols without resistance . . . without fighting to the last drop of their blood?"[121] After this exchange, Yalálag gobernador don Juan de la Cruz conferred with García and arrested Zárate, Paz, and four other Betaza and Lachitaa officials present at the fair. Initially, Betaza interpreted these arrests as a direct attack from Yalálag: some of the prisoners' wives left Betaza with one of their alcaldes to complain to the alcalde mayor,[122] and Zárate had a nephew spread the news about the arrests. Thus, one of Yalálag's couriers, who carried a notification of these events for the alcalde mayor, was seized in Betaza by an angry crowd. After learning about this development from an informant, Cotes ordered his alguacil mayor to lead